What Is Legal Education For?

How we interpret and understand the historical contexts of legal education has profoundly affected how we understand contemporary educational cultures and practices. This book, the result of a Modern Law Review seminar, both celebrates and critiques the lasting impact of Peter Birks' influential edited collection, *Pressing Problems in the Law: Volume 2: What are Law Schools For?* Published in 1996, his book addresses many critical issues that are hauntingly present in the twenty-first century, amongst them the impact of globalisation, technological disruption, and the tension inherent in law schools as they seek to balance the competing interest of teaching, research and administration. Yet Birks' collection misses key issues such as the role of well-being, of emotion or affect, the relation of legal education to education, the status of legal education in what, since his volume, have become the devolved jurisdictions of Northern Ireland, Wales and Scotland; these and many other issues are absent from the research agenda of the book.

Today, legal educators face new challenges. We are still recovering from the effects of the Covid-19 pandemic on our universities. In 1996, Birks was keen to stress the importance of comparative research within Europe. Today, legal researchers are dismayed at the possibility of losing valuable EU research funding when the UK leaves the EU, and at the many other negative effects of Brexit on legal education. The proposed Solicitors Qualifying Examination takes legal education regulation and professional learning into uncharted waters. This book discusses these and related impacts on our legal educations.

As law schools approach an existential crossroads post-Covid-19, it seems timely to revisit Birks' fundamental question: what are law schools for?

Rachel Ann Dunn is a Course Director of Pro Bono and Employability at the Leeds Law School, Leeds Beckett University, UK. She was awarded her PhD, focused on Legal Education, in 2018. Her thesis explored the knowledge, skills and attributes which are considered necessary to start legal practice competently and whether live client legal clinics can develop them. Rachel has extensive experience of research methods, both empirical and doctrinal, and has collected research in various countries across the globe.

She is a reviewer for the *International Journal of Clinical Legal Education* and regularly attends international conferences to present her research.

Paul Maharg is Distinguished Professor of Practice – Legal Education at Osgoode Hall Law School in York University, Ontario, Canada, and part-time Professor of Practice at Newcastle University Law School, England. He is Honorary Professor of Law in The Australian National University College of Law, Canberra, where he was Director of the PEARL (Profession, Education and Regulation in Law) centre. He publishes widely in the field of legal education, particularly in international and interdisciplinary educational design, and in the use of technology-enhanced learning. He is a Principal Fellow of the Higher Education Academy (2015), a National Teaching Fellow (2011) and a Fellow of the RSA (2009). He holds Visiting Professorships in Hong Kong University Faculty of Law, the Chinese University of Hong Kong Faculty of Law, and was 2014 Distinguished Professor of Teaching and Learning at Denver University Sturm College of Law. He is Consultant Editor of the *European Journal of Law and Technology*, and blogs at https://paulmaharg.com.

Victoria Roper is an Associate Professor and Director of Postgraduate Education for the Law School. She holds several external roles, including being the Chair of the Law Society for England and Wales' Education and Training Committee and a Deputy Editor of the *Law Teacher Journal*. Victoria is also a Senior Fellow of the HEA and an external examiner. Victoria is widely published in legal education, is a reviewer for a number of journals and regularly attends international conferences to present her research. She is currently supervising a number of legal education and substantive law PhDs and professional doctorates. Victoria is the convenor of Northumbria's Legal Education and Professional Skills Research Group (LEAPS). LEAPS was established in 2013 as an inclusive, collegiate, group dedicated to the promotion and enhancement of legal education scholarship. Victoria has a wide variety of teaching experience, including supervising case work in Northumbria's Student Law Office and delivering teaching annually at a partner institution in Hong Kong.

Emerging Legal Education

Series Editors:
Paul Maharg, Osgoode Hall Law School, York University, ON, Canada,
Elizabeth Mertz, University of Wisconsin-Madison/American Bar
Foundation, USA and
Meera Deo, Thomas Jefferson School of Law, San Diego, CA, USA

Emerging Legal Education is a forum for analysing the discourse of legal education and creating innovative ways of learning the law. The series focuses on research, theory and practice within legal education, drawing attention to historical, interdisciplinary and international characteristics, and is based upon imaginative and sophisticated educational thinking. The series takes a broad view of theory and practice. Series books are written for an international audience and are sensitive to the diversity of contexts in which law is taught, learned and practised.

Some other titles in this series:

Affect and Legal Education
Emotion in Learning and Teaching the Law
Edited by Paul Maharg and Caroline Maughan

Imperatives for Legal Education Research
Then, Now and Tomorrow
Edited by Ben Golder, Marina Nehme, Alex Steel and Prue Vines

Better Law for a Better World
New Approaches to Law Practice and Education
Liz Curran

Public Legal Education
The Role of Law Schools in Building a More Legally Literate Society
Richard Grimes

Clinical Legal Education
Philosophical and Theoretical Perspectives
Omar Madhloom and Hugh McFaul

https://www.routledge.com/Emerging-Legal-Education/book-series/ELE

What Is Legal Education For?
Re-Assessing the Purposes of Early Twenty-First Century Learning and Law Schools

Edited by
Rachel Ann Dunn,
Paul Maharg and
Victoria Roper

LONDON AND NEW YORK

First published 2022
by Routledge
4 Park Square, Milton Park, Abingdon, Oxon OX14 4RN

and by Routledge
605 Third Avenue, New York, NY 10158

Routledge is an imprint of the Taylor & Francis Group, an informa business

© 2022 selection and editorial matter, [Rachel Ann Dunn, Paul Maharg and Victoria Roper]; individual chapters, the contributors

The right of [Rachel Ann Dunn, Paul Maharg and Victoria Roper] to be identified as the author[s] of the editorial material, and of the authors for their individual chapters, has been asserted in accordance with sections 77 and 78 of the Copyright, Designs and Patents Act 1988.

All rights reserved. No part of this book may be reprinted or reproduced or utilised in any form or by any electronic, mechanical, or other means, now known or hereafter invented, including photocopying and recording, or in any information storage or retrieval system, without permission in writing from the publishers.

Trademark notice: Product or corporate names may be trademarks or registered trademarks, and are used only for identification and explanation without intent to infringe.

British Library Cataloguing-in-Publication Data
A catalogue record for this book is available from the British Library

ISBN: 978-1-032-10073-9 (hbk)
ISBN: 978-1-032-34427-0 (pbk)
ISBN: 978-1-003-32209-2 (ebk)

DOI: 10.4324/9781003322092

Typeset in Times New Roman
by codeMantra

For law school students of the future and in memory of Tina Bond

Contents

List of figures and tables	xi
List of contributors	xiii
Preface	xvii
Acknowledgements	xxxvii
List of abbreviations	xxxix

1 The unitary idea of 'the' law school and other issues when defining 'problems' in legal education 1
ELAINE HALL AND SAMANTHA RASIAH

2 What are law teachers for? Finding ways to introduce law teachers' voices through the TEF in the ever-changing HE sector in England 25
MARIBEL CANTO-LOPEZ

3 Beyond the jurisdiction: law schools, the LLB and 'global' education 60
CHLOË WALLACE

4 Reinventing possibility: a reflection on law, race and decolonial discourse in legal education 85
FOLUKE IFEJOLA ADEBISI AND KATIE BALES

5 Who are law schools for? A story of class and gender 111
JESSICA GUTH AND DOUG MORRISON

6 A change in outfit? Conceptualising legal skills in the contemporary law school 138
EMMA JONES

x *Contents*

7 **'Originary intimacy': a thought experiment in jurisprudential legal education inquiry** 167
PAUL MAHARG

8 **Three authors in search of phenomenologies of learning and technology** 195
LYDIA BLEASDALE, PAUL MAHARG AND CRAIG NEWBERY-JONES

9 **What is the law school for in a post-pandemic world?** 231
MARGARET THORNTON

Index 261

Figures and Tables

Figures

1.1	Forms of disciplinary learning, from Broudy et al., 1964	16
8.1	Digital lecture, Civil Procedure, Glasgow Graduate School of Law, c. 2004	213
8.2	Identity frame	214
8.3	Navigation frame	215
8.4	Knowledge frame	215
8.5	Layers of engagement	216

Table

8.1	Threefold views of knowledge acquisition	219

Contributors

Foluke Ifejola Adebisi is a Senior Lecturer at the University of Bristol, UK. Her scholarship focuses on decolonial thought in legal education. In 2017, she co-designed a Law and Race unit, which is one of the very few of its kind within the UK. In September 2019, she convened the first 'Decolonisation and the Law' conference at the University of Bristol. Her decolonial scholarship, which is pedagogical as well as jurisprudential, examines what happens at the intersection of legal education, law, society and a history of changing ideas of what it means to be human. She is also the founder of Forever Africa Conference and Events (FACE), a Pan-African interdisciplinary conference hosted in Bristol. She blogs about her scholarship, pedagogy and interrelated ideas on her website 'Foluke's African Skies' at https://FolukeAfrica.com.

Katie Bales is a Senior Lecturer at University of Bristol, UK. Her research and teaching focus on issues of forced migration, political economy, labour law and the welfare state. She is a trustee for the Bristol City of Sanctuary charity, co-editor of the interdisciplinary Futures of Work blog and a working group member of the Sanctuary Scholarships team at the University of Bristol.

Lydia Bleasdale is a Professor of Legal Education at the University of Leeds, UK. Her research focuses on wellness and belonging within the legal academy and the legal professions. She is the co-founder of the Advancing Wellness in Law Network and Connecting Legal Education. For over ten years Lydia directed the Law School's community engagement projects, such as the award-winning Welfare Rights project assisting litigants in person. In 2018, she was awarded the national Oxford University Press Law Teacher of the Year Award.

Maribel Canto-Lopez is a Teaching Dominant Associate Professor at the Law School, University of Leicester, UK, and a senior fellow of the HEA. She leads and mentor colleagues to attain UKPSF accreditations and has enhanced the Law curriculum by including opportunities in it where students may improve their employability skills (particularly

xiv *Contributors*

group work and professional writing). For this work, she was awarded the University Distinguished Teaching Fellowship. She has led various pedagogical projects, and is a member of the Association of Law Teachers (ALT) and the Legal Education Research Network (LERN). She is also a member of the Editorial Board of the legal education journal *REJIE* (Spain).

Rachel Ann Dunn is a Course Director of Pro Bono and Employability at the Leeds Law School, Leeds Beckett University, UK. She was awarded her PhD, focused on Legal Education, in 2018. Her thesis explored the knowledge, skills and attributes that are considered necessary to start legal practice competently and whether live client legal clinics can develop them. Rachel has extensive experience of research methods, both empirical and doctrinal, and has collected research in various countries across the globe. She is a reviewer for the *International Journal of Clinical Legal Education* and regularly attends international conferences to present her research.

Jessica Guth is the Head of the School of Law, Birmingham City University, UK. Her research interests include feminist approaches to Law and legal education broadly conceived and she is currently working on a project looking to re-imagine the neo-liberal university and law school as well as on projects to enhance students' critical thinking and writing skills.

Elaine Hall is a Professor in Legal Education, whose career spans more than 20 years. Since joining Northumbria Law School, she has seen various successful legal education PhD students through to completion. Elaine is the Editor in Chief of the *International Journal of Clinical Legal Education* and leads the organisation of its annual conference. Professor Hall has worked on numerous funded research projects and is currently contributing to a funded HEA project looking at Reward and Recognition in Higher Education.

Emma Jones is a Senior Lecturer and the Director of Student Wellbeing at the University of Sheffield's School of Law. Her research interests focus on the role of emotion and well-being in legal education and the legal profession. She is a Senior Fellow of the HEA and current Vice-Chair of the Association of Law Teachers.

Paul Maharg is a Distinguished Professor of Practice – Legal Education at Osgoode Hall Law School, York University, Ontario, Canada; and part-time Professor of Practice, Newcastle University Law School, England. He is an Honorary Professor of Law in The Australian National University College of Law, Canberra, where he was Director of the PEARL (Profession, Education and Regulation in Law) centre. He publishes widely in the field of legal education, particularly in international and interdisciplinary educational design, and in the use of technology-enhanced learning. He is a Principal Fellow of the Higher Education Academy (2015), a National Teaching Fellow (2011) and a Fellow of the RSA (2009). He holds visiting professorships in Hong Kong University Faculty of Law, the Chinese University of Hong Kong Faculty of Law, and was 2014 Distinguished Professor of Teaching and Learning at Denver University Sturm College of Law. He is Consultant Editor of the *European Journal of Law and Technology*, and blogs at https://paulmaharg.com.

Doug Morrison is a Senior Lecturer at the Leeds Law School, Leeds Beckett University, UK. His research interests cover healthcare law, health rights, legal education and bio-politics. He is currently working with Jessica Guth on neoliberal university, vulnerability and has just completed work with Prof Simon Gardiner and Prof Simon Robinson, around duty of candour and integrity in public life.

Craig Newbery-Jones is a Lecturer of Legal Education and Deputy Director of Student Education in University of Leeds School of Law, UK. He has a keen research interest in pedagogic theory, and has led multiple projects exploring experiential learning, technology-enhanced learning and problem-based learning. He also engages with work around how law programmes can better embed employability skills into the curriculum and the transitional experiences of students coming to study law at university.

Samantha Rasiah is a Lecturer at the Institute of Policing, Staffordshire University, UK. Her research interests lie in higher education, professional education, employability skills and curriculum design. She is currently involved in module and course design for UK and overseas universities. She is pursuing her PhD in Legal Education under the supervision of Elaine Hall at Northumbria University. Her PhD research investigates the impact that Covid-19 has had on the increased use of technologies in employment and the challenges involved in equipping undergraduate law students with transferrable employability skills.

Victoria Roper is an Associate Professor and the Director of Postgraduate Education for the Law School, Northumbria University, UK. She holds several external roles, including being the Chair of the Law Society for England and Wales' Education and Training Committee and a Deputy Editor of the *Law Teacher Journal*. Victoria is also a Senior Fellow of the HEA and an external examiner. Victoria is widely published in legal education, is a reviewer for a number of journals and regularly attends international conferences to present her research. She is currently supervising a number of legal education and substantive law PhDs and professional doctorates. Victoria is the convenor of Northumbria's Legal Education and Professional Skills Research Group (LEAPS). LEAPS was established in 2013 as an inclusive, collegiate, group dedicated to the promotion and enhancement of legal education scholarship. Victoria has a wide variety of teaching experience, including supervising case work in xvi *Contributors*

Northumbria's Student Law Office and delivering teaching annually at a partner institution in Hong Kong.

Margaret Thornton is an Emerita Professor of Law at the Australian National University College of Law, Canberra. Her research interests span feminist legal theory, discrimination law, legal education, the legal profession and the corporatisation of universities. Her publications include *Privatising the Public University: The Case of Law* (Routledge, 2012) and edited collections, *Through a Glass Darkly: The Social Sciences Look at the Neoliberal University* (ANU Press, 2014); and with Schultz, Shaw and Auchmuty, *Gender and Careers in the Legal Academy* (Hart, 2021). Her internationally recognised work has led to her election as a Fellow of the Academy of Social Sciences in Australia and a Foundation Fellow of the Australian Academy of Law, together with the award of an Australian Research Council Professorial Fellowship, in addition to international fellowships.

Chloë Wallace is an Associate Professor of Law at the School of Law, University of Leeds, UK, and the Co-Director of the Centre for Innovation and Research in Legal Education. She leads law with languages programmes and study abroad programmes at Leeds, and is currently conducting research on the pedagogic experience of study abroad and the role of narrative and imagination in the process of legal education.

Preface

This is an unusual book in legal education literature. It is at once a homage to and critique of another book written quarter of a century ago, and which has been influential on the thinking around legal education since then. That book was entitled *Pressing Problems in the Law: Volume 2: What Are Law Schools For?* (henceforth, 'Birks' collection') – a collection of chapters largely on legal education, edited by Peter Birks.[1] The arresting title gives a sense of the book's ambition to seek answers to one of the most fundamental questions that we can ask about our lives as legal academics. Twenty-five years later, we are seeking answers to the same question, and our book comprises one set of responses.

In this introduction, we shall set out some of the context of Birks' collection, describe some of the methodology of our own text and preview the shape and content of this book.

Publication context

Its publication context and history is important to understanding the purpose and content of Birks' collection. Two years before, Birks had edited an earlier book, entitled *Reviewing Legal Education*,[2] published also by OUP and in the same A4 softback format as the later collection. Published in July 1994, this earlier book arose from a Society of Public Teachers of Law

---

1 Peter Birks (ed), *Pressing Problems in the Law, Volume 2: What Are Law Schools For?* (Oxford University Press 1996, 2003 reprint). It was preceded by the earlier *Pressing Problems in the Law. Volume 1, Criminal Justice & Human Rights: Reshaping the Criminal Justice System, Fraud and the Criminal Law, Freedom of Expression* (Oxford University Press 1995). Both were published in a plain black cover, softback, A4 two-column format more commonly used for conference proceedings. The titles and formats express the sense of urgency and crisis in the domains of criminal justice and legal education that is part of content of the volumes.

  Birks (1941–2004) was Regius Professor of Civil Law at the University of Oxford and Fellow of All Souls College. His principal area of scholarship was in the English law of restitution, but his interests extended to many other topics, including legal education.

2 Peter BH Birks, Reviewing Legal Education (Oxford University Press 1994).

xviii *Preface*

(SPTL) seminar held at All Souls College in April 1994. The seminar papers were published as a response to the Lord Chancellor's Advisory Committee on Legal Education and Conduct (ACLEC). The first publication of ACLEC in June 1994 was a 49-question consultation paper on 'The Initial Stage' of legal education.[3] The earlier edited collection thus did not take the form of a learned society's report. Instead, it is a gathering of articles on aspects of legal education arising from the SPTL seminar.

The later collection, published by Birks and which went to press just before publication of the ACLEC report, takes a similar approach. As Birks himself points out in the Preface, the aims of both collections were 'to provide a forum in which to air a series of personal views as to the nature and purpose of some or all of the functions of a modern law school'.[4] There are strategic differences however between the two books. The later collection, it is made plain, while arising out of the efforts by the SPTL to engage with ACLEC's process, includes 'personal insights into the life and purposes of law schools set out with the intention of enriching the debate as it enters the crucial stage *after* the publication of the ACLEC report'.[5] In other words, the earlier volume was designed to influence ACLEC while it was gathering information – hence the first word of the title, which sought to establish perspectives on law school history and context which Birks (and he was probably not alone in this amongst the contributors) was certain would not be properly understood by regulators.[6] The later volume sought to influence developments after the publication of what was seen at the time as an important milestone in the history of law schools in England and Wales.

---

3 Lord Chancellor's Advisory Committee on Legal Education and Conduct (ACLEC), *First Report on Legal Education and Training* (1996) <https://ials.sas.ac.uk/ukcle/78.158.56.101/archive/law/files/downloads/407/165. c7e69e8a.aclec.pdf> accessed 7 January 2022.

4 Peter Birks (ed), *Pressing Problems in the Law, Volume 2: What Are Law Schools For?* (Oxford University Press 1996, 2003 reprint), vi. We should note that while Birks intended to widen the focus of the later collection, he does not achieve this aim. The titles are revealing in this respect. The second volume asks the question 'what are law schools for' rather than stating, as does the first volume, that the book will review legal education. In this respect, Birks opens up for debate many of the functions of a law school, not just legal education. It is fair to say, however, that the chapters in the later volume still deal overwhelmingly with legal education as its subject. In shaping our own responses to Birks' question in this book, we have taken the same approach – a wide-angled focus, but our subject is still largely legal education – and our title reflects that.

5 Ibid, our emphasis.

6 Birks' Preface was finished on 12 July 1994; respondents to the 49 questions of ACLEC's consultation paper had till the end of that year to respond. As Birks acknowledges in his Preface, the SPTL seminar contributions which gave rise to the book were never intended as direct answers to the 49 ACLEC questions, for the questions had still to be formulated at the time the seminar was held (April 1994) [p. iii]. As a result of this timing, the purpose of *Reviewing Legal Education* to influence ACLEC was diluted.

Preface xix

The difference is significant, for it is clear that Birks, who was the driving force behind both books, had learned the lesson from the Ormrod Report. He regarded the *post*-report period as being at least as important as the consultation leading up to the composition of that report. In this he was undoubtedly right. The post-report period of any significant report is the stage when public perception of the report is formed, when regulatory responses are made and become policy; and in many respects that period *post*-Ormrod Report was a lost opportunity.[7]

While *Reviewing Legal Education* was cited in ACLEC, it is doubtful if it had much influence (ACLEC's committee already had academic representation well able to articulate many of the views of the edited collection).[8] Nor is it clear that the later Birks' collection had any influence on the agenda-setting post-ACLEC. It appeared just prior to the publication of the ACLEC report, whose recommendations were not implemented but which, like Birks' collection, became regarded as touchstone for a vision of university legal education founded upon liberal principles. Indeed, ACLEC was radical amongst legal education reports in that it was the first to present a vision at all. Its critique took in the whole spectrum of legal education.[9] As

---

7 We might compare that moment with the period post-LETR, where the responses from the regulatory stakeholders involved in that report (LSB, BSB, SRA, CILEX) effectively and relatively swiftly set the tone and direction of their legal educational agendas for the foreseeable future. The LETR Report authors noted this point more generally: 'The relative failure of previous reports to make substantial changes to LSET [legal services education and training] has often reflected an inability to mobilise the support of key stakeholders, despite the excellence of many of those reports and no lack of endeavour in the attempts to institute reforms'. Webb J, et al., *Setting Standards: The Future of Legal Services Education and Training Regulation in England and Wales (The Legal Education and Training Review (LETR)* (2013). SRA, London. Para 7.3. <https://letr.org.uk/the-report/chapter-5/compea

8 Birks himself (ACLEC p.23); Robert Stevens, Law School: *Legal Education in America from the 1850s to the 1980s* (University of North Carolina Press, 1987); Dawn Oliver, 'Teaching and Learning Law: Pressures on the Liberal Law Degree' in Peter Birks (ed), *Reviewing Legal Education* (Oxford University Press 1994), at p. 44 ACLEC) were cited.

9 It is interesting to note that in his article on the Benson Report, (Sir H Benson, *Royal Commission on Legal Services* (Cmnd 7648, 1979)) Alan Paterson criticised the report for being 'not so much a blueprint for the future as a snapshot of the status quo' (Alan Paterson, 'Legal Services for All?' (1980) 2 (6) The Journal of Social Welfare Law, 321–329, 321). He drew the contrast with the Royal Commission on Legal Services in Scotland (Cmnd 7846), known as the Hughes Report after its Chair, which took a 'more visionary stance' that was more social, looking beyond the profession to provide 'guidelines for progress rather than stagnation' (p. 321). The Hughes Report in many respects prefigures the ACLEC Report in this regard. ACLEC focused on the changing needs of legal practice, the need for a new vision of legal education in the context of HE in England & Wales, access and funding, the qualifying law degree, professional legal studies practice courses for barristers and solicitors, and quality assurance. Being a unitary report rather than a collection of academic

xx *Preface*

was noted in LETR, it advocated liberalisation of the academic curriculum, which found voice in the Joint Statement. Flexibility was key:

> In shaping its proposals for legal education and training ACLEC [...] asserted that 'the growing variety of practice settings, the need to respond to rapid changes and to take opportunities as they arise [...] suggest that a pluralistic approach should be encouraged, with providers of legal education and training having greater discretion than they are currently allowed'.[10]

This liberalising pluralism was adopted by Birks, too, and contributed to his editorial methods. Neither of the volumes he edited states any methodology. Birks' later collection itself has no programmatic intent: it does not take an explicitly specific line on education or jurisprudential educational analysis, for example. If its stated aim was to present the thoughts of 'leading experts' on legal education, there is no description of how 'leading' is defined in the editorial choice of authors, a number of whom espouse views similar to those of Birks. Given the lack of information about methodology, we must look to Birks' Preface to fill the gap. There he outlines the background of English law schools in recent decades in the form of an extended essay on the place, activities and cultures of law schools.[11]

In focusing thus on the social milieux of law schools, ACLEC and Birks' collection were part of a growing literature on the gathering speed of significant changes in higher education (HE). Developments have been fast paced.[12] They include the massive increase in student numbers, the creation of new universities from polytechnics and colleges, the gradual erosion of

---

    voices in an edited book, it has had as much if not more influence on subsequent legal education literatures as Birks' collection.

10 Julian Webb, et al., *Setting Standards: The Future of Legal Services Education and Training Regulation in England and Wales (The Legal Education and Training Review (LETR)* (2013)). SRA, London. Para 5.45. <https://letr.org.uk/the-report/chapter-5/competence-and-flexibility/index.html> accessed 7 January 2022.

11 *Reviewing Legal Education* contained a similar piece entitled 'The Historical Context' (Peter Birks, 'The Historical Context' in Peter BH Birks (ed), Reviewing Legal Education (Oxford University Press 1994) 1–9) which deals with some of the pre-twentieth century background. Birks' Preface serves to update this chapter in Peter Birks (ed), *Pressing Problems in the Law, Volume 2: What Are Law Schools For?* (Oxford University Press 1996, 2003 reprint). It is written in the form of a general introduction, with no footnotes or references – clearly it is meant to be read as a personal statement upon recent law school history in England. It is an interesting rhetorical device – more below on why he may have adopted it.

12 Twining stated in his 2018 Upjohn Lecture that he had "underestimated the acceleration of the pace of change in education, legal services, information technology, globalisation and so on". William Twining, 'Rethinking Legal Education' (2018) 52 (3) The Law Teacher, 241, 250. The extent to which law schools have, under huge pressure, struggled to create online digital versions of study programmes during the lockdowns and closures of the Covid-19 pandemic is a particularly salient contemporary example.

Preface xxi

fiscal resources provided by the state, the rise of neoliberalist New Public Management, entrepreneurialism and corporatised approaches to knowledge, learning and the university, and the increase of both governmental and professional regulatory intervention. Birks' collection also deals with the rolling impact of globalisation[13]; technological disruption[14]; and the balance of the competing interests of teaching, research, administration and research funding.[15]

In this sense, Birks helped to define a generation of research directions about the shifting identity of law schools. Since his collection, for example, commentators have identified how the law school has become a commercial corporation, highlighting how we are compelled to entrepreneurialism, forced to seek private funding in the form of fee-paying postgraduate programmes, undergoing deep restructuring in our undergraduate programmes. In the UK, we are now measured in ever more granularised detail in our research, teaching and knowledge exchange performances.[16] International commentators such as Thornton have shown how the massification and the corporatisation of HE has 'helped shift the orientation and purpose of universities generally from intellectual inquiry to instrumentalism and vocationalism', and how that has affected legal education.[17] Indeed the lasting influence of Birks' book was to be within the late twentieth- and early twenty-first-century development of law schools in England where it became a key statement of a liberal law school values framework in a period when those values were under pressure. To that extent, Birks' authors presaged many of the future challenges for law schools. It was a powerful warning to law schools of their future in the new century.

Yet Birks' collection misses some things too, for instance the role of well-being, of emotion or affect; the status of gender and ethnicity; the relation of legal education to education itself in other places and times; the jurisdictional differentials of legal education in what, since Birks' collection, have become the devolved polities of Northern Ireland, Wales and Scotland; these and many more issues are absent from what appears to be the research agenda of the book.[18] Further, law schools are no longer 'isolated from other

---

13 See, for example, the discussion in Eugene Clark and Martin Tsamenyi, 'Legal Education in the Twenty-First Century: A Time of Challenge' in Peter Birks (ed), *What Are Law Schools For?* (Oxford University Press 1996, 2003 reprint).

14 Ibid.

15 Peter Birks, *Pressing Problems in the Law, Volume 2: What Are Law Schools For?* (Oxford University Press, 1996, 2003 reprint) vi.

16 Richard Collier, 'The Liberal Law School, the Restructured University and the Paradox of Socio-Legal Studies' (2005) 68 (3) Modern Law Review, 475.

17 Margaret Thornton, 'The Demise of Diversity in Legal Education: Globalisation and the New Knowledge Economy' (2001) 8 (1) International Journal of the Legal Profession, 37, 43.

18 Birks takes a peculiarly English-centred approach to the other jurisdictions of these isles. He attributes, for example (Peter Birks, *Pressing Problems in the Law, Volume 2: What Are Law Schools For?* (Oxford University Press 1996, 2003 reprint), v), the formation in

xxii *Preface*

parts of the university. Virtually every department in the social sciences and the humanities has been raided or visited by those in law schools'.[19] We have also seen the rise of movements such as socio-legal studies, empirical studies, critical legal studies and other unique legal research areas, a diversity which was present to some degree in the mid-1990s, and which Birks himself was keen to encourage.[20]

Today, we view Birks' collection across a very changed landscape: extensive growth in the indicia of neoliberalism, a global financial crisis, Brexit, fresh regulatory interventions such as the SRA's Solicitors Qualifying Examination (SQE), growing environmental crises, the transformative effects of digital upon whole industries and the effects of viral epidemics such as Covid-19 upon universities worldwide, unfolding as our own edited collection was being written. In 1996, Birks was keen to stress the importance of comparative research within Europe, given the UK's status a member state[21]; yet today legal researchers are dismayed at the possibility of losing valuable EU research funding as a result of the UK leaving the EU. The passage of time and the force of history create their own ironies. In 1996, Birks was highlighting the inflexibility created by stringent commands of the regulating bodies as to what a law degree should include,[22] whilst more than two decades later we are adjusting to a future where solicitors in England and Wales will not be required to have any formal legal education at all.[23]

In the face of all this, Birks' fundamental question remains as relevant as ever: what are law schools *for*? As law schools approach an existential

---

Scotland of the Diploma in Legal Practice in the 1980s to the influence of the English Ormrod Report (*Report of the Committee on Legal Education* (Cmnd 4595 (1971)), when in fact there were many other local pressures and drivers from Scots legal culture and society for the development of the course, not least the Royal Commission of 1980 (Lord Hughes of Hawkhill, *Royal Commission on Legal Services in Scotland* (Cmnd 7846, 1980) Hughes Report). As Michael Zander pointed out in his comparison of this Report with the English Royal Commission that reported the previous year (Sir H Benson, *Royal Commission on Legal Services* (Cmnd 7648, 1979) Benson Report), 'the Scots [were] considerably more radical than the English'. The Scots report was also the more warmly welcomed, and arguably implemented more than the proposals of the Benson Report [Michael Zander, 'Scottish Royal Commission on Legal Services Report' (1980) 66 American Bar Association Journal, 1092–1095, 1092].

19 Anthony Bradney, *Conversations, Choices and Chances: The Liberal Law School in the Twenty-First Century* (Bloomsbury Publishing, 2003) 10.

20 Peter Birks, *Pressing Problems in the Law, Volume 2: What Are Law Schools For?* (Oxford University Press 1996, 2003 reprint), viii.

21 Ibid.

22 Ibid, xvii.

23 Under the SRA's proposals solicitors will be required to have a degree (but not necessarily a law degree) and to have passed the Solicitors Qualifying Examination (SQE) but the mode of preparing for the SQE is not prescribed – Solicitors Regulation Authority, Draft Authorisation of Individuals Regulations Post Consultation, Regulation 2.1. <https://www.sra.org.uk/solicitors/standards-regulations/authorisation-individuals-regulations/> accessed 7 January 2022.

Preface xxiii

crossroads *post*-Covid, it seems timely to revisit the question, not least because, as Clark and Tsamenyi observe in the Birks collection, 'like it or not *all* law academics are involved and affected by such issues'.[24] This book contains both our answers and more questions.

Methodology of our book

We start from the position that legal education is a socially complex phenomenon. This is hardly a novel approach, but it is as well to state it from the start. Moreover, and drawing from the work of a risk analyst, Sydney Dekker, we would draw a distinction between a complicated object and a complex object. Dekker uses the example of a jet liner. It is a hugely complicated object with its assemblage of hundreds of thousands of parts, but can be disassembled and reassembled from its component parts because it is 'understandable and describable in principle'.[25] By contrast, a complex system works in real time, with components working in local relation only, and the manufacturer would be unaware of the behaviour of other components in real-time action, in multiple, complex environmental contexts.[26] When the jet liner is in operation, the complicated object becomes a complex object. The same is true of legal education in law schools. Described as curricula, syllabi, modules with learning outcomes and assessment criteria, knowledge and skills components, it is a complicated artefact. When performed and operated in real time, however, it becomes a much more complex object, where (for example) module descriptors are only a small part of a much larger experiential whole, for students as well as academic staff. Indeed, like music, we must experience it in real-time performance for its dense, woven complexity to be revealed; and every experience of it is different: in every iteration, we step into Heraclitus' river anew.

If complexity theory matters significantly in legal education, then the form of inquiry is almost as important. There is a variety of methods by which we can understand social complexity and intellectual changes in law schools. One is the general history – Robert Steven's history of US legal education is one such example.[27] Or a history of concepts or *begriffgeschichte* –

---

24 Eugene Clark and Martin Tsamenyi, 'Legal Education in the Twenty-First Century: A Time of Challenge' in Peter Birks (ed), *What Are Law Schools For?* (Oxford University Press 1996, 2003 reprint) 44.

25 Sidney Dekker, et al. 'The Complexity of Failure: Implications of Complexity Theory for Safety Investigations' (2011) 49 *Safety Science* 939. Quoted in Paul Maharg 'The Gordian Knot: Regulatory Relationship and Legal Education' (2017) 4 (2) Asian Journal of Legal Education, 79–94, 82.

26 Ibid.

27 Robert Stevens, *Law School: Legal Education in America from the 1850s to the 1980s* (North Carolina Press 1987).

xxiv *Preface*

curriculum, for example, or assessment[28]; or a history of the development of areas of law such as Twining's *Theories of Evidence: Bentham and Wigmore.*[29] We might undertake a review of the research findings of a topic in a particular period.[30] Another method is through the history of our institutions – Cownie and Cock's history of the SPTL / Society of Legal Scholars is an example.[31] Yet another approach is to track specific changes in detail over a span of time, empirically examining their aetiologies of change, their causes, symptoms and effects – the many studies carried out on the case method in US legal education is an example of such historical educational literatures. Or we can undertake a detailed anthropological study of aspects of law school culture, rather as Beth Mertz does in her study of the case method in US legal education, using sociolinguistic studies of the discourses used in legal classrooms.[32]

Another method involves the study of a prior text that is recognised as being influential in the discipline. It employs historical approaches that are well understood in the canons of Arts disciplines, in literary analysis or historiography for instance. Augustine's *Confessions* is often seen as an *ur-* or meta-text for northern and western autobiography, and the study of its interpretation can tell us much about the genre and its place in literary canons. In genre studies, Scott's *Waverley* has been critiqued as a source of both historical fiction and fictional history. It has been studied for its Europe-wide influence on the genre of historical novels and the part that such narratives can play, for example, in the development of nationalist movements.[33] In history, historiographers have noted how the nineteenth-century histories of Ranke, Michelet and Burckhardt, those *grands récits* that wove claims of the arcs of social progress and decline around great events, persuaded contemporary readers by creating historical spaces and characters that spoke not just of their own historical time, but to the time

---

28 Alison Bone and Paul Maharg (eds), *Assessment and Legal Education: Critical Perspectives on the Scholarship of Learning and Assessment in Law*, volume one: England (ANU Press 2019).

29 William L Twining, *Theories of Evidence: Bentham and Wigmore* (Weidenfeld & Nicolson 1985).

30 Paul Maharg and Emma Nicol, 'Simulation and Technology in Legal Education: A Systematic Review and Future Research Programme' in Caroline Strevens, Richard Grimes and Edward Phillips (eds), *Legal Education: Simulation in Theory and Practice* (Emerging Legal Education Series, Ashgate Publishing 2014).

31 Fiona Cownie and Raymond Cocks, *A Great and Noble Occupation! The History of the Society of Legal Scholars* (Hart Publishing 2009).

32 Elizabeth Mertz, *The Language of Law School: Learning to 'Think Like a Lawyer'* (Oxford University Press 2007).

33 See for example Karen O'Brien and Susan Manning 'Historiography, Biography and Identity' in Susan Mannin, Ian Brown, Thomas Owen Clancy and Murray Pittock (eds), *The Edinburgh History of Scottish Literature: Enlightenment, Britain and Empire* (1707–1918), volume two (Edinburgh University Press 2007).

Preface xxv

and place of the reader, too.[34] In the field of literary criticism itself, a major work such as Erich Auerbach's *Mimesis: The Representation of Reality in Western Thought* has become the focus of critical analysis, and the subject of symposia and conferences.[35] In the canon of literary criticism, its hegemonic status stimulates critical reflection upon its method and its influences.

Our method follows this critical tradition. It involves the re-interpretation of Birks' collection – effectively a recognition of Birks' achievement and a celebration by critique. It is a form that is relatively rare in legal education. We have chosen this text not just because in England Birks' collection is still cited in publications in legal education, not just because it addresses critical issues that are, hauntingly, still present for us now, albeit in forms and shapes that the original authors may not have envisaged, but also because the method of re-reading a text tells us much about our own times as well as the time of the original authors. Indeed, we cannot but read Birks' collection except with twenty-first-century eyes: we can only, in Harold Bloom's terms, 'misread' Birks' collection, even over the relatively short passage of time since its publication. Such a process of misreading, though, is creative: in re-reading, remembering and interpreting Birks' collection, we can re-interpret anew our own particular stances in legal education theory and practice, and with regard not just to our present, but to the pasts and futures of legal education. Above all, it is a methodology that acknowledges and explores the essential effects of time and change within a research domain.

A good example of this is the question of technology in law schools. Digital technology was the focus of a chapter by Hugh Collins in *Reviewing Legal Education*, and was discussed in a section in Clark and Tsamenyi's overview

34 Hayden White, *Metahistory: The Historical Imagination in Nineteenth Century Europe* (Fortieth Anniversary Edition, Johns Hopkins University Press 1973, 2014 reprint); Hayden White 'The fictions of factual representation' in Donald Preziosi and Claire Farago (eds), *Grasping the World: The Idea of the Museum* (Routledge 2004).

35 The text was written by Auerbach in Istanbul while in exile from Nazi Germany between May 1942 and April 1945. It was first published in German in Berne, Switzerland in 1946 by A. Francke Ltd Co. The English translation, by Willard Trask, appeared in 1953, published by Princeton University Press. The best current edition is that containing Edward Said's extensive Introduction to the 50th anniversary edition of Auerbach's work – an edition that also included Auerbach's own responses to his critics. See Erich Auerbach, *Mimesis: The Representation of Reality in Western Thought* (Princeton University Press 2003: reprinted First Princeton Classics Edition, 2013). See also Hyeryung Hwang, *Said and the Mythmaking of Auerbach's Mimesis*. CLCWeb: Comparative Literature and Culture 18.1 (2016) <https://doi.org/10.7771/1481-4374.2776> accessed 7 January 2022. See also William Calin and Erich Auerbach, 'Mimesis – 'Tis Fifty Years Since: A Reassessment' (1999) 33 (3) Style, 463–474 (and note how Calin nods to the title of Scott's *Waverley* in the title of his own article, implying the status of Auerbach's text in criticism is equivalent to the status of Scott's novel in nineteenth century historical fiction). All this and much else illustrates the creative, interpretative work that can surround a classic in the canon.

xxvi *Preface*

of Australian legal education in Birk's collection.[36] The focus was limited to applications and their integration with prior legal education pedagogies. The larger questions of the effects of digital on education and knowledge were not raised. As an example of these larger questions, we might take one of the fundamental paradoxes of the internet, whereby it makes visible the *centrality* of knowledge (as well as raising questions about how we access it, verify it and who owns it). But it also *de-centres* the university and its scholarly communities as the once-privileged sites of knowledge production and dissemination. As Weinberger pointed out, the vast expansion of access to knowledge that the internet entails reveals much more the actual extent of contestation about knowledge claims than the shared truths of insight, overturning Enlightenment claims to knowledge as the basis of shared understanding.[37] These and similar processes were already being observed and theorised by the mid-1990s.[38] But it is only by looking back at their absence in Birks' collection that we can begin to appreciate the immense changes we have experienced since 1997, and how those changes will affect our law school futures, our law school purposes.

Birks' blunt title question therefore is a constant challenge to all generations of teachers and learners. Our response, arguing from a view of legal education as contingent and socially complex, cannot hope to capture the huge complexity of law school cultures within our volume, but we can begin to unpack the deceptive simplicity of Birks' title and recognise that the question may be cast differently. Or that it contains, like a *matryoshka* doll, many other questions: *who* are law schools for? *Where* are law schools? *What* is learned in law schools? *How* do we learn and teach in law schools? Indeed, what is there of value in the wider fields of education – kindergarten, primary school, secondary school, college and other disciplines in HE, e.g. medical education, adult and lifelong education – that we can draw upon? *When* are law schools? The last is especially resonant. What were law schools like in the past and what might we see of value in them for our present reflection and practices? This includes unearthing the forgotten, almost invisible 'shadow' pedagogies of the past that can be recast, re-formed for the future.

It is a methodology that also, with its background in the Arts, pays special attention to what is unsaid as well as what is said in Birks; who is missing from among the list of authors (especially as regards gender and ethnic

---

36 Eugene Clark and Martin Tsamenyi, 'Legal Education in the Twenty-First Century: A Time of Challenge' in Peter Birks (ed), Pressing Problems in the Law, Volume 2: What Are Law Schools For? (Oxford University Press 1996, 2003 reprint) 29–32.

37 David Weinberger, *Too Big to Know* (Basic Books 2012) 174–175.

38 See for instance New London Group, 'A Pedagogy of Multiliteracies: Designing Social Futures' (1996) 66 (1) Harvard Educational Review, 60–92; Cliff McKnight, Andrew Dillon and John Richardson, *Hypertext in Context* (Cambridge University Press 1991); Manuel Castells, The Rise of the Network Society, Volume 1 of The Information Age: Economy, Society and Culture (Blackwell 1996).

Preface xxvii

diversity) as well as who was chosen to be present; and what could have been written instead of what was written. In this regard, the concept of the 'implied narrative' in textual theory is important to our project in this book. Just as there can be an implied audience, an implied author, so can there be an implied narrative – one that is not made overt or *ad longam* but which is implied or hinted at through various devices within a text. Where narratives often link past, present and future in conclusive causation, implied narratives present a single instance or event that gestures to the existence of an event before or after (or both) the one that is described.[39]

In our interpretation, the implied narrative of Birks' text is the emergence and ethical presence of the liberal law school. It cannot be made programmatic in his text largely because his authors disagree about the nature of the concept. Compare, for instance, the views on law schools that Goodrich held over against Toddington or any other author, and you begin to see the problem that Birks faced as the editor of his authors. It is for this reason that Birks eschews explicit programmatic intent, but uses implied narratives throughout the Preface to signal the book's allegiances. That subtle Preface, which manages to be stylistically both a careful summary of selected aspects of the recent history of law schools and an apparently bluff personal opinion piece, lays down the markers of such an approach for the book.[40] Arguing from a substructure of implied beliefs about law school, the Preface's structure inhibits counter-arguing; and it creates the space for Birks to tell a story about the liberal law school which is by no means applicable to all but with many recognisably visible traits in actual law schools. In its way, the Preface is both a powerful vision for law schools, imaginative, creative and complex; and a strategy in which Birks attempts to influence the direction of law schools' future *post*-ACLEC and the practical implementation of that future.[41]

We would argue that it is one of the rhetorical strengths of Birks' collection, and which sustained it as a key text for the development of the liberal law school framework of values. Our book in a variety of ways and in a number of chapters (see below) questions that implied narrative.

---

39 See for example Sky Marsen, *Narrative Dimensions of Philosophy: A Semiotic Exploration in the Work of Merleau-Ponty, Kierkegaard and Austin, chapter 2*, passim (Palgrave Macmillan 2006). Twitter is an example of a text genre that thrives on implication and implied narratives. See Laila Al Sharaqi and Irum Abbasi, 'Twitter Fiction: A New Creative Literary Landscape' (2016) 7 (4) Advances in Language and Literary Studies, 16–19.

40 Peter Birks (ed), *Pressing Problems in the Law, Volume 2: What Are Law Schools For?* (Oxford University Press 1996, 2003 reprint).

41 For a discussion of this narrative strategy, see, for example, Sonya Dal Cin, Mark P Zanna and Geoffrey T Fong, 'Narrative Persuasion and Overcoming Resistance' in Eric S Knowles and Jay A Linn (eds), *Resistance and Persuasion* (Routledge 2013, first published Lawrence Erlbaum Associates 2004) 175–192.

xxviii *Preface*

After his untimely death in 2004, Birks was the subject of two *festschriften* in his memory.[42] Neither dealt with legal education. In a sense this is appropriate: Birks himself was not an original contributor to the literature, or much of an innovator in educational practices. Birks' collection, however, is a watershed, bringing together as it did a range of important critiques of legal education, and an important text in the canon. Our methodology accords the passage of time and change a central role. Understandings of the past and visions for the future are intimately bound up each with the other. As Maharg and others point out, though, too many aspects of legal education remain undocumented, historyless, forgotten.[43] This book is therefore a rescue archaeology where we understand the past by critiquing Birks' collection and its place in our discipline's canon. But it also asks Birks' question anew: what are law schools for, today, in the first quarter of the twenty-first century, and for the foreseeable future? What visions do we have for our law schools and our legal educations?

Above all, our chapters question the constructions we form of the past and future of legal education that depend upon our multiple identities as academics, and the tensions that arise from those roles. If legal education is a complex object, it is so partly because of three general characteristics that operate simultaneously in real time. First, the many roles that academics can play: tutor, lecturer, facilitator, assessor, designer, learner, manager, leader, administrator, team-player, consultant, discipline expert, researcher, writer, disciplinary (inter)national collaborator, funding-seeker and more; and often playing several roles simultaneously. Second, law schools are conservative institutions in a number of ways, not least in that they are conservationist: part of their essential role is to conserve and pass on legal academic cultures, ways of thinking and modes of being. Third, they are also committed to critique, to changing the way we think about law and justice, and striving to achieve that change.

Legal education can be in the forefront of such change, with experimental experiential forms of learning, radical initiatives, collaborations beyond the law school and much else; but legal education is also highly conservative too, strongly attracted by the gravitational pull of the *status quo*.[44] Many

---

42 Charles Rickett and Ross Grantham, Structure and Justification in Private Law: Essays for Peter Birks (Hart Publishing 2008); Andrew Burrows and Alan Rodger, Mapping the Law: Essays in Memory of Peter Birks (Oxford University Press 2006).

43 Paul Maharg, 'Prometheus, Sisyphus, Themis: Three Futures for Legal Education Research' in Ben Golder, Marina Nehme, Alex Steel and Prue Vines (eds), *Imperatives for Legal Education Research: Then, Now and Tomorrow* (Emerging Legal Education Book Series, Routledge 2020) 271–288. See also Webb J, et al., *Setting Standards: The Future of Legal Services Education and Training Regulation in England and Wales (The Legal Education and Training Review (LETR)* (2013)). SRA, London. Paras 1.30, 1.46. <https://letr.org.uk/the-report/chapter-5/competence-and-flexibility/index.html> accessed 7 January 2022.

44 Webb J, et al., *Setting Standards: The Future of Legal Services Education and Training Regulation in England and Wales (The Legal Education and Training Review (LETR)* (2013)).

Preface xxix

of the narratives of change and innovation in the modern period reveal how difficult it is to bring about sustainable change in legal education when conservation and critique are prioritised within the law school, and when our roles are so kaleidoscopically fractured. As a result, it is difficult to discern the purposes of our legal educations. How we resolve those tensions and uncertainties each for ourselves and also for our legal education communities, and shape our purposes, is also part of this book's project.

Chapter overviews

Our book grew out of a funded *Modern Law Review* seminar held at Northumbria University Law School, in collaboration with Nottingham Trent University Law School, in June 2019. The seminar brought legal academics from different parts of the world, with different perspectives, arguments and experiences.[45] Its focus was wide, and many topics were explored. We organised the day into various streams which had a specific focus on the current landscape of legal education. Margaret Thornton gave the first keynote address, outlining how legal education is becoming increasingly marketised and the impacts this has on institutions and the staff and students who work in them. Among much else there were streams exploring skills and practices in legal education training; exploration of clinical legal education; how law can adapt through globalising the curriculum and becoming more inter-disciplinary; who law schools are for; and the profiles of academics and the loss of law teacher views in regulatory changes brought about by, for example, the Solicitors Qualifying Examination (SQE) and the Teaching Excellence Framework (TEF). Stephen Vaughan explored how we teach core modules in his keynote and whether it was time for law schools to be more creative in their curriculum design. Paul Maharg gave the final keynote, exploring how hermeneutics can help us question how we explore law schools and understand their cultures, histories and epistemologies. He outlined ways we can change this hermeneutic focus. Not all speakers have contributed to this edited collection, though their presentations were invaluable to the seminar. We also recruited some authors to the book who did not contribute to the seminar, to provide a holistic overview of the current landscape of legal education and more recent phenomena and issues that were crucial to include.

The book begins with Elaine Hall and Samantha Rasiah's chapter that deals with snapshots of the history and evolution of the concept of the law school. Throughout, Hall and Rasiah discuss the place, purpose and attitudes of law schools. They observe for example the effect of a generalising

---

SRA, London. Para 1.21. <https://letr.org.uk/the-report/chapter-5/competence-and-flexibility/index.html> accessed 7 January 2022.

45 See Victoria Roper, Rachel Dunn and Samantha Rasiah, 'Revisiting *Pressing Problems in the Law: What Is the Law School for?* 20 Years on' (2020) 54 (3) The Law Teacher, 455–464.

xxx *Preface*

tendency when talking about law schools: 'Talking about "the" law school ignores [...] inequalities within and between each law school and is therefore potentially a serious distraction from one of our more pressing problems'. They also question 'who is law school (apparently and actually) for?' and discuss how we might move from a conventional 'replication / application' mode of learning and teaching to a more radical 'interpretation / association' mode. They draw striking parallels between the Berytus law school foundation in the second century CE and contemporary law schools, particularly in the idea of plurality within unitary foundation, and the relations between law school and government, both local and imperial. The result is an overview that helps us to think beyond the parochial boundary issues of our law school thinking about purpose.

The theme of governmental pressure upon law schools is continued in Maribel Canto-Lopez's retrospective on the place and effect of the TEF in law schools in England. As her title suggests, the model for TEF was the Research Excellence Framework (REF), and Canto-Lopez tracks in detail the origins and the implementation and effects of TEF. She reveals the relations between governmental policy and the marketisation of higher education (HE) and the employability agendas that are a key focus of such market-based pivots in HE. Canto-Lopez is unsparing in her analysis: TEF creates busyness around education; it increases stress levels across the board; it creates more 'administrative bureaucracy'; it endorses the concept of students as consumers. She also observes TEF as a silencing intervention: how law teachers' voices have been silenced or unheard in the introduction of the TEF. She notes this as a theme in Birks' collection and investigates closely why this has happened much more so since the mid-1990s. She notes the need for less management and more leadership, management based on trust not power relations, the lack of real consultation and much else. She ends by emphasising the need for staff to regain their identities and values that are 'lost to competitiveness and productivity indoctrination'.

Internationalisation of law and legal education was discussed in Birks' collection, though not necessarily the versions of it that we encounter today. Chapters by Grief, and Clark and Tsamenyi made arguments and predictions for a more international focus of legal education and scholarship. Chloe Wallace outlines the need for a more internationalised legal curriculum, not just because of the exigencies of the global legal labour market, but also because *au fond,* the purpose of HE should be to create good citizens. In order to achieve this, Wallace argues, we should be moving towards a curriculum that builds in legal systems and rules from other jurisdictions, for our students to understand why our system is the way it is. In so doing our students can better understand any particular jurisdiction's imperfections and the alternatives that may be available elsewhere. This chapter complements arguments made by Adebisi and Bales, below, in holding that it is only by understanding our own legal system alongside others that we

Preface xxxi

can create graduates who are global citizens, with potentially decolonising and anti-racist attitudes.

The racialisation of law schools is discussed in more depth in the chapter by Foluke Adebisi and Katie Bales. Birks' authors were writing at a time when the Scarman report on the Brixton riots[46] was still relatively fresh in memory, and the Macpherson report[47] was ongoing. Yet there is little or no mention of the effects of race from most of the authors in his collection. More recently, racialisation has become a current pressing issue following the growth of the Black Lives Matter movement. Adebisi and Bales present the reader with a history and overview of how law and legal structures have impacted on racialised groups, the prior lack of acknowledgement of this in legal education and why it is imperative that we include colonial histories, antiracist and decolonial discourses within law school curricula. They provide practical examples of modules that do this at Bristol Law School to allow students to reflect upon the racialising consequences of our legal systems and to give them 'tools to properly understand their social realities'.

Neither class nor gender was explicitly discussed in Birks' collection to any great extent. Some of our authors have framed their chapters around this, questioning *who* law schools are for, as well as how this impacts *what* they do in legal education. Jessica Guth and Doug Morrison analyse class, gender and race, using an autoethnographic methodology. They begin by highlighting that no women contributed to Birks' collection in 1996. In asking *who* are law schools for, Guth and Morrison explore the law schools beyond the physical space and instead focus on the people who inhabit them. Their chapter argues that the superficial differences between our contemporary law schools and those of the mid-1990s belie the underlying continuity that *who* law schools are for has not really changed since the publication of Birks' collection.

Since Birks' collection, one element of law school educational discourse that has substantially increased is the literature on skills. That this was already happening in the 1990s is evident in Birks' collection, with Toddington's chapter in particular focusing on legal skills. Emma Jones draws upon this chapter and how skills are currently characterised and used within legal education, and questions the nature of authentic legal skills. Where Thornton highlights in her chapter that HE has moved towards marketisation, Jones analyses a particular example of this in the relation between skills and employability. She argues that the perception of legal skills has significantly changed since Toddington's chapter was written. She argues for a different conceptualisation of legal skills, one that has a greater focus on emotional

---

46 The Scarman Report into *The Brixton Disorders 10–12 April 1981* (1981) (Cmnd. 8427).
47 *The Stephen Lawrence Inquiry: Report of an Inquiry by Sir William Macpherson of Cluny* (1999) (Cmnd. 4262).

xxxii *Preface*

and social competencies, with a shift towards online, blended and flipped models of teaching.

Paul Maharg makes a case for the 'originary intimacy' between legal method and educational method to be revived. He claims that the uneasy status of legal education stems not just from its multidisciplinary origins but from it having no apparent place in the foundational methods and knowledge structures within the legal academy, and he advocates for the reclamation of legal education as a core jurisprudential activity. To explore this, he carries out a thought experiment. Taking a legal realist approach, he constructs an argument for his claim from the materials and debates historically available to Birks' authors, exploring the relations between jurisprudential and educational debates, and demonstrating the epistemic cross-overs between the two.

Digital technology was the focus of a chapter in *Reviewing Legal Education*, and was discussed in a section in Clark and Tsamenyi's overview of Australian legal education in Birks' later collection.[48] While both Birks' collections acknowledged that there would be a need to adapt, the extent of the reach and power of the ongoing digital revolution in society at large as well as law schools was not anticipated in Birks' collection. Lydia Bleasdale, Paul Maharg and Craig Newbery-Jones explore two aspects of recent developments, namely the spatio-temporal challenges to legal education embodied in Bakhtin's concept of the chronotope, and the problems of creating and sustaining identity and community within a curriculum that is powerfully bounded by digital technologies. Both topics are of key interest to the post-pandemic law school. In the third section of the chapter, they use a lecture as a case study, in both its analogue and digital formats, and conclude with an analysis of the future of digital within our law schools.

Margaret Thornton ends our edited collection by outlining how law schools have been 'beset with a sense of schizophrenia', with their identities even more uncertain in light of the neoliberal turn. Though authors in Birks' collection did discuss the marketisation and corporatisation of legal education, the full impacts on law schools had yet to manifest themselves. Drawing upon her recent work, Thornton depicts the current situation law schools find themselves in – for instance state disinvestment in public education, more pressure on income generation, increasing governmental regulation, the creation of consumerist cultures, league tables driving the operation of universities, the commercialisation of research and the disappearing space for HE to act and be perceived as a public good. With such constraints, she questions whether law schools have a choice as to what they are for. Drawing upon the work of Foucault, Thornton analyses the 'contemporary role of both law students and legal academics'. In spite of all the challenges to their

---

48 Eugene Clark and Martin Tsamenyi, 'Legal Education in the Twenty-First Century: A Time of Challenge' in Peter Birks (ed), *Pressing Problems in the Law, Volume 2: What Are Law Schools For?* (Oxford University Press 1996, 2003 reprint) 29–32.

Preface xxxiii

cultures and practices, legal academics are praised for their commitment to creating new legal scholarship and inspiring generations of law students.

Assembled in this way, there are many adjacencies and comparisons between the chapters. For example, the first chapter deals in part with the distant past of law school, while the last, chapter 9, deals with the future, i.e. post-pandemic, institution; but both are grounded in a critique of present law schools and their cultural contexts. The next five (chapters 2–6: Canto-Lopez; Wallace; Adebisi and Bales; Guth and Morrison; Jones) are fascinating comparisons in change cultures. All are critical about the changes that have or have not taken place since Birks' collection. There are contrasts in these chapters, too – the absence of voice in the narrative around the TEF (Canto-Lopez) over against the place of voice in global education (Wallace), for example. Chapters 5 and 7 (Guth and Morrison; Maharg), though very different in topic, have similar yet contrasting methodologies. Chapters 7 and 8 (Maharg, and Bleasdale, Maharg, Newbery-Jones) deal with interdisciplinarity in different ways but are similar in that they engage in close readings of specific forms of legal education – scholarly writing and lectures, respectively. Throughout all chapters, there are also general themes, e.g. neoliberalist infiltration into legal education. The structure makes the book more powerful between the book-ends of chapters 1 and 8, allowing us to use the sociolegal cultural and linguistic turns of our method as a set of tools in order to understand the social complexity of legal education.

There is no conclusion to our book because it seemed to us that no conclusion could encompass the varied sophistication of our authors' contributions. Birks' collection structure, too, leaves us with the authorial kaleidoscope of views: he made it clear in his Preface that that was the aim of his book. We seem to have replicated the Birks' collection structure in leaving the last word to all our authors. And yet, however brilliant the individual critiques in Birks' collection may be – and in truth they are a mixed bag – there is no meta-critique of the law school, or legal education and its purpose in Birks' collection. Goodrich's chapter, a profoundly critical reading of Twining's *Blackstone's Tower*, comes closest to performing this function in Birks' collection:

> As to the teaching relation and the institutional development of the law school, the absence of any history or even mention of class, gender, race or oppression reflects an altogether more immediate isolation and arrogance on the part of the academy and its historians.[49]

As editors, we feel a responsibility to address this in our relation to Birks' challenging question. It seemed to us as the book was taking shape that if

---

49 Peter Goodrich, 'Of Blackstone's Tower: Metaphors of Distance and Histories of the English Law School' in Peter Birks (ed), *What Are Law Schools For?* (Oxford University Press, 1996) 67.

xxxiv *Preface*

there were a single theme weaving itself throughout our book, it is that the liberal law school framework of values is an *essential but insufficient foundation* for the contemporary law school in the first half of the twenty-first century. That framework emerged from and described a moment in law school history in England, post-WWII to the late twentieth century. In the quarter century since the publication of Birks' collection, law schools have changed significantly, and the speed of transformation is not showing signs of slowing down. If anything, law schools have become more fragile and precarious places, post-Covid-19. In our view, the *post*-liberal law school, whose cultures, problems and opportunities are outlined in part in this book, in addition to acknowledging the achievements of the liberal framework, has to recognise how little progress has been made by law school since Birks' collection. The *post*-liberal law school needs to become more transgressive, more relational with regard to students, more dynamic in its collaborations, more porous in its interdisciplinarities and more global in its outlooks.

This of course still leaves us all with the final question as to what an essential *and* sufficient structure may look like for each of us, in our individual law school, regardless of what roles and positions we hold within it. Our book presents versions, imaginings, wireframes, and fragmentary narratives – in effect, and in Dekker's sense, visions of complex law schools that move beyond the 'culture and non-relation of law school'.[50] But on the shaping detail of those versions and their working out in your lives and careers – over to you, dear reader.

Bibliography

Al Sharaqi L and Abbasi I, 'Twitter Fiction: A New Creative Literary Landscape' (2016) 7(4) *Advances in Language and Literary Studies* 16–19.

Auerbach E, *Mimesis: The Representation of Reality in Western Thought* (Princeton University Press 2003: reprinted First Princeton Classics Edition, 2013).

Birks P, *Pressing Problems in the Law. Volume 2: What are Law Schools For?* (OUP 1996: 2003 reprint).

Birks P, *Pressing Problems in the Law. Volume 1, Criminal Justice & Human Rights: Reshaping the Criminal Justice System, Fraud and the Criminal Law, Freedom of Expression* (OUP 1995).

Birks P, *Reviewing Legal Education* (OUP 1994).

Birks P, 'The Historical Context' in Peter B H Birks (ed), Reviewing Legal Education (OUP 1994).

Bone A and Maharg P (eds), *Assessment and Legal Education: Critical Perspectives on the Scholarship of Learning and Assessment in Law*, volume one: England (ANU Press 2019).

Bradney A, *Conversations, Choices and Chances: The Liberal Law School in the Twenty-First Century (Bloomsbury Publishing, 2003)*.

---

50 Ibid.

Preface xxxv

Burrows A and Rodger A, *Mapping the Law: Essays in Memory of Peter Birks* (OUP 2006).

Calin W and Auerbach E, 'Mimesis – "Tis Fifty Years Since: A Reassessment"' (1999) 33(3) *Style* 463–474.

Cin S D, Zanna M P, and Fong, G T, 'Narrative Persuasion and Overcoming Resistance' in Eric S Knowles and Jay A Linn (eds), *Resistance and Persuasion* (Routledge 2013, first published Lawrence Erlbaum Associates 2004) 175–92.

Clark E and Tsamenyi M, 'Legal Education in the Twenty-First Century: A Time of Challenge' in Peter Birks (ed), *What Are Law Schools For?* (OUP 1996: 2003 reprint).

Collier R, 'The Liberal Law School, the Restructured University and the Paradox of Socio-Legal Studies' (2005) 68(3) *Modern Law Review* 475.

Cownie F and Cocks R, *A Great and Noble Occupation! The History of the Society of Legal Scholars* (Hart Publishing 2009).

Dekker S, et al., 'The Complexity of Failure: Implications of Complexity Theory for Safety Investigations' (2011) 49 *Safety Science* 939.

Goodrich P, 'Of Blackstone's Tower: Metaphors of Distance and Histories of the English Law School' in Peter Birks (ed), *What are Law Schools For?* (OUP 1996).

Hwang H, *Said and the Mythmaking of Auerbach's Mimesis* (2016) CLCWeb: Comparative Literature and Culture 18.1 <https://doi.org/10.7771/1481-4374.2776> accessed 7 January 2022.

Lord Chancellor's Advisory Committee on Legal Education and Conduct, *First Report on Legal Education and Training* (1996) <https://ials.sas.ac.uk/ukcle/78.158.56.101/archive/law/files/downloads/407/165.c7e69e8a.aclec.pdf> accessed 7 January 2022.

Lord Hughes of Hawkhill, *Royal Commission on Legal Services in Scotland* (Cmnd 7846, 1980).

Maharg P, 'The Gordian Knot: Regulatory Relationship and Legal Education' (2017) 4(2) *Asian Journal of Legal Education* 79–94.

Maharg P and Nicol E, 'Simulation and Technology in Legal Education: A Systematic Review and Future Research Programme' in Caroline Strevens, Richard Grimes, and Edward Phillips (eds), *Legal Education: Simulation in Theory and Practice* (Emerging Legal Education series, Ashgate Publishing 2014).

Manuel Castells, *The Rise of the Network Society, Volume 1 of The Information Age: Economy, Society and Culture* (Blackwells 1996).

Marsen S, *Narrative Dimensions of Philosophy: A Semiotic Exploration in the Work of Merleau-Ponty, Kierkegaard and Austin,* chapter 2, *passim* (Palgrave Macmillan 2006).

McKnight C, Dillon A, and Richardson J, *Hypertext in Context* (CUP 1991).

Mertz E, The Language of Law School: Learning to 'Think Like a Lawyer' (OUP 2007).

New London Group, 'A Pedagogy of Multiliteracies: Designing Social Futures' (1996) 66(1) *Harvard Educational Review* 60–92.

O'Brien K and Manning S, 'Historiography, Biography and Identity' in Susan Mannin, Ian Brown, Thomas Owen Clancy and Murray Pittock (eds), *The Edinburgh History of Scottish Literature: Enlightenment, Britain and Empire (1707–1918)*, volume two (Edinburgh University Press 2007).

Oliver, D 'Teaching and Learning Law: Pressures on the Liberal Law Degree' in Peter Birks (ed) *Reviewing Legal Education* (OUP 1994).

xxxvi *Preface*

Paterson A, 'Legal Services for All?' (1980) 2(6) *The Journal of Social Welfare Law* 321–329.

Rickett C and Grantham R, *Structure and Justification in Private Law: Essays for Peter Birks* (Hart Publishing 2008).

Roper V, Dunn R and Rasiah S, 'Revisiting "Pressing Problems in the Law: What is the Law School For?" 20 Years On' (2020) 54(3) *The Law Teacher* 455–464.

Sir H Benson, *Royal Commission on Legal Services (Cmnd 7648, 1979).*

Solicitors Regulation Authority, Draft Authorisation of Individuals Regulations Post Consultation, Regulation 2.1 <https://www.sra.org.uk/solicitors/standards-regulations/authorisation-individuals-regulations/> accessed 7 January 2022.

Stevens R, *Law School: Legal Education in America from the 1850s to the 1980s* (University of North Carolina Press 1983).

Stevens R, *Law School: Legal Education in America from the 1850s to the 1980s* (University of North Carolina Press 1987).

The Scarman Report into *The Brixton Disorders 10–12 April 1981* (Cmnd 8427, 1981).

The Stephen Lawrence Inquiry: Report of an Inquiry by Sir William Macpherson of Cluny (Cmnd 4262, 1999).

Thornton M, 'The Demise of Diversity in Legal Education: Globalisation and the New Knowledge Economy' (2001) 8(1) *International Journal of the Legal Profession 37.*

Twining W, 'Rethinking legal education' (2018) 52(3) *The Law Teacher 241.*

Twining WL, *Theories of Evidence: Bentham and Wigmore* (Weidenfeld & Nicolson 1985).

Webb J, et al., *Setting Standards: The Future of Legal Services Education and Training Regulation in England and Wales (The Legal Education and Training Review (LETR)* (2013)). SRA, London. Para 5.45 <https://letr.org.uk/the-report/chapter-5/competence-and-flexibility/index.html> accessed 7 January 2022.

White H, *Metahistory: The Historical Imagination in Nineteenth Century Europ* (Fortieth Anniversary Edition, Johns Hopkins University Press 1973: 2014 reprint).

White H, 'The Fictions of Factual Representation' in Donald Preziosi and Claire Farago (eds), *Grasping the World: The Idea of the Museum* (Routledge 2004).

Zander M, 'Scottish Royal Commission on Legal Services Report' (1980) 66 *American Bar Association Journal* 1092–1095.

Acknowledgements

As with all academic work, there are many who have worked on this edited collection throughout one of the most difficult and unprecedented of times. We acknowledge the funding provided by the *Modern Law Review* that underpinned the seminar and without which it could not have happened. We thank the seminar participants for their stimulating and unique contributions on the day. We would also like to thank Samantha Rasiah, our research assistant at the time, who worked tirelessly on the seminar's organisation.

On the development of the book, we would like to acknowledge the work of all authors, who met tight deadlines through the trauma of the Covid-19 pandemic. We thank our Routledge editors, Meera Deo and Beth Mertz, for their wise counsel, and Siobhan Poole of Routledge for her endless patience as we editors worked our way through Covid-related difficulties. Lastly, we would like to acknowledge the work of our book's research assistant Lauren Napier for her excellent work in preparing the text ready for submission.

Abbreviations

ACLEC	Lord Chancellor's Advisory Committee on Legal Education and Conduct
BSB	Bar Standards Board
CUS	Critical University Studies
DfE	Department for Education
DLHEA	Destination of Leavers Survey from HE
ERA	Excellence in Research for Australia
f2f	Face-to-Face
GCSE	General Certificate of Secondary Education
GFC	Global Financial Crisis
Go8	Group of Eight
HE	Higher Education
HECS	Higher Education Contribution Scheme
HEFCE	Higher Education Funding Council for England
HEI	Higher Education Institutions
HELP	Higher Education Loan Programme
HERA	Higher Education and Research Act
HESA	Higher Education Statistics Agency
IMF	International Monetary Fund
JD	Juris Doctorate
LACC	Law Admissions Consultative Committee
LEO	Longitudinal Education Outcome
LLB	Bachelor of Laws
LPC	Legal Practice Course
LT	Law Teachers
LTV	Law Teachers' Voices
NSS	National Student Survey
OECD	Organisation for Economic Co-operation and Development
OfS	Office for Students
PGR	Post Graduate Research
PGT	Post Graduate Taught
QAA	Quality Assurance Agency
QLD	Qualifying Law Degree

xl *Abbreviations*

RAE	Research Assessment Exercise
REF	Research Excellence Framework
ROI	Return on Investment
SOAS	School of Oriental and African Studies
SPTL	Society of Public Teachers of Law
SQE	Solicitors Qualifying Examination
SRA	Solicitors Regulation Authority
STEM	Science, Technology, Engineering and Math
TEF	Teaching Excellence Framework
UCL	University College London
UCLA	University of California Los Angeles
UCU	University and College Union

1 The unitary idea of 'the' law school and other issues when defining 'problems' in legal education

Elaine Hall[1] and Samantha Rasiah[2]

Introduction

The title of the seminar funded by the Modern Law Review was *Revisiting "Pressing Problems in the Law: What is the Law School for?" 20 years on*[3] and I was invited by the organisers to welcome the participants with some framing remarks: this chapter picks up on those and sets out to develop some of the ideas which had begun to form, were highly stimulated by the seminar and continue to develop offshoots and tangential turns to this day. However, then and now, my discomfort with the role of 'Framing Professor Authority Figure' led me to suggest that we should hear from some others – those undergoing legal education and those passionately involved in studying it – so this chapter is leavened by the work of doctoral candidate Samantha Rasiah and the voices of undergraduates from Northumbria and Nottingham Universities.[4] The structure of the chapter therefore moves back and forth between these three perspectives: what students think about their experience in law school; the way in which law academics with an interest in legal education frame the field and name the problems besetting it; and my own position as an education researcher only latterly settled in a School of Law.

I am writing this chapter as an outsider who has been invited inside and decided to stay. My background in education and professional learning led me to a role supporting the Legal Education and Professional Skills research group at Northumbria University and I am now Professor of Legal Education. I am not being disingenuous when I say that this is a recurrent source of surprise to others and to me. I am not supposed to have this job: I

---

1 Elaine Hall is Professor of Legal Education at Northumbria Law School.
2 Samantha Rasiah is completing her PhD candidature at Northumbria Law School and is a Lecturer at Staffordshire Law School.
3 Summarised here: Victoria Roper, Rachel Dunn and Samantha Rasiah, 'Revisiting "Pressing Problems in the Law: What Is the Law School For?" 20 years on' (2020) 54 (3) The Law Teacher, 455–464, using Peter Birks (ed), *Pressing Problems in the Law. Vol 2. What Are Law Schools For?* (Oxford University Press 1996) as the stimulus text.
4 With that in mind, sections written in the first-person singular are Elaine, unless specified as Samantha, our joint endeavours are first person plural.

DOI: 10.4324/9781003322092-1

2 Elaine Hall and Samantha Rasiah

have no legal qualification or training, no practice experience, no specialist doctrinal knowledge. The former Dean of the Faculty who appointed me did so as a conscious act of disruption, my lack of cultural capital as a law academic balanced by my understanding of curriculum design, pedagogy and assessment; of professional learning cultures; of reflexive practice and research methodologies. I have become acculturated in many ways over the past seven years, but I try to maintain some of my helpful ignorance, my ability to ask why some things are constantly sites for enquiry whilst others remain relatively undisturbed and unquestioned. With that in mind, I approached the seminar with questions about the definition of problems, about whose voices are heard and whether or not there is, was or ever shall be such a thing as 'the' law school.

I am aware that it's a pedantic move to take issue with the wording used by a previous author and then to insist that if only everyone else would join them at this point of definitional clarity, then the progress of the issue at hand would proceed smoothly. Given that awareness, it's perhaps a shame that this chapter is going to do quite a bit of that, and the reader's only consolation may be that I'm only going to do the 'taking issue' part and worry away at some of the wording with the goal of disrupting any normative perspective we might have about legal education. This is not so that we settle on rigid definitions and ideas so as to proceed in problem-solving, in fact the opposite: the position taken by each actor on the meanings attributed to key words opens up for them a series of agentic choices which may diverge significantly from the choices available to, or favoured by, other actors. Exploring 'what we talk about when we talk about'[5] *Pressing Problems in the Law School* is not, in my view, mere academic noodling; rather it is an opportunity to consider questions which we hope will linger in the readers' minds as they engage with other chapters of this book: After all, Boon and Webb noted in 2008 "an underlying epistemic uncertainty about the nature of the English Legal education project and a tendency to respond ad hoc to national, regional and globalising pressures",[6] so, we need, for example, to keep interrogating whether we are focusing on 'our' problems, that is the problems closest to our experiences and values rather than the problems that others wish us to take on. It's a chance to ask who the 'we' are – a homogeneous tribe or an opportunistic band of fellow-travellers? Which problems might require systemic solutions, and which might be best served by variation? Can we agree on the relative urgency of different problems? Can alliances based on our hierarchies of urgency emerge?

---

5 Raymond Carver, *What We Talk About When We Talk About Love* (Knopf 1981).
6 Andrew Boon and Julian Webb, 'Legal Education and Training in England and Wales: Back to the Future?' (2008) 58 (1) Journal of Legal Education, 79–121, 79.

Missing voices from the debate– what do students think in retrospect, what might they know in advance?

As Paul Maharg pointed out in his reflective blogpost,[7] in Birks' collection *'Student views are almost entirely absent from a book on legal education'* and student views were still significantly under-represented in our seminar. It seems important to start, therefore, with the student voice that we did manage to include via an online survey that was circulated among second- to fourth-year undergraduate law degree students at the seminar hosting organisations, Northumbria Law School and Nottingham Law School. First year students were excluded from this research as it was believed that they might not have experienced enough of the law school yet to answer some of the questions on the online survey (i.e., questions on experiential/clinical modules). The online survey consisted of 25 questions that were a mixture of multi-answer, single-answer, rating options and free-text answers regarding module content, delivery, assessments, and preparation for life after law school. Samantha presented the findings in the opening session in an attempt to focus the academics' attention on student experience and preference across a number of factors,[8] with the explicit caveat that this brief survey was not significantly superior to the blunt instruments[9] used to gauge student satisfaction within and between universities. Nevertheless, we include the data here as a potentially compelling snapshot:

- Only one respondent selected the option 'If I could remodel Law School, I wouldn't change a thing' regarding course delivery and assessment.
- All respondents felt the core subjects were 'essential' or 'important', the majority found their option choices 'strengthened research skills'.
- There was a strong preference for experiential learning: as a positive experience, in developing a range of skills and as a preparation for employment and they were the most popular option for potential change to the balance of the curriculum; nevertheless, traditional lectures and seminars were judged to have value.
- This was mirrored in the responses to assessment: respondents liked practical coursework, e.g. drafting, and participatory assessments, e.g.

---

7 See Paul Maharg, 'Pressing Problems MLR Seminar, Final Thoughts' (Paul Maharg, 09 July 2019) <https://paulmaharg.com/2019/07/09/pressing-problems-mlr-seminar-final-thoughts/> accessed 15 November 2021.

8 Reported in full in Victoria Roper, Rachel Dunn and Samantha Rasiah, 'Revisiting "Pressing Problems in the Law: What Is the Law School For?" 20 years on' (2020) 54 (3) The Law Teacher, 455–464.

9 Aftab Dean, Moade Shubita and Julia Claxton, 'What Type of Learning Journey Do Students Value Most? Understanding Enduring Factors from the NSS Leading to Responsible Decision-Making' (2020) 11 (4) Journal of Global Responsibility, 347–362. Most universities nevertheless paste the data prominently on websites, without undertaking the nuanced analysis necessary.

4   Elaine Hall and Samantha Rasiah

advocacy, more than traditional coursework, open and closed book exams. Without wishing to erase the traditional methods, they wanted more of the experiential and one respondent specified so as to build those skills over time: "I believe 0 credit advocacy modules in years 1 and 2 would benefit students, giving them the knowledge whether advocacy is something they enjoy whilst also receiving constructive feedback from trained professionals".

There was, however, some ambiguity evident between the respondents' ideas about curriculum design and their reports of their behaviour and motivation with regard to lecture and seminar attendance and participation:

- Lectures are regarded by the majority as useful sources of new information and of clarification for material already met and by a minority as pointless because they can be watched back at any time and/or material has to be revisited. Half of respondents combine these views, considering value and pointlessness as coexisting.
- Not attending lectures is most often attributed to external *force majeure* (illness, other commitments) but also to the previously mentioned time flexibility, pointlessness and the lack of (perceived) attendance policing[10]; respondents also considered having attendance count towards grades as the most useful incentive.
- Seminars are considered more valuable, providing deeper insight and opportunities to prepare for assessment, with only one respondent finding them pointless; simultaneously they are seen as a source of stress with pressures relating to preparation and performance: *Stressful when it appears that I am the only student who has done any prep and is therefore able to engage with the tutor.*
- Not attending seminars, apart from external circumstances, focuses on not feeling prepared for the session, dreading the interaction or not considering that they will benefit from it; yet again, the extrinsic motivation of attendance counting towards grades is considered the most effective way to encourage attendance.
- In redesigning the curriculum, while respondents rank other activities higher, they also want more lectures and seminars.

The responses suggest that students do not want fundamental changes to the core curriculum and delivery of their law courses while simultaneously wanting to increase the amount of preferred elements. We interpret these

---

10 As in other institutions, attendance is monitored. However, the dashboard is not visible to students, so only when non-attendance reaches a critical threshold is the institution's awareness shared with the student. Would the knowledge of this surveillance make a difference to behaviour, particularly if the thresholds were public? Would everyone drive at 29 mph?

The unitary idea of 'the' law school and other issues   5

preferred elements as thematically grouped around key constructivist pedagogical ideas: experiential and dialogic learning experiences that build skills and knowledge as part of membership of a community of practice, assessed in ways that constructively align both with academic and professional practice.[11] We assume that this is what students' reflections reveal that *they would have wanted* so it occurred to us to wonder whether, had they known this at the outset, they would have been able to select law courses based on these preferences. We had not considered this decision process when designing the survey, so we fell back on a hypothetical exploration.

To try to engage with this problem, we conducted a scoping survey of law courses in 2019 from the perspective of three prospective students. Each student had different predicted grades and using the Guardian University Guide, we selected a shortlist of five institutions that might be that student's first choice.[12] Ali predicted A*AA (which translates to 176 points) had options including Warwick, Nottingham, Manchester, Exeter, Newcastle; Jo predicted ABB (148 points) had City, Lancaster, Kent, Surrey, Liverpool; and Nat predicted CCC (96 points) had Bedfordshire, Northampton, Bolton, London Met, Wolverhampton. We considered the ways in which the degree as a whole was presented, the module structures and option choices and any information about how each module was taught and assessed. Clearly, choice of institution is based on multiple factors unconnected to the learning experience but the purpose of our scoping was to gauge how much information students might have about the curricular variation between law schools when making this choice.

At first glance, the idea of 'the law school' is semiotically unchallenged: the visual presentation of law degrees conforms to the cliche of 'wigs on websites'[13]; apparently we understand lawyering through the image of the formally wigged and robed barrister. This is the sign that indicates the law section of the Higher Education market, the overarching signifier to draw in everyone who wants something law-flavoured. Once the consumer enters the

---

11 See, for example, Elaine Hall and Cath Sylvester, 'Clinic as the Crucible for Theorised Practice and the Practice of Theory in Legal Education' in Linden Thomas, Steven Vaughan, Bharat Malkani and Theresa Lynch (eds), *Reimagining Clinical Legal Education* (Bloomsbury Publishing 2018) for a discussion of how these ideas fit and chafe alongside the traditional legal curriculum.

12 In this hypothetical work, we have focused on English universities, since elsewhere in the chapter, we focus on the legal education landscape in the context of the access to practitioner status rules of England and Wales and we have also excluded the 'elite' universities, since decisions to study there are based in different understandings of quality as explored by Wittek and Kvernbekk, focused on the reputation of the institution itself (quality as exception) rather than on the detail of curricular design (quality as perfection/ transformation). Line Wittek and Tone Kvernbekk, 'On the Problems of Asking for a Definition of Quality in Education' (2011) 55 (6) Scandinavian Journal of Educational Research, 671–684.

13 Although the law undergraduate to barrister pathway will be a reality for only 7%–8% of students.

6   Elaine Hall and Samantha Rasiah

law section, it becomes important particularly to the individual university vendor that the consumer differentiates between institutions and while there is a common core of marketing language, each university seeks to position itself as different. This 'sub-branding' positioning uses a combination of factors which speak both to the history and values of that university and what they think prospective students are looking for. We note universities making much of the connection to and relationship with the local legal profession or specific opportunities for elements of the course in partnership with employers; for clinical placements; for specialist modules tailored to commercial or interdisciplinary work; for activism and policy work. Some law schools highlight their employability statistics,[14] and others their student satisfaction scores, some emphasise the large number of optional modules available, each hoping that this combination will draw the student and their funding to their stall.

Once the consumer starts to click through to more detailed descriptions of modules, options and assessment, it becomes clear that there are considerable and significant differences between law schools. Students attending different universities will encounter significant variation of both what is taught beyond the 'common core' of the Qualifying Law Degree (QLD)[15] subjects and how all law subjects are taught and assessed. All courses surveyed by the authors offer the QLD subjects but the length of the module and the extent to which subjects are combined vary so that the space left in a typical three-year degree also varies. Thus, at some universities, the core dominates and there are a small number of specialised options in later years whilst some universities offer significant levels of divergence within their degrees, with optional subjects in every year. Demonstrating the coverage of the QLD subjects in terms of module credits conceals huge variation in what students will do on each programme and how they will demonstrate the knowledge and skills acquired, though not a variation in quality, since

---

14 Law graduates' employability overall is in line with other non-science graduates both in terms of rates of employment and mean and median salaries. Going by this 2019 data, law graduates don't seem to outperform other social scientists, so this may be another reputational ambiguity. See HESA, 'Figure 10: Percentage of UK Domiciled Leavers Entering Employment in the UK in Professional Occupations by Subject Area and Personal Characteristics' (*HESA*, June 2018) <https://www.hesa.ac.uk/data-and-analysis/sfr250/figure-10> accessed 05 November 2021; HESA, 'Figure 14: UK Domiciled Leavers Who Obtained First Degree Qualifications and Entered Full-Time Paid Work in the UK by Subject Area and Salary' (*HESA*, August 2018) <https://www.hesa.ac.uk/data-and-analysis/sfr250/figure-14> accessed 05 November 2021.
15 The QLD rests upon the 1999 Joint Academic Stage Board Statement from the regulators – at the time this was the Law Society and the General Council of the Bar, latterly the Solicitors Regulation Authority and the Bar Standards Board available in Appendix 1. See Solicitors Regulation Authority and Bar Standards Board, 'Academic Stage handbook' (2014) <https://www.sra.org.uk/globalassets/documents/students/academic-stage/academic-stage-handbook.pdf?version=4a1ac3> accessed 05 November 2021, Appendix 1, 15–20.

The unitary idea of 'the' law school and other issues 7

all these programmes are quality approved and externally examined. Therefore, it is incredibly important to emphasise that this finding of diversity is not a criticism; rather it is a celebration of the creativity of academics and variety offered to students beneath a surface similarity. Our one concern was about how much insider knowledge was needed to read the websites in this way, how many pages had to be clicked through to get all the information – particularly about modes of assessment – and therefore, how many students would be able (or motivated) to access this information and make it part of their decision-making process.[16] Indeed, how informed would those decisions be before the programme commences – how well can someone predict their preferences for longer or shorter modules, for coursework assessment over examinations, for multiple module choices that might depend on an academic not having a sabbatical that semester over the certainty of fewer modules with larger teams?

It would seem that law schools are already quite different from one another in how they frame and deliver the curriculum. We may wish to consider then, for universities marketing law degrees as an economically safe option given its consistent popularity as a course choice and for students choosing a place to study law, how important is the homogeneity of the 'law brand'? Should we continue to speak of 'the law school'? Does it matter that law schools are different? The answer could be both yes and no: difference provides more space for diversity but also encourages comparison and hierarchy that often has little to do with substantive difference. Whether we opt (or are pushed) into greater homogeneity or variety, we need to ask: how do these spaces benefit and exclude? How do hierarchies and the denial of them coexist in the legal academic marketplace? If law schools are like cats, are some cats 'better' than others and is that construction of 'better' an artefact of the curriculum and pedagogy of that law school (the power of the tiger, the speed of the cheetah) or of other accidents, such as being a fairly average bobcat in the most prestigious zoo?

Defining the law school and its problems

In order to explore some of these ideas without getting too bogged down in twenty-first-century context, we draw on useful threads from scholarship on the origins of university legal education.

Berytus (Beirut), the 'mother of laws', provides us with points of comparison for our own practices in terms of – to apply anachronistic terms –

---

16 At Northumbria, we like to think that one of our Unique Selling Points is our clinical module – the Student Law Office – which is a required module on most routes. It is therefore galling how many of our students are surprised to learn this when we have option discussions with them in first and second year.

8   Elaine Hall and Samantha Rasiah

'university mission', 'target markets', 'pedagogy and publishing'. Berytus[17] sits in the contemporary accounts as not only a unitary law school but as the pre-eminent example so, for our purposes, can be examined in greater detail to separate (insofar as this is ever possible) reputation, reality and contextual factors. Berytus was not, prior to the establishment of the Roman military colony, a particularly important settlement and certainly not a centre of power, governance or scholarship. The development of the heavily 'Romanised' city and, in the late second or early third century AD of the law school as a centre of scholarship happened within a context of imperial strategy, financial investment and political preferment. Then[18] as now, the development of universities could be a conscious and deliberate part of the state's operational goals, principally in this case to cement the status and impact of the Justinian law reforms in the Eastern empire.[19] The Roman law *Digest* was largely developed by the scholars of Berytus and from this flowed a tradition of hermeneutic scholarship, commentary and teaching. Berytus was well established by AD 361 when Libanius writes of sending his student to 'the mother of laws' and at its height in the fifth century is lauded by the Egyptian poet Nonnus: "the unshakeable wall of laws by which Beirut and only Beirut, fortified the cities of the world".[20]

However, even at this early stage of our ancestry, we do not have 'the' law school at Berytus. Despite the impression given by Libanius of a single, maternal entity, Millar cautions that "we should speak of 'law schools' rather than of 'the Law School'".[21] Rather, Berytus is best seen as an example of the tutelary model, where professors had client relationships with elite students from across the empire and they formed many schools in co-location. The incredible reputation of the Berytus 'professors of universal compass'[22] was collective and reputational rather than part of the lived experience

---

17 Kathleen McNamee, 'Another Chapter in the History of Scholia' (1998) 48 (1) Classical Quarterly, 269–288.

18 The notable exception to this, of course, is Bologna, where the formation of the University by the students is characterised as a flowering of independent (from the state) scholarship, though of course this formation was at least partly a defensive move against the city state's interesting method of making all/any 'foreigners' responsible for the malefactions of any one non-native. Peter Denley, '"Medieval", "Renaissance", "modern". Issues of Periodization in Italian University History' (2013) 27 (4) Renaissance Studies, 487–503.

19 Fergus Millar, 'The Roman Colonies of the Near East. A Study of Cultural Relations' in Heikki Solin and Mika Kajava (eds), *Roman Eastern Policy and Other Studies in Roman History: Proceedings of a Colloquium at Tvarminne* (The Finish Society of Sciences and Letters, 1990) 7–58.

20 Ibid, 270.

21 Fergus Millar, 'The Roman Colonies of the Near East. A Study of Cultural Relations' in Heikki Solin and Mika Kajava (eds), *Roman Eastern Policy and Other Studies in Roman History: Proceedings of a Colloquium at Tvarminne* (The Finish Society of Sciences and Letters, 1990) 7–58, 23; Kathleen McNamee, 'Another Chapter in the History of Scholia' (1998) 48 (1) Classical Quarterly, 269–288, 269.

22 Also referred to as 'heroes' and 'teachers of exceptional distinction' in the *Basilica*, the tenth-century summary of Justinian's codification. See Kathleen McNamee, 'Another Chapter in the History of Scholia' (1998) 48 (1) Classical Quarterly, 269–288, 271.

of individual professors or students. Each professor/school had a distinct identity, based on individual expertise and constituting a 'school' much in the same way that Renaissance artists' schools developed,[23] so one might study adjacent to those exploring discrete aspects of the law without oneself studying them. It is very likely, as with artistic schools, that there would have been significant exchange of ideas and influence between professorial schools without those schools blurring into homogeneity and losing their individual character. The reputational need for the idea of 'the' law school has arguably two drivers: first, the familiar, ancient and persistent market effect whereby specialists cluster in one place order to attract more customers but maintain their differences in order to compete once the customers are in view (discussed further in our look at pedagogy and student experience) and, less often examined, the relationship of the state to legal scholarship and education. States in their codification role[24] tend to operate in an imagined present where the current law becomes 'the law' despite the historical evidence and lived experience that law is mutable and constantly adjusting to circumstance and culture. It is useful, therefore, for states (sometimes) to think about the law school as similarly unitary.

Law schools in Berytus were places where laws were recorded and codified for the state(s) and other authorities, initially the Roman Empire and later the early Christian church whose jurisdiction/influence they found themselves in/under. They were places where laws were subjected to analysis and commentary in service to those lawmakers[25] and this political preferment was explicit: Berytus had permissions to hold and work on documents only otherwise held in the capitals of Rome and Constantinople and overt protection from the Imperial government to the extent that similar law school developments were halted and prohibited by Justinian in Alexandria and Caesarea. While law schools in England and Wales continue the work of analysis and commentary the transactional relationship with the state and other authorities is more diffuse and opportunistic than for the scholars of Berytus: legal academics participate in joint research and policy development as partners and contractors but also contribute to law reform as independent critics and stakeholders. Legal academics *as a group* do these things; it is vital to point out that individuals have significantly different opportunities and capital, depending both on their position in the academic hierarchy of precarity and status and on the culture, capital and resource of

---

23 Fergus Millar, 'The Roman Colonies of the Near East. A Study of Cultural Relations' in Heikki Solin and Mika Kajava (eds), *Roman Eastern Policy and Other Studies in Roman History: Proceedings of a Colloquium at Tvarminne* (The Finish Society of Sciences and Letters, 1990) 7–58.

24 Gunther Weiss, 'The Enchantment of Codification in the Common-Law World' (2000) 25 (2) Yale Journal of International Law, 435–532.

25 Or despite them, or under tacit protection. Justinian's official prohibition on commentary was widely ignored by the Berytus scholars but none were prosecuted, though scholars elsewhere were suppressed. See Kathleen McNamee, 'Another Chapter in the History of Scholia' (1998) 48 (1) Classical Quarterly, 269–288, 271.

10 Elaine Hall and Samantha Rasiah

their particular institution.[26] Talking about 'the' law school ignores these inequalities within and between each law school and is therefore potentially a serious distraction from one of our more pressing problems.[27] Our relationship to different agencies of the state is also a complicating factor: there are tensions between our duties to the professional regulators[28] – broadly conceptualised as 'maintaining standards' via the mechanism of the Qualifying Law Degree (QLD) – and our role within the broader provision of higher education places for larger numbers of students.

Here I think we have alighted on a pressing problem, an academic culture which has not recognised or is reluctant to acknowledge the lack of fit between its traditional assumptions about both purpose and actors and the current Higher Education and legal-professional landscapes. The massification of Higher Education[29] has opened up opportunities for engagement and study so significantly as to change young people's expectations of their life course within a generation, such that going to university is an expected rite of passage in the twenty-first century, instead of a minority activity in the 1980s. Law schools with their lack of expensive laboratories, high status professional links and cultural capital have been significant beneficiaries *and* victims of this massification process. Our university overlords have been keen for us to expand, there are larger departments, more academic posts and more opportunities for aspirant legal scholars but the pace and extent of that expansion have changed the job, in particular the modes of engagement with students, though these changes have been primarily driven by practicalities rather than pedagogical reflection. This has been particularly evident in the rapid adoption of hybrid technological solutions during the Covid-19 pandemic where the imitation of practices developed over years and rigorously evaluated by colleagues at the Open University has not necessarily transplanted the contextual awareness and intent of those approaches.[30] However, more fundamentally we have yet as a community of

---

26 This is before we begin to consider the intersectional elements of disability, race, gender, sexuality, culture and class that shape the space within which individual academics can operate. Sara Ahmed, *On Being Included: Racism and Diversity in Institutional Life* (Duke University Press 2012).

27 For further discussion of these issues, see Jessica Guth and Doug Morrison, 'Who Are Law Schools For? A Story of Class and Gender'; Foluke Adebisi and Katie Bales, 'Reinventing Possibility: A Reflection on Law, Race and Decolonial Discourse in Legal Education' in this book.

28 The Solicitors Regulation Authority (SRA) and the Bar Standards Board (BSB).

29 David J Hornsby and Ruksana Osman, 'Massification in Higher Education: Large Classes and Student Learning' (2014) 67 (6) Higher Education, 711–719; Ceryn Evans, Gareth Rees, Chris Taylor and Stuart Fox, 'A Liberal Higher Education for All? The Massification of Higher Education and Its Implications for Graduates' Participation in Civil Society' (2021) 81, Higher Education 521–535; See also Margaret Thornton, 'What Is the Law School For in a Post-Pandemic World?' in this book.

30 For example, Francine Ryan, 'Rage Against the Machine? Incorporating Legal Tech into Legal Education' (2020) 55 (3) The Law Teacher, 392–404; Hugh McFaul, Liz Hardie, Francine Ryan, Keren Lloyd Bright and Neil Graffin, 'Taking Clinical Legal Education

The unitary idea of 'the' law school and other issues   11

legal educators to significantly explore the way in which we understand our curriculum. This is not to discount the considerable work published[31]; it is just that we do not seem ready to discuss and operationalise it. Can we, as individual law teachers, as collective groups in law schools and across the law teacher community articulate to ourselves where that knowledge comes from, how theoretically commensurate it is with our understanding of what the law is and what law school is for? Can we map and interrogate how that translates to our structures and practices?

The QLD[32] in England and Wales has until recently[33] acted as the gateway to the profession; aspirant lawyers must acquire the requisite knowledge and skills either through their first degree or through a graduate conversion course before undertaking the professional aspects of training (typically through the Legal Practice Course (LPC) for solicitors and the Bar Course for barristers offered both by law schools and specialist providers). The espoused aim of the QLD was to ensure that the 'foundations of legal knowledge' as well as 'key skills' were held in common by all law graduates and, presumably, by all to an appropriate standard.[34] This move can be interpreted in a number of ways. From one perspective, this demonstrates a high

---

Online: Songs of Innocence and Experience' (2020) 27 (4) International Journal of Clinical Legal Education, 27, 4, 6–38; Francine Ryan and Hugh McFaul, 'Innovative Technologies in UK Legal Education' in Emma Jones and Fiona Cownie (eds), *Key Directions in Legal Education: National and International Perspectives* (Routledge 2020).

31 By *inter alia,* Fiona Cownie and Anthony Bradney, 'An Examined Life: Research into University Legal Education in the United Kingdom and the Journal of Law and Society' (2017) 44 (S1) Journal of Law and Society, S129–S143; Luke Mason, 'SQEezing the Jurisprudence Out of the SRA's Super Exam: The SQE's Bleak Legal Realism and the Rejection of Law's Multimodal Truth' (2018) 52 (4) The Law Teacher, 409–424; Chloe J Wallace, 'The Pedagogy of Legal Reasoning: Democracy, Discourse and Community' (2018) 52 (3) The Law Teacher, 260–271.

32 The QLD rests upon the 1999 Joint Academic Stage Board Statement from the regulators – at the time, this was the Law Society and the General Council of the Bar, latterly the Solicitors Regulation Authority and the Bar Standards Board. See Solicitors Regulation Authority and Bar Standards Board, 'Academic Stage Handbook' (2014) <https://www. sra.org.uk/globalassets/documents/students/academic-stage/academic-stage-handbook. pdf?version=4a1ac3> accessed 08 November 2021, Appendix 1.

33 I have expressed my reservations elsewhere Elaine Hall, John Hodgson, Caroline Strevens and Jessica Guth, '"What We Did Over the Summer": Updates on Proposed Reforms to Legal Education and Training in England and Wales and the Republic of Ireland' (2019) 53 (4) The Law Teacher, 536–546; Elaine Hall, 'Glass Houses: How Might We Decide on a 'Good Enough' Assessment to Become a Solicitor?' (2018) 53 (4) The Law Teacher, 453–466; Elaine Hall, 'Notes on the SRA Report of the Consultation on the SQE: Comment Is Free, but Facts Are Sacred' (2017) 41 (1) The Law Teacher, 364–372.

34 It is clear that even in 1999, the issue of standards was tricky: the baseline was set as the Quality Assurance Agency (QAA) threshold that applies to all degrees but footnote 4 plaintively says *"It is hoped at all institutions will set their standards above the Benchmark"* Joint statement, Solicitors Regulation Authority and Bar Standards Board, 'Academic Stage Handbook' (2014) <https://www.sra.org.uk/globalassets/documents/students/ academic-stage/academic-stage-handbook.pdf?version=4a1ac3> accessed 08 November 2021, Appendix 1.

level of trust between the regulators and 'the' law school, a belief that a common understanding of foundational knowledge was explicitly shared and that therefore multiple routes could safely be charted towards a common destination. This position of trust and belief was not likely to be disrupted by experience, since the regulators did not undertake systematic reviews of curriculum or inspections of teaching, relying on the self-report of institutions about the number of credits and the subjects covered in each degree.

However, it does not appear that the common understanding exists, nor that there is much conceptual clarity about the genesis of or justification for the 'foundation', as Cherry and Koo point out:

> The BSB consultation on Future Bar Training 2015 summarising the current position in relation to core states at para 60: "Under the present arrangements, students must study certain subjects that began as a list of what were regarded as 'core' over 40 years ago, plus some that have been added since then in an ad hoc manner. The list of required subjects contains things that some barristers may never use (for example trusts, crime) and does not contain other subjects which are of great importance."
>
> And the consultation goes on, para 61:
>
> It is hard to find concrete evidence that knowledge of most of the required subjects is any more 'essential' than knowledge of many other subjects. These arrangements tend to give prominence to the acquisition of knowledge, rather than understanding of principles and concepts and the development of transferable intellectual and legal skills.[35]

Nevertheless, we have been operating with the apparent confidence of shared assumptions for some time and these have been presented as part of the legal professional identity: "the systematic knowledge base of a profession is thought to have four essential properties. It is specialised, firmly bounded, scientific and standardised".[36] The QLD might possibly be characterised as specialised and bounded – we question the designation 'scientific' because of the lack of first principles exploration of essence and accidence in the legal curriculum and we will explore in more depth the extent to which standardisation has been attempted below.

---

35 Cherry James and John Koo, 'The EU Law "Core" Module: Surviving the Perfect Storm of Brexit and the SQE' (2018) 52 (1) The Law Teacher, 68–84, citing Bar Standards Board, 'Future Bar Training: Consultation on the Future of Training for the Bar: Academic, Vocational and Professional Stages of Training' (2015) <https://www.barstandardsboard.org.uk/uploads/assets/e85659f2-9dce-453c-9cc1ce640677c227/fbttripleconsultation-july2015.pdf> accessed 15 November 2021.

36 Donald Schon, *The Reflective Practitioner: How Professionals Think in Action* (Basic Books 1983) 23, cited by Michael Eraut, *Developing Professional Knowledge and Competence* (Routledge 1994) 101.

The unitary idea of 'the' law school and other issues 13

The 'lightly prescribed'[37] diet of subjects and the diversity of methods by which the QLD ingredients could be combined both in terms of whether subjects are taught individually or in combination as well as autonomy in designing modes of assessment suggests that the regulators were content to set broad parameters and to leave details to the discretion of each institution. It may be inferred that their trust in academics' compliance was justified: Boon and Webb estimated in 2008 that the Foundation accounted around one third of the average degree curriculum; in 2019, Steven Vaughan noted that this had not changed significantly[38] despite the 'bonfire of regulations'.[39] John Flood commented: "This will give the universities and colleges plenty of scope to innovate, **should they choose to do so.** Unfortunately, the British academy is slow in this area, not always recognising that change has occurred".[40] Why have they not so chosen? Is it simply a question of inertia, as Flood suggests or are there multiple constraints at work? In other areas of education, we have seen the development of guidance (e.g. the literacy and numeracy 'hour' recommended in the National Strategy[41]) into prescriptive practice (expected by Ofsted and rigidly applied in timetables nationwide) despite there being no actual requirement. One possible explanation is that it is easier to demonstrate compliance by imitation of a model, rather than having to explain or defend how your idiosyncratic approach meets the criteria. Also, there are strong cultural traditions at work which use memory to reinforce and justify practice: for example, all law schools teach crime and most of them do so within a very similar frame, with a strong focus on crimes against the person, with an emphasis on murder, grievous and actual bodily harm and assault. This frame appears to be one that has accreted, rather than having been designed, either from a theoretical or practice

---

37 Andrew Boon and Julian Webb, 'Legal Education and Training in England and Wales: Back to the Future?' (2008) 58 (1) Journal of Legal Education, 79–121, 79.

38 Andrew Boon and Julian Webb, 'Legal Education and Training in England and Wales: Back to the Future?' (2008) 58 (1) Journal of Legal Education, 79–121; Steven Vaughan, Pressing Problems keynote "The lies we tell ourselves: problematising the (s)hallow foundations of the core of legal education", cited in Victoria Roper, Rachel Dunn and Samantha Rasiah, 'Revisiting "Pressing Problems in the Law: What Is the Law School For?" 20 years on' (2020) 54 (3) The Law Teacher, 455–464.

39 Announced by the SRA's Anthony Townsend in 2013, the 'bonfire' was positioned as the removal of most significant constraints in the teaching of Qualifying Law Degree subjects in terms of curriculum content, module design and assessment. It was seen as liberating and reported on widely, though prompted little actual change in classrooms, as noted with particularly trenchant comment from John Flood on his blog. John Flood, 'One Size Doesn't Fit All in Legal Education' (*John Flood's Random Academic Thoughts*, 15 October 2013) <http://johnflood.blogspot.com/2013/10/one-size-doesnt-fit-all-in-legal.html> accessed 08 November 2021

40 Ibid, my emphasis.

41 Maria Mroz, Fay Smith and Frank Hardman, 'The Discourse of the Literacy Hour' (2000) 30 (3) Cambridge Journal of Education, 379–390.

standpoint[42] and tends to be defended on the grounds that this content is engaging and popular with students, which is an extremely compelling argument but not one that satisfies those interested in curriculum design, who argue that if curricular structures have emerged ecologically, then they are likely to be healthiest in a constant state of reaction and renewal. As the ecology of Higher Education and society changes, these structures deserve critical analysis. This critical analysis must, importantly, avoid overstating the speed and extent of change: "changes [in the legal profession] have been neither uniform nor uncontested. In sites of multiprofessional work strong disciplinary connections to law survive, despite regulatory liberalisation and increased external control. Furthermore, the profession retains a large proportion of legal work".[43]

It appears from our scoping survey that the top line content of law degrees is very similar, although the fine detail reveals differences that may well be significant in terms of student experience and we consider that the idea of 'the' law school is real because of a common heritage and also due to ecological constraints, external factors such as requirements driven by professional recognition, that reinforce our points of similarity. Despite this common ancestry and ecological constraints and the surface impression of curricular similarity, there is nevertheless a strong phenomenological testimony from legal educators that there is considerable diversity between schools and that this difference is important[44] because it enables the richness and diversity of the law – as scholarly practice; as critical engagement; as professional endeavour – to be differentially privileged across law schools.

Another perspective is that possibly the governing bodies did not have that trust or belief but did not consider this to be problematic: the undergraduate diet might not be critical to professional standards, which would rather be maintained by the LPC/ Bar Course training and by the acculturation and assimilation that took place in the early stages of employment (the solicitor's training contract or the barrister's pupillage). It is here that we need to consider what other mechanisms might have been/ be contributing to and maintaining the 'expected' routes into practice – by which we mean both that employers get the employees they expect and that aspirants who expect, based on experience and privilege, to access the profession are able to do so. It is arguable that the governing bodies assumed that the existing

---

42 See the fantastic text, *The Teaching of Criminal Law: The Pedagogical Imperatives*, for an extended discussion of the problem and a range of approaches to solutions. Kris Gledhill and Ben Livings (eds), *The Teaching of Criminal Law: The Pedagogical Imperatives'* (Routledge 2018).

43 Hilary Sommerlad, Andrew Francis, Joan Loughrey and Steven Vaughan, 'England and Wales: A Legal Profession in the Vanguard of Professional Transformation?' in Richard L Abel, Ole Hammerslev and Hilary Sommerlad (eds), *Lawyers in 21st Century Societies: Vol. 1 National Reports* (Bloomsbury 2020).

44 Jessica Guth and Chris Ashford, 'The Legal Education and Training Review: Regulating Socio-Legal and Liberal Legal Education?' (2014) 48 (1) The Law Teacher, 5–19, 5.

The unitary idea of 'the' law school and other issues 15

hierarchy of class and its mirror in the hierarchy of universities[45] would maintain the status quo and here, I think we have alighted upon one of our significant 'pressing problems': access.

Who is law school (apparently and actually) for?

Access to justice, particularly since the reforms to Legal Aid in England and Wales,[46] is a societal pressing problem and the decline in funding for all aspects of the civil and criminal legal system exacerbates the inequalities that citizens face when engaging with the law. However, there is a broader inequity: some citizens look to judges, to barristers, to solicitors and see themselves mirrored and others do not.[47] Representation of diversity in the law is low: apart from gender where universities recruit a balance of male and female students, even at undergraduate level we are less likely to see people from minoritised groups. Only a minority of law graduates enter the profession[48] and as we move into employment and up the various hierarchies within law firms, at the Bar and in the judiciary, even the impact of more female graduates appears to evaporate and we see an increasingly

---

45 In England and Wales, the hierarchy begins with Oxford and Cambridge, descends to a self-appointed and gatekeeping set called the Russell Group which mainly contains the older-established institutions but also includes later creations. Outside the Russell group, 'Red-brick' institutions claim longevity (and sometimes other kinds of) status over 'concrete' and 'post-92' universities, a move which is only partially undermined by league tables (noting that those metrics are highly problematic) since reputation and performance are not and have never been the same thing.

46 For analysis of the impacts of this reform Legal Aid, Sentencing and Punishment of Offenders Act 2012, commonly abbreviated to LASPO see, *inter alia*, Pascoe Pleasence, Nigel J Balmer and Catrina Denvir, 'Wrong about Rights: Public Knowledge of Key Areas of Consumer, Housing and Employment Law in England and Wales' (2017) 80 (5) Modern Law Review, 836–859; Chris Barton, 'MacLean, Mavis and Eekelaar, John, After the Act: Access to Family Justice After LASPO' (2019) 82 (6) Modern Law Review, 1176–1179; Jess Mant and Julie Wallbank, 'The Mysterious Case of Disappearing Family Law and the Shrinking Vulnerable Subject' (2017) 26 (5) Social and Legal Studies, 629–648.

47 See, inter alia, Alexandra Wilson, *In Black and White: A Young Barrister's Story of Race and Class in a Broken Justice System* (Endeavour 2020); I Stephanie Boyce, 'Presidential Address' (The Law Society, 24 March 2021) <https://www.lawsociety.org.uk/en/topics/news-articles/i-stephanie-boyce-presidential-address> accessed 08 November 2021; Lady Hale, 'Lord Upjohn Lecture 2021 – "When There Are 12": Legal Education and a Diverse Judiciary' (2021) The Law Teacher <https://www.tandfonline.com/doi/full/10.1080/030694 00.2021.1966251> accessed 08 November 2021.

48 The Law Society, 'Entry Trends' (*The Law Society*, 25 November 2020) <https://www.lawsociety.org.uk/en/career-advice/becoming-a-solicitor/entry-trends> accessed 08 November 2021 notes 25,575 UK and Overseas students commencing law degrees in 2019/20. Accepted onto the roll of solicitors by the SRA were 6,972 people in the year to 31 July 2019, making the total on the roll 195,821. Called to the Bar were 1,004 people in 2019–2020, joining a community of 17,078 practising barristers in 2020.

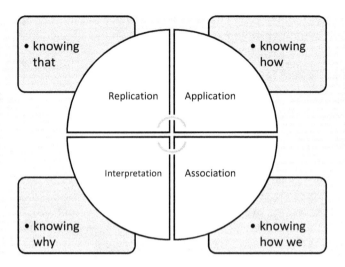

Figure 1.1 Forms of disciplinary learning, from Broudy et al., 1964.

homogenous white, male, abled, wealthy group.[49] This process is equally at work in universities, where intersectional advantage ensures that the same people rise more fluidly, while others meet barriers.[50] The traditional structures are strong and based on what Eraut notes as a 'relationship of tension' between the academy and the profession, nascent here in the "two distinct historical traditions"[51]: the Replication/Application forms of knowing which encompass the codification and collation of laws (and the translation for students) and the Association/Interpretation forms which include critical and cultural hermeneutic analysis (and the translation for students)[52] (Figure 1.1).

Most law teachers might intend that for genuinely foundational concepts (for example 'intent' or 'reasonableness') all elements of the cycle would be visited, explored and ingested, reflected upon internally to gain ownership of the concept and reflected back to the student through assessment and that the process would be repeated within and between modules to build up confidence and accuracy in Replication/Application and sophistication and tolerance for ambiguity in Association/Interpretation. If that were

---

49 Lady Hale, 'Lord Upjohn Lecture 2021 – "When There Are 12": Legal Education and a Diverse Judiciary' (2021) The Law Teacher <https://www.tandfonline.com/doi/full/10.1080/03069400.2021.1966251> accessed 08 November 2021
50 Sara Ahmed, *On Being Included: Racism and Diversity in Institutional Life* (Duke University Press 2012).
51 Michael Eraut, *Developing Professional Knowledge and Competence* (Routledge 1994) 101.
52 Harry S Broudy, Bunnie Othanel Smith and Joe R Burnett, *Democracy and Excellence in American Secondary Education: A Study in Curriculum Theory* (Rand McNally 1964).

operationalised in our courses, I suspect that we might see very different practices in terms of our interactions with students and, in particular, our forms of assessment. The curriculum, rather than focusing on 'covering' intent in Crime (often a first-year subject), would set up spaces for explicit dialogue whenever intent returns, or indeed where it might be assumed to be present but is not. Since 'intent' in Contract is parsed as 'intent to create' the legal relationship but does not carry the same weight of causality of 'intent to cause harm', we may not specify to our students that this concept that was crucial last semester is now subordinate, even though, as students struggle to master the new language of contract law, this remains a common conceptual error. We may not, when discussing the remedies for breach of contract, have lecture or tutorial space to explore the considerable practical difficulties of obtaining these remedies after judgment. However, we could point to the places in our curriculum – Streetlaw, Human Rights and Justice, Clinic (advice and/or representation) – where this will be explored and critiqued. The role of the law teacher needs to include an empathetic awareness of what the student has just encountered and what they will go on to encounter. This awareness can manifest in clear scaffolding and signposting, making explicit to all students the threshold concepts and key connections that some students make but that many struggle with. In other words, it is not adequate for law teachers to treat their module as a sealed unit but to actively seek out the connections and make them clear.

The traditional legal pedagogies, replication models based on the memorisation of case studies and limited application exercises of 'dogmatic *interpretatio*'[53] had a number of disadvantages for the Berytus professors and their elite students: the time spent on lecturing, the need to translate texts from Latin to Greek to reflect a more internationalised student body and the awareness that only some of the students wished to 'apprentice' as lawyers or professors. In what can be seen as a pragmatic pedagogical as well as a smart academic publishing move, the professors of Berytus created annotated *papyri* for their students, demonstrated by McNamee to be the first examples of critical syntheses of the law and how to acquire mastery of it in one annotated artefact[54]: 'the preferred hybrid vehicle for legal instruction'.[55] These early legal textbooks, with their helpful annotations – glosses of key words, cross-referencing and didactic instructions 'learn this', 'skip this' and 'mark this' – returned with the students to their home cities, setting up a cultural rippling effect of both legal knowledge and the presentation and transmission of that knowledge, one that is mirrored in the contemporary uses of religious commentaries[56] and laying bare the shared

---

53 Kathleen McNamee, "Another Chapter in the History of Scholia" (1998) 48 (1) Classical Quarterly, 269–288, 274.
54 Ibid, 283.
55 Ibid, 274.
56 Ibid, 284.

hermeneutic traditions of legal and religious scholarly work. As 'people of the book', scholars of religious and secular law begin by developing replication and application skills in relation to their text(s). They perform activities of maintenance, recording and dissemination, so that the laws are visible and the legal actors' decisions are reflected. This process of conservation of and service to legal structures remains a key part of legal education and training. It is here perhaps that we can see the roots of Langdell's framing of law being a discoverable truth and that 'everything you would wish to know can be obtained from printed books'.[57] But what of these books? As Gledhill and Livings warn "there is little material to suggest that law school curricula in general or criminal law courses in particular are designed on a foundation of research that supports how best to secure an understanding of how criminal law operates".[58] We might fruitfully consider, therefore, the processes of choice that go into setting textbooks, is it more than tradition or contiguity? Given the potentially symbiotic relationship between text, lecture, seminar and assessment, one that increases over time for both students and staff, has that choice been made with reference to 'an understanding of *how* law *operates*'? What do we mean when we talk about 'how' – is this practice-oriented, theoretically driven, political? How do we conceptualise 'operation' – a realist framing, an idealist one (and which or whose ideals?)?

Resting upon the texts and the structures of a course and bringing it to vibrant life are the interactions between students and tutors. The pedagogic practice of the Berytus 'professors of universal compass' goes much beyond their educational publishing, centred on the day-to-day activities and particularly the Associative and Interpretative elements of the learning. These were explored in what we might recognise as seminars or supervisions in which the cultural constraints of practice and the philosophical ideals (apparently) underpinning laws were subject to critical analysis. These conversations therefore were highly relational and specific, whilst leaving little historical trace so, while the political intent and the publicity related to Berytus appear to be about convergence and homogeneity, the reality of the 'student experience' may have been considerably more variable. This variation based on specialism and passion persists, arguably to the present day when we reflect upon the range of options offered in the various curricula offered to students at different universities, revealed in our scoping survey. As in Berytus, individual interest and preferred style have fostered in English law schools the development of diverse educational cultures, sometimes because of professional governing bodies and sometimes despite them. Such discussions form the basis for our more interesting teaching and learning encounters to this day, and we highlight these parts of our professional practice as legal educators; it is these 'higher order' and more specialised aspects

---

57 David R Barnhizer, 'The University Ideal and Clinical Legal Education' (1990) 35 (1) New York Law School Law Review, 87, citing Langdell 1887.

58 Kris Gledhill and Ben Livings (eds), *The Teaching of Criminal Law: The Pedagogical Imperatives'* (Routledge 2018) 5.

The unitary idea of 'the' law school and other issues 19

that we point to as vital and important, that distinguish what we do from mere 'training' and that make our own law school most uniquely itself.[59]

The traditional focus in terms of the university legal curriculum in England was on highly focused erudition, with a disdain for generalist or, heaven forfend, foundational knowledge[60]; we can more meaningfully understand this as an artefact of barristers and, to a certain extent, solicitors being quite separate from the class of legal clerks, whose considerable expertise in Replication and Application forms of knowledge acquired through apprenticeship supported the endeavours of the elite. As Eraut notes, the possession of a university education was much more a marker of class, rather than competence: "70 per cent of practising barristers were graduates in 1875, degrees did not become compulsory until 1975".[61] We can see this even further back with the Law students of Berytus, who were not neophyte/undergraduate legal scholars but already 'qualified' and engaged in further study as part of elite replication. Legal studies at university until arguably the mid-twentieth century were for those privileged males who were being prepared to transition from existing privilege into positions of greater power, within and beyond their *familia*. These students entered Berytus schools often with goals other than that of operating (at a more specialist level) in the legal profession: Liebeschuetz notes "a steady increase in the popularity of Latin and legal studies... caused by the government's policy of giving preference, when making appointments to the civil service, to applicants who had knowledge of Latin and Roman Law".[62] The historical roots of the law degree as a 'passport to employability',[63] albeit in this elite context, are evident here.

Problems, what is pressing, hidden and visible hierarchies

The discourse within Birk's collection, in the seminar and more widely in legal education, has strong overtones of frustration: if only we had better

---

59 Luke Mason's reflections on 'bleak legal realism' and on the development of legal science approaches explored at the Pressing problems seminar developed further in this blogpost. Luke Mason, 'SQEezing the Jurisprudence Out of the SRA's Super Exam: The SQE's Bleak ertments, more academic posts,mber (GLOBAL; Legal Realism and the Rejection of Law's Multimodal Truth' (2018) 52 (4) The Law Teacher, 409–424; Luke Mason, 'Decolonisation, Law and Legal Education: A Multimodal View' (*African Legal Studies Blog*, 30 July 2021) <https://africanlegalstudies.blog/2021/07/30/decolonisation-law-and-legal-education-a-multimodal-view/ > accessed 08 November 2021.

60 Paul McKeown and Elaine Hall, 'If We Could Instil Social Justice Values Through Clinical Education, Should We?' (2018) 5 (1) Journal of International and Comparative Law, 143–179.

61 Michael Eraut, *Developing Professional Knowledge and Competence* (Routledge 1994) 8.

62 J H W G Liebeschuetz, *Antioch: City and Imperial Adminstration in the Later Roman Empire* (Oxford University Press 1971) 246, cite by Kathleen McNamee, 'Another Chapter in the History of Scholia' (1998) 48 (1) Classical Quarterly, 269–288, 273.

63 Jill Alexander and Carol Boothby, 'Stakeholder Perceptions of Clinical Legal Education within an Employability Context' (2018) 25 (3) International Journal of Clinical Legal Education, 53–84.

20 *Elaine Hall and Samantha Rasiah*

students; more time, resources and technologies; more pedagogically inclined academic staff; if certain constraints were lifted, then much greater progress could be made. Powerful actors position the issues as problems but are these law school *problems* (as opposed to phenomena sometimes perceived as problematic)? We would argue that all of these issues listed are both complicated problems (with potentially practical solutions) and complex problematic issues (in that each element is in relationship with many others with unpredictable results). However, these issues are subordinate to unresolved questions of purpose and value. At this point in our explorations, it is our contention that the pressing problems of the law school are not primarily pragmatic but conceptual and centred on who the law school serves.

Our conception of service in this chapter is politically driven: we therefore set out to highlight the idea of 'the' law school since we consider that it serves to erase inequalities within the academy and the profession. We chose to focus on access both to the law school and to what the law school purports to offer since the serious inequalities in society are reinforced by the institutional structures of universities and professions[64] and the alignment of the curriculum with the implicit goals of the law school and the desires of students since without that careful constructive alignment we are merely tinkering. In choosing these to be presented as most pressing, this is, in itself, another example of the way in which academics use their privileged position to present one way of framing an issue as paramount.[65]

Even within our self-assigned choices, we have created more questions rather than definitive answers. For example, the commercial and regulatory relationships between the state, the law schools, the students and the legal employers are portrayed as highly problematic but these discussions are mainly from the perspective of insiders to the academy and legal hierarchies and the idea of 'pressing' is driven by proximal economic and political changes, with much less focus on underlying purpose. We wonder: does it matter that while law schools are bigger and more people get to study law, that only some people get to be lawyers and they are still mostly the people who got to be lawyers 50 years ago? Only when all citizens can see themselves at all levels of the legal system can we talk about genuine access to

---

64 Tina McKee, Rachel Anne Nir, Jill Alexander, Elisabeth Griffiths, Paul Dargue and Tamara Hervey, 'The Fairness Project: The Role of Legal Educators as Catalysts for Change. Engaging in Difficult Dialogues on the Impact of Diversity Barriers to Entry and Progression in the Legal Profession' (2021) 55 (3) The Law Teacher, 283–313.

65 Are these the pressing problems? We consider them to be problematic, they do require our attention. And yet, in Berytus, no doubt there were problems considered equally pressing until the city was destroyed by the earthquake of AD 551. The survivors moved their activities to Constantinople but the power and reach of Berytus was not replicated. The 'mother of laws' and her professors of 'universal compass' became legend. Today, we consider issues of access to law school, scale and form of the experience and the role of the lawyer in society. Meanwhile, the seas burn.

justice: are we headed in that direction and if so, is the speed of change more than geological? Is it ok to market law degrees with 'wigs on websites' – does the student-consumer really understand that they have a less than 1 in 12 chance of wearing a wig? Is our role, as many legal academics believe, to reproduce an epistemological tribe of hermeneuts who, regardless of their actual job, are capable of bringing a legal sensibility to their lives and communities? If so, how could we communicate that to prospective students on a website? Would they be interested?

Students themselves seem concerned to improve the system that exists rather than to remake it (though of course we haven't really asked them those questions, that might well be a dangerous move) and primarily they seem to want more relational and exploratory opportunities, whilst demonstrating the gap between this aspiration and practice by taking pragmatic or extrinsic approaches to attendance and engagement. This is often presented as a problem, though we wonder if it is more fundamental to human learning, perhaps a feature that cannot be avoided? Can curriculum and pedagogy ever really 'design out' key elements:

- that to learn is to be vulnerable and it is natural to shy away from this at times;
- that the most effective learning environments are also those that are the most exposing for teacher and learner;
- that many complicated and complex things rest on quite dull foundations and that these foundations need to be present before/alongside the interesting complexity;
- that nobody really listens to the whole lecture because human attention spans don't work like that;
- that Socratic questioning and seminar discussions privilege more extroverted students;
- that most of our assessments are of individual performance when working life is much more about collaborative endeavour, and so on.

Our problems with students and students' problems with us are fundamentally relational and, whilst capable of local and temporary amelioration, probably eternal. However, the end goal of work in inequalities is not to 'fix' things but to be constantly, passionately, interested in them. Rather, we may delight in the temporary ameliorations and welcome the return of perennial paradoxes, in anticipation of different insights next time around.

Bibliography

Ahmed S, *On Being Included: Racism and Diversity in Institutional Life* (Duke University Press 2012).

Alexander J and Boothby C, 'Stakeholder Perceptions of Clinical Legal Education within an Employability Context' (2018) 25(3) *International Journal of Clinical Legal Education* 53–84.

Bar Standards Board, 'Future Bar Training: Consultation on the Future of Training for the Bar: Academic, Vocational and Professional Stages of Training' (2015) <https://www.barstandardsboard.org.uk/uploads/assets/e85659f2-9dce-453c-9cc1ce640677c227/fbttripleconsultationjuly2015.pdf> accessed 15 November 2021.

Barnhizer D, 'The University Ideal and Clinical Legal Education' (1990) 35(1) *New York Law School Law Review* 87.

Barton C, 'MacLean, Mavis and Eekelaar, John, After the Act: Access to Family Justice After LASPO' (2019) 82(6) *Modern Law Review* 1176–1204.

Birks P (ed) *Pressing Problems in the Law. Vol 2. What Are Law Schools For?* (Oxford University Press 1996).

Boon A and Webb J, 'Legal Education and Training in England and Wales: Back to the Future?' (2008) 58(1) *Journal of Legal Education* 79–121.

Boyce S, 'Presidential Address' (the Law Society, 24 March 2021) <https://www.lawsociety.org.uk/en/topics/news-articles/i-stephanie-boyce-presidential-address> accessed 08 November 2021.

Broudy H, Smith B, and Burnett J, *Democracy and Excellence in American Secondary Education: A Study in Curriculum Theory* (Rand McNally 1964).

Carver R, *What We Talk About When We Talk About Love* (Knopf 1981).

Cownie F and Bradney A, 'An Examined Life: Research into University Legal Education in the United Kingdom and the Journal of Law and Society' (2017) 44(S1) *Journal of Law and Society* 129–143.

Dean A, Shubita M, and Claxton J, 'What Type of Learning Journey Do Students Value Most? Understanding Enduring Factors from the NSS Leading to Responsible Decision-Making' (2020) 11(4) *Journal of Global Responsibility* 347–362.

Denley P, '"Medieval", "Renaissance", "modern". Issues of Periodization in Italian University History" (2013) 27(4) *Renaissance Studies* 487–503.

Eraut M, *Developing Professional Knowledge and Competence* (Routledge 1994).

Evans C, Rees G, Taylor C, and Fox S, 'A Liberal Higher Education for All? The Massification of Higher Education and Its Implications for Graduates' Participation in Civil Society' (2021) 81 *Higher Education* 521–535.

Flood J, 'One Size Doesn't Fit All in Legal Education' (*John Flood's Random Academic Thoughts*, 15 October 2013) <http://johnflood.blogspot.com/2013/10/one-size-doesnt-fit-all-in-legal.html> accessed 08 November 2021.

Gledhill K and Livings B (eds), *The Teaching of Criminal Law: The Pedagogical Imperatives'* (Routledge 2018).

Guth J and Ashford C, 'The Legal Education and Training Review: Regulating Socio-Legal and Liberal Legal Education?' (2014) 48(1) *The Law Teacher* 5–19.

Hale L, 'Lord Upjohn Lecture 2021— "When There Are 12": Legal Education and a Diverse Judiciary' (*The Law Teacher* 2021) <https://www.tandfonline.com/doi/full/10.1080/03069400.2021.1966251> accessed 08 November 2021

Hall E, 'Glass Houses: How Might We Decide on a "Good Enough" Assessment to Become a Solicitor?' (2018) 53(4) *The Law Teacher* 453–466.

Hall E, 'Notes on the SRA Report of the Consultation on the SQE: Comment Is Free, but Facts Are Sacred' (2017) 41(1) *The Law Teacher* 364–372.

Hall E and Sylvester C, 'Clinic as the Crucible for Theorised Practice and the Practice of Theory in Legal Education' in Linden Thomas, Steven Vaughan, Bharat Malkani and Theresa Lynch (eds) *Reimagining Clinical Legal Education* (Bloomsbury Publishing 2018)

Hall E, Hodgson J, Strevens C, and Guth J, '"What We Did Over the Summer": Updates on Proposed Reforms to Legal Education and Training in England and Wales and the Republic of Ireland' (2019) 53(4) *The Law Teacher* 536–546.

HESA, 'Figure 10: Percentage of UK Domiciled Leavers Entering Employment in the UK in Professional Occupations by Subject Area and Personal Characteristics' (*HESA*, June 2018) <https://www.hesa.ac.uk/data-and-analysis/sfr250/figure-10> accessed 05 November 2021.

HESA, 'Figure 14: UK Domiciled Leavers Who Obtained First Degree Qualifications and Entered Full-Time Paid Work in the UK by Subject Area and Salary' (*HESA*, August 2018) <https://www.hesa.ac.uk/data-and-analysis/sfr250/figure-14> accessed 05 November 2021.

Hornsby D and Osman R, 'Massification in Higher Education: Large Classes and Student Learning' (2014) 67(6) *Higher Education* 711–719.

James C and Koo J, 'The EU Law "Core" Module: Surviving the Perfect Storm of Brexit and the SQE' (2018) 52(1) *The Law Teacher* 68–84.

Liebeschuetz J, *Antioch: City and Imperial Administration in the Later Roman Empire* (Oxford University Press 1971).

Maharg P, 'Pressing Problems MLR Seminar, Final Thoughts' (*Paul Maharg*, 09 July 2019) <https://paulmaharg.com/2019/07/09/pressing-problems-mlr-seminar-final-thoughts/> accessed 15 November 2021.

Mant J and Wallbank J, 'The Mysterious Case of Disappearing Family Law and the Shrinking Vulnerable Subject: The Shifting Sands of Family Law's Jurisdiction' (2017) 26(5) *Social and Legal Studies* 629–648.

Mason L, 'Decolonisation, Law and Legal Education: A Multimodal View' (*African Legal Studies Blog*, 30 July 2021) <https://africanlegalstudies.blog/2021/07/30/decolonisation-law-and-legal-education-a-multimodal-view/ > accessed 08 November 2021.

Mason L, 'SQEezing the Jurisprudence Out of the SRA's Super Exam: The SQE's Bleak Legal Realism and the Rejection of Law's Multimodal Truth' (2018) 52(4) *The Law Teacher* 409–424.

McFaul H, Hardie L, Ryan F, Bright K, and Graffin N, 'Taking Clinical Legal Education Online: Songs of Innocence and Experience' (2020) 27(4) *International Journal of Clinical Legal Education* 6–38.

McKee T, Nir R, Alexander J, Griffiths E, Dargue P, and Hervey T, 'The Fairness Project: The Role of Legal Educators as Catalysts for Change. Engaging in Difficult Dialogues on the Impact of Diversity Barriers to Entry and Progression in the Legal Profession' (2021) 55(3) *The Law Teacher* 283–313.

McKeown P and Hall E, 'If We Could Instil Social Justice Values Through Clinical Education, Should We?' (2018) 5(1) *Journal of International and Comparative Law* 143–179.

McNamee K, 'Another Chapter in the History of Scholia' (1998) 48(1) *Classical Quarterly* 269–288.

Millar F, 'The Roman Colonies of the Near East. A Study of Cultural Relation' in Heikki Solin and Mika Kajava (eds) *Roman Eastern Policy and Other Studies in Roman History: Proceedings of a Colloquium at Tvarminne* (The Finish Society of Sciences and Letters, 1990) 7–58.

Mroz M, Smith F, and Hardman F, 'The Discourse of the Literacy Hour' (2000) 30(3) *Cambridge Journal of Education* 379–390.

Pleasence P, Balmer N, and Denvir C, 'Wrong about Rights: Public Knowledge of Key Areas of Consumer, Housing and Employment Law in England and Wales' (2017) 80(5) *Modern Law Review* 836–859.

Roper V, Dunn R and Rasiah S, 'Revisiting "Pressing Problems in the Law: What Is the Law School For?" 20 Years on' (2020) 54(3) *The Law Teacher* 455–464.

Ryan F, 'Rage Against the Machine? Incorporating Legal Tech into Legal Education' (2020) 55(3) *The Law Teacher* 392–404.

Ryan F and McFaul H, 'Innovative Technologies in UK Legal Education' in Emma Jones and Fiona Cownie (eds) *Key Directions in Legal Education: National and International Perspectives* (Routledge 2020).

Schon D, *The Reflective Practitioner: How Professionals Think in Action* (Basic Books 1983).

Solicitors Regulation Authority and Bar Standards Board, 'Academic Stage Handbook' (2014) <https://www.sra.org.uk/globalassets/documents/students/academic-stage/academic-stage-handbook.pdf?version=4a1ac3> accessed 05 November 2021.

Sommerlad H, Francis A, Loughrey J, and Vaughan S, 'England and Wales: A Legal Profession in the Vanguard of Professional Transformation?' in Richard L Abel, Ole Hammerslev and Hilary Sommerlad (eds) *Lawyers in 21st Century Societies: Vol. 1 National Reports* (Bloomsbury 2020).

The Law Society, 'Entry Trends' (*The Law Society*, 25 November 2020) <https://www.lawsociety.org.uk/en/career-advice/becoming-a-solicitor/entry-trends> accessed 08 November 2021.

Wallace C, 'The Pedagogy of Legal Reasoning: Democracy, Discourse and Community' (2018) 52(3) *The Law Teacher* 260–271.

Weiss G, 'The Enchantment of Codification in the Common-Law World' (2000) 25(2) *Yale Journal of International Law* 435–532.

Wilson A, *In Black and White: A Young Barrister's Story of Race and Class in a Broken Justice System* (Endeavour 2020).

Wittek L and Kvernbekk T, 'On the Problems of Asking for a Definition of Quality in Education' (2011) 55(6) *Scandinavian Journal of Educational Research* 671–684.

2 What are law teachers for? Finding ways to introduce law teachers' voices through the TEF in the ever-changing HE sector in England

Maribel Canto-Lopez

Introduction

As discussed in Thornton's chapter, the signs of a marketised neo-liberal higher education (HE) are becoming entrenched into academics' daily lives,[1] including ideas like productivity, control, employability, metrics, audits and profits.[2] Birks, Clark and Tsamenyi's contribution discussed how legal education's challenges in the twenty-first century would affect law teachers (LTs) and their values.[3] The authors stated that the life of LTs was becoming gradually more stressful; for example, growing numbers of students, notions of 'students as consumers', more audits and their related paperwork, new administrative duties and the imposition of a management culture over leadership in law schools.[4] All these factors have thrived because of the marketisation of the HE sector.[5]

England saw a new regulatory system for Higher Education Institutions (HEIs) that is based on consumer protection values.[6] The new regulations were grounded on market and audit principles, extending governmental

---

1 Mike Molesworth, Richard Scullion and Elizabeth Nixon (eds), *The Marketisation of Higher Education and the Student as a Consumer* (Routledge 2011) 3; see Margaret Thornton, 'What Is the Law School for in a Post-Pandemic World?' in this book.
2 Ian McNay, 'From the Collegial Academy to the Corporate Enterprise: The Changing Cultures of Universities in the Changing University' in Tom Schuller (ed), *The Changing University* (SRHE 1995); Maurice Kogan and Stephen Hanney, *Reforming Higher Education* (Jessica Kingley Publisher 1999).
3 Eugene Clark and Martin Tsamenyi, 'Legal Education in the Twenty-First Century: A Time of Challenge' in Peter Birks (ed), *Pressing Problems in the Law, Volume 2: What Are Law Schools For?* (Oxford University Press 1996, 2003 reprinting) 17.
4 Ibid, 35–36.
5 Gill Wyness, 'Policy Changes in UK Higher Education Funding, 1963–2009' (2010) DoQSS Working Paper no. 10–15, 1 <https://www.researchgate.net/publication/46463033_Policy_changes_in_UK_higher_education_funding_1963-2009> accessed 02 November 2021; Kathleen Lunch, 'Neo-Liberalism and Marketisation: The Implications for Higher Education' (2006) 5 European Education Research Journal, 2.
6 Raewyn Connell, 'The Neoliberal Cascade and Education: An Essay on the Market Agenda and Its Consequences' (2013) 54 (2) Critical Studies in Education 99.

DOI: 10.4324/9781003322092-2

26 Maribel Canto-Lopez

control into research and teaching in HEIs.[7] The transformation is well under way; HEIs are to become business and revenue generators,[8] and students are taking a new role as consumers[9] under the Consumer Right Act (CRA, 2015) and the Higher Education and Research Act (HERA, 2017).[10] The 'student-consumer' shift has arguably driven the quality of HEIs provision up, by challenging universities and enabling students to attend HEIs that offer the highest quality teaching.[11] However, the changes affecting LTs in England come not only from the governmental agenda of control and accountability of HEIs, but have penetrated the management of individual HEIs, which have adopted new efficiency targets, novel distribution of their income and increased the administrative duties of academic staff.[12]

Some of the transformations occurring in HE and legal education specifically were predicted many years ago and had started to take form when Birks' edited collection was published. Birks identified two changes in legal education: (1) the creeping control of the government into the research of law schools[13]; and (2) that the representatives of the law profession would edge towards resisting the requirement of law degrees for practising lawyers as a sign of their contempt towards Law Schools.[14] A full exploration of these two predictions is beyond the scope of this chapter, and they are briefly mentioned as examples. Regarding Birks' first prediction, the Research Excellence Framework (REF) was introduced in 2014 to assess the

---

7 Simon Marginson, 'The Impossibility of Capitalist Markets in Higher Education' (2013) 28 (3) Journal of Education Policy 353.

8 Sue Hubble, David Foster and Paul Bolton, 'Higher Education and Research Bill 2016 [Bill No 004 of 2016-17]' (Briefing Paper No 7608, 2016) <https://www.timeshighereducation.com/sites/default/files/breaking_news_files/he_bill_briefing.pdf> accessed 02 November 2021.

9 Louise Bunce, Amy Baird and Sian Jones, 'The Student-as-a-Consumer Approach in Higher Education and Its Effect on Academic Performance' (2017) 42 (11) Studies in Higher Education 1958, 1976; Tony Woodall, Alex Hiller and Sheilagh Resnick, 'Making Sense of Higher Education: Students as Consumers and the Value of the University Experience' (2014) 39 (1) Studies in Higher Education, 48.

10 John Morgan, 'Higher Education and Research Bill Passed by UK Parliament' (*Times Higher Education*, 27 April 2017) <https://www.timeshighereducation.com/news/higher-education-and-research-bill-passed-uk-parliament#survey-answer accessed 25/12/2017> accessed 13 January 2021.

11 Michael Tomlinson, Jurgen Enders and Rajani Naidoo, 'The Teaching Excellence Framework: Symbolic Violence and the Measured Market in Higher Education' (2020) 61 (5) Critical Studies in Education 627.

12 John Dearlove, 'The Academic Labour Process: From Collegiality and Professionalism to Managerialism and Proletarianisation?' (1997) 30 (1) Higher Education Review 56.

13 This could be done through the prioritisation of some projects, in the name of value for money, Peter Birks, 'Preface' in Peter Birks (ed), *Pressing Problems in the Law, Volume 2: What Are Law Schools For?* (Oxford University Press 1996, 2003 reprinting) vi.

14 Ibid, xvi.

quality of research in UK HE Institutions (HEIs).[15] The REF system influences the status of the HEIs, impacting the allocated research funds for each HEI as determined by their rankings.[16] REF has increased the research outputs in HEIs, and academics are under intense pressure to publish.[17] Within the REF (and while recognising that participation is voluntary, at least nominally), there seems to be a move towards greater governmental control of research affecting HEIs and the academics working in them.[18] For some, the REF appears to dictate the type of research that is being accounted as valuable.[19]

In addition, Birks' concerns regarding removal of the necessity of a law degree have materialised to some extent in the form of the new Solicitors Qualifying Examination (SQE) route to qualification, proposed by the Solicitors Regulation Authority (SRA) in 2016.[20] The SQE does not require a law degree for applicants to sit the centrally set exam.[21] The impact of the SQE on LTs is unknown, and it will affect some law schools, and their HEIs, more than others depending on their outlook on vocationality and other issues,[22] and the pressure they feel to stay competitive[23] by creating SQE-friendly curricula.[24] It is noteworthy that views expressed by LTs during the SQE 'consultation' did not make much of a difference to the SRA's

---

15 It substituted the Research Assessment Exercise (RAE), which was introduced in 1986, to evaluate quality of publications produced by academics working at universities.

16 Peter Tymms and Steve Higgins, 'Judging Research Papers for Research Excellence' (2018) 43 (9) Studies in Higher Education 1548.

17 Richard Watermeyer, 'Impact in the REF: Issues and Obstacles' (2016) 41 (2) Studies in Higher Education 199.

18 Hugh Willmott, 'Commercialising Higher Education in the UK: The State, Industry and Peer Review' (2003) 28 (2) Studies in Higher Education 2.

19 Doug Morrison and Jessica Guth, 'Rethinking the Neoliberal University: Embracing Vulnerability in English Law Schools?' (2021) 55 (1) The Law Teacher 47.

20 Jenny Gibbons 'Policy Recontextualisation: The Proposed Introduction of a Multiple-Choice Test for the Entry-Level Assessment of the Legal Knowledge of Prospective Solicitor in England and Wales, and the Potential Effect on University-Level Legal Education' (2017) 24 (3) International Journal of the Legal Profession 227. Note that the proposal comes, in fact, from the regulator, rather than the legal profession at large as Birks predicted.

21 'To become a solicitor after September (2021), everyone must have a degree (or equivalent) but it doesn't have to be a law degree' in Solicitors Regulation Authority, Degree or Equivalent. See Solicitors Regulation Authority, 'Degree or Equivalent' (SRA, September 2021) <https://www.sra.org.uk/students/sqe/degree-equivalent/> accessed 02 November 2021.

22 'The impact of (SQE) is likely to be significant for those law schools traditionally focuses on a more vocation approach to legal education' in Doug Morrison and Jessica Guth, 'Rethinking the Neoliberal University: Embracing Vulnerability in English Law Schools?' (2021) 55 (1) The Law Teacher 42, 49.

23 Lucinda Ferguson, 'Complicating the 'Holy Grail', Simplifying the Search: A Critique of the Conventional Problematisation of Social Immobility in Elite Legal Education and the Profession' (2017) 41 (4) The Law Teacher 377, 378.

24 DE Morrison, 'The SQE and Creativity: A Race to the Bottom?' (2018) 52 (4) The Law Teacher 467, 469.

28 Maribel Canto-Lopez

final plans.[25] The SQE was introduced in September 2021, despite the disruption caused to law schools by Covid-19.[26]

Writing back in 1996, Clark and Tsamenyi envisioned what has become the central theme of this chapter, which is that LTs need to think about ways to reconnect with their institutions and with regulatory policies in order to make their voices heard and count. Clark and Tsamenyi warned LTs that some of the challenges faced by legal education were down to a disconnect between their values and aspirations and the goals of the new HE schemes.[27] I would also argue that all LTs, regardless of their position, level of seniority, contract or the type of law school in which they work, should be interested in their voices being heard and engaged within their HEIs. In sum, all LTs should want to feel included in HE policies, whichever type of academic life they live.[28] As LTs we can only speculate about the future, but we have a responsibility to decide what we stand for in the current changing and unpredictable HE landscape.

This chapter will analyse how LTVs have not been heard in the context of the introduction of the Teaching Excellence Framework (TEF). The TEF is a government evaluative framework of teaching quality that brings a level of scrutiny and competition between HEIs as never seen before. The TEF has fitted well in the new overwhelming HE metrics culture.[29] The TEF uses the results of the National Student Survey (NSS) in its metrics,[30] itself a measure that for some has strengthened the students-as-consumers role

---

25 Luke Mason and Jessica Guth, 'Re-Claiming Our Discipline' Editorial in 'Special Issue: From LETR to SQE: Reforming Legal Education and Training in England and Wales' (2018) 52 (4) The Law Teacher 379; Maribel Canto-Lopez, 'New Challenges in the UK Legal Education Landscape: TEF, SQE and the Law Teacher' (2018) 18 Revista Jurídica de Investigación e Innovación Educativa (REJIE Nueva época), 11.

26 Solicitors Regulation Authority, 'Coronavirus Update – Education and Training Q & A' (*SRA*, 27 May 2021) <https://www.sra.org.uk/sra/news/coronavirus-questions-answers/> accessed 02 November 2021.

27 Eugene Clark and Martin Tsamenyi, 'Legal Education in the Twenty-First Century: A Time of Challenge' in Peter Birks (ed), *Pressing Problems in the Law, Volume 2: What Are Law Schools For?* (Oxford University Press 1996, 2003 reprinting) 18.

28 Whatever else legal academics do, one matter that should concern them is the nature of their lives. In Fiona Cownie and Anthony Bradney, 'An Examined Life: Research into University Legal Education in the United Kingdom and the *Journal of Law and Society*' (2017) 44 (1) Journal of Law and Society 129.

29 Cris Shore, 'Audit Culture and Illiberal Governance: Universities and the Politics of Accountability' (2008) 8 (3) Anthropological Theory 278; James Wilsdon, Eleonora Belfiore, Liz Allen and Philip Campbell, 'The Metric Tide: Report of the Independent Review of the Role of Metrics in Research Assessment and Management' (2015) <https://www.researchgate.net/publication/279402178_The_Metric_Tide_Report_of_the_Independent_Review_of_the_Role_of_Metrics_in_Research_Assessment_and_Management> accessed 02 November 2021

30 Duna Sabri, 'Student Evaluations of Teaching as 'Fact-Totems': The Case of the UK National Student Survey' (2013) 18 (4) Sociological Research Online <https://journals.sagepub.com/doi/full/10.5153/sro.3136> accessed 02 November 2021

in universities.[31] I argue that the TEF is a clear example of the increased bureaucracy, endorsement of the notion of students as consumers, and escalation of the government's control over LTs academic activities related to teaching and learning practices and their quality assurance.[32] Moreover, HEIs' management teams have implemented the TEF with little input from academics.[33] The chapter will conclude by evaluating the role that LTs can play to challenge their fading control over their future, within the current HE arena by finding a way to broadcast their Law Teachers' Voices (LTVs), and thus participate in institutional and public debates. As Clark and Tsamenyi note: 'the success of legal education in meeting challenges... will depend, more than anything else, on the willingness of legal educators to be involved and lend their collective voice to the values of law and legal education'.[34]

The silence of academic and LTVs in HE policies

Clark and Tsamenyi were right to highlight that LTs are central to the sustainable functioning of their law schools and, in turn, their HEIs.[35] For some, law schools are 'cash generators' amidst other disciplines in HEIs, particularly in the social sciences.[36]

The quest to introduce academic and LTVs in educational policies at any level is not an easy task. First, the need for LTs to have their voices heard by HEIs and the government is relatively new, so they need to create new pathways. Second, governments' education policies have not included academic voices and instead, they listen exclusively to the HEIs, and to voices that are predominantly managerial. Finally, the growing disconnect between HEIs' management and academics is silencing LTVs and so far, arguably, it has been easy to keep this *status quo* for the HEIs.

---

31 Tony Woodall, Alex Hiller and Sheilagh Resnick, 'Making Sense of Higher Education: Students as Consumers and the Value of the University Experience' (2014) 39 (1) Studies in Higher Education 48; Stefan Collini, 'Who Are the Spongers Now?' (2016) 38 (2) London Review of Books 33.

32 Mike Neary, 'Teaching Excellence Framework: A Critical Response and an Alternative Future' (2016) 12 (3) Journal of Contemporary European Research 690.

33 Vanessa Cui, Amanda French and Matt O'Leary, 'A Missed Opportunity? How the UK's Teaching Excellence Framework Fail to Capture the Voice of University Staff' ((2019) 46(9) *Studies in Higher Education* 1756.

34 Eugene Clark and Martin Tsamenyi, 'Legal Education in the Twenty-First Century: A Time of Challenge' in Peter Birks (ed), *Pressing Problems in the Law, Volume 2: What Are Law Schools For?* (Oxford University Press 1996, 2003 reprinting), 44.

35 Ibid, 35.

36 Alastair Hudson, 'Two Futures for Law Schools' (2021) 55 (1) The Law Teacher 101, 104; Anthony Bradney, 'The Success of University Law Schools in England and Wales: Or How to Fail' (2018) 52 (4) The Law Teacher 490, 491; Doug Morrison and Jessica Guth, 'Rethinking the Neoliberal University: Embracing Vulnerability in English Law Schools?' (2021) 55 (1) The Law Teacher 42.

30 *Maribel Canto-Lopez*

There has been criticism regarding the apathy of LTs towards HE changes; even Birks noted a 'worrying lack of articulated resistance' from LTs towards government policy on HE.[37] In addition, Twining has described LTs as remarkably submissive, or indolent or unimaginative.[38] Post WWII, LTs were relatively free from interferences in their academic lives from regulator and government, and some have inferred from this that LTVs were not present in HE policy because they did not need to be.[39] I would argue that LTVs, and those of other academics, are necessary for educational policies at regulatory and institutional level to protect autonomy in teaching and research of academic lives in general. Lack of voice, I claim, has led to a lack of democratic engagement for many LTs,[40] caught in a mesh of metrics, accountability, competition and performance management.[41]

It has been argued recently that input from academics tends to be absent from the formulation of HE policies.[42] Sabri concluded after interviewing individuals working for HE agencies in the UK, between 2003 and 2005, that HE policy makers rarely mentioned academics in their conversations.[43] For the policy makers, the main 'interlocutors' worth listening to were those in HEIs' management.[44] It seems HE policy makers then were also uninterested in engaging with academics to understand their perceptions about HE policies.[45] However, this fact is arguably unwise as it cultivates and expands the mistrust of academics and LTs towards HE policies; they are the policy implementers in their everyday teaching.[46] Even more worryingly, as HE policies do not include LTVs, the signal is that HEIs can do the same in their institutional policies. Smith inferred after evaluating learning and teaching strategies from different HEIs in the UK (written between 2002 and 2010)

---

37 Peter Birks, 'Preface' in Peter Birks (ed), *Pressing Problems in the Law, Volume 2: What Are Law Schools For?* (Oxford University Press 1996, 2003 reprinting), x.

38 William Twining, 'Lord Upjohn Lecture 2017: Rethinking Legal Education' (2018) 52 (3) The Law Teacher 241, 257.

39 Ian McNay, 'From the Collegial Academy to the Corporate Enterprise: The Changing Cultures of Universities in the Changing University' in Tom Schuller (ed), *The Changing University* (SRHE 1995); See Duna Sabri, 'Absence of the Academic from Higher Education Policy' (2010) 25 (2) Journal of Education Policy 191, 200.

40 J Clare Wilson and Caroline Strevens, 'Perceptions of Psychological Well-Being in UK Law Academics' (2018) 52 (3) The Law Teacher 335, 343; Ailsa Kolsaker, 'Relocating Professionalism in an English University' (2014) 36 (2) Journal of Higher Education Policy and Managements 129, 131.

41 Hugo Horta and Joao M Santos, 'Organisational Factors and Academic Research Agendas: an Analysis of Academics on the Social Sciences' (2020) 45(12) Studies in Higher Education 2382, 2396.

42 Duna Sabri, 'Absence of the Academic from Higher Education Policy' (2010) 25 (2) Journal of Education Policy 191.

43 Ibid, 199.

44 Ibid, 201.

45 Ibid, 202.

46 Ibid, 203.

What are law teachers for? 31

that the voices of those who teach were ignored.[47] The educational strategies only mentioned HEIs management, for example the pro-vice chancellors for education.[48] By silencing academics and LTVs in HEIs educational strategies, institutions disempower and alienate the very people who implement the strategies to reach the centrally proposed targets through their everyday efforts.[49]

Ignoring LTs voices in HEIs policies will only exacerbate the arguably growing gap between HEIs and LTs. Following the advice of Clark and Tsamenyi, LTs need to engage in public debates to adapt to the challenges of the HE sector of the twenty-first century.[50] Clark and Tsamenyi blamed LTs for their growing precarious situation and the HEIs that needed more leadership and less management. Leadership was described in terms of engaging with others and finding ways to listen and discuss with academics a possible joint mission for the HEI.[51]

Since Clark and Tsamenyi's chapter in the mid-1990s, academics have noted the controlling nature of HEI management structures and the increasing pressures on their performance as academics.[52] Consequently, the new relations between academics and the institutions' management seem to be based on power rather than trust.[53] In one study, Kuznetsova explored the development of employee relations of academics in HEIs between 1996 and 2017.[54] The author analysed the University and College Union (UCU)[55] branch archives of the HEIs. Kuznetsova discovered that since the beginning of the 2000s, the institutional documents labelled as 'university policy' hardly included academics in negotiations or consultations, prior to presenting them to all the HEI.[56] An example of the progressive disempower-

---

47 Karen Smith, 'Who Do You Think You Are Talking to? The Discourse of Learning and Teaching Strategies' (2018) 56 (4) Higher Education 395.

48 Ibid, 401.

49 Ibid, 405.

50 Eugene Clark and Martin Tsamenyi, 'Legal Education in the Twenty-First Century: A Time of Challenge' in Peter Birks (ed), *Pressing Problems in the Law, Volume 2: What Are Law Schools For?* (Oxford University Press 1996, 2003 reprinting), 44.

51 Ibid, 43.

52 Katherine Sang, Abigail Powell, Rebecca Finkel and James Richards, '"Being an Academic Is Not a 9–5 Job": Long Working Hours and the "Ideal Worker" in UK Academia' (2015) 25(3) Labour & Industry: A Journal of the Social and Economic Relations of Work 235.

53 Paul S Adler, 'Market, Hierarchy and Trust: The Knowledge Economy and the Future of Capitalism' (2001) 12(2) *Organizational Science* 215

54 Olga Kuznetsova and Andrei Kuznetsova, 'And Then There Were None: What a UCU Archive Tells Us about Employee Relations in Marketising Universities' (2020) 45 (12) Studies in Higher Education 2439, 2450.

55 The UCU claims to be the largest further and higher education union in the world.

56 Olga Kuznetsova and Andrei Kuznetsova, 'And Then There Were None: What a UCU Archive Tells Us about Employee Relations in Marketising Universities' (2020) 45 (12) Studies in Higher Education 2439, 2444.

32 *Maribel Canto-Lopez*

ment of academic voices is demonstrated by the fact that one HEI ignored a staff survey showing that 78% of the staff could not meet workload demands. However, when the NSS score of a department was 67%, a red alert was issued accompanied by many actions design to improve the result.[57] If the empowerment continues to be one-sided in favour of HEIs management only, it may lead to an unsustainable HE sector.[58] And there is no more striking example of one-sided managerial implementation than the TEF, which we will analyse in detail.

Law teachers and teaching: what's TEF got to do with it?

As noted above, Birks warned about the change in the nature of university life and predicted a growing sense of government intrusion and increasing accountability targeted at LTs research; this would affect the unchallenged respect for academic freedom.[59] There was previously some evaluation of the quality of research undertaken by HEIs, by the Research Assessment Exercise (RAE), the forerunner to the REF.[60] However, at that time, there was no sign that this kind of government control would also be extended to evaluate the quality of teaching in HEIs. This section will explore TEF, still a relatively new framework, which aims to assess the quality of teaching in English HEIs. TEF is a governmental initiative seen as a further example of the marketisation of HE.[61] Many neo-liberal principles inspire TEF, such as value for money degrees, employability, students as consumers, accountability of the HE sector and encouraging competition between HEIs.[62]

Consequently, TEF's requirements and goals have filtered down to HEIs' management, which has imposed these aims top-down on academics without any real meaningful engagement with them.[63] As a result, many LTs, like academics in other disciplines, have suffered the consequences of

---

57 Ibid, 2445.
58 Colin Mayer, 'Whose Responsible for Irresponsible Business? An Assessment' (2017) 33 (2) Oxford Review of Economic Policy 157.
59 Peter Birks, 'Preface' in Peter Birks (ed), *Pressing Problems in the Law, Volume 2: What Are Law Schools For?* (Oxford University Press 1996, 2003 reprinting), ix–x.
60 Lewis Elton, 'The UK Research Assessment Exercise: Unintended Consequences' (2000) 54(3) Higher Education Quarterly 274, 276.
61 Adam Matthews and Ben Kotzee, 'The Rhetoric of the UK Higher Education Teaching Excellence Framework: A Corps-Assisted Discourse Analysis of TEF2 Provider Statements' (2019) 73 (5) Educational Review 523.
62 Michael Tomlinson, Jurgen Enders and Rajani Naidoo, 'The Teaching Excellence Framework: Symbolic Violence and the Measured Market in Higher Education' (2020) 61 (5) Critical Studies in Education 627, 629.
63 Vanessa Cui, Amanda French and Matt O'Leary, 'A Missed Opportunity? How the UK's Teaching Excellence Framework Fail to Capture the Voice of University Staff' (2019) 46(9) Studies in Higher Education 1756.

implementing the TEF in their HEIs[64]; they had to embed conceptions of employability and student satisfaction on their teaching and learning practices and feel more controlled and accountable to management implementing those practices.[65] Not many academics have escaped from the increase in scrutiny of academic performance through module evaluations and student's satisfaction feedback.[66] There are also reports of more standardisation of teaching and assessment practices together with the curriculum.[67] In practical terms, this has meant more bureaucracy and increasing administrative workloads, negatively impacting working conditions for LTs and other academics,[68] and paradoxically less time for preparing and developing teaching.[69] More importantly, I argue that the effect of TEF's implementation in HEIs is to create disengagement between HEIs and academics.[70] Academics feel the consequences of a framework that ignores their views

---

64 Karen Gravett and Ian Kinkchin, 'Revisiting A "Teaching Excellence" for the Times We Live in: Posthuman Possibilities' (2020) 25 (8) Teaching in Higher Education 1028.

65 Matt O'Leary, Vanessa Cui and Amanda French, 'Understanding, Recognising and Rewarding Teaching Quality in Higher Education: An Exploration of the Impact and Implications of the Teaching Excellence Framework' (2019) Project Report for UCU (UCU TEF Report) <https://www.ucu.org.uk/media/10092/Impact-of-TEF-report-Feb-2019/pdf/ImpactofTEFreportFEb2019> accessed 02 November 2021, 5.

66 Pieter Spooren, Bert Brockx and Dimitri Mortelmans, 'On the Validity of Student Evaluation of Teaching' (2013) 83(4) Review of Educational Research 598; Vanessa Cui, Amanda French and Matt O'Leary, 'A Missed Opportunity? How the UK's Teaching Excellence Framework Fail to Capture the Voice of University Staff' (2019) 46 (9) Studies in Higher Education, 8–9 <https://www.tandfonline.com/doi/full/10.1080/03075079.2019.1704721> accessed 02 November 2021.

67 Vanessa Cui, Amanda French and Matt O'Leary, 'A Missed Opportunity? How the UK's Teaching Excellence Framework Fail to Capture the Voice of University Staff' (2019) 46(9) Studies in Higher Education 1756.

68 Matt O'Leary, Vanessa Cui and Amanda French, 'Understanding, Recognising and Rewarding Teaching Quality in Higher Education: An Exploration of the Impact and Implications of the Teaching Excellence Framework' (2019) Project Report for UCU (UCU TEF Report) <https://www.ucu.org.uk/media/10092/Impact-of-TEF-report-Feb-2019/pdf/ImpactofTEFreportFEb2019> accessed 02 November 2021, 5; Vanessa Cui, Amanda French and Matt O'Leary, 'A Missed Opportunity? How the UK's Teaching Excellence.' (2019) 46(9) Studies in Higher Education 1756

69 Matt O'Leary, Vanessa Cui and Amanda French, 'Understanding, Recognising and Rewarding Teaching Quality in Higher Education: An Exploration of the Impact and Implications of the Teaching Excellence Framework' (2019) Project Report for UCU (UCU TEF Report) <https://www.ucu.org.uk/media/10092/Impact-of-TEF-report-Feb-2019/pdf/ImpactofTEFreportFEb2019> accessed 02 November 2021, 63.

70 It has been argued that new changes, brought by HEI administrations in learning and teaching because of TEF, may not all be negative. Some have welcomed the increased focus and investments from HEIs towards teaching and learning. See Matt O'Leary, Vanessa Cui and Amanda French, 'Understanding, Recognising and Rewarding Teaching Quality in Higher Education: An Exploration of the Impact and Implications of the Teaching Excellence Framework' (2019) Project Report for UCU (UCU TEF Report) <https://www.ucu.org.uk/media/10092/Impact-of-TEF-report-Feb-2019/pdf/ImpactofTEFreportFEb2019> accessed 02 November 2021, 5

34 *Maribel Canto-Lopez*

and increases their workload.[71] Put simply, if teachers are not protected or happy, the quality of the teaching in HE will be adversely affected.[72]

In this context, we should mention in passing how Covid-19 pandemic has aggravated in many cases, the situation of an already discontent and disengaged academic workforce in HE.[73] The pandemic has, and continues to have, a considerable impact on the HE sector worldwide.[74] In England, Covid-19 has meant a transformation in teaching and learning approaches, an unprecedented fast revamp of curricula, and new activities to deliver teaching online in HEIs.[75] Many academics quickly had to adapt to new technologies while trying to adopt untried pedagogies in their institutions.[76] What happened with TEF has happened with the pandemic: academics had little input on the teaching and learning changes imposed by the management of HEIs. In place of such disempowerment and disengagement, I advocate for the need to find ways in which academics and LTVs could be included in educational policies such as the TEF. This quest is not easy, for in the case of the TEF, we are looking at a framework that is constantly evolving, as illustrated in the next section.

71 Alan M Skelton, 'A "Teaching Excellence" for the Times We Live in?' (2009) 14(1) Teaching in Higher Education, 107, 109.
72 Paula Baron, 'Thriving in the Legal Academy' (2007) 17(1) Legal Education Review 27, 52; Clare Wilson and Caroline Strevens, 'Perceptions of Psychological Well-Being in UK Law Academics' (2018) 52(3) The Law Teacher 335; Matt O'Leary, Vanessa Cui and Amanda French, 'Understanding, Recognising and Rewarding Teaching Quality in Higher Education: An Exploration of the Impact and Implications of the Teaching Excellence Framework' (2019) Project Report for UCU (UCU TEF Report) <https://www.ucu. org.uk/media/10092/Impact-of-TEF-report-Feb-2019/pdf/ImpactofTEFreportFEb2019> accessed 02 November 2021, 64.
73 Richard Watermeyer, Tom Crick, Cathryn Knight and Janet Goodall, 'Covid-19 and Digital Disruption in UK Universities: Afflictions and Affordances of Emergency Online Migration' (2021) 81 Higher Education 623, 638.
74 Giorgio Marinoni, Hilligje van't Land and Trine Jensen, 'The Impact of Covid-19 on Higher Education around the World: IAU Global Survey Report' (2020) <https://www. iau-aiu.net/IMG/pdf/iau_covid19_and_he_survey_report_final_may_2020.pdf> accessed 02 November 2021.
75 Joseph Crawford, Kerryn Butler-Henderson, Jurgen Rudolph, Bashar Malkawi, Matt Glowatz, Rob Burton, Paola A Magni and Sophia Lam, 'COVID-19: 20 Countries' Higher Education Intra-Period Digital Pedagogy Responses' (2020) 3 (1) Journal of Applied Learning and Teaching, 3 <https://eprints.utas.edu.au/34123/2/138340%20-%20COVID-19.%2020%20countries%27%20higher%20education%20intra-period%20 digital%20pedagogy%20responses.pdf> accessed 02 November 2021.
76 Andy Pitchford and Ed Stevens, 'Covid Disrupts Our Academic Identities, and That's Something We Should Embrace' (*WonkHE*, 18 December 2020) < ttps://wonkhe. com/blogs/covid-disrupts-our-academic-identities-and-thats-something-we-should-embrace-2/> accessed 02 November 2021.

The TEF: an ever-changing evaluative framework on teaching excellence

Since its introduction in 2016, the TEF has not included LTVs in a meaningful way.[77] For example, after the outcome of the TEF 2 (2017), there was a consultation on 'Lessons learned', which primarily focused on the practical operation of the TEF so far.[78] The feedback and survey were directed mainly at the HEIs participants in the TEF 2, and their view on the application process.[79] The exercise of 'Lessons learned', arguably, facilitated the inclusion of the views of HEIs management and the staff already involved in the TEF 2 submission: to the exclusion of those less senior staff that probably still dealing with the TEF consequences on their workloads. The only genuine attempt to have academic voices heard, regarding TEF's implications in their academic lives, was made by an independent research study commissioned by the UCU on the impact of the TEF on HE staff (UCU Report), in 2019.[80]

TEF is constantly changing, and currently under review. TEF originated in the green paper 'Fulfilling Our Potential: Teaching Excellence, Social Mobility and Student's Choice' published in 2015.[81] One year later, this paper was ratified. The white paper presented the two-fold purpose of TEF: (1) 'to provide clear information to students about where the best provision can be found', and (2) 'to drive up the standard of teaching in all universities'.[82] The Department for Education (DfE) asked the Higher Education Funding Council for England (HEFCE) to manage the TEF at that time.

---

77 Matt O'Leary, Vanessa Cui and Amanda French, 'Understanding, Recognising and Rewarding Teaching Quality in Higher Education: An Exploration of the Impact and Implications of the Teaching Excellence Framework' (2019) Project Report for UCU (UCU TEF Report) <https://www.ucu.org.uk/media/10092/Impact-of-TEF-report-Feb-2019/pdf/ImpactofTEFreportFEb2019> accessed 02 November 2021, 3.

78 UK Department of Education, 'Teaching Excellence and Student Outcomes Framework: Lessons Learned from Year Two' (October 2017) <https://webarchive.nationalarchives.gov.uk/ukgwa/20180313174804/https://www.gov.uk/government/publications/teaching-excellence-framework-lessons-learned> accessed 02 November 2021.

79 Ibid, 59.

80 Matt O'Leary, Vanessa Cui and Amanda French, 'Understanding, Recognising and Rewarding Teaching Quality in Higher Education: An Exploration of the Impact and Implications of the Teaching Excellence Framework' (2019) Project Report for UCU (UCU TEF Report) <https://www.ucu.org.uk/media/10092/Impact-of-TEF-report-Feb-2019/pdf/ImpactofTEFreportFEb2019> accessed 02 November 2021, 3

81 UK Department for Business Innovations and Skills, 'Fulfilling Our Potential: Teaching Excellence, Social Mobility and Student Choice' (Green Paper, Cm 9141, November 2015) <https://assets.publishing.service.gov.uk/government/uploads/system/uploads/attachment_data/file/474227/BIS-15-623-fulfilling-our-potential-teaching-excellence-social-mobility-and-student-choice.pdf> accessed 02 November 2021.

82 UK Department for Business Innovations and Skills, 'Success as a Knowledge Economy: Teaching Excellence, Social Mobility and Students Choice' (White Paper, Cm 9258, 16 May 2016).

36 *Maribel Canto-Lopez*

Soon after this, the government created the Office for Students (OfS); The OfS is now the 'Single Market Regulator' in HE, which aims to protect the interests of students, employers and taxpayers.[83] The OfS is now fully responsible for the implementation of the TEF, after adopting the TEF in January 2018 under HERA's Section 25 (2017). In 2016, TEF 1 offered one level of award, 'meets expectations', based on the Quality Assurance Agency for HE (QAA) rating. This first TEF allowed 430 HE institutions in England to increase their fees up to a limit of £9,250.[84] In 2017, TEF's name changed to the 'Teaching Excellence and Students Outcomes Framework', yet the branded acronym TEF remained. During that same year, TEF 2 presented the 'Olympian' rating for HEIs: gold, silver and bronze.[85] The metrics for TEF would now include two elements: an institutional statement, 15 pages long, submitted by the HEI, and common sector indicators.[86] The TEF collects information and builds the picture of the HEI for the examiners panel, based on qualitative and quantitative data.

The statement was the qualitative data submitted by the HEI and could include whatever narrative the institution wished to present, from learning analytics to employer engagement, staff pedagogical qualifications or enterprise activities.[87] The quantitative data was based on three core data sets: teaching quality[88]; learning environment[89]; and student outcomes and learning gain.[90] The common sectors indicators that formed the quantitative data included: student's employment and earnings data from the Destination of Leavers Survey from HE (DLHE[91]; students' retention and

---

83 Department for Education, 'Office for Students: Regulatory Framework for Higher Education' (19 October 2017) <https://assets.publishing.service.gov.uk/government/uploads/system/uploads/attachment_data/file/683616/Regulatory_Framework_DfE_government_response.pdf > accessed 18 November 2021.

84 Linda Barkas, Jonathan M Scott, Nicola J Poppitt and Paul J Smith, 'Tinker, Tailor, Policy-Maker: Can the UK Government's Teaching Excellence Framework Deliver Its Objectives?' (2017) 43(6) *Journal of Further and Higher Education* 801, 804.

85 In TEF 2 295 institutions were assessed, with 59 achieving gold, 116 silver, 56 bronze and 64 provisional.

86 UK Department for Education, 'Teaching Excellence and Students' Outcomes Framework Specifications' (2017) <https://assets.publishing.service.gov.uk/government/uploads/system/uploads/attachment_data/file/658490/Teaching_Excellence_and_Student_Outcomes_Framework_Specification.pdf> accessed 02 November 2021.

87 Diana Beech, 'Going for Gold: Lessons from the TEF Provider Submissions' (2017) HEPI Report 99 <https://www.hepi.ac.uk/wp-content/uploads/2017/10/FINAL-HEPI-Going-for-Gold-Report-99-04_10_17-Screen.pdf> accessed 02 November 2021, 57.

88 Includes student engagement, valuing teaching, rigour and feedback.

89 Includes resources, scholarship, research and professional practice and personalised learning.

90 Includes employment and further study, employability and transferrable skills and positive outcomes for all.

91 The DLHEA is in the process of being replaced by the Graduate Outcome Survey. The (GO) survey was first run by HESA in December of 2018. It will be used by TEF to provide data on what students do after they graduate. In UK Department of Education, 'Independent Review of the Teaching Excellence and Student Outcomes Framework (TEF):

What are law teachers for? 37

continuation statistics from the HE Statistics Agency (HESA); and, students' satisfaction information from the NSS.[92] 2018 brought some slight changes and data refinement to TEF introduced by the regulator, such as the addition of the more comprehensive Longitudinal Education Outcome (LEO) data, which measures the extent to which a graduate-level education increases and influences employability and earning power,[93] and a different weighting of the NSS down to 5% from the previous 10%.[94] Trialled alongside the TEF 3 was the subject-level TEF pilot, which explored the value of assessing provision at subject rather than institutional level.[95]

There was originally an intention to implement a subject-level TEF for the academic year 2019–2020.[96] In the interim, in January 2019, an independent review of TEF was launched.[97] Its purpose was to assess the impact of TEF, whether it was fit for informing students and employers and enhancing teaching excellence in HEIs.[98] In August 2019, Dame Shirley Pearce

---

Report to the Secretary of State for Education' (August 2019) <https://assets.publishing.service.gov.uk/government/uploads/system/uploads/attachment_data/file/952754/TEF_Independent_review_report.pdf> accessed 02 November 2021, 110.

92 NSS is an annual UK-wide survey of final-year undergraduates.

93 After TEF 3, in June 2018, LEO was introduced. LEO data refers to education data records joined to tax and benefits. It allows the tracking of students through school, college, University and into the labour market. It shows whether students were employed after graduating and how much they were paid. It also shows if they subsequently studied on another course. In UK Department of Education, 'Independent Review of the Teaching Excellence and Student Outcomes Framework (TEF): Report to the Secretary of State for Education' (August 2019) <https://assets.publishing.service.gov.uk/government/uploads/system/uploads/attachment_data/file/952754/TEF_Independent_review_report.pdf> accessed 02 November 2021, 111.

94 Ant Bagshaw and David Karnohan, 'TEF: The Incredible Machine Remixed' (*WonkHE*, 22 June 2017) <https://wonkhe.com/blogs/the-incredible-machine-remixed/> accessed 02 November 2021.

95 UK Department of Education, 'Teaching Excellence Framework: Subject-Level Pilot Specification' (July 2017) <https://assets.publishing.service.gov.uk/government/uploads/system/uploads/attachment_data/file/629976/Teaching_Excellence_Framework_Subject-level_pilot_specification.pdf> accessed 02 November 2021.

96 Office for Students, 'The Impact of the Coronavirus Crisis Means That We Do Not Currently Have a Date for the Next TEF Exercise' Letter of 14 April 2020 (2020) <https://www.officeforstudents.org.uk/publications/letter-to-providers-tef-update/> accessed 18 November 2021; Office for Students, 'Report: Teaching Excellence and Student Outcomes Framework (TEF): Findings from the Second Subject-Level Pilot 2018–19' (21 January 2021) <https://www.officeforstudents.org.uk/publications/tef-findings-from-the-second-subject-level-pilot-2018-19/> accessed 18 November 2021.

97 UK Department for Education, 'Higher Education Expert to Review TEF' (*gov.uk*, 20 November 2018) <https://www.gov.uk/government/news/higher-education-expert-to-review-tef> accessed 02 November2021.

98 UK Department of Education, 'Independent Review of the Teaching Excellence and Student Outcomes Framework (TEF): Report to the Secretary of State for Education' (August 2019) <https://assets.publishing.service.gov.uk/government/uploads/system/uploads/attachment_data/file/952754/TEF_Independent_review_report.pdf> accessed 02 November 2021, 23.

38 *Maribel Canto-Lopez*

reported the review's findings to the government (Pearce Review).[99] The Review was welcomed because it engaged with the HE sector's concerns and sought to improve TEF.[100] The Pearce Review ran a public consultation,[101] various listening sessions,[102] focus groups and some desktop review of research regarding TEF, to gather a wide range of views from across the whole HE sector.[103] The views of academics were included in the Pearce Review through the aforementioned UCU report.[104] The UCU report stated how only one in ten of the participants in the report welcomed TEF.[105] Interestingly, the Pearce Review recognised how academics was the only group of HE stakeholders that did not support TEF's aim of assessing the quality of teaching in HE.[106] This independent Review exposed for the first time how unpopular the TEF was with a majority of academics working in HE. More importantly, the Pearce Review unveiled the dissonance between the views of academics and HEI's management on TEF's impact on teaching excellence. For example, looking at the Pearce Review public consultation, the question of endorsing the TEF's aim of auditing teaching excellence, 90% of HEIs answered yes. In comparison, only 42% of academics responded positively.[107] Another example was the answer to the statement that the

99 Ibid.
100 Paul Ashwin, 'The Government's Response to the Pearce Review of TEF Doesn't Do Justice to It' (*WonkHE*, 8 February 2021) <https://wonkhe.com/blogs/the-governments-response-to-the-pearce-review-of-tef-doesnt-do-justice-to-it/> accessed 02 November 2021.
101 Those views were analysed by an independent organisation 'Analysis of Responses to the call for views for the Independent Review of the TEF' Commissioned by the UK Dept. of Education on behalf of the TEF Independent Review. See Philip Wilson, Kate Crosswaite and Sophie Elliott, 'Analysis of Responses to the Call for Views for the Independent Review of the Teaching Excellence and Student Outcomes Framework (TEF)' (York Consulting, June 2019) <https://assets.publishing.service.gov.uk/government/uploads/system/uploads/attachment_data/file/935306/York_Consulting_TEF_call_for_views_analysis_-_accessible.pdf> accessed 02 November 2021
102 Around 60 separate events were organised, meetings were held in Birmingham, and Leeds as well as London to ensure a good geographic spread.
103 UK Department of Education, 'Summary of the Listening Sessions for the TEF Independent Review' (2021) <https://assets.publishing.service.gov.uk/government/uploads/system/uploads/attachment_data/file/947204/Listening_sessions_summary.pdf> accessed 02 November 2021.
104 Matt O'Leary, Vanessa Cui and Amanda French, 'Understanding, Recognising and Rewarding Teaching Quality in Higher Education: An Exploration of the Impact and Implications of the Teaching Excellence Framework' (2019) Project Report for UCU (UCU TEF Report) <https://www.ucu.org.uk/media/10092/Impact-of-TEF-report-Feb-2019/pdf/ImpactofTEFreportFEb2019> accessed 02 November 2021, 73.
105 Ibid, 4.
106 UK Department of Education, 'Independent Review of the Teaching Excellence and Student Outcomes Framework (TEF): Report to the Secretary of State for Education' (August 2019) <https://assets.publishing.service.gov.uk/government/uploads/system/uploads/attachment_data/file/952754/TEF_Independent_review_report.pdf> accessed 02 November 2021, 23.
107 Ibid.

TEF does not improve students' educational experience. Only 31% of HEIs agreed with this assertion, in contrast with the agreement of 79% of the academics participating.[108] Arguably, academics in the frontline may have a better perception of the TEF's impact on the students' learning experience. In any case, the Pearce Review reveals for the first-time academic voices, which were brought directly into the discussions and consultations about the TEF. No other general consultations about the TEF were launched after the aforementioned 'Lessons learned' project.[109] It would have been helpful if the Pearce Review had shone more light onto the *reasons* why so many academics did not agree with TEF's aim and implementation. However, the Pearce Review's remit was limited to assessing whether the TEF was a good system for providing information to applicants and employers and if it supported the enhancement of teaching quality, which seems to be the sole responsibility of HEI's management.[110] The disengagement between academics and their institutions regarding TEF is unlikely to be part of the government's policies or goals for HE. It is the role of academics and LTs to elucidate on this dissonance, if there is a genuine intention by the government to enhance teaching excellence in a sustainable way in the HE sector. Dame Pearce indicated her hopes for HEIs to share their expertise with the OfS to shape the future of TEF[111] – a statement that will be greeted with some scepticism given the limited opportunity for academics to engage with TEF to date.

The government produced a response to the Pearce report in January 2021.[112] It indicated that it agreed with the Pearce Review's recommendation that TEF's primary purpose should be 'enhancing' learning and teaching; this means that informing student choice about the provision available in

---

108 Ibid, 71.
109 UK Department of Education, 'Teaching Excellence and Student Outcomes Framework: Lessons Learned from Year Two' (October 2017) <https://webarchive.nationalarchives. gov.uk/ukgwa/20180313174804/https://www.gov.uk/government/publications/teaching-excellence-framework-lessons-learned> accessed 02 November 2021.
110 During the interview to the then Chair of the TEF (2018), Professor Sir Chris Husbands, stated that one of the solid impacts of the TEF was to 'made senior leaders think more seriously about teaching', in Matt O'Leary, Vanessa Cui and Amanda French, 'Understanding, Recognising and Rewarding Teaching Quality in Higher Education: An Exploration of the Impact and Implications of the Teaching Excellence Framework' (2019) Project Report for UCU (UCU TEF Report) <https://www.ucu.org.uk/media/10092/ Impact-of-TEF-report-Feb-2019/pdf/ImpactofTEFreportFEb2019> accessed 02 November 2021, 74.
111 Shirley Pearce, 'The Value of a National TEF Is in Enhancing University Learning and Teaching' (*WonkHE*, 8 February 2021) <https://wonkhe.com/blogs/the-value-of-a-national-tef-is-in-enhancing-university-learning-and-teaching/> accessed 02 November 2021.
112 UK Department of Education, 'Government Response to Dame Shirley Pearce's Independent Review of the Teaching Excellence and Student Outcomes Framework (TEF)' (January 2021) <https://assets.publishing.service.gov.uk/government/uploads/system/ uploads/attachment_data/file/953306/Goverment_response_to_the_independent_ review_of_TEF_.pdf> accessed 02 November 2021, 6.

40 *Maribel Canto-Lopez*

HE will become now a secondary purpose.[113] Another recommendation from the Pearce Review related to underpinning the TEF with the principles of transparency, relevancy and robustness to improve respect in the framework; the three principles were explained by reference to the needs of students and HEIs, not academics[114] (with little input into the TEF). The government added another principle in its response, the principle of proportionality, which may reduce the bureaucratic burden and cost that the TEF signified for HEIs.[115] However, as expected there was neither a mention, nor an acknowledgement of the burden and increase in workload the TEF brings to many academics in HEIs. Linked to the idea of the proportionality and cost, the government has endorsed the proposal to abandon the subject-level assessment as part of the TEF. The subject-level TEF has been held to be a non-cost-effective initiative.[116] There will not be an opportunity now, to gather or analyse data relating specifically to a law subject TEF.

Finally, TEF's rating system (gold, silver and bronze) is to be substituted for a new four-level rating.[117] The government subscribes to this recommendation and the OfS will decide on the new level names. The government agreed that the TEF should take place every four to five years.[118] In June 2021, the OfS sent a letter to HEIs indicating that the new provisional timeline for submission will open in summer 2022 and the outcomes should be announced in early 2023.[119] HEIs should not use their existing TEF awards

113 Shirley Pierce, 'The Value of a National TEF Is in Enhancing University Learning and Teaching' (*WonkHE*, 8 February 2021) <https://wonkhe.com/blogs/the-value-of-a-national-tef-is-in-enhancing-university-learning-and-teaching/> accessed 22 February 2021/> accessed 02 November 2021.

114 UK Department of Education, 'Independent Review of the Teaching Excellence and Student Outcomes Framework (TEF): Report to the Secretary of State for Education' (August 2019) <https://assets.publishing.service.gov.uk/government/uploads/system/uploads/attachment_data/file/952754/TEF_Independent_review_report.pdf> accessed 02 November 2021, 29–30.

115 UK Department of Education, 'Government Response to Dame Shirley Pearce's Independent Review of the Teaching Excellence and Student Outcomes Framework (TEF)' (January 2021) <https://assets.publishing.service.gov.uk/government/uploads/system/uploads/attachment_data/file/953306/Goverment_response_to_the_independent_review_of_TEF_.pdf> accessed 02 November 2021, 7.

116 Ibid, 8.

117 The Pearce Review recommended the following names: Meets UK Quality Requirements, Commended, Highly Commended and Outstanding. UK Department of Education, 'Independent Review of the Teaching Excellence and Student Outcomes Framework (TEF): Report to the Secretary of State for Education' (August 2019) <https://assets.publishing.service.gov.uk/government/uploads/system/uploads/attachment_data/file/952754/TEF_Independent_review_report.pdf> accessed 02 November 2021, 11.

118 Ibid, 8.

119 Office for Students, 'Letter to Providers: TEF Update' (*OfS*, 10 June 2021) <https://www.officeforstudents.org.uk/publications/letter-to-providers-tef-update/> accessed 02 November 2021, 2; David Kernohan, 'Another Pause for TEF, More Consultation on Regulation' (*WonkHE*, 10 June 2021) <https://wonkhe.com/wonk-corner/another-pause-for-tef-more-consultation-on-regulation/> accessed 28 June 2021.

for marketing from September 2021. In the meantime, there will be a few consultations for providers and students.[120] I would speculate that by 'providers', the OfS will mean HEIs management: this will not include many academics or LTVs, as evidenced by previous consultations. TEF will still be part of the education quality system of HE for years to come.[121] More importantly, while TEF started as a voluntary scheme, participation is now a condition of registration[122] for those English institutions[123] with more than 500 undergraduates.[124] TEF has undergone many changes since its creation; unfortunately, none of those included more engagement with academics or LTs. It seems LTs need to find ways to have their LTVs included meaningfully in the TEF's planning and implementation in HEIs.

LTs and the TEF: the good the bad and the future

Early in the process, many academics feared that the TEF was nothing more than another evidence-gathering exercise; part of the New Public Management wave HE has been dealing with in the last two decades.[125] Many LTs do not believe that the TEF was the right instrument to audit excellence in teaching in HEIs[126]; particularly, as the metrics were based on governmental economic targets such as student employability and

---

120 Office for Students, 'Letter to Providers: TEF Update' (*OfS*, 10 June 2021) <https://www.officeforstudents.org.uk/publications/letter-to-providers-tef-update/> accessed 02 November 2021, 2.

121 UK Department of Education, 'Government Response to Dame Shirley Pearce's Independent Review of the Teaching Excellence and Student Outcomes Framework (TEF)' (January 2021) <https://assets.publishing.service.gov.uk/government/uploads/system/uploads/attachment_data/file/953306/Goverment_response_to_the_independent_review_of_TEF_.pdf> accessed 02 November 2021, 6.

122 All HE institutions in England who want to access public funding for teaching or research must be registered with the OfS.

123 Providers in Scotland, Wales and Northern Ireland can also apply with the consent of the relevant devolved administration.

124 UK Department of Education, 'Independent Review of the Teaching Excellence and Student Outcomes Framework (TEF): Report to the Secretary of State for Education' (August 2019) <https://assets.publishing.service.gov.uk/government/uploads/system/uploads/attachment_data/file/952754/TEF_Independent_review_report.pdf> accessed 02 November 2021, 17.

125 Margaret Wood and Feng Su, 'What Makes an Excellent Lecturer? Academics' Perspectives on the Discourse of "Teaching Excellence" in Higher Education' (2017) 22 (4) Teaching in Higher Education 451, 460.

126 Sally Weston and Sarah McKeown, 'After the TEF and Consumer Law-Based Interventions- Are Prospective HE Students Now Able to Make Informed Choices?' (2020) 54 (3) The Law Teacher 414.

42 *Maribel Canto-Lopez*

postgraduate earnings.[127] Academics and LTs have little direct control over those factors.[128] As Frankham stated: 'doing better will be judged by metrics developed from outside the academy. Failings will be laid at the door of academics'.[129] It can be said that LTs may not want to engage with an evaluative framework based on values of which they disapprove.[130] But as outlined before, the problem is not just one of not agreeing with the values the TEF represents but also how these values were imposed by HEIs management without involving LTVs.[131]

According to the UCU report, more than 80% of the staff were not consulted about implementing TEF in their HEIs. Therefore, some academics felt just as 'passive recipients' of the TEF's demands in their own HEI.[132] The UCU report used information from 5,895 participants, 88% came from 154 English HEIs. Of those participants 5,512 were academics[133] (93.51%), 258 were professional services (4.38%) and 86 were management (1.46%).[134] It is clear from the UCU report that the voices of academics were not included in TEF policies, for example, the methodologies of data gathering or

---

127 Wendy Robinson and Angelique Hilli, 'The English 'Teaching Excellence Framework' and Professionalising Teaching and Learning in Research-Intensive Universities: and Exploration of Opportunities, Challenges, Rewards and Values from a Recent Empirical Study' (2016) 14 (21) Foro de Educacion 151, 153.

128 Ewart Keep and Ken Mayhew, 'Inequality – "Wicked Problems", Labour Market Outcomes and the Search for Silver Bullets' (2014) 40(6) Oxford Review of Education 764; Philip Wilson, Kate Crosswaite and Sophie Elliott, 'Analysis of Responses to the Call for Views for the Independent Review of the Teaching Excellence and Student Outcomes Framework (TEF)' (York Consulting, June 2019) <https://assets.publishing.service.gov.uk/government/uploads/system/uploads/attachment_data/file/935306/York_Consulting_TEF_call_for_views_analysis_-_accessible.pdf> accessed 02 November 2021, Section 5.172, 69–70.

129 Jo Frankham, 'Employability and Higher Education: The Follies of the 'Productivity Challenge' in the Teaching Excellence Framework' (2017) 32 (5) Journal of Education Policy, 637.

130 Matt O'Leary, Vanessa Cui and Amanda French, 'Understanding, Recognising and Rewarding Teaching Quality in Higher Education: An Exploration of the Impact and Implications of the Teaching Excellence Framework' (2019) Project Report for UCU (UCU TEF Report) <https://www.ucu.org.uk/media/10092/Impact-of-TEF-report-Feb-2019/pdf/ImpactofTEFreportFEb2019> accessed 02 November 2021, 2.

131 Ibid, 4.

132 Ibid, 7.

133 3,805 teaching and research, 785 teaching-focused, 473 teaching and scholarship and 449 research-focused.

134 Vanessa Cui, Amanda French and Matt O'Leary, 'A Missed Opportunity? How the UK's Teaching Excellence Framework Fail to Capture the Voice of University Staff' (2019) 46 (9) Studies in Higher Education 1756; Matt O'Leary, Vanessa Cui and Amanda French, 'Understanding, Recognising and Rewarding Teaching Quality in Higher Education: An Exploration of the Impact and Implications of the Teaching Excellence Framework' (2019) Project Report for UCU (UCU TEF Report) <https://www.ucu.org.uk/media/10092/Impact-of-TEF-report-Feb-2019/pdf/ImpactofTEFreportFEb2019> accessed 02 November 2021, 103–106.

in the TEF institution statement; or in any other institutional consultations relating to the TEF policies or its practices.[135] Surprisingly, seven in ten academics in teaching-focused positions had no involvement or awareness of the TEF in their institutions.[136] Only 12.48% of academics in teaching-focused roles reported some involvement with the TEF institutional consultations, compared to 64.19% of staff in management roles.[137]

Cui states that this data highlights two problems.[138] First, the different level of involvement between academics and the HEIs management in TEF translates into different perceptions of TEF and increases the distance between both groups. Second, there remains the issue of how HEI management will construct the narrative of their institution's teaching provision without the voices of those that carry out the everyday teaching and learning in their institutions.[139] On this latter point, Beech had looked at the TEF's statements submitted in TEF 2 (2017) by 12 HEIs.[140] These were all TEF statements, which helped their HEIs move up on the TEF rankings from the original rank indicated by the quantitative data alone.[141] Beech's report presents good examples of the TEFs panel being persuaded to award TEF gold. After reading some of the extracts from the institutions' statements, it seems reasonable to conclude that they are likely written mainly by the HEI management. For example, employment contracts are one of the criteria included in 'teaching quality', which was one of the three quantitative core data sets of the TEF. HEIs tend to recognise in TEF's statement that teaching quality is linked to academic staff career development.[142] However, there was one institution where 9% of the staff were on non-permanent contracts and there was a high proportion of hourly paid staff. The HEI's narrative explained how this contract situation was favourable, as it was their way to bringing in 'practitioners' expertise. According to Beech justifying the

---

135 Ibid, 3, 71–72.

136 Ibid, 4.

137 Vanessa Cui, Amanda French and Matt O'Leary, 'A Missed Opportunity? How the UK's Teaching Excellence Framework Fail to Capture the Voice of University Staff' (2019) 46 (9) Studies in Higher Education 1756.

138 Ibid, 10.

139 Ibid.

140 University of the Arts London, University of Bedfordshire, University of Birmingham, Bournemouth University, University of Bristol, University of Derby, Edge Hill University, Imperial College London, Leeds Becket University, Newcastle University, Royal Veterinary College and University College London. These institutions reflect, according to the author, the variety of the English HE sector, in Diana Beech, 'Going for Gold: Lessons from the TEF Provider Submissions' (2017) HEPI Report 99 <https://www.hepi. ac.uk/wp-content/uploads/2017/10/FINAL-HEPI-Going-for-Gold-Report-99-04_10_17-Screen.pdf> accessed 02 November 2021, 19.

141 Diana Beech, 'Going for Gold: Lessons from the TEF Provider Submissions' (2017) HEPI Report 99 <https://www.hepi.ac.uk/wp-content/uploads/2017/10/FINAL-HEPI-Going-for-Gold-Report-99-04_10_17-Screen.pdf> accessed 02 November 2021, 19.

142 Ibid, 25–26.

44 *Maribel Canto-Lopez*

employment methods under a veil of 'honesty' enhanced the HEIs' statements.[143] Perhaps it would be better to have testimonies and the real voices of those working on those hourly or non-permanent contracts reflected in the statement. I would argue that including the voices of academics and their narrative, positive or negative, about the type of contract they are on, would tell a more inclusive and transparent story in the HEI statement. The introduction of these narratives in the TEF statement may not help with elevating the HEI in the TEF ranking, yet this could initiate honest and much-needed conversation between academics and HEI management.

On the issue of academics and LTs' career development, it is true that as part of the government goal of refocusing the HEIs on teaching, the TEF brought some benefits for those on teaching-focused contracts.[144] Some academics on teaching-dominant contracts have seen a rise in status within their HEIs and the possibility of better career prospects.[145] It was reported that TEF panels tend to commend HEIs that create teaching dominant career paths.[146] However, Cui observes that the TEF has also meant offering institutions a 'leverage' to redirect some of their academic staff into teaching-intensive workloads by increasing teaching-only contracts.[147] The UCU report stated that it was generally felt that teaching-focused contracts were less highly regarded than research ones. More worrying is that some academics reported HEIs were switching their contracts, from research into teaching as a punitive response, after receiving low REF scores.[148]

---

143 Ibid, 26.
144 Pat Young, 'Out of Balance: Lecturers' Perception of Differential Status and Rewards in Relation to Teaching and Research' (2006) 11(2) Teaching & Higher Education 191.
145 Wendy Robinson and Angelique Hilli, 'The English 'Teaching Excellence Framework' and Professionalising Teaching and Learning in Research-Intensive Universities: and Exploration of Opportunities, Challenges, Rewards and Values from a Recent Empirical Study' (2016) 14(21) Foro de Educacion 151, 159.
146 Diana Beech, 'Going for Gold: Lessons from the TEF Provider Submissions' (2017) HEPI Report 99 <https://www.hepi.ac.uk/wp-content/uploads/2017/10/FINAL-HEPI-Going-for-Gold-Report-99-04_10_17-Screen.pdf> accessed 02 November 2021, 25.
147 Vanessa Cui, Amanda French and Matt O'Leary, 'A Missed Opportunity? How the UK's Teaching Excellence Framework Fail to Capture the Voice of University Staff' (2019) 46 (9) Studies in Higher Education 1756; Matt O'Leary, Vanessa Cui and Amanda French, 'Understanding, Recognising and Rewarding Teaching Quality in Higher Education: An Exploration of the Impact and Implications of the Teaching Excellence Framework' (2019) Project Report for UCU (UCU TEF Report) <https://www.ucu.org.uk/media/10092/Impact-of-TEF-report-Feb-2019/pdf/ImpactofTEFreportFEb2019> accessed 02 November 2021, 65.
148 Matt O'Leary, Vanessa Cui and Amanda French, 'Understanding, Recognising and Rewarding Teaching Quality in Higher Education: An Exploration of the Impact and Implications of the Teaching Excellence Framework' (2019) Project Report for UCU (UCU TEF Report) <https://www.ucu.org.uk/media/10092/Impact-of-TEF-report-Feb-2019/pdf/ImpactofTEFreportFEb2019> accessed 02 November 2021, 65.

The UCU report stated that a quarter of all participants agreed it was positive that there has been greater recognition of the importance of teaching.[149] The problem with that statement is again the different perception between academics and the HEIs on what teaching excellence means. I would argue that recognition and rewarding of teaching can only be welcomed if, in refocusing on teaching, there is engagement with academics and LTs, which results in greater support. High teaching workloads and high student-staff ratios will not help teaching excellence. According to Morrison and Guth, LTs need resources and time to create the right learning environment that would empower them and the learning experience of their students.[150]

According to UCU's report data, TEF ignores the experience, concerns, expertise, values and hope of many LTs, consequently, the disengagement between LTs and their institutions was aggravated.[151] The UCU report recommends more involvement of academics in the TEF preparation and implementation in HEIs.[152] Without their involvement, there cannot be a sustainable improvement of the teaching and learning quality in the HEIs. Academics and LTs are central to the everyday delivery, development and improvement of the teaching and learning experience in HEIs.[153] This has proven true during Covid-19.

Interestingly, Clark and Tsamenyi mentioned in their chapter that integrating technology was a future challenge for LTs. According to them, to succeed in integrating technology, there was a need for pedagogical principles to base that integration. They also added that incorporating new technologies into law schools requires managerial and LTs support.[154] Undoubtedly, Clark and Tsamenyi could never have envisaged the speed at which LTs had to embrace digital pedagogy to teach under the pressures of a pandemic and the continually changing HE landscape. Nevertheless, HEIs need to be more transparent and inclusive on how they want to push for digitalisation and the seemingly irreversible change into a new technological HE era.[155] LTVs need to find their way into the discussions about the future of HEIs post-Covid, or arguably, the outcome would be unsustainable. LTs should

---

149 Ibid, 73.
150 Doug Morrison and Jessica Guth, 'Rethinking the Neoliberal University: Embracing Vulnerability in English Law Schools?' (2021) 55 (1) The Law Teacher 42.
151 Ibid, 76.
152 Ibid, 3.
153 Vanessa Cui, Amanda French and Matt O'Leary, 'A Missed Opportunity? How the UK's Teaching Excellence Framework Fail to Capture the Voice of University Staff' (2019) 46 (9) Studies in Higher Education 1756.
154 Eugene Clark and Martin Tsamenyi, 'Legal Education in the Twenty-First Century: A Time of Challenge' in Peter Birks (ed), *Pressing Problems in the Law, Volume 2: What Are Law Schools For?* (Oxford University Press 1996, 2003 reprinting), 30.
155 Richard Watermeyer, Tom Crick, Cathryn Knight and Janet Goodall, 'Covid-19 and Digital Disruption in UK Universities: Afflictions and Affordances of Emergency Online Migration' (2021) 81 Higher Education 623, 638.

46 *Maribel Canto-Lopez*

seize these disrupted times to start thinking about how to be part of real consultations and collaborate with HEIs to plan the future.[156]

Pressing needs for LTs: finding a way to have LTVs present in HE policies through the TEF

Since Birks' assessment to the present day, there is a common denominator: the absence of academic and LTVs from governmental and HEIs policies.[157] This lack of LTVs is more evident now because HE policies are increasingly affecting the working conditions of all stakeholders in HE, particularly academics.[158] These new pressures in HE, like the ones originating in the TEF, are upsetting the identity and well-being of many academics and LTs.[159] This situation will, arguably, have negative repercussions for the sustainability of the HE sector. Clark and Tsamenyi advocated for the participation of LTVs in public debate as a way to challenge the changes that more than 20 years ago were already endangering the values of legal education, the HE sector and society in general.[160] Based on that notion, there is an urgent pressing need for LTs to think about practical ways to engage and make themselves heard within their institutions and government policies.

For some, education unions have a pivotal role in ensuring HEIs and the government recognise the role of academics in advancing education in a post-TEF and post-pandemic era.[161] I suggest all LTs, members of the UCU or not,[162] need to start finding bottom-up collaborative solutions inside their HEIs, to help everyone in the institution cope with the effects of the

---

156 Andy Pitchford and Ed Stevens 'Covid Disrupts Our Academic Identities, and That's Something We Should Embrace' (*WonkHE*, 18 December 2020) <https://wonkhe.com/blogs/covid-disrupts-our-academic-identities-and-thats-something-we-should-embrace-2/ > accessed 15 August 2021.

157 Duna Sabri, 'Absence of the Academic from Higher Education Policy' (2010) 25(2) Journal of Education Policy 191, 205.

158 Ibid, 201.

159 Jon Nixon, 'Not Without Dust and Heat: The Moral Bases of the 'New' Academic Professionalism' (2001) 49(2) British Journal of Educational Studies 173; J Clare Wilson and Caroline Strevens, 'Perceptions of Psychological Well-Being in UK Law Academics' (2018) 52(3) The Law Teacher 335.

160 Eugene Clark and Martin Tsamenyi, 'Legal Education in the Twenty-First Century: A Time of Challenge' in Peter Birks (ed), *Pressing Problems in the Law, Volume 2: What Are Law Schools For?* (Oxford University Press 1996, 2003 reprinting), 35.

161 Rob Copland, 'Addressing the Challenges of the Covid-19 Pandemic: A View from Higher Education Staff' in Sjur Bergan, Tony Gallagher, Ira Harkavy, Ronaldo Munck and Hilligje van't Land (eds), Higher Education's Response to the Covid-19 Pandemic: Building a More Sustainable and Democratic Future (Council of Europe Higher Education Series No 25, 2021), 287; Graham Ferris, 'Undermining Resilience: How the Modern UK University Manufactures Heightened Vulnerability in Legal Academics and What Is to Be Done' (2021) 55(1) The Law Teacher 24, 40.

162 In total, 48.7% of employees in education are part of the union. In UK Department for Business, Energy & Industrial Strategy, 'Trade Union Memberships, UK 1995–2019: Statistical Bulletin' (2020).

TEF and Covid-19 in the future.[163] In practical terms, at institutional level, LTs can, for example, include their demands for participation in all the TEF stages of consultation and implementation in the law schools' meetings, alert their heads of school about these pleas, and use twitter[164] and blogs[165] to disseminate the need to have LTVs heard. Doing nothing arguably will perpetuate the increasing workloads and bureaucracy TEF brings to HEIs. At governmental level, LTs can also publicise the idea of including 'staff satisfaction' as a new independent metric for the TEF. LTs can broadcast this idea through the UCU and with the help of their own community,[166] for example, through the Association of Law Teachers.[167]

At an institutional level, it seems TEF's consultations and implementation are written in a one-sided fashion by the HEIs management.[168] Introducing academic voices in the TEF will arguably help to align the values of academics with the values of the HEIs management. According to Shields and Watermeyer, the values of academics and the values of HE management are in competition, at least from the point of view of 'institutional logics'.[169] The concept of 'Institutional logics' relates, in principle, to the beliefs, values and shared understanding of practices inside a particular HEI, which help its members articulate their purpose.[170] Academic's institutional logics are more aligned with values of autonomy; HE management institutional

---

<https://assets.publishing.service.gov.uk/government/uploads/system/uploads/attachment_data/file/887740/Trade-union-membership-2019-statistical-bulletin.pdf> accessed 03 November 2021, 9.

163 Simone Buitendijk. 'Covid-19: Universities Can't Fix Everything and That Should Be OK', (*WonkHE*, 9 November 2020) <https://wonkhe.com/blogs/covid-19-universities-cant-fix-everything-and-that-should-be-ok/> accessed 03 November2021; David Jones and Dean Patton, 'An Academic Challenge to the Entrepreneurial University: The Spatial Power of the "Slow Swimming Club"' (2020) 45(2) Studies in Higher Education 375, 386.

164 The Association of Law Teachers, Twitter <https://twitter.com/TheLTjournal?ref_src=twsrc%5Egoogle%7Ctwcamp%5Eserp%7Ctwgr%5Eauthor> accessed 18 November 2021.

165 James Richards, 'Because I Need Somewhere to Vent': The Expression of Conflict Through Work Blogs' (2008) 23 (1–2) New Technology, Work and Employment 95; The Association of Law Teachers, Blog <http://lawteacher.ac.uk/alt-blog-2/> accessed 18 November 2021.

166 Chris Ashford, 'Editorial – Turning Points' (2019) 53(2) The Law Teacher 133.

167 The Association of Law Teachers, 'Membership Benefits' (2021) < http://lawteacher.ac.uk/join/> accessed 03 November 2021.

168 Adam Matthews and Ben Kotzee, 'The Rhetoric of the UK Higher Education Teaching Excellence Framework: A Corps-Assisted Discourse Analysis of TEF2 Provider Statements' (2019) 73 (5) Educational Review 523.

169 Robin Shields and Richard Watermeyer, 'Competing Institutional Logics in Universities in the United Kingdom: Schism in the Church of Reason' (2020) 45(1) Studies in Higher Education 3, 13.

170 Alistair Mutch, 'Practice, Substance, and History: Reframing Institutional Logics' (2018) 43(2) Academy of Management Review 242, 244.

48 *Maribel Canto-Lopez*

logics are more grounded on neo-liberal principles.[171] And it is argued that those in management positions in HEIs tend to be in charge of the institutional logics of the HEIs.[172]

For some, institutional logics are very difficult to change in HEIs, because HEIs managers perceive that external pressures such as diminishing funding, market pressures, competition, over which they do not have control, stop any possibility of changes they may want to implement in their HEIs.[173] However according to Graham and Donaldson, changes in 'practices' inside the HEIs can occur with much more ease. Perhaps using this hypothesis, some of the aforementioned practical suggestions to include LTVs in the institutional TEF's doings, may help in time to change the HEIs institutional logic. For example, if LTs can include LTVs in the HEI TEF statement, this change in practice can be the 'low hanging fruit' that may start some more important changes in the HEI.[174] It may help HEIs management understand how LTs perceptions can be included in practice, and in time change, the management perceived rigidity of the institutional logics.[175]

The inclusion of more LTVs in the TEF's statement, possibly, will help LTs regain some sense of autonomy, well-being and collegiality.[176] It may also enable HEIs to understand what teaching excellence means from an academics' perspective.[177] HEIs can learn about the need to give more time to academics to research pedagogy.[178] Research that can help with a long-term sustainable institutional logic that will be shared across the whole HEI, helping other academics, and improving the student learning experience.[179] Academics and the HEIs' management can debate together solutions to any

---

171 Robin Shields and Richard Watermeyer, 'Competing Institutional Logics in Universities in the United Kingdom: Schism in the Church of Reason' (2020) 45(1) Studies in Higher Education 3, 13.

172 Steven W Graham and Joe F Donaldson, 'Academic Leaders' Response to the Volatility of Higher Education: The Influence of Institutional Logics' (2020) 45(9) Studies in Higher Education 1864, 1876.

173 Ibid, 1874–1876.

174 Ibid, 1876.

175 Ibid.

176 Nikos Macheridis and Alexander Paulson, 'Professionalism between Profession and Governance: How University Teachers' Professionalism Shapes Coordination' (2019) 44(3) Studies in Higher Education 470, 482.

177 Margaret Wood and Feng Su, 'What Makes an Excellent Lecturer? Academics' Perspectives on the Discourse of "Teaching Excellence" in Higher Education' (2017) 22(4) Teaching in Higher Education 451.

178 Anne Tierney, 'The Scholarship of Teaching and Learning and Pedagogic Research between the Disciplines: Should It Be Included in the Research Excellence Framework?' (2020) 45(1) Studies in Higher Education 176.

179 Sue Cherrington, Anne Macaskill, Rhian Salmon, Suzanne Boniface, Sydney Shep and Jonny Flutey, 'Developing a Pan-University Professional Learning Community' (2018) 23(4) International Journal for Academic Development 298.

of the challenges TEF brings to the HEIs in a creative and dynamic way.[180] It may help academics and the HEIs find a shared interpretation and a common mission particular to their HEI, because not all HEIs are the same.[181]

At a governmental level, academics and LTs could push for an independent metric, which will measure staff (i.e. academics') satisfaction. The Pearce Review recommended that the TEF submission process should include a way for the student body to contribute independently.[182] I would propose that the academic body can do the same. It has been argued that HEIs and their management do not have many incentives to listen to academics, because no one is monitoring universities' performance on the grounds of being good employers.[183] If staff satisfaction was measured, perhaps HEIs would be encouraged to listen to academic voices,[184] and reduce the engagement with precarious contracts practices.[185] Students will also benefit by being informed about the HEIs in which the staff feel more fulfilled and more motivated to excel at teaching and learning.[186] More importantly, if HEIs reconnect with their staff, they will help create HEIs with a 'satisfied'

---

180 Michael Tomlinson, Jurgen Enders and Rajani Naidoo, 'The Teaching Excellence Framework: Symbolic Violence and the Measured Market in Higher Education' (2020) 61(5) Critical Studies in Education 627, 639.

181 Daniel Berger and Charles Wild, 'The Teaching Excellence Framework: Would You Tell Me, Please, Which Way I Ought to Go from Here?' (2016) 48(3) Higher Education Review 5.

182 UK Department of Education, 'Independent Review of the Teaching Excellence and Student Outcomes Framework (TEF): Report to the Secretary of State for Education' (August 2019) <https://assets.publishing.service.gov.uk/government/uploads/system/uploads/attachment_data/file/952754/TEF_Independent_review_report.pdf> accessed 02 November 2021, 7.

183 Olga Kuznetsova and Andrei Kuznetsova, 'And Then There Were None: What a UCU Archive Tells Us about Employee Relations in Marketising Universities' (2020) 45(12) Studies in Higher Education 2439, 2448.

184 Daryl Dugas, Amy E Stich, Lindsay N Harris and Kelly H Summers, '"I'm Being Pulled in Too Many Different Directions": Academic Identity Tensions at Regional Public Universities in Challenging Economic Times' (2020) 45(2) Studies in Higher Education 312, 314–315.

185 Rosemary Deem and Kevin J Brehony 'Management as Ideology: The Case of "New Managerialism" in Higher Education' (2005) 31(2) Oxford Review of Education 217; Alysia Blackham, 'Unpacking Precarious Academic Work in Legal Education' (2020) 54(3) The Law Teacher 426; Colin Bryson, 'What about the Workers? The Expansion of Higher Education and the Transformation of Academic Work' (2001) 35(1) Industrial Relations Journal 38; Diana Beech, 'Going for Gold: Lessons from the TEF Provider Submissions' (2017) HEPI Report 99 <https://www.hepi.ac.uk/wp-content/uploads/2017/10/FINAL-HEPI-Going-for-Gold-Report-99-04_10_17-Screen.pdf> accessed 02 November 2021, 25.

186 Gary Anderson and Michael Cohen, 'Redesigning the Identities of Teachers and Leaders: A Framework for Studying New Professionalism and Educator Resistance' (2015) 23(91) Education Policy Analysis Archives 1.

50 *Maribel Canto-Lopez*

workforce[187] and a sustainable future for the whole of the HE sector. The OfS could consult academics about the new metric, which will genuinely help improve teaching excellence, as motivated and happy academics are central to protecting HE,[188] and student learning experiences.[189]

The pandemic has presented a crossroad in which many academics had to reflect upon their responsibility to find ways to recover their identities and values.[190] If academics believe their voices matter, it will improve their resilience and the HEIs' resilience.[191] For LTs, I argue that the need of finding ways to include LTVs into education policies is urgent; to stop the array of top-down pressures from frameworks like the TEF, at HEIs and government levels. These pressures are leaving many LTs exhausted and demotivated.[192] During the pandemic, LTs have shown their spirit; they quickly and tirelessly transformed learning and teaching provisions to help students, HEIs and society.[193] This seminal year has also encouraged collegiality[194] and a sense of community. Undeniably, LTs have a common interest with the rest of academics working in HE, for reasserting academic values and a sustainable future of the HE sector.[195] A better prospect for LTs will mean a better future for their HEIs and all involved in them. Indeed, LTs can use

187 ' ...HEIs often boast of being ...employers of choice... (it would help) to acquire a new competitive advantage – one rooted in staff satisfaction' in Liz Morrish, 'Pressure Vessels: The Epidemic of Poor Mental Health among Higher Education Staff' (*HEPI*, Occasional Paper 20, 2019) <https://www.hepi.ac.uk/2019/05/23/pressure-vessels-the-epidemic-of-poor-mental-health-among-higher-education-staff/> accessed 03 November 2021, 11.

188 Peter Birks, 'Preface' in Peter Birks (ed), *Pressing Problems in the Law, Volume 2: What Are Law Schools For?* (Oxford University Press 1996, 2003 reprinting), xiv.

189 Michael Tomlinson, 'Conceptions of the Value of Higher Education in a Measured Market' (2018) 75 Higher Education 711.

190 Kate Tapper, 'Getting through Covid-19 Means Rethinking Resilience' (*WonkHE*, 9 November 2020) <https://wonkhe.com/blogs/getting-through-covid-19-means-rethinking-resilience/> accessed 03 November 2021.

191 Michael Unger 'Put Down the Self-Help Books. Resilience Is Not at DIY Endeavour' (*The Globe and Mail*, 25 May 2019) <https://www.theglobeandmail.com/opinion/article-put-down-the-self-help-books-resilience-is-not-a-diy-endeavour/#:~:text=The%20 notion%20that%20your%20resilience,is%20not%20a%20DIY%20endeavour.> accessed 03 November 2021.

192 J Clare Wilson and Caroline Strevens, 'Perceptions of Psychological Well-Being in UK Law Academics' (2018) 52(3) The Law Teacher 335.

193 Chris Ashford, 'Editorial: Law Teaching and the Coronavirus Pandemic' (2020) 54(2) The Law Teacher 167; Richard Watermeyer, Tom Crick, Cathryn Knight and Janet Goodall, 'Covid-19 and Digital Disruption in UK Universities: Afflictions and Affordances of Emergency Online Migration' (2021) 81 Higher Education 623, 626.

194 Emma Flint, Michael Doherty and Lydia Bleasdale, 'Connecting Legal Education: Building Communities' (*Association of Law Teachers*, 14 April 2020) <http://lawteacher.ac.uk/connecting-legal-education/connecting-legal-education-building-communities/> accessed 03 November 2021.

195 Graham Ferris, 'Undermining Resilience: How the Modern UK University Manufactures Heightened Vulnerability in Legal Academics and What Is To Be Done' (2021) 55(1) The Law Teacher 24, 40.

What are law teachers for? 51

the pandemic as the springboard to lend their collective voices[196] to HE policies, to remind policy makers and HEIs about the importance of academic autonomy, social values and the public good.

Conclusion

The last two decades have brought many changes to HE, principally the increased marketisation and corporatisation of the sector and HEIs.[197] Some of the changes were already present in an emergent phase when the Birks' collection was released. Other events and changes, such as the TEF, could not be predicted or even imagined.

The TEF as a HE evaluative framework of the teaching quality in HE institutions is still evolving and the sector is waiting for the latest design of this initiative. TEF emphasises the economic value of HE,[198] which is conceptually different to academics and LTs ideas of teaching quality.[199] The TEF has not only resulted in more bureaucracy, control and accountability through institutions top-down diktats, but it has done this without including academics or LTVs into its implementation.[200] This has only increased the gap of disengagement between institutions and LTs. Now is the time for LTs to find ways to start bottom-up conversations with HE institutions to reconnect. There are practical ideas, at an institutional level, to help reconnect with the HEIs management, such as being part of the TEF institutional consultations or drafting collaboratively the TEF institutions' statement. This will help the institution understand how it can promote fundamental pedagogical research and develop scholarly attitudes to learning and teaching. More importantly, it will help LTs motivation,

---

196 Eugene Clark and Martin Tsamenyi, 'Legal Education in the Twenty-First Century: A Time of Challenge' in Peter Birks (ed), *Pressing Problems in the Law, Volume 2: What Are Law Schools For?* (Oxford University Press 1996, 2003 reprinting), 44.

197 Robin Shields and Richard Watermeyer, 'Competing Institutional Logics in Universities in the United Kingdom: Schism in the Church of Reason' (2020) 45(1) Studies in Higher Education 3, 15.

198 Michael Tomlinson, Jurgen Enders and Rajani Naidoo, 'The Teaching Excellence Framework: Symbolic Violence and the Measured Market in Higher Education' (2020) 61(5) Critical Studies in Education 627, 638.

199 John Canning 'The UK Teaching Excellence Framework (TEF) as an Illustration of Baudrillard's Hyperreality' (2019) 40(3) Discourse: Studies in the Cultural Politics of Education 319, 328.

200 Vanessa Cui, Amanda French and Matt O'Leary, 'A Missed Opportunity? How the UK's Teaching Excellence Framework Fail to Capture the Voice of University Staff' (2019) 46(9) Studies in Higher Education 1756.; Matt O'Leary, Vanessa Cui and Amanda French, 'Understanding, Recognising and Rewarding Teaching Quality in Higher Education: An Exploration of the Impact and Implications of the Teaching Excellence Framework' (2019) Project Report for UCU (UCU TEF Report) <https://www.ucu.org.uk/media/10092/Impact-of-TEF-report-Feb-2019/pdf/ImpactofTEFreportFEb2019> accessed 02 November 2021.

52 Maribel Canto-Lopez

which has been bruised under TEF's scrutiny. At a sector level, LTs could push collectively to introduce staff satisfaction as an independent metric in TEF, which will also help embed LTVs into HE education policy. The OfS could take forward the redevelopment of TEF including academic voices in a brand new TEF metric.

This moment, at what might be regarded as a pivot point for TEF and in a return to campus-based higher education after the pandemic, is the right time for LTs to start broadcasting their voices and regaining their identities and values,[201] lost to competitiveness and productivity indoctrination.[202] HEIs should realise that LTs and their colleagues need time and space to build their communities and support their teaching up with pedagogic research and share them widely to enhance students' learning experience in a way that employers expect, and society deserves.[203] For this reason, there may be a chance to answer more positively the question of what LTs are for moving forward.

Bibliography

Adler P, 'Market, Hierarchy and Trust: The Knowledge Economy and the Future of Capitalism' (2001) 12(2) *Organizational Science Journal* 215–234.

Anderson G and Cohen M, 'Redesigning the Identities of Teachers and Leaders: A Framework for Studying New Professionalism and Educator Resistance' (2015) 23(91) *Education Policy Analysis Archives* 1–25.

Ashford C, 'Editorial: Law Teaching and the Coronavirus Pandemic' (2020) 54(2) *The Law Teacher* 167–168.

Ashford C, 'Editorial: Turning Points' (2019) 53(2) *The Law Teacher* 133–135.

Ashwin P, 'The Government's Response to the Pearce Review of TEF Doesn't Do Justice to It' (*WonkHE*, 8 February 2021) <https://wonkhe.com/blogs/the-governments-response-to-the-pearce-review-of-tef-doesnt-do-justice-to-it/> accessed 02 November 2021.

Bagshaw A and Karnohan D, 'TEF: The Incredible Machine Remixed' (*WonkHE*, 22 June 2017) <https://wonkhe.com/blogs/the-incredible-machine-remixed/> accessed 02 November 2021.

Barkas L, Scott J, Poppitt N, and Smith P, 'Tinker, Tailor, Policy-Maker: Can the UK Government's Teaching Excellence Framework Deliver Its Objectives?' (2017) 43(6) *Journal of Further and Higher Education* 801–813.

Baron P, 'Thriving in the Legal Academy' (2007) 17(1) *Legal Education Review* 27–52.

---

201 Richard M Ryan and Edward L Deci, 'Self-Determination Theory and the Facilitation of Intrinsic Motivation, Social Development, and Well-Being' (2000) 55 (1) American Psychologist 68, 76.

202 Hugo Horta and Joao M Santos, 'Organisational Factors and Academic Research Agendas: An Analysis of Academics on the Social Sciences' (2020) 45(12) Studies in Higher Education 2382, 2396.

203 Paula Baron, 'Thriving in the Legal Academy' (2007) 17(1) Legal Education Review 27, 52.

Beech D, 'Going for Gold: Lessons from the TEF Provider Submissions' (2017) HEPI Report 99 <https://www.hepi.ac.uk/wp-content/uploads/2017/10/FINAL-HEPI-Going-for-Gold-Report-99-04_10_17-Screen.pdf> accessed 02 November 2021.

Berger D and Wild C, 'The Teaching Excellence Framework: Would You Tell Me, Please, Which Way I Ought to Go from Here?' (2016) 48(3) *Higher Education Review* 5–22.

Birks P, 'Preface' in Peter Birks (ed) *Pressing Problems in the Law, Volume 2: What Are Law Schools For?* (Oxford University Press 1996, 2003 reprinting).

Blackham A, 'Unpacking Precarious Academic Work in Legal Education' (2020) 54(3) *The Law Teacher* 426–442.

Bradney A, 'The Success of University Law Schools in England and Wales: Or How to Fail' (2018) 52(4) *The Law Teacher* 490–498.

Bryson C, 'What about the Workers? The Expansion of Higher Education and the Transformation of Academic Work' (2001) 35(1) *Industrial Relations Journal* 38–57.

Buitendijk S, 'Covid-19: Universities Can't Fix Everything and That Should Be OK', (*WonkHE*, 9 November 2020) < https://wonkhe.com/blogs/covid-19-universities-cant-fix-everything-and-that-should-be-ok/> accessed 03 November 2021.

Bunce L, Baird A, and Jones S, 'The Student-as-a-Consumer Approach in Higher Education and Its Effect on Academic Performance' (2017) 42(11) *Studies in Higher Education* 1958–1978.

Canning J, 'The UK Teaching Excellence Framework (TEF) as an Illustration of Baudrillard's Hyperreality' (2019) 40(3) *Discourse: Studies in the Cultural Politics of Education* 319–330.

Canto-Lopez M, 'New Challenges in the UK Legal Education Landscape: TEF, SQE and the Law Teacher' (2018) 18 *Revista Jurídica de Investigación e Innovación Educativa (REJIE Nueva época)* 11–30.

Cherrington S, Macaskill A, Salmon R, Boniface S, Shep S, and Flutey J, 'Developing a Pan-University Professional Learning Community' (2018) 23(4) *International Journal for Academic Development* 298–311.

Clark E and Tsamenyi M, 'Legal Education in the Twenty-First Century: A Time of Challenge' in Peter Birks (ed) *Pressing Problems in the Law, Volume 2: What Are Law Schools For?* (Oxford University Press 1996, 2003 reprinting).

Collini S, 'Who Are the Spongers Now?' (2016) 38(2) *London Review of Books* 33–37.

Connell R, 'The Neoliberal Cascade and Education: An Essay on the Market Agenda and Its Consequences' (2013) 54(2) *Critical Studies in Education* 99–112.

Copland R, 'Addressing the Challenges of the Covid-19 Pandemic: A View from Higher Education Staff' in Sjur Bergan, Tony Gallagher, Ira Harkavy, Ronaldo Munck and Hilligje van't Land (eds) *Higher Education's Response to the Covid-19 Pandemic: Building a More Sustainable and Democratic Future* (Council of Europe Higher Education Series No 25, 2021).

Cownie F and Bradney A, 'An Examined Life: Research into University Legal Education in the United Kingdom and the *Journal of Law and Society*' (2017) 44(1) *Journal of Law and Society* 129–143.

Crawford J, Butler-Henderson K, Rudolph J, Malkawi B, Glowatz M, Burton R, Magni P, and Lam S, 'COVID-19: 20 Countries' Higher Education Intra-Period Digital Pedagogy Responses' (2020) 3(1) *Journal of Applied Learning and Teaching* <https://eprints.utas.edu.au/34123/2/138340%20-%20COVID-19.%2020%20

54 *Maribel Canto-Lopez*

countries%27%20higher%20education%20intra-period%20digital%20peda-gogy%20responses.pdf> accessed 02 November 2021.

Cui V, French A and O'Leary M, 'A Missed Opportunity? How the UK's Teaching Excellence Framework Fail to Capture the Voice of University Staff' (2019) 46(9) *Studies in Higher Education* 1756–1770.

Dearlove J, 'The Academic Labour Process: From Collegiality and Professionalism to Managerialism and Proletarianisation?' (1997) 30(1) *Higher Education Review* 56–75.

Deem R and Brehony K, 'Management as Ideology: The Case of "New Managerialism" in Higher Education' (2005) 31(2) *Oxford Review of Education* 217–235.

Dugas D, Stich A, Harris L and Summers K, '"I'm Being Pulled in Too Many Different Directions": Academic Identity Tensions at Regional Public Universities in Challenging Economic Times' (2020) 45(2) *Studies in Higher Education* 312–326.

Elton L, 'The UK Research Assessment Exercise: Unintended Consequences' (2000) 54(3) *Higher Education Quarterly* 274–283.

Ferguson L, 'Complicating the 'Holy Grail', Simplifying the Search: A Critique of the Conventional Problematisation of Social Immobility in Elite Legal Education and the Profession' (2017) 41(4) *The Law Teacher* 377–400.

Ferris G, 'Undermining Resilience: How the Modern UK University Manufactures Heightened Vulnerability in Legal Academics and What Is to Be Done' (2021) 55(1) *The Law Teacher* 24–41.

Flint E, Doherty M, and Bleasdale L, 'Connecting Legal Education: Building Communities' (*Association of Law Teachers*, 14 April 2020) <http://lawteacher.ac.uk/connecting-legal-education/connecting-legal-education-building-communities/> accessed 03 November 2021.

Frankham J, 'Employability and Higher Education: The Follies of the 'Productivity Challenge' in the Teaching Excellence Framework' (2017) 32(5) *Journal of Education Policy* 628–641.

Gibbons J, 'Policy Recontextualisation: The Proposed Introduction of a Multiple-Choice Test for the Entry-Level Assessment of the Legal Knowledge of Prospective Solicitor in England and Wales, and the Potential Effect on University-Level Legal Education' (2017) 24(3) *International Journal of the Legal Profession* 227–241.

Graham S and Donaldson J, 'Academic Leaders' Response to the Volatility of Higher Education: The Influence of Institutional Logics' (2020) 45(9) *Studies in Higher Education* 1864–1877.

Gravett K and Kinkchin I, 'Revisiting A "Teaching Excellence" for the Times We Live in: Posthuman Possibilities' (2020) 25(8) *Teaching in Higher Education* 1028–1034.

Horta H and Santos J, 'Organisational Factors and Academic Research Agendas: An Analysis of Academics on the Social Sciences' (2020) 45(12) *Studies in Higher Education* 2382–2397.

Hubble S, Foster D, and Bolton P, 'Higher Education and Research Bill 2016 [Bill No 004 of 2016–17]' (Briefing Paper No 7608, 2016) <https://www.timeshigher-education.com/sites/default/files/breaking_news_files/he_bill_briefing.pdf> accessed 02 November 2021.

Hudson A, 'Two Futures for Law Schools' (2021) 55(1) *The Law Teacher* 101–104.

Jones D and Patton D, 'An Academic Challenge to the Entrepreneurial University: The Spatial Power of the "Slow Swimming Club"' (2020) 45(2) *Studies in Higher Education* 375–389.

What are law teachers for? 55

Keep E and Mayhew K, 'Inequality – "Wicked Problems", Labour Market Outcomes and the Search for Silver Bullets' (2014) 40(6) *Oxford Review of Education* 764–781.

Kernohan D, 'Another Pause for TEF, More Consultation on Regulation' (*WonkHE*, 10 June 2021) <https://wonkhe.com/wonk-corner/another-pause-for-tef-more-consultation-on-regulation/> accessed 28 June 2021.

Kogan M and Hanney S, *Reforming Higher Education* (Jessica Kingsley Publisher 1999).

Kolsaker A, 'Relocating Professionalism in an English University' (2014) 36(2) *Journal of Higher Education Policy and Managements* 129–142.

Kuznetsova O and Kuznetsova A, 'And Then There Were None: What a UCU Archive Tells Us about Employee Relations in Marketising Universities' (2020) 45(12) *Studies in Higher Education* 2439–2450.

Lunch K, 'Neo-Liberalism and Marketisation: The Implications for Higher Education' (2006) 5(1) *European Education Research Journal* 1–17

Macheridis N and Paulson A, 'Professionalism between Profession and Governance: How University Teachers' Professionalism Shapes Coordination' (2019) 44(3) *Studies in Higher Education* 470–485.

Marginson S, 'The Impossibility of Capitalist Markets in Higher Education' (2013) 28(3) *Journal of Education Policy* 353–370.

Marinoni G, van't Land H, and Jensen T, 'The Impact of Covid-19 on Higher Education around the World: IAU Global Survey Report' (2020) <https://www.iau-aiu.net/IMG/pdf/iau_covid19_and_he_survey_report_final_may_2020.pdf> accessed 02 November 2021.

Mason L and Guth J, 'Re-Claiming Our Discipline' Editorial in 'Special Issue: From LETR to SQE: Reforming Legal Education and Training in England and Wales' (2018) 52(4) *The Law Teacher* 379–383.

Matthews A and Kotzee B, 'The Rhetoric of the UK Higher Education Teaching Excellence Framework: A Corps-Assisted Discourse Analysis of TEF2 Provider Statements' (2021) 73(5) *Educational Review* 523–543.

Mayer C, 'Whose Responsible for Irresponsible Business? An Assessment' (2017) 33(2) *Oxford Review of Economic Policy* 157–175.

McNay I, 'From the Collegial Academy to the Corporate Enterprise: The Changing Cultures of Universities in the Changing University' in Tom Schuller (ed) *The Changing University* (SRHE 1995).

Molesworth M, Scullion R, and Nixon E (eds), *The Marketisation of Higher Education and the Student as a Consumer* (Routledge 2011).

Morgan J, 'Higher Education and Research Bill Passed by UK Parliament' (*Times Higher Education,* 27 April 2017) <https://www.timeshighereducation.com/news/higher-education-and-research-bill-passed-uk-parliament#survey-answer accessed 25/12/2017> accessed 13 January 2021.

Morrish L, 'Pressure Vessels: The Epidemic of Poor Mental Health among Higher Education Staff' (*HEPI*, Occasional Paper 20, 2019) <https://www.hepi.ac.uk/2019/05/23/pressure-vessels-the-epidemic-of-poor-mental-health-among-higher-education-staff/> accessed 03 November 2021.

Morrison D, 'The SQE and Creativity: A Race to the Bottom?' (2018) 52(4) *The Law Teacher* 467–477.

Morrison D and Guth J, 'Rethinking the Neoliberal University: Embracing Vulnerability in English Law Schools?' (2021) 55(1) *The Law Teacher* 42–56.

56 Maribel Canto-Lopez

Mutch A, 'Practice, Substance, and History: Reframing Institutional Logics' (2018) 43(2) *Academy of Management Review* 242–258.

Neary M, 'Teaching Excellence Framework: A Critical Response and an Alternative Future' (2016) 12(3) *Journal of Contemporary European Research* 690–695.

Nixon J, 'Not Without Dust and Heat: The Moral Bases of the 'New' Academic Professionalism' (2001) 49(2) *British Journal of Educational Studies* 173–186.

Office for Students, 'Letter to Providers: TEF Update' (*OfS*, 10 June 2021) <https://www.officeforstudents.org.uk/publications/letter-to-providers-tef-update/> accessed 02 November 2021.

Office for Students, 'Report: Teaching Excellence and Student Outcomes Framework (TEF): Findings from the Second Subject-Level Pilot 2018–19' (21 January 2021) <https://www.officeforstudents.org.uk/publications/tef-findings-from-the-second-subject-level-pilot-2018-19/> accessed 18 November 2021.

Office for Students, 'The Impact of the Coronavirus Crisis Means That We Do Not Currently Have a Date for the Next TEF Exercise' Letter of 14 April 2020 (2020) <https://www.officeforstudents.org.uk/publications/letter-to-providers-tef-update/> accessed 18 November 2021.

O'Leary M, Cui V, and French A, 'Understanding, Recognising and Rewarding Teaching Quality in Higher Education: An Exploration of the Impact and Implications of the Teaching Excellence Framework' (2019) Project Report for UCU (UCU TEF Report) <https://www.ucu.org.uk/media/10092/Impact-of-TEF-report-Feb-2019/pdf/ImpactofTEFreportFEb2019> accessed 02 November 2021.

Pearce S, 'The Value of a National TEF Is in Enhancing University Learning and Teaching' (*WonkHE*, 8 February 2021) <https://wonkhe.com/blogs/the-value-of-a-national-tef-is-in-enhancing-university-learning-and-teaching/> accessed 02 November 2021.

Pitchford A and Stevens E, 'Covid Disrupts Our Academic Identities, and That's Something We Should Embrace' (*WonkHE* 18 December 2020) <https://wonkhe.com/blogs/covid-disrupts-our-academic-identities-and-thats-something-we-should-embrace-2/> accessed 02 November 2021.

Richards J, 'Because I Need Somewhere to Vent': The Expression of Conflict Through Work Blogs' (2008) 23(1–2) *New Technology, Work and Employment* 95–110.

Robinson W and Hilli A, 'The English 'Teaching Excellence Framework' and Professionalising Teaching and Learning in Research-Intensive Universities: And Exploration of Opportunities, Challenges, Rewards and Values from a Recent Empirical Study' (2016) 14(21) *Foro de Educacion* 151–165

Ryan R and Deci E, 'Self-Determination Theory and the Facilitation of Intrinsic Motivation, Social Development, and Well-Being' (2000) 55(1) *American Psychologist* 68–78.

Sabri D, 'Absence of the Academic from Higher Education Policy' (2010) 25(2) *Journal of Education Policy* 191–205.

Sabri D, 'Student Evaluations of Teaching as 'Fact-Totems': The Case of the UK National Student Survey' (2013) 18(4) *Sociological Research Online* <https://journals.sagepub.com/doi/full/10.5153/sro.3136> accessed 02 November 2021.

Sang K, Powell A, Finkel R, and Richards J, '"Being an Academic Is Not a 9–5 Job": Long Working Hours and the "Ideal Worker" in UK Academia' (2015) 25(3) *Labour & Industry: A Journal of the Social and Economic Relations of Work* 235–249.

Shields R and Watermeyer R, 'Competing Institutional Logics in Universities in the United Kingdom: Schism in the Church of Reason' (2020) 45(1) *Studies in Higher Education* 3–17.

Shore C, 'Audit Culture and Illiberal Governance: Universities and the Politics of Accountability' (2008) 8(3) *Anthropological Theory* 278–298.

Skelton A, 'A "Teaching Excellence" for the Times We Live in?' (2009) 14(1) *Teaching in Higher Education* 107–112.

Smith K, 'Who Do You Think You Are Talking to? The Discourse of Learning and Teaching Strategies' (2008) 56(4) *Higher Education* 395–406.

Solicitors Regulation Authority, 'Coronavirus Update – Education and Training Q & A' (*SRA*, 27 May 2021) <https://www.sra.org.uk/sra/news/coronavirus-questions-answers/> accessed 02 November 2021.

Solicitors Regulation Authority, 'Degree or Equivalent' (*SRA*, September 2021) <https://www.sra.org.uk/students/sqe/degree-equivalent/> accessed 02 November 2021.

Spooren P, Brockx B, and Mortelmans D, 'On the Validity of Student Evaluation of Teaching' (2013) 83(4) *Review of Educational Research* 598–642.

Tapper K, 'Getting through Covid-19 Means Rethinking Resilience' (*WonkHE*, 9 November 2020) <https://wonkhe.com/blogs/getting-through-covid-19-means-rethinking-resilience/> accessed 03 November 2021.

The Association of Law Teachers, Blog <http://lawteacher.ac.uk/alt-blog-2/> accessed 18 November 2021.

The Association of Law Teachers, 'Membership Benefits' (2021) <http://lawteacher.ac.uk/join/> accessed 03 November 2021.

The Association of Law Teachers, Twitter <https://twitter.com/TheLTjournal?ref_src=twsrc%5Egoogle%7Ctwcamp%5Eserp%7Ctwgr%5Eauthor> accessed 18 November 2021.

Tierney A, 'The Scholarship of Teaching and Learning and Pedagogic Research between the Disciplines: Should It Be Included in the Research Excellence Framework?' (2020) 45(1) *Studies in Higher Education* 176–186.

Tomlinson M, 'Conceptions of the Value of Higher Education in a Measured Market' (2018) 75 *Higher Education* 711–727.

Tomlinson M, Enders J, and Naidoo R, 'The Teaching Excellence Framework: Symbolic Violence and the Measured Market in Higher Education' (2020) 61(5) *Critical Studies in Education* 627–642.

Twining W, 'Lord Upjohn Lecture 2017: Rethinking Legal Education' (2018) 52(3) *The Law Teacher* 241–260.

Tymms P and Higgins S, 'Judging Research Papers for Research Excellence' (2018) 43(9) *Studies in Higher Education* 1548–1560.

UK Department for Business, Energy & Industrial Strategy, 'Trade Union Memberships, UK 1995–2019: Statistical Bulletin' (2020) <https://assets.publishing.service.gov.uk/government/uploads/system/uploads/attachment_data/file/887740/Trade-union-membership-2019-statistical-bulletin.pdf> accessed 03 November 2021.

UK Department for Business Innovations and Skills, 'Fulfilling Our Potential: Teaching Excellence, Social Mobility and Student Choice' (Green Paper, Cm 9141, November 2015) <https://assets.publishing.service.gov.uk/government/uploads/system/uploads/attachment_data/file/474227/BIS-15-

58 Maribel Canto-Lopez

623-fulfilling-our-potential-teaching-excellence-social-mobility-and-student-choice.pdf> accessed 02 November 2021.

UK Department for Business Innovations and Skills, 'Success as a Knowledge Economy: Teaching Excellence, Social Mobility and Students Choice' (White Paper, Cm 9258, 16 May 2016).

UK Department of Education, 'Government Response to Dame Shirley Pearce's Independent Review of the Teaching Excellence and Student Outcomes Framework (TEF)' (January 2021) <https://assets.publishing.service.gov.uk/government/uploads/system/uploads/attachment_data/file/953306/Goverment_response_to_the_independent_review_of_TEF_.pdf> accessed 02 November 2021.

UK Department for Education, 'Higher Education Expert to Review TEF' (*gov. uk*, 20 November 2018) <https://www.gov.uk/government/news/higher-education-expert-to-review-tef> accessed 02 November2021.

UK Department of Education, 'Independent Review of the Teaching Excellence and Student Outcomes Framework (TEF): Report to the Secretary of State for Education' (August 2019) <https://assets.publishing.service.gov.uk/government/uploads/system/uploads/attachment_data/file/952754/TEF_Independent_review_report.pdf> accessed 02 November 2021.

UK Department for Education, 'Office for Students: Regulatory Framework for Higher Education' (19 October 2017) <https://assets.publishing.service.gov.uk/government/uploads/system/uploads/attachment_data/file/683616/Regulatory_Framework_DfE_government_response.pdf > accessed 18 November 2021.

UK Department of Education, 'Summary of the Listening Sessions for the TEF Independent Review' (2021) <https://assets.publishing.service.gov.uk/government/uploads/system/uploads/attachment_data/file/947204/Listening_sessions_summary.pdf> accessed 02 November 2021.

UK Department of Education, 'Teaching Excellence and Student Outcomes Framework: Lessons Learned from Year Two' (October 2017) <https://webarchive.nationalarchives.gov.uk/ukgwa/20180313174804/https://www.gov.uk/government/publications/teaching-excellence-framework-lessons-learned> accessed 02 November 2021.

UK Department for Education, 'Teaching Excellence and Students' Outcomes Framework Specifications' (2017) <https://assets.publishing.service.gov.uk/government/uploads/system/uploads/attachment_data/file/658490/Teaching_Excellence_and_Student_Outcomes_Framework_Specification.pdf> accessed 02 November 2021.

UK Department of Education, 'Teaching Excellence Framework: Subject-Level Pilot Specification' (July 2017) <https://assets.publishing.service.gov.uk/government/uploads/system/uploads/attachment_data/file/629976/Teaching_Excellence_Framework_Subject-level_pilot_specification.pdf> accessed 02 November 2021.

Unger M, 'Put Down the Self-Help Books. Resilience Is Not at DIY Endeavour' (*The Globe and Mail,* 25 May 2019) <https://www.theglobeandmail.com/opinion/article-put-down-the-self-help-books-resilience-is-not-a-diy-endeavour/#:~:text=The%20notion%20that%20your%20resilience,is%20not%20a%20DIY%20endeavour.> accessed 03 November 2021.

Watermeyer R, 'Impact in the REF: Issues and Obstacles' (2016) 41(2) *Studies in Higher Education* 199–214.

Watermeyer R, Crick T, Knight C, and Goodall J, 'Covid-19 and Digital Disruption in UK Universities: Afflictions and Affordances of Emergency Online Migration' (2021) 81 *Higher Education* 623–641.

Weston S and McKeown S, 'After the TEF and Consumer Law-Based Interventions-Are Prospective HE Students Now Able to Make Informed Choices?' (2020) 54(3) *The Law Teacher* 414–425.

Willmott H, 'Commercialising Higher Education in the UK: The State, Industry and Peer Review' (2003) 28(2) *Studies in Higher Education* 129–141.

Wilsdon J, Belfiore E, Allen L, and Campbell P, 'The Metric Tide: Report of the Independent Review of the Role of Metrics in Research Assessment and Management' (2015) <https://www.researchgate.net/publication/279402178_The_Metric_Tide_Report_of_the_Independent_Review_of_the_Role_of_Metrics_in_Research_Assessment_and_Management> accessed 02 November 2021.

Wilson P, Crosswaite K, and Elliott S, 'Analysis of Responses to the Call for Views for the Independent Review of the Teaching Excellence and Student Outcomes Framework (TEF)' (York Consulting, June 2019) <https://assets.publishing.service.gov.uk/government/uploads/system/uploads/attachment_data/file/935306/York_Consulting_TEF_call_for_views_analysis_-_accessible.pdf> accessed 02 November 2021.

Wilson C and Strevens C, 'Perceptions of Psychological Well-Being in UK Law Academics' (2018) 52(3) *The Law Teacher* 335–349.

Wood M and Su F, 'What Makes an Excellent Lecturer? Academics' Perspectives on the Discourse of "Teaching Excellence" in Higher Education' (2017) 22(4) *Teaching in Higher Education* 451–466.

Woodall T, Hiller A, and Resnick S, 'Making Sense of Higher Education: Students as Consumers and the Value of the University Experience' (2014) 39(1) *Studies in Higher Education* 48–67.

Wyness G, 'Policy Changes in UK Higher Education Funding, 1963–2009' (2010) DoQSS Working Paper No. 10-15 <https://www.researchgate.net/publication/46463033_Policy_changes_in_UK_higher_education_funding_1963-2009> accessed 02 November 2021.

Young P, 'Out of Balance: Lecturers' Perception of Differential Status and Rewards in Relation to Teaching and Research' (2006) 11(2) *Teaching & Higher Education* 191–202.

3 Beyond the jurisdiction

Law schools, the LLB and 'global' education

Chloë Wallace

Introduction

In Birks' collection, Clarke and Tsamenyi, writing from an Australian perspective, painted a picture of increasing interest in internationalisation within the curriculum, largely deriving from the increased importance of international law and cross-border issues in professional practice.[1] Over 20 years later, many UK law schools are international in composition, with large numbers of students and staff originating from around the globe.[2] The 2014 Research Excellence Framework (REF) statement comments that both public international law and EU law were fields in which large numbers of outputs had been submitted,[3] although, echoing Birks' collection in 1996, they also commented that comparative work tended to focus more on common law than civil law systems.[4] All law schools are, and should be, seeking to take a global view: in an interconnected world, where technology of all types brings us closer together, and where destructive populist politics at times seeks to push us further apart, one of the things that law schools should be for is the building of international connections and global citizens. However, despite much discussion of the necessity of an internationalized curriculum, most undergraduate curricula at law schools in England

---

1 Eugene Clark and Martin Tsamenyi, 'Legal Education in the Twenty-First Century: A Time of Challenge' in Peter Birks (ed), *Pressing Problems in the Law Volume 2. What Are Law Schools For?* (Oxford University Press 1996).
2 According to the Higher Education Statistical Agency data of 2019/2020, 27% of law school staff and 22% of law students are not UK nationals. HESA, 'Where do they work, come from and go to?' (*HESA*) <https://www.hesa.ac.uk/data-and-analysis/staff/location> accessed 3 May 2021. The statistics do not break down to show distribution between institutions, but anecdotally, there are more international students at more traditional 'pre-92' law schools than at more modern institutions.
3 The REF is a periodic review of research outputs, impact and culture within UK institutions of higher education. For the report, see: Research Excellence Framework, 'REF 2014 Panel Overview Reports' (2015) <https://www.ref.ac.uk/2014/panels/paneloverviewreports/> (main panel C subpanel 20) accessed 12 September 2021.
4 Peter Birks, 'Editors Preface' in Peter Birks (ed), *Pressing Problems in the Law Volume 2. What Are Law Schools For?* (Oxford University Press 1996) viii.

DOI: 10.4324/9781003322092-3

Beyond the jurisdiction 61

and Wales remain predominantly, and determinedly, focused on the single jurisdiction of England and Wales.

In this chapter, I argue that it is essential for the credibility of the undergraduate law degree as a good general education and as an education for citizenship that we consider critically the implications of the failure of the discipline to respond effectively to the call to internationalise. This is in addition to the important professional reasons for the internationalisation of the law degree framed by Clark and Tsamenyi and argued well elsewhere.[5] We need to consider manageable and realistic concrete steps to improve the situation; proposals for entirely new and radical curricula are exciting but rarely possible to implement across the board, particularly given the current approach of the regulator in England and Wales, the Solicitors Regulation Authority (SRA). I therefore go on to draw on literature on intercultural education to propose an approach which is more modest than an entire curriculum change, but more effective than simply proposing individual modules, compulsory or otherwise. In doing so, I suggest that the most significant way in which an LLB degree can develop a global perspective is, perhaps counter-intuitively, not to teach about 'other' legal systems but to teach more deeply and critically about the one in which we are based.

The internationalisation of (legal) higher education

In order to understand the need for internationalisation within law schools, and within the curriculum in particular, we need first to consider what internationalisation means within the higher education context as a whole. Knight has argued that internationalisation is a complex concept within higher education, traditionally referring to schemes and networks which connect universities across the globe, both research and student education focused, but which also covers student recruitment and the content of academic programmes.[6] Within this varied activity, Harrison observes that attempts to internationalise curricula and pedagogy have generally been less successful than the processes of building international networks and schemes. In particular, ambitions to expose students who do not travel to the personal development benefits of exposure to cultural diversity have largely been unrealised. The drivers for internationalisation are multiple both at the sectoral and institutional levels and include the need to educate students to participate in a global labour market, the building of transnational alliances, the need to generate income for universities and the attraction

---

5 For example, Ana Speed, 'Academic Perspectives on Teaching International Family Law in Higher Education Institutions in England and Wales' (2020) 54 (1) The Law Teacher, 69–102.

6 Jane Knight, 'Internationalization Remodelled: Definition, Approaches and Rationales' (2004) 8 Journal of Studies in International Education, 5–31.

62 Chloë Wallace

for universities to develop a global 'brand'.[7] Whilst economic drivers have become increasingly predominant,[8] Stier has identified ideologies of internationalisation around idealism – the solving of global problems – and educationalism – the value for individual growth – which move beyond the straightforward needs of the labour market.[9] The achievement of the goals of these ideologies require not just the creation of international networks and programmes, such as exchange programmes, but also the internationalisation of the curriculum itself.

Within the higher education sector, law is no exception to this drive for internationalisation. The extent of a law school's commitment to internationalisation may depend on the position of the institution in which it is situated and whether that institution is seeking to engage internationally, develop a global brand, and recruit students from overseas. In addition to the observations about the international composition of staff and students in law schools,[10] it is not unusual to see law schools with significant international networks and activity; the 2014 REF statement refers to work having international impact and to impressive international collaborations in some law schools.[11] However, notwithstanding institutional priorities, the increased globalization of the legal labour market means that, for some time, including in more than one chapter in Birks' collection, arguments have been made that the undergraduate curriculum in law needs to have more international content, no matter the composition of the student body within the law school or the ambitions of the institution in which it is situated.[12]

---

7 Philip G. Altbach and Jane Knight, 'The Internationalization of Higher Education: Motivations and Realities' (2007) 11 Journal of Studies in International Education, 290–305.
8 Jane Knight, 'Internationalization Remodelled: Definition, Approaches and Rationales' (2004) 8 Journal of Studies in International Education.
9 Jonas Stier, 'Taking a Critical Stance toward Internationalization Ideologies in Higher Education: Idealism, Instrumentalism and Educationalism' (2004) 2 (1) Globalisation, Societies and Education, 1–28.
10 HESA, 'Where Do They Work, Come From and Go To?' (*HESA*) <https://www.hesa.ac.uk/data-and-analysis/staff/location> accessed 3 May 2021.
11 Research Excellence Framework, 'REF 2014 Panel Overview Reports' (2015) <https://www.ref.ac.uk/2014/panels/paneloverviewreports/> (main panel C subpanel 20) accessed 12 September 2021.
12 Eugene Clark and Martin Tsamenyi, 'Legal Education in the Twenty-First Century: A Time of Challenge' in Peter Birks (ed), *Pressing Problems in the Law Volume 2. What Are Law Schools For?* (Oxford University Press 1996); Ana Speed, 'Academic Perspectives on Teaching International Family Law in Higher Education Institutions in England and Wales' (2020) 54 The Law Teacher; See also Nicholas Grief, 'The Pervasive Influence of European Community Law in the United Kingdom' in Peter Birks (ed), *Pressing Problems in the Law Volume 2. What Are Law Schools For?* (Oxford University Press 1996); William Twining, 'A Cosmopolitan Discipline? Some Implications of "Globalisation" for Legal Education' (2001) 8 (1) International Journal of the Legal Profession, 23–36; Jessica Guth and Tamara Hervey, 'Threats to Internationalised Legal Education in the Twenty-First Century UK' (2018) 52 (3) The Law Teacher, 350–370; Danielle Ireland-Piper. 'Teaching

These arguments tend to focus on either the labour market for legal professionals, or the nature of the discipline itself. The first task of this chapter is to make a further specific case for the internationalisation of the legal curriculum: that it is necessary in order to achieve the objective of developing global citizens. The LLB degree in England and Wales is a three-year general undergraduate degree, which forms one way of fulfilling the first, academic, stage of qualification as a barrister and, until 2021, as a solicitor. It is well documented that only a minority of law graduates in England and Wales go on to practice law,[13] and therefore, attention needs to be paid to the broader labour market, not just the needs of the legal professions, and to the overall objectives of undergraduate higher education. This means that the non-economic drivers of internationalisation also need to be considered: the importance of a global mindset for individual educational development, and for the achievement of non-economic national and global goals.[14] In the next section, it will be argued that the first obstacle to the achievement of those objectives through an undergraduate law degree is the extent to which the law degree in England and Wales, unlike most other academic degrees, has traditionally been and continues to be explicitly jurisdictional and thus tied to a particular place.

Out of the ordinary: the resistance to internationalising the undergraduate legal curriculum

Law is a discipline where learning at undergraduate level is tied to a particular jurisdiction, a place and a set of people. Whilst introductory books about law as a subject of study often highlight the discipline's breadth in terms of areas of life covered, they rarely mention that the concepts and ideas studied are likely to be, at least partially, those developed in one small part of the world only.[15] 'Introduction to Law' books may highlight the need to learn how to find European or international legal materials, but in

---

Public Law in a Comparative Paradigm: Virtues and Vices' (2019) 53 (1) The Law Teacher, 102–118.

13 See The Law Society entry trends: in 2019–2020, over 25,000 students were accepted onto undergraduate law degrees, whilst 6,344 traineeships were registered. Law Society, 'Career Advice Becoming a Solicitor' (*Law Society*, 25 November 2020) <https://www.lawsociety.org.uk/en/career-advice/becoming-a-solicitor/entry-trends> accessed 12 September 2021. In the same year, 402 trainee (pupil) barristers started their first six months pupillage, and 522 started their second six months. Bar Standards Board, 'Pupillage Statistics' (*Bar Standards Board*, 22 July 2021) <https://www.barstandardsboard.org.uk/news-publications/research-and-statistics/statistics-about-the-bar/pupillage.html> accessed 12 September 2021.

14 Jonas Stier, 'Taking a Critical Stance toward Internationalization Ideologies in Higher Education: Idealism, Instrumentalism and Educationalism' (2004) 2 *Globalisation, Societies and Education*.

15 McBride's well known introductory book specifically refers to studying English Law. Nicholas J. McBride, *Letters to a Law Student* (Pearson 2007) 3–4.

64 Chloë Wallace

general skills such as legal research and legal reasoning are presented with no explicit indication that this is not a universal way of doing it, but one confined to a particular jurisdiction and legal culture.[16] This is by no means intended as a criticism but rather as a sign of how implicit the geographical and jurisdictional limitation of the law degree is. In this section, I want to make this point explicit: the jurisdictional nature of the undergraduate law degree is not an inevitable state of affairs and in some respects, it is extremely unusual. It is unusual even within law degrees. Postgraduate taught degrees tend to be much more international in scope, at least in terms of content, and attract more students from outside the UK largely because they are aimed at those students. Many PhD theses are on EU or international law or take comparative or cross-jurisdictional approaches.[17]

A good indication of the specificity of this focus is a comparison with the requirements of other university subjects, as expressed through the Subject Benchmark statements produced by the UK's Quality Assurance Agency (QAA), which are intended to set a baseline across the UK of what graduates should be able to "know, do and understand" at the end of studying a particular degree.[18] The Subject Benchmark Statement for Law promotes a jurisdictional approach to the study of the law, stating in its contextual statement that

> the study of law may focus on one or more jurisdictions ...(requiring) knowledge of the main features and principles of whatever legal system is (or systems are) being considered.[19]

It does refer to understanding the law in a global context but gives no indication of what that might mean. This permission to focus on one country or area only is extremely unusual amongst disciplines; other Subject Benchmark Statements either assume that the discipline is not tethered to one territorial space (e.g. scientific disciplines,[20] but also sociology and politics)

---

16 For example, Emily Finch and Stefan Fafinski, *Legal Skills* (Oxford University Press 2015).

17 The Higher Education Statistical Education data for 2019/2020 indicate that, whilst 17.5% of undergraduate law students in the UK were from outside the UK, that figure rises to 31% for taught postgraduate students and that over half of UK law PhD students are from outside the UK. HESA, 'Where Do They Work, Come from and Go to?' (*HESA*) <https://www.hesa.ac.uk/data-and-analysis/staff/location> accessed 3 May 2021.

18 QAA, 'Subject Benchmark Statements' (*QAA*, 03 December 2020) <https://www.qaa.ac.uk/quality-code/subject-benchmark-statements> accessed 30 July 2021.

19 QAA, 'Subject Benchmark Statement: Law' (*QAA*, November 2019) <https://www.qaa.ac.uk/docs/qaa/subject-benchmark-statements/subject-benchmark-statement-law.pdf?sfvrsn=b939c881_18> accessed 9 February 2021.

20 Sawir has argued that academics in scientific disciplines are more likely to assume that their discipline is inherently international and thus require no particular effort to 'internationalise' curriculum or pedagogy: Erlenawati Sawir, 'Academic Staff Response to

Beyond the jurisdiction 65

or specifically insist that the curriculum stretch beyond one country or state (e.g. business management, English and history). Even in area studies – degrees with an interdisciplinary curriculum focusing on a particular area of the world, and thus necessarily tethered in space – the Benchmark Statement requires some element of comparison with other areas and some reference to transnational links.[21] And for degrees in languages, cultures and societies, which may focus on one particular country where the target language is spoken, the Benchmark Statements emphasise the benefits of learning about a culture and language other than one's own cultural starting point.[22] It seems, therefore, that, amongst degree programmes where it would seem possible to constrain the subject of study to one geographical space that is the cultural starting point of most of the students on the degree programme, law is the only discipline where this is explicitly permitted, and no international or comparative element required. This removes one important pressure to internationalise curriculum content: the QAA simply does not require it.

Thornton and Shannon have argued that what internationalisation in legal education is there exists because the professions seek it.[23] One obvious explanation for the lack of international focus of the undergraduate law degree in England and Wales is, therefore, the fact that the legal profession in England and Wales, particularly acting through their regulator, does not seek it. Indeed, Menis has argued that, historically, the legal academy has never really delivered on the promise of a liberal legal education overall because the need to comply with professional regulations is too strongly felt and compliance with the professional requirements takes too much time to make space for other elements in the curriculum.[24] In order to fulfil the requirements of professional qualification, a law degree has needed to be designated a Qualifying Law Degree (QLD), meaning that it complies with the requirements of a Joint Statement of the Law Society and the Bar in terms of programme content and skills taught.[25] Notably, the Joint Statement

---

International Students and Internationalising the Curriculum: The Impact of Disciplinary Differences' (2011) 16 (1) International Journal for Academic Development, 45–57.

21 QAA, 'Subject Benchmark Statement: Area Studies' (*QAA*, December 2019) <https://www.qaa.ac.uk/docs/qaa/subject-benchmark-statements/subject-benchmark-statement-area-studies.pdf?sfvrsn=1ee2cb81_5> accessed 3 May 2021.

22 QAA, 'Subject Benchmark Statement: Languages, Cultures and Societies' (*QAA*, December 2019) https://www.qaa.ac.uk/docs/qaa/subject-benchmark-statements/subject-benchmark-statement-languages-cultures-and-societies.pdf?sfvrsn=4ce2cb81_4> accessed 3 May 2021.

23 Margaret Thornton and Lucinda Shannon, '"Selling the Dream": Law School Branding and the Illusion of Choice' (2013) 23 (2) Legal Education Review, 249.

24 Susanna Menis, 'The Liberal, the Vocational and Legal Education: A Legal History Review – from Blackstone to a Law Degree' (2000) 54 (2) The Law Teacher, 285–299.

25 The Joint Statement can be found here: Solicitors Regulation Authority, 'Joint Statement on the Academic Stage of Training' (*SRA*) <https://www.sra.org.uk/students/academic-stage/academic-stage-joint-statement-bsb-law-society/> accessed 3 May 2021.

has required that 50% of a QLD must be spent on the foundations of legal knowledge: public law, EU law, criminal law, law of obligations, property law and equity. It also explicitly refers to the need to learn the law of England and Wales and the rules of English law. Only one of the foundations requires a focus outside of the UK and the position of EU law remains in question following the UK's departure from the European Union on 31st January 2020.[26] This has in itself limited the amount of international and comparative content that has traditionally been able to be included in an LLB.

From 2021 onwards, the route to qualifying as a solicitor will move away from the QLD approach and will instead require candidates to have an undergraduate degree (although not necessarily a law degree) or equivalent qualification or experience, to take and pass the Solicitors Qualifying Examination (SQE), in two parts, and to undertake two years qualifying work experience.[27] The impact, which this will have on undergraduate law degrees, is likely to be variable and remains unclear; research by Gilbert in September 2020 demonstrated that, at that point, three-quarters of law school websites did not indicate that the SQE would have any impact on their degrees.[28] In particular, law schools which have an internationally diverse undergraduate student body and who thus have a high number of students who wish to have their law degree recognised as part of qualification in another country are unwilling to make changes that affect the willingness of those overseas regulators who had previously recognized the QLD to recognize any new degrees. Ironically, therefore, until the position of those regulators becomes clear, more internationalised law schools may be less willing to take the opportunities for curriculum reform which the SQE theoretically offers. And, whilst the number of law students progressing to careers as barristers is extremely small, it is not yet clear what the attitude of the bar will be to law degrees which depart from the framework of the QLD. All of this may disincentivise the removal or reduction in coverage of existing core subjects which is theoretically permitted by the SQE, with the notable exception of EU law, which is barely covered in the

---

26 For discussion of the impact of Brexit on the curriculum, see Jessica Guth and Tamara Hervey, 'Threats to internationalised legal education in the twenty-first century UK' (2018) 52 (3) The Law Teacher; Chloë J. Wallace and Tamara K. Hervey, 'Brexit and the Law School: From Vacillating Between Despair and Hope to Building Responsibility and Community' (2019) 53 (2) The Law Teacher.

27 For further information, see Solicitors Regulation Authority, 'Solicitors Qualifying Examination (SQE)' (*SRA*, May 2021) <https://www.sra.org.uk/students/sqe/> accessed 30 July 2021 During a transitional period, students who have started their degree before the end of 2021 or accepted a place on a degree before 21 September 2021 will be able to opt for the 'new' or 'old' qualification routes.

28 Andrew Gilbert, 'Preparing for the Exam? – Law School Websites and the SQE' (*Association of Law Teachers*, 9 October 2020) <http://lawteacher.ac.uk/sqe/preparing-for-the-exam-law-school-websites-and-the-sqe/ > accessed 25 April 2021.

Statement of Legal Knowledge on which the SQE is based,[29] and which regulators outside of the EU typically do not require as a core qualifying subject. Guth and Hervey have argued, therefore, that 'elite' institutions which recruit the bulk of non-UK students and whose students are most frequently recruited by global law firms, are likely to make fewer changes to their curricula as a result of the SQE, whereas other institutions may be more likely to develop degrees that promise that graduates will be SQE-ready.[30] As Gilbert notes, however, this is currently speculation, and the Covid-19 pandemic may have further hindered the future planning of law schools. Therefore, it remains unclear whether and to what extent the SQE will change law degrees and, in particular, will give law schools more effective choice in their curriculum.

Birks argued in his preface to *What Are Law Schools For?* that a besetting problem for legal education was the fact that the legal profession, in his view, whilst retaining substantial control over access to the legal profession, shows a lack of respect for the value of university legal education.[31] Here, I would add that many regulators, including the SRA, show a particular lack of understanding of the need for an internationalised legal curriculum, in terms of the needs of the profession.[32] The point can be made by means of a comparison with the Scottish situation. Da Lomba, Fletcher and Zahn argue that the Scottish law degree tends to have a more international and comparative perspective than that of England and Wales because, in part, of the relative openness which the Scottish legal system has traditionally had towards external influences.[33] Whilst the SRA require very little attention to be paid either to transnational law or to conceptual or theoretical legal

---

29 Solicitors Regulation Authority, 'Statement of Knowledge' (*SRA*, February 2021) < https://www.sra.org.uk/solicitors/resources/cpd/competence-statement/statement-legal-knowledge/ > accessed 3 May 2021

30 Jessica Guth and Tamara Hervey, 'Threats to Internationalised Legal Education in the Twenty-First Century UK' (2018) 52 (3) The Law Teacher.

31 Peter Birks, 'Editors Preface' in Peter Birks (ed), *Pressing Problems in the Law Volume 2. What Are Law Schools For?* (Oxford University Press 1996) viii.

32 Eugene Clark and Martin Tsamenyi, 'Legal Education in the Twenty-First Century: A Time of Challenge' in Peter Birks (ed), *Pressing Problems in the Law Volume 2. What Are Law Schools For?* (Oxford University Press 1996); Ana Speed, 'Academic Perspectives on Teaching International Family Law in Higher Education Institutions in England and Wales' (2020) 54 The Law Teacher; See also Nicholas Grief, 'The Pervasive Influence of European Community Law in the United Kingdom' in Peter Birks (ed) *Pressing Problems in the Law Volume 2. What Are Law Schools For?* (Oxford University Press 1996); William Twining, 'A Cosmopolitan Discipline? Some Implications of "Globalisation" for Legal Education' (2001) 8 (1) International Journal of the Legal Profession, 23–36; Jessica Guth and Tamara Hervey, 'Threats to Internationalised Legal Education in the Twenty-First Century UK' (2018) 52 (3) The Law Teacher, 350–370; Danielle Ireland-Piper, 'Teaching Public Law in a Comparative Paradigm: Virtues and Vices' (2019) 53 (1) The Law Teacher, 102–118.

33 Sylvie Da Lomba, Maria Fletcher and Rebecca Zahn, 'Scottish Legal Education after Brexit' (2019) 53 (2) The Law Teacher, 138–147.

68   *Chloë Wallace*

study, the Law Society of Scotland appears to have a rather more positive view towards extra-jurisdictional learning. Da Lomba, Fletcher and Zahn speculate that Brexit could push the Scottish curriculum to even greater coverage of international law, and a rejection of the notion that a legal education could or should be limited to one jurisdiction.[34] The problem in England and Wales therefore is not so much that the profession, through its regulator, continues to have an influence on the undergraduate law degree, but rather that the relevant regulator(s), including those outside the UK, have a narrow view of what legal education and training require, paying little attention to extra-jurisdictional learning and the study of supranational and intergovernmental legal orders and legal pluralism. Despite all the arguments that a global law degree is necessary for global legal practice, the professional regulators do not seem to be requiring it at undergraduate level, and it is thus harder to make the case that it is necessary and that space for it needs to be found. If we are therefore to assume that the attitude of the SRA is unlikely to change, and that the impact of the arrival of the SQE is unclear but does not give rise to optimism, this leads us to the conclusion that, compared with other university disciplines, the law degree has an additional hurdle to face in achieving the already difficult task of a genuinely internationalised curriculum.[35] In the next part of this chapter, I will consider why it is imperative for that hurdle to be crossed, and through the framework of Nussbaum's concept of educating for world citizenship, what we can focus on in order to achieve it.

Towards global citizenship: the need for a global law degree

In the first section of this chapter, it was argued that the internationalisation of legal education needs to be focused not only on the legal labour market but also on the ability of the degree to deliver the kind of general intellectual training that any degree requires, and that the QAA Subject Benchmark Statement for Law particularly highlights as the goal of an undergraduate law degree.[36] Degrees are not just about employment prospects and the labour market. Even the 2019 Augur Review, with its controversial references to 'low-value HE' and troubling reliance on efficiency savings rather than government support, takes as a premise that amongst the key purposes of a university education is improving citizens' ability to fulfil their potential in non-employment related ways, including engaging with civic and political

---

34 Ibid.
35 Neil Harrison, 'Practice, Problems and Power in 'Internationalisation at Home': Critical Reflections on Recent Research Evidence' (2015) 20 Teaching in Higher Education.
36 QAA, 'Subject Benchmark Statement: Law' (*QAA*, November 2019) <https://www.qaa. ac.uk/docs/qaa/subject-benchmark-statements/subject-benchmark-statement-law.pdf?s-fvrsn=b939c881_18> accessed 9 February 2021.

life.[37] The Browne Review, which led to the current English higher education funding system, begins by asserting: "Higher Education matters. It helps to create the knowledge, skills and values that underpin a civilised society."[38] This suggests an often-used formulation; that a university education creates and develops good citizens as well as good workers. This is replicated in the literature around the internationalisation of the curriculum; Harrison refers to two, often opposing, paradigms of 'global worker' and 'global citizen'[39] and it is certainly common nowadays for universities to claim to provide a global citizenship education, however that is defined.[40] This position is supported by Nussbaum, who has argued that a liberal university education which cultivates and develops the whole person must educate for world citizenship.[41]

Nussbaum's emphasis on global rather than national citizenship alone is, however, particularly important for undergraduate legal education. Citizenship is frequently conceptualised as tethered to a nation state, and as a project of belonging to that state.[42] National citizenship plays a role in policing boundaries between people; if some are citizens, then others are not. The law does a lot of the work of maintaining those boundaries around local/national citizenship. In the UK, as in many countries, it does so in ways which give privileged access to citizenship through money and education. The law also authorises heavy monitoring and policing of naturalised citizens and those from migrant backgrounds.[43] More broadly, when faced with a diverse and/or international student body, it makes no sense to argue that a law degree is about creating good citizens of England and Wales alone. Expressing

---

37 UK Secretary of State for Education, 'Independent Panel Report to the Review of Post-18 Education and Funding' (May 2019) <https://www.gov.uk/government/publications/post-18-review-of-education-and-funding-independent-panel-report> accessed 10 February 2021, 15.

38 Lord Browne, 'Securing a Sustainable Future for Higher Education: An Independent Review of Higher Education Funding and Student Finance [Browne Report]' (*UK Department for Business, Innovation and Skills*, 12 October 2020) <https://www.gov.uk/government/publications/the-browne-report-higher-education-funding-and-student-finance> accessed 10 February 2021, 14.

39 Neil Harrison, 'Practice, Problems and Power in 'Internationalisation at Home': Critical Reflections on Recent Research Evidence' (2015) 20 Teaching in Higher Education

40 For discussion see Gerardo L. Blanco, "Global Citizenship Education as a Pedagogy of Dwelling: Re-Tracing (mis)Steps in Practice During Challenging Times" (2021) 19 (4) Globalisation, Societies and Education; For an analysis of the divergent typologies of what is meant by global citizenship education, see Karen Pashby, Marta da Costa, Sharon Stein and Vanessa Andreotti, "A Meta-Review of Typologies of Global Citizenship Education" (2000) 56 (2) Comparative Education, 144–164.

41 Martha Nussbaum, *Cultivating Humanity: A Classical Defense of Reform in Liberal Education* (Harvard University Press 1997).

42 See for example Nira Yuval-Davies, *The Politics of Belonging: Intersectional Contestations* (Sage 2011), particularly Chapter 2.

43 See for example Devyani Prabhat, *Britishness, Belonging and Citizenship: Experiencing Nationality Law* (Policy Press 2018).

70   Chloë Wallace

it in those terms makes clear the colonial roots of the reach of higher education and particularly the connection between the 'exportability' of English legal education and the relationship between common law and empire. A focus on the global does not automatically avoid these risks: critical literature on global citizenship highlights the extent to which globalism and internationalism can and often do entrench colonialist relations.[44] However, without a clear and deliberate focus on a critical and decolonised concept of world citizenship, English legal education remains in that colonial space, teaching non-British citizens, many of whom come from formally colonised countries, how to be British citizens. A change in focus is thus essential.

Nussbaum's manifesto for education for global citizenship emphasises the development of three things through a curriculum: the capacity for critical examination of oneself and one's own traditions; the ability to see oneself as a human being bound to all other human beings, rather than simply as part of one region or group; and the capacity to put oneself into the shoes of another through what she refers to as narrative imagination.[45] The first, she argues, needs to happen through a requirement to study philosophy; the second through a required course of study relating to other cultures, as well as ensuring that discipline-focused courses are not restricted to the study of one perspective or culture; and the third through the study of subjects such as literature which require the use of the imagination.

Nussbaum further observes that the US system, which requires two years of general education at university prior to specialisation, is more suited to the development of world citizens, because she sees a single discipline focus as lacking in the diversity of perspectives which is necessary to develop global citizenship.[46] This is true although, arguably, fixable; as she shows herself, it is possible to set curricula within disciplines which achieve the goals that she is aiming at. Within a law curriculum, it is possible to devise relevant compulsory courses in philosophy and jurisprudence; this has at least in the past been common in English universities,[47] and remains quite

---

44 Sharon Stein, "The Persistent Challenges of Addressing Epistemic Dominance in Higher Education: Considering the Case of Curriculum Internationalization" (2017) 61 (S1) Comparative Education Review S25–S50; Karen Pashby, Marta da Costa, Sharon Stein, and Vanessa Andreotti, "A Meta-Review of Typologies of Global Citizenship Education" (2000) 56 (2) Comparative Education.

45 Martha Nussbaum, *Cultivating Humanity: A Classical Defense of Reform in Liberal Education* (Harvard University Press 1997) 9–10.

46 Martha Nussbaum, 'Educating for Citizenship in an Era of Global Connection' (2002) 21 Studies in Philosophy and Education, 289–303, 292.

47 In 2000, Roger Cotterell wrote that "...jurisprudence has a moderately secure place in undergraduate law curricular in the UK at present..." Roger Cotterell, "Pandora's Box: Jurisprudence in Legal Education" (2000) 7 (3) International Journal of the Legal Profession, 179–187, 179.

Beyond the jurisdiction 71

usual in legal education systems of continental Europe.[48] It is also possible to develop the narrative imagination through courses in law and literature and law and film.[49] These are all additional courses which call on increasingly tight resources, and Twining's preference for a four-year degree is understandable,[50] but, whilst this approach is disincentivised and has practical issues, it remains possible.

The focus of this chapter, however, is on Nussbaum's second requirement: the development of the ability to see oneself as a human being bound to all other human beings, by ensuring that the study of other cultures is required, and study is not focused solely on one perspective or culture. This second requirement is extremely challenging, if not impossible, for a legal education which fixes itself firmly within the boundaries of a single jurisdiction. Such a curriculum cannot and should not present the law of one jurisdiction as relevant to all human beings, but, because only one jurisdiction is taught, no connection can be made between the law and values of one jurisdiction and one legal culture, and those of others. Indeed, Husa has argued that there is a 'hidden curriculum' within a nationally focused law degree that the law taught is to be preferred.[51]

One illustration of this problem can be found in the teaching of the rule of law within an English law degree. The rule of law is typically taught as a specific principle[52]; one of a number of principles that underlies the UK constitution. Because it is presented as a feature of the UK constitution, the fact that the same principle applies in other jurisdictions is not highlighted. On top of this, nowadays, English-educated students will also have been subject during their school days to the teaching of Ofsted-mandated 'British Values.'[53] These values include a number that are demonstrably not

---

48 Eva Steiner, *French Law: A Comparative Approach* (Oxford University Press 2010) 201–204. For discussion of the place of the sociology of law in German law degrees, see Stefan Machura, 'Milestones and Directions: Socio-Legal Studies in Germany and the United Kingdom' (2020) 21 (7) German Law Journal, 1318.

49 For further discussion of this aspect of Nussbaum's work, see Ian Ward, 'Legal Education and the Democratic Imagination' (2009) 3 (1) Law and Humanities, 87–112.

50 William Twining, *Blackstone's Tower: The English Law School* (Sweet and Maxwell 1994) Chapter 3; See also Peter Birks, 'Editors Preface' in Peter Birks (ed), *Pressing Problems in the Law Volume 2. What Are Law Schools For?* (Oxford University Press 1996) viii for a suggestion that the three-year law degree is under considerable pressure.

51 Jaakko Husa, 'Turning the Curriculum Upside Down: Comparative Law as an Educational Tool for Constructing the Pluralistic Legal Mind' (2009) 10 (6–7) German Law Journal 913–926.

52 One of the most popular constitutional law textbooks refer to it as "an envelope that contains a set of more specific principles." Mark Elliott and Robert Thomas, *Public Law* (Oxford University Press 2017) 65.

53 UK Department of Education, 'Promoting Fundamental British Values as Part of SMSC in Schools: Department Advice for Maintained Schools' (2014) <https://assets.publishing.service.gov.uk/government/uploads/system/uploads/attachment_data/file/380595/SMSC_Guidance_Maintained_Schools.pdf> accessed 11 February 2021. It is particularly

72 *Chloë Wallace*

specifically British, and no more visible in the UK than in other places: democracy; individual liberty; mutual respect and tolerance. But in that list of 'British values' is the rule of law. Might this mean that some students will come to their university studies with a view already in place that the rule of law is a peculiarly British concept? If no comparative or international perspective is presented, some students could easily come to believe that the rule of law is a British conception which, because it has been presented to them as self-evidently good, demonstrates the superiority of Britishness over other cultures or identities. This may also support the development of an embedded notion that the rule of law is unequivocally positive, making them resistant to its many critiques. This is unlikely to be the intention of many contemporary teachers of constitutional law, but it is, likely be the outcome for at least some students of a focus on one jurisdiction. It serves as a significant barrier to effectiveness not only of a global legal education but also to a critical, decolonised and anti-racist curriculum.

This example illustrates the difficulty of fostering world citizenship, in Nussbaum's terms, within a single jurisdictional law degree as it is traditionally taught. The inclusion of 'foreign' or international or global law for instrumental reasons related to the jurisdiction of England and Wales or to the practice of law within England and Wales does not necessarily address this point because it remains jurisdiction-centric. Even if this were not so, token courses on 'foreign law' or 'international law' do not achieve what Nussbaum is trying to achieve, because teaching them as disconnected from the core of what is being studied means that they are presented or perceived as an 'exotic other' or an extra.[54] And, as Harrison observes, an internationalized curriculum is not just about content but also about affecting students' ways of thinking and of seeing the world.[55]

In the final part of this chapter, I want to suggest a rethinking of what we centre when we build a law curriculum, in order to support the development of an internationalized curriculum in these terms. This reorientation may in some cases be quite subtle, and certainly need not require a major change in what is taught, or increase in the quantity of what is taught, which is often a point of resistance in discussions about introducing a more comparative element into the curriculum.[56] Done carefully, however, such a reorientation

---

notable that, according to this document, respect for English law forms part of British values. The guidance applies only in England, but this juxtaposition makes clear the illogical nature of the construction.

54 For discussion of the problems with these types of courses, particularly when taught in upper years of study, see Jaakko Husa, 'Turning the Curriculum Upside Down: Comparative Law as an Educational Tool for Constructing the Pluralistic Legal Mind' (2009) 10 (6–7) German Law Journal.

55 Neil Harrison, 'Practice, Problems and Power in 'Internationalisation at Home': Critical Reflections on Recent Research Evidence' (2015) 20 Teaching in Higher Education.

56 Danielle Ireland-Piper, 'Teaching Public Law in a Comparative Paradigm: Virtues and Vices' (2019) 53 (1) The Law Teacher.

Beyond the jurisdiction 73

will be sufficient to create a law curriculum much more suitable for the task of developing world citizens.

Towards a model of intercultural legal education

In order to understand what this reorientation might look like, we need to consider the field of intercultural education. Intercultural education is "designed to teach people how to live and function in cultures other than their own"[57] and, more generally, to work effectively across cultures. It is usually particularly focused on 'sojourners' – people who, for one reason or another, are living in a culture other than the one they feel most part of – but can be relevant to everyone. It is a specialist field of education, however, because of the highly practical nature of what is being learned: it is not learning about other cultures in a theoretical or textbook sense, but learning how to move between cultures, change one's behaviour and respond to different cultural orientations and approaches. Intercultural education is intended to inculcate a quality known as intercultural sensitivity: an awareness of cultural difference combined with the skills to respond effectively to that cultural difference. People with this kind of intercultural sensitivity can also develop intercultural competence: the ability to work and live with people from different cultural backgrounds and to function within different cultures.

This emphasis on sojourners and on intercultural sensitivity ought to give a sense of how intercultural education can apply to jurisdictional legal education. If we accept that in most cases an undergraduate legal education will be focused on a 'home' jurisdiction, to become the basis of world citizenship that education must enable students to move from the cultural context of the 'home' jurisdiction into the cultural context of other jurisdictions. Law graduates need not become 'natives' of more than one jurisdictional culture; as Twining has observed, there is a difference between transnational specialists in the legal profession, which is a very specific category of practitioners, and of making students properly aware of the geographical spread of legal systems and concepts.[58] The process and experience of intercultural education will be very different for law students and graduates trying to understand the complexities of global law than for, for example, international students or migrants trying to navigate the challenges of social interaction

---

57 R. Michael Paige, 'On the Nature of Intercultural Experiences and Intercultural Education' in R. Michael Paige (ed), *Education for the Intercultural Experience* (Intercultural Press 1993) 1.

58 William Twining, 'A Cosmopolitan Discipline? Some Implications of "Globalisation" for Legal Education' (2001) 8 (1) International Journal of the Legal Profession; Faulconbridge and Muzio suggest that much of the training to develop specific transnational specialism takes place within law firms, not law schools: James R Faulconbridge and Daniel Muzio, 'Legal Education, Globalization, and Cultures of Professional Practice' (2009) 22 Georgetown Journal of Legal Ethics, 1335–1360.

74 *Chloë Wallace*

and friendships within a new culture. Nevertheless, intercultural educators argue that a tendency towards ethnocentrism – the assumption that the world view of your own culture, or of one particular culture, is universal or at least more widely spread than it actually is – makes working within a different culture a more emotionally intense and difficult experience and makes it harder to get it right.[59] Thus, a student in an English law school who assumes that the rules, institutions and culture of English law are the norm will find working in a global legal context equally difficult and find it equally hard to get right. It ought, therefore, to be an objective of a law degree to move students beyond legal ethnocentrism.

The framework used in this chapter to reflect on this issue is Milton Bennett's developmental model of intercultural sensitivity.[60] This is a model of growth of intercultural competence, derived through grounded theory, which indicates increasingly sophisticated ways of dealing with cultural differences, moving from an ethnocentric position to what Bennett refers to as a position of ethnorelativity, where one can move easily between cultures. What is important and extremely helpful for the purposes of this argument is the way in which, rather than focusing on learning about 'the other culture', Bennett's framework emphasises the importance of focus on oneself and one's own positioning.

We can start to understand this framework by looking at the two extremes of the continuum. At one end of the spectrum, Bennett places denial – a state of lack of awareness of any cultural difference.[61] Extreme ethnocentricity is created by isolation or by separation. Nowadays, isolation is relatively rare, in the sense that very few people are completely isolated from other cultures, but separation can be created within closed communities of dominant cultures that choose to have relatively little contact with those outside and to make little effort to learn about them. People in denial will not perceive differences because they are not prepared to accept that they exist or, if they cannot avoid accepting their existence, they are likely to see them as overgeneralised binaries. At the other end of Bennett's spectrum is integration.[62] A fully integrated individual is someone who functions outside of any particular culture and therefore can move easily between them – the much-discussed 'citizen of nowhere'.[63] An integrated individual has no cultural 'default' and makes choices within each cultural context

---

59 R. Michael Paige, 'On the Nature of Intercultural Experiences and Intercultural Education' in R. Michael Paige (ed), *Education for the Intercultural Experience* (Intercultural Press 1993) 6.

60 Milton J. Bennett, "Towards Ethnorelativism: A Developmental Model of Intercultural Sensitivity" in R. Michael Paige (ed), *Education for the Intercultural Experience* (Intercultural Press 1993).

61 Ibid, 30–34.

62 Ibid, 59–65.

63 See then-Prime Minister Theresa May's speech to the Conservative Party Conference 5th October 2016: BBC, 'Conservative Conference: Theresa May's Speech in Full' BBC

as appropriate to the activity and context. On the negative side, fully integrated individuals in fact do not belong to any culture and can feel marginalised within all of them, which can create significant psychological trauma in some circumstances.

Bennett's spectrum is about an individual journey, and his approach builds a series of educational interventions, which supports people moving in a healthy way from one stage to another to avoid trauma and alienation. Like any developmental model, this linearity can be criticised. However, this chapter does not propose the design of a curriculum to move students along this spectrum, if only because individuals within diverse student bodies will have very different starting points. What this spectrum can usefully be used for, however, is to diagnose where our curricula might sit on it, and from there to suggest changes in approach to teaching which can support the development of law students into global citizens with an intercultural competence as far as legal systems are concerned.

Many, if not most, English law degrees, it is contended, remain at the cultural denial stage at the far end of Bennett's continuum. They exist in an isolated space, often demonstrating little awareness of cultural approaches to law beyond that of England and Wales, and lead students to assume that all legal systems are the same as 'our' legal system. Students who have studied A level law, for example, will have studied a syllabus entirely focused on the legal system of England and Wales. Those who have not may be getting the bulk of their knowledge about the legal system from the news and from popular culture, neither of which gives anything more than an anecdotal impression of legal diversity, if that.[64] This is understandable; we should not expect students starting our degree programmes to know a lot about the subject. The concern, however, is when our degrees do not do much to challenge this. Specific legal subjects – contract law, tort law, criminal law – are often taught without explicit mention or recognition that this is the law of England and Wales, and that other systems or traditions may do things differently, let alone any understanding of what those differences might be. When aspects of our law come from, or are influenced from, 'outside', notably from EU law, this is frequently not mentioned, cementing the perception of laws which are untouched by external influence.[65] And, as Stychin suggests, when that influence must be confronted, it presents 'the other' as

---

(London, 5 October 2016) <https://www.bbc.co.uk/news/av/uk-politics-37563510> accessed 14 February 2021.

64 For discussion of the popular cultural tendency to present law as culturally homogenous and the challenges that this creates for legal education, see Chloë J. Wallace, 'Law, Culture and Euro-Crime: Using *Spiral* to Teach French Law' (2014) 48 (2) The Law Teacher, 154–165.

65 For a specific discussion of the issues this poses in the context of Brexit see Chloë J. Wallace and Tamara K. Hervey, 'Brexit and the Law School: from Vacillating between Despair and Hope to Building Responsibility and Community' (2019) 53 (2) The Law Teacher, 221–229.

76   Chloë Wallace

a threat to a harmonious legal or constitutional order, rather than as something which may enhance it.[66]

A slightly different case here is constitutional law, where, because of the nature of the UK constitution, courses typically start with an explanation of why the UK constitution is 'different'. Even there, however, is a temptation to move swiftly onto why the British approach might be seen to be better or has been preferred. This remains a very ethnocentric approach to teaching the subject but equates more to Bennett's second stage: defence.[67] Here, other approaches are recognised as existing but place them in a hierarchy with, typically, our approach at the top. Guth and Hervey argue, for example, that a traditional legal education curriculum risks presenting domestic law, implicitly, as the best, thus reinforcing damaging colonialism and nationalism in its various forms.[68] Bennett suggests that the defence stage can also incorporate reversal where we see other cultures as superior to our own. This might be seen in an approach of seeing codified constitutions, or entrenched human rights declarations, as inherently desirable without clearly analysing the weaknesses of systems which incorporate this element.

Bennett's work, therefore, helps to identify a way of addressing the ethnocentricity of the undergraduate law curriculum. Between the two extremes of denial and integration, discussed above, Bennett moves through six stages and shows what types of educational interventions are necessary to move from one step to another. This movement has an overarching theme: that what matters is an increasingly complex understanding of 'otherness.' In terms of individual intercultural education, the more people become aware of the fact that difference is complex, and that 'other' experience or perspective is just as varied and nuanced as our own, the better people are at being culturally sensitive and thus recognising and adapting to difference. Applying that to an undergraduate law curriculum suggests that the more students

---

66 For discussion, see Carl F. Stychin, 'Rethinking Legal Methods after Brexit' (2019) 53 (2) The Law Teacher, 212–220.

67 Milton J. Bennett, "Towards Ethnorelativism: A Developmental Model of Intercultural Sensitivity" in R. Michael Paige (ed), *Education for the Intercultural Experience* (Intercultural Press 1993) 34, 41.

68 Eugene Clark and Martin Tsamenyi, 'Legal Education in the Twenty-First Century: A Time of Challenge' in Peter Birks (ed), *Pressing Problems in the Law Volume 2. What Are Law Schools For?* (Oxford University Press 1996); Ana Speed, 'Academic Perspectives on Teaching International Family Law in Higher Education Institutions in England and Wales' (2020) 54 The Law Teacher; See also Nicholas Grief, 'The Pervasive Influence of European Community Law in the United Kingdom' in Peter Birks (ed), *Pressing Problems in the Law Volume 2. What Are Law Schools For?* (Oxford University Press 1996); William Twining, 'A Cosmopolitan Discipline? Some Implications of "Globalisation" for Legal Education' (2001) 8 (1) International Journal of the Legal Profession, 23–36; Jessica Guth and Tamara Hervey, 'Threats to Internationalised Legal Education in the Twenty-First Century UK' (2018) 52 (3) The Law Teacher, 350–370; Danielle Ireland-Piper, 'Teaching Public Law in a Comparative Paradigm: Virtues and Vices' (2019) 53 (1) The Law Teacher, 102–118.

Beyond the jurisdiction 77

learn to be aware of complex differences between one's own legal system and that of another, the more graduates will show cultural sensitivity and cultural competence and be able to operate within a global environment.

To understand further how this might work, we need to look more closely at Bennet's step by step approach. Generally speaking, movement within the ethnocentric side of the spectrum requires ridding oneself bit by bit of the idea that one's own culture is the default. So, to move out of denial, it is necessary simply to discover that cultural differences exist, by means of cultural awareness activities. This takes us to defence, where we are aware of cultural differences but tend to hierarchise cultures and, usually but not always, place our culture at the top of that hierarchy. At its worst, this can look like overt colonialism or white supremacy. Bennett emphasises that the cause of this problem is not simply misunderstanding the 'other' but having a mindset which insists on hierarchies and rankings, with an instinctive necessity either to demonstrate that 'our' approach is better than the others or, conversely, that another approach is necessarily better than ours. To move beyond this, we need to maintain awareness of difference, but shift the focus onto similarity, equivalence and globalism; developing an understanding of the ways in which diverse people, cultures or systems can co-operate and the common ground they have available to do so. This is an important step but contains within it a dangerous tendency to revert back to semi-denial by what Bennett refers to as 'minimisation.'[69] Minimising involves forgetting that difference does not prevent co-operation and thus seeks to minimise and draw focus from diversity out of fear that common ground will be lost. The risk of cycling from minimisation back to full denial means that the next phase is particularly important. Indeed, Bennett refers to it as a 'paradigmatic barrier' because, he argues, it requires us to move from absolutism and binaries (good/bad; right/wrong) to relativism; a major cognitive shift within Western thought. Knowledge of others can take us up to this barrier, but it can take us no further. To cross it and enter the more ethnorelative acceptance phase, we need cultural self-awareness: a recognition that we too operate within a culture that is distinctive, complex and open to criticism. This self-awareness is what moves us away from seeing our own culture as the norm, default or ideal-type, and others as different, special and divergent. It should move us, if we have already absorbed the existence of difference and of common ground, towards an acceptance that cultures provide different methods of understanding, ordering and interpreting what is around us and that one culture is not more real or true than any other. It is this realisation, in turn, that helps with understanding the complexity of the other because, once we accept that our complex and nuanced culture is

---

69 Ibid, 41–46; Milton J. Bennett, "Towards Ethnorelativism: A Developmental Model of Intercultural Sensitivity" in R. Michael Paige (ed), *Education for the Intercultural Experience* (Intercultural Press 1993) 34, 41–46.

no more true or normative than any other, we need to accept that all other cultures are also complex and nuanced. And once this is done, it is much more straightforward to move from one cultural frame to another without essentialising and with instead an effort to understand the complexities and nuances of the unfamiliar cultural frame.

How, then, should this apply within an undergraduate law curriculum? There is insufficient space within this chapter to launch a complete argument that law can be equated to the kinds of cultural systems that Bennett is talking about. However, a good working definition of culture would cover behaviours and norms of societies and organisations. The concept of legal culture is contested, but Blankenberg, for example, considers legal cultures to include legal norms and institutions as explanatory of the way in which people within, and impacted by, legal systems behave.[70] Ehrmann considers legal rules to be cultural rules, in so far as they are rules which condition behaviour, together with ideas about what the law is and how it ought to work which are conditioned by history and by social circumstances.[71] Even if one does not accept that legal cultures exist or that legal rules are cultural rules, it is argued here that there are sufficient similarities between legal systems and cultural systems to make it possible to equate the two. At the very least, it is a useful exercise to look at Bennett's three ethnocentric phases and how to move out of them and consider how they might apply within a law curriculum.

To move out of denial, we need cultural awareness; to be aware of approaches other than the ones we are most familiar with. At its most basic, this suggests that early on in any law curriculum, some introduction to legal diversity needs to be included. Avoiding the temptation to propose new compulsory courses, which is what causes the problem of overload referred to above, this can simply involve drawing attention to the specificity of what is being taught by making it clear that other systems do things differently. This is already done by necessity within most constitutional law courses, which usually teach in a limited way that other Western approaches to constitutions are available. A similar thing could be done in other subjects, simply by introducing students to the notion that, for example, the doctrine of consideration does not exist in many systems that derive from Roman law, or that the concepts of *actus reus* and *mens rea* are not used in the analysis of criminal offences in all systems. More ambitiously, the opportunities offered by technology to bring students across the globe together can be used to model and demonstrate legal diversity and allow students to learn from each other.[72]

---

70 Erhard Blankenburg, 'Civil Litigation Rates as Indicators for Legal Cultures' in David Nelken (ed), *Comparing Legal Cultures* (Routledge 1997).
71 Henry Ehrmann, *Comparative Legal Cultures* (Prentice-Hall 1976).
72 For a good example of how this might work, see Bronwen Jones, Yasser Gadallah and Shaimaa Lazem, 'Facebook Debate: Facilitating International, Intercultural Knowledge Exchange and Collaboration in the Field of International Intellectual Property Law' (2019) 53 (3) The Law Teacher, 279–297.

Beyond the jurisdiction 79

Such a curriculum should avoid the tendency to hierarchise by asking questions about 'best' or 'preferred' legal solutions. However, students are quite likely to do this anyway. Instead, to move from this defence stage onto an understanding of common endeavour despite differences, there is value in learning about not only supranational legal orders, such as the EU and aspects of international law, but also of legal pluralism, to understand how individuals operate with multiple legal orders and the particular intersections between state and non-state law. Crucially, the role here is to emphasise commonalities which may in legal terms either be concepts used or, more likely, the human problems which need to be solved by the law and then ways in which solutions to those problems are found. This suggests an approach to teaching EU and international law, as well as other forms of supranationalism and legal pluralism which pays attention to the different legal traditions which come together by, for example, understanding how the procedures of supranational courts are influenced by more than one legal tradition, that the content of supranational rules may be taken sometimes from one system and sometimes from another, and the ways in which legal pluralism can work.

Here we come to the paradigmatic barrier, which I argue the law curriculum needs to cross in order for it to be a genuinely liberal university education for world citizenship. Once the existence of differences and respect for common endeavour is established, the next step, according to Bennett, is looking back to one's legal system or culture, to understand why things are as they are. This might suggest a need for a revival in the teaching of legal history, at least in some form, and of the legal cultures which have significantly impacted English law: notably EU law but perhaps also Roman law and Islamic law.[73] Bennett's insight makes it clear that, whilst it may seem paradoxical, it is vitally important if the law of one jurisdiction is to be treated as the basis of an education for global citizenship that the cultural and historical specificity of that law be understood. More in-depth exposure to other legal cultures is useful as part of this process but needs to be carefully managed to avoid falling back into a state of defence or minimalism: the point is to observe, note and accept difference, rather than to essentialise, hierarchise or minimise.

Conclusion

In this chapter, I have argued that a global perspective within the legal curriculum is important for a range of reasons, including the needs of the global

---

73 For suggestions to this effect, see Carl F. Stychin, 'Rethinking Legal Methods after Brexit' (2019) 53 (2) The Law Teacher; John Cotter and Elaine Dewhurst, 'Lessons from Roman Law: EU Law in England and Wales after Brexit' (2019) 53 (2) The Law Teacher, 173–188; Imranali Panjwani, 'The Ignored Heritage of Western Law: The Historical and Contemporary Role of Islamic Law in Shaping Law Schools' (2020) 54 (4) The Law Teacher 562–577.

80 *Chloë Wallace*

legal labour market but also relating to drivers shared within the higher education sector as a whole and relating to claims that an undergraduate degree provides a general intellectual education for global, or world citizens. Many law schools have been able to engage successfully with sector-wide internationalisation strategies and processes by focusing on networks and student recruitment but have tended to focus less on developing an internationalised curriculum and, even there, have tended to focus on content, rather than approach: introducing specific modules or topics within modules, rather than on an overall approach and the building of an international mindset or intercultural competence. I have suggested that a key reason for this is that neither the SRA as regulator of the solicitors' profession nor the QAA as the regulator for higher education require law degrees to be internationalised as to content or approach, and that this places the discipline of law apart from other disciplines taught at university level. Without those external pressures, and with the competing pressures of space required for the QLD subjects, there seems to have been little impetus to internationalise the content of undergraduate law degrees, and in many respects, things have not moved on since the publication of Birks' collection. This needs to change, not only to fulfil the promise of a law degree as a good general education, but also as a necessary, if not sufficient, step towards a critical and decolonised legal education system.

To propose a new approach to internationalisation, which may have more chance of success, I have further suggested that an internationalised law degree is not necessarily one which teaches certain sorts of international or supranational subjects, or teaches more than one jurisdiction in depth, but rather one which takes a particular approach to the jurisdiction which is being studied; developing legal intercultural awareness by learning about differences and by learning about the cultural and historical development and specificity of the jurisdiction studied. Much of what I have suggested can be done within the confines of a law degree as currently structured, particularly by moving a Foundations of Law or Introduction of Law course away from a focus on the specifics of the English Legal System and towards a more conceptual, global and decolonised approach, or by taking a different angle on both core and optional modules within the curriculum. There is a strong case for creating core modules on international law and legal pluralism, in order to avoid placing too much weight on introductory modules, and many law schools will have sufficient expert staff to do this well, but this is not strictly necessary. Of course, as Twining has argued, a four-year programme would make it easier to fit all of this in, and we can see the benefits of this within Scottish legal education,[74] but equally it is not necessary. The most important thing is to position the English Legal System, not as

---

74 Sylvie Da Lomba, Maria Fletcher and Rebecca Zahn, 'Scottish Legal Education after Brexit' (2019) 53 (2) The Law Teacher, 138–147.

the norm from which all other systems derive or deviate, but as one system amongst many, with its own history, peculiarities, and flaws, many of which can only be seen when the English system is contrasted with others.

It is, I suggest, only in doing this that we can move away from the tradition of an insular, colonial and uncritical curriculum towards one that not only contributes to the development of global citizens but also has the potential to be decolonised, anti-racist and emancipatory. For that reason, whilst curriculum changes of this nature can be best justified at institutions with diverse cohorts in terms of the nationality/home country of students, they are essential to all legal curricula.

Bibliography

Altbach P and Knight J, 'The Internationalization of Higher Education: Motivations and Realities' (2007) 11 *Journal of Studies in International Education* 290–305.

Bar Standards Board, 'Pupillage Statistics' (Bar Standards Board, 22 July 2021) <https://www.barstandardsboard.org.uk/news-publications/research-and-statistics/statistics-about-the-bar/pupillage.html> accessed 12 September 2021.

BBC, 'Conservative Conference: Theresa May's Speech in Full' BBC (London, 5 October 2016) <https://www.bbc.co.uk/news/av/uk-politics-37563510> accessed 14 February 2021.

Bennett, M 'Towards Ethnorelativism: A Developmental Model of Intercultural Sensitivity' in R. Michael Paige (ed) *Education for the Intercultural Experience* (Intercultural Press 1993).

Birks P, 'Editors Preface' in Peter Birks (ed) *Pressing Problems in the Law Volume 2. What Are Law Schools For?* (Oxford University Press 1996).

Blanco G, 'Global Citizenship Education as a Pedagogy of Dwelling: Re-Tracing (mis)Steps in Practice during Challenging Times' (2021) 19(4) *Globalisation, Societies and Education* 1–11

Blankenburg E, 'Civil Litigation Rates as Indicators for Legal Cultures' in David Nelken (ed) *Comparing Legal Cultures* (Routledge 1997).

Browne L, 'Securing a Sustainable Future for Higher Education: An Independent Review of Higher Education Funding and Student Finance [Browne Report]' (*UK Department for Business, Innovation and Skills*, 12 October 2020) <https://www.gov.uk/government/publications/the-browne-report-higher-education-funding-and-student-finance> accessed 10 February 2021.

Clark E and Tsamenyi M, 'Legal Education in the Twenty-First Century: A Time of Challenge' in Peter Birks (ed) *Pressing Problems in the Law Volume 2. What Are Law Schools For?* (Oxford University Press 1996).

Cotter J and Dewhurst E, 'Lessons from Roman Law: EU Law in England and Wales after Brexit' (2019) 53(2) *The Law Teacher* 173–188.

Cotterell R, 'Pandora's Box: Jurisprudence in Legal Education' (2000) 7(3) *International Journal of the Legal Profession* 179–187.

Da Lomba S, Fletcher M, and Zahn R, 'Scottish Legal Education after Brexit' (2019) 53(2) *The Law Teacher* 138–147.

Ehrmann H, *Comparative Legal Cultures* (Prentice-Hall 1976).

Elliott M and Thomas R, *Public Law* (Oxford University Press 2017).

Faulconbridge J and Muzio D, 'Legal Education, Globalization, and Cultures of Professional Practice' (2009) 22 *Georgetown Journal of Legal Ethics* 1335–1360.

Finch E and Fafinski S, *Legal Skills* (Oxford University Press 2015).

Gilbert A, 'Preparing for the Exam? – Law School Websites and the SQE' (*Association of Law Teachers*, 9 October 2020) <http://lawteacher.ac.uk/sqe/preparing-for-the-exam-law-school-websites-and-the-sqe/ > accessed 25 April 2021.

Grief N, 'The Pervasive Influence of European Community Law in the United Kingdom' in Peter Birks (ed) *Pressing Problems in the Law Volume 2. What Are Law Schools For?* (Oxford University Press 1996).

Guth J and Hervey T, 'Threats to Internationalised Legal Education in the Twenty-First Century UK' (2018) 52(3) *The Law Teacher* 350–370.

Harrison N, 'Practice, Problems and Power in 'Internationalisation at Home': Critical Reflections on Recent Research Evidence' (2015) 20 *Teaching in Higher Education*.

HESA, 'Where Do They Work, Come from and Go to?' (*HESA*) <https://www.hesa.ac.uk/data-and-analysis/staff/location> accessed 3 May 2021.

Husa J, 'Turning the Curriculum Upside Down: Comparative Law as an Educational Tool for Constructing the Pluralistic Legal Mind' (2009) 10(6–7) *German Law Journal* 913–926.

Ireland-Piper D, 'Teaching Public Law in a Comparative Paradigm: Virtues and Vices' (2019) 53(1) *The Law Teacher* 102–118.

Jones B, Gadallah Y, and Lazem S, 'Facebook Debate: Facilitating International, Intercultural Knowledge Exchange and Collaboration in the Field of International Intellectual Property Law' (2019) 53(3) *The Law Teacher* 279–297.

Knight J, 'Internationalization Remodelled: Definition, Approaches and Rationales' (2004) 8 *Journal of Studies in International Education* 5–31.

Law Society, 'Career Advice Becoming a Solicitor' (*Law Society*, 25 November 2020) <https://www.lawsociety.org.uk/en/career-advice/becoming-a-solicitor/entry-trends> accessed 12 September 2021.

Machura S, 'Milestones and Directions: Socio-Legal Studies in Germany and the United Kingdom' (2020) 21(7) *German Law Journal* 1318.

McBride N, *Letters to a Law Student* (Pearson 2007).

Menis S, 'The Liberal, the Vocational and Legal Education: A Legal History Review – From Blackstone to a Law Degree' (2000) 54(2) *The Law Teacher* 285–299.

Nussbaum M, *Cultivating Humanity: A Classical Defense of Reform in Liberal Education* (Harvard University Press 1997).

Nussbaum M, 'Educating for Citizenship in an Era of Global Connection' (2002) 21 *Studies in Philosophy and Education* 289–303.

Paige M, 'On the Nature of Intercultural Experiences and Intercultural Education' in R. Michael Paige (ed), *Education for the Intercultural Experience* (Intercultural Press 1993).

Panjwani I, 'The Ignored Heritage of Western Law: The Historical and Contemporary Role of Islamic Law in Shaping Law Schools' (2020) 54(4) *The Law Teacher* 562–577.

Pashby K, da Costa M, Stein S, and Andreotti V, 'A Meta-Review of Typologies of Global Citizenship Education' (2000) 56(2) *Comparative Education* 144–164.

Prabhat D, *Britishness, Belonging and Citizenship: Experiencing Nationality Law* (Policy Press 2018).

QAA, 'Subject Benchmark Statements' (*QAA*, 03 December 2020) <https://www.qaa.ac.uk/quality-code/subject-benchmark-statements> accessed 30 July 2021.

QAA, 'Subject Benchmark Statement: Area Studies' (*QAA*, December 2019) <https://www.qaa.ac.uk/docs/qaa/subject-benchmark-statements/subject-benchmark-statement-area-studies.pdf?sfvrsn=1ee2cb81_5> accessed3 May 2021.

QAA, 'Subject Benchmark Statement: Languages, Cultures and Societies' (*QAA*, December 2019)<https://www.qaa.ac.uk/docs/qaa/subject-benchmark-statements/subject-benchmark-statement-languages-cultures-and-societies.pdf?sfvrsn=4ce2cb81_4> accessed 3May 2021.

QAA, 'Subject Benchmark Statement: Law' (*QAA*, November 2019) <https://www.qaa.ac.uk/docs/qaa/subject-benchmark-statements/subject-benchmark-statement-law.pdf?sfvrsn=b939c881_18> accessed 9 February 2021.

Research Excellence Framework, 'REF 2014 Panel Overview Reports' (2015) <https://www.ref.ac.uk/2014/panels/paneloverviewreports/> (main panel C subpanel 20) accessed 12 September 2021.

Sawir E, 'Academic Staff Response to International Students and Internationalising the Curriculum: The Impact of Disciplinary Differences' (2011) 16(1) *International Journal for Academic Development* 45–57.

Solicitors Regulation Authority, 'Joint Statement on the Academic Stage of Training' (*SRA*) <https://www.sra.org.uk/students/academic-stage/academic-stage-joint-statement-bsb-law-society/> accessed 3 May 2021.

Solicitors Regulation Authority, 'Solicitors Qualifying Examination (SQE)' (*SRA*, May 2021) <https://www.sra.org.uk/students/sqe/> accessed 30 July 2021.

Solicitors Regulation Authority, 'Statement of Knowledge' (*SRA*, February 2021) <https://www.sra.org.uk/solicitors/resources/cpd/competence-statement/statement-legal-knowledge/ > accessed 3 May 2021.

Speed A, 'Academic Perspectives on Teaching International Family Law in Higher Education Institutions in England and Wales' (2020) 54(1) *The Law Teacher* 69–102.

Stein S, 'The Persistent Challenges of Addressing Epistemic Dominance in Higher Education: Considering the Case of Curriculum Internationalization' (2017) 61(S1) *Comparative Education Review* S25–S50.

Steiner E, *French Law: A Comparative Approach* (Oxford University Press 2010).

Stier J, 'Taking a Critical Stance toward Internationalization Ideologies in Higher Education: Idealism, Instrumentalism and Educationalism' (2004) 2(1) *Globalisation, Societies and Education* 1–28.

Stychin C, 'Rethinking Legal Methods after Brexit' (2019) 53(2) *The Law Teacher* 212–220.

Thornton M and Shannon L, '"Selling the Dream": Law School Branding and the Illusion of Choice' (2013) 23(2) *Legal Education Review* 249.

Twining W, 'A Cosmopolitan Discipline? Some Implications of "Globalisation" for Legal Education' (2001) 8(1) *International Journal of the Legal Profession* 23–36.

Twining W, *Blackstone's Tower: The English Law School* (Sweet and Maxwell 1994) Chapter 3.

UK Department of Education, 'Promoting Fundamental British Values as part of SMSC in Schools: Department Advice for Maintained Schools' (2014) <https://assets.publishing.service.gov.uk/government/uploads/system/uploads/attachment_data/file/380595/SMSC_Guidance_Maintained_Schools.pdf> accessed 11 February 2021

UK Secretary of State for Education, 'Independent Panel Report to the Review of Post-18 Education and Funding' (May 2019) <https://www.gov.uk/government/publications/post-18-review-of-education-and-funding-independent-panel-report> accessed 10 February 2021.

Wallace C, 'Law, Culture and Euro-Crime: Using *Spiral* to Teach French Law' (2014) 48(2) *The Law Teacher* 154–165.

Wallace C and Hervey T, 'Brexit and the Law School: From Vacillating between Despair and Hope to Building Responsibility and Community' (2019) 53(2) *The Law Teacher* 221–229.

Ward I, 'Legal Education and the Democratic Imagination' (2009) 3(1) *Law and Humanities* 87–112.

Yuval-Davies N, *The Politics of Belonging: Intersectional Contestations* (Sage 2011).

4 Reinventing possibility

A reflection on law, race and decolonial discourse in legal education

Foluke Ifejola Adebisi and Katie Bales

Introduction

The relationship between law and race has become one of the most pressing issues of the lockdown era following the murder of George Floyd in Minneapolis in May 2020.[1] Floyd's death drew widespread outrage after policeman Derek Chauvin placed his knee on Floyd's neck and refused to remove it for 9 minutes and 29 seconds, despite repeated pleas from Floyd to do so. The recording of this act spurred a new generation of antiracism activists to join the global Black Lives Matter movement and other worldwide protests demanding justice for Floyd, his family and other victims of racism and police brutality.[2] Alongside this movement, there has been a growing demand from students to 'decolonise the University' which gained traction in 2015 following efforts from students at University College London (UCL) and the School of Oriental and African Studies (SOAS), among others.[3] Whilst these developments have thrown scholarship and discourse on race and racism under the spotlight once more, contestation over the relationship between law and race is nothing new and builds upon a long global history of antiracism struggles and critique of the imperial project.

The fact that antiracism and decolonial scholarship has been largely absent from university and law school agendas reflects the reality that systemic racism remains prevalent within our higher education institutions which privilege patriarchal, middle-class and Eurocentric epistemologies over other cultural, political or class-based perspectives and knowledge systems. This is further elucidated by the lacunae of colonial history and antiracism

---

1 Oxiris Barbot, 'George Floyd and Our Collective Moral Injury' (2020) 110 (9) American Journal of Public Health, 1253–1253.
2 Aleem Maqbool, 'Black Lives Matter: From Social Media Post to Global Movement' (*BBC News*, 9 July 2020) <https://www.bbc.com/news/world-us-canada-53273381> accessed 23 March 2021.
3 Ahmed Raza Memon and Suhraiya Jivraj, 'Trust, Courage and Silence: Carving Out Decolonial Spaces in Higher Education through Student–Staff Partnerships' (2020) 54 The Law Teacher, 475.

DOI: 10.4324/9781003322092-4

86 *Foluke Ifejola Adebisi and Katie Bales*

within Birks' collection,[4] which was published in 1996 following the murder of Stephen Lawrence in 1993. Lawrence's murder highlighted the structural racism present within our legal and police practices, yet many other British events preceded Birks' collection, including the Bristol bus boycott and the Brixton and Toxteth riots. Despite addressing the seemingly elevated separation of the epistemic knowledge of law schools in the Anglo-American tradition from everyday human experience, Birks' collection neglects to include any discussion of race as both a significant aspect of British and legal history, as well as the impact of racism on our everyday interactions with law.[5] In places, issues with race and colonisation are alluded to but not explicitly discussed. For example, Clark and Tsamenyi's chapter discusses the challenges of cultural sensitivity, outlining specific issues prevalent in Australia at that time. They argued for the need of legal education to address the 'issues of the appropriateness of the law in given circumstances'.[6] Whilst there is no mention of 'decolonising the curriculum' explicitly, they highlight the need for law schools to educate students in cultural issues, building cultural diversity into the curriculum. Further, Birks himself highlights the importance of the relationship between law schools, judges and the legislators, in order to help those making laws understand the problems between law and policy and to properly understand the existing law, its background and deficiencies.[7] This neglecting of proper discussion of issues with race, however, may be a result of a book written predominantly by men racialised as white, whose experience of race and racism would be minimal and therefore not considered particularly significant. The authors feel that, because of this, there is a certain irony to framing this chapter fully around Birks' collection, and thus there will be minimal further discussion of it.

Accordingly, this chapter argues that it is the responsibility of all law schools to reflect upon the role of law in shaping inequalities both historically and in the present to reveal the significant harms that law causes (and has caused) to people racialised as non-white in the UK and abroad. History tells us that this harm is largely a product of the colonial-capitalist enterprise where European powers manufactured dehumanising and hierarchical discourses of race and racialisation to justify the exploitation and expropriation of indigenous peoples and populations in what is currently designated the Global South. These discourses then go on to influence knowledge construction as well as present laws, policymaking and legal enforcement,

---

4 Peter Birks, *What Are Law Schools For?* (University Press 1996).
5 Peter Goodrich, 'Of Blackstone's Tower: Metaphors of Distance and Histories of the English Law School" in Peter Birks (ed), *What Are Law Schools For?* (Oxford University Press, 1996).
6 Eugene Clark and Martin Tsamenyi, 'Legal Education in the Twenty-First Century: A Time of Challenge' in Peter Birks (ed), *What Are Law Schools For?* (University Press 1996) 41.
7 Peter Birks, *What Are Law Schools For? Editors Preface* (University Press 1996).

including legal practitioners' interactions with people of colour. These epistemologies also affect the world in other ways, for example, the commodification of labour and space. As legal 'teachers', it is our responsibility to ensure that these histories, harms and epistemologies are not overlooked but rather connected and unveiled to help to shape our understanding of the ways in which law and legal education function to create, maintain and reproduce inequalities. This is important if we wish to use legal education and practice to imagine and bring to fruition new worlds in which these histories and harms are not reproduced.

The chapter begins by centring the negative impact that law and legal structures have had upon racial minoritised groups both historically and in the present. We argue that the role of law in causing such harms on both national and global scales, as well as legacies of racism, makes imperative the inclusion of colonial histories, antiracist and decolonial discourses in law school curricula throughout the country. The chapter then moves to address ways in which law schools can centre antiracism within their practice, drawing lessons from: writings on decolonial thought generally and decolonial thought in legal knowledge particularly; wider 'decolonise the curriculum' campaigns; and our own practices at the University of Bristol. We note that in taking an antiracist/decolonial approach, achievements will not necessarily be simply measured by metrics or statistics, especially when such measurements rely on colonial paradigms of success. Rather, we are seeking to create a culture within law schools where all students, racially minoritised or otherwise, understand that racialisation is not a handicap but a source and knowledge, allowing them to reflect upon 'the racial consequences of dominant values, concepts, and rules'.[8] In addition, it is especially important for our students who are racialised as white to gain critical knowledge of colonial histories. This includes the ways in which the exploitation and expropriation of Global South populations form an integral part of the story of capitalism and how lasting legacies of class and race-based oppression and systems of privilege benefit whiteness. In affirming an antiracist/decolonial discourse, we give our students tools to properly understand their social realities. Thus, it is hoped that our students will be able to influence the direction and culture of the legal profession and beyond.

Defining terms

Before embarking on the proceeding discussion, it is necessary to set out some of the relevant definitions which inform our core argument. First, we understand 'race' as a social relational construct, meaning it is produced by

---

8 Kimberle Williams Crenshaw, 'Toward a Race-Conscious Pedagogy in Legal Education' (1988) 11 National Black Law Journal, 8 <https://escholarship.org/uc/item/0qp9p46c> accessed 22 March 2021.

88 *Foluke Ifejola Adebisi and Katie Bales*

people rather than referring solely to a physical or biological characteristic. Theorists such as Franz Boas and W.E.B. Du Bois reject the idea that 'race' has biological meaning. Throughout the twentieth century and culminating with the end of the human genome project at the start of the twenty-first century, the scientific validity of 'race' having any biological meaning was debunked.[9] Thus, for Paul Gilroy, the term 'race' does not mean physical differences or variations coded in, on or around the body. Rather 'race' refers to the 'impersonal, discursive arrangement, the brutal result of the raciological ordering of the world, not its cause'.[10] Accordingly, as a social construct, it is the value-meaning attached to 'race' which is then politically, socially and economically enforced. Therefore, the artificial production and historical use of 'race' as a technology creates and reproduces contrived material distinctions between groups of humanity.[11] Without the desire to use 'race' to hierarchise, dehumanise and dispossess, it serves no legitimate categorising purpose on its own. Contemporary racial categorisation is, more often than not, used to measure disparities between racialised groups within a particular jurisdiction. Racial categories consequently measure the effect of structural, historical and present racism produced across space and time. Social construction thus has no significance without law and society which creates the system which gives racialising epistemologies and technologies power and meaning. Accordingly, Gilroy notes that it is the power of racism that needs to be taken seriously and not the concept of 'race'. To put it differently, racism reifies and gives 'race' its place.

Thus, Grosfoguel defines racism as 'a global hierarchy of superiority and inferiority, organized along the lines of the human that have been politically, culturally and economically produced and reproduced for centuries'.[12] It is not 'just a question of prejudice or stereotypes, but above all an institutional/structural hierarchy related to the materiality of domination'.[13] Whereas people racially categorised as 'human' gain social recognition and access to rights, as well as recognition of their subjectivities, identities, epistemologies and spiritualities, those racialised as non-human, have their humanity questioned and their rights and recognition denied.[14] It is important to remember however, that due to their dependence on social constructs for meaning, both race and racism are fluid concepts. Racism is influenced

---

9 Patricia McCann-Mortimer, Martha Augoustinos and Amanda LeCouteur. '"Race" and the Human Genome Project: Constructions of Scientific Legitimacy" (2004) 15 (4) *Discourse & Society*, 409–432, 410–412.

10 Paul Gilroy, *After Empire: Melancholia or Convivial Culture?* (Routledge 2004).

11 Kamna Patel, 'Race and a Decolonial Turn in Development Studies' (2020) 41 (9) Third World Quarterly, 1463–1475, 1464.

12 Ramon Grosfoguel, 'What Is Racism?' (2016) 22 Journal of World-Systems Research, 9.

13 Ramon Grosfoguel, 'Decolonizing Post-Colonial Studies and Paradigms of Political-Economy: Transmodernity, Decolonial Thinking and Global Coloniality' (2011) 1 Transmodernity: Journal of Peripheral Cultural Production of the Luso-Hispanic World, 1.

14 Charles W Mills, *The Racial Contract* (Cornell University Press 2014).

Reinventing possibility 89

by different colonial histories, in different ways, in different regions of the world and is marked differently by colour, ethnicity, language, culture and/ or religion. Racial categorisation differs by jurisdiction as does the material manifestations of being racialised 'below the line of the human'. Taking an expansive approach to unpacking racism is important as it avoids reductionism to particular racial markers and methodological nationalism which 'obscures the broader and world-systemic understanding of a modern/colonial problem such as racism'.[15] This structural understanding of racism takes us beyond a focus on individual prejudice and allows us to examine the complicity of law, the state and ancillary power structures in the production and reproduction of the conditions of racism. It is this complicity that informs Gilmore's definition of racism as 'the state-sanctioned or extralegal production and exploitation of group-differentiated vulnerability to premature death'.[16] Therefore, an antiracist praxis in legal education and knowledge very deliberately and intentionally goes beyond non-racism, as it recognises the embedded and societal/structural nature of racism and its propensity to reproduce itself (i.e. group-differentiated vulnerability to premature death) in the status quo. Antiracist education can thus be described as 'active resistance to the ways in which knowledge, status, value, and competence have been framed to give preference to white interests'.[17]

Another vital term used throughout this chapter is 'racialisation'. Racialisation, according to Grosfoguel, occurs through the marking of bodies – with some racialised as superior and others as inferior.[18] Indeed, Shilliam uses racialisation to consider the shifting distinctions between those deserving and undeserving of welfare provision. For him, the term 'racialisation' refers to 'the way in which racist attributes and hierarchies come to determine the everyday meaning and common-sense valuation of an entity or phenomenon'.[19] Considering that 'race' is arguably not a legitimate categorisation of humanity, but rather marks the ways in which social forces produce hierarchies, 'racialisation' is a more useful term to describe this production and reproduction. It is also important to note that racialisation marks both sides of the dividing line – those racialised above and below the line. In the context of Critical Race Theory, for example, Whiteness exemplifies the meanings attached to being racialised as White that exceed

---

15 Ramon Grosfoguel, 'Decolonizing Post-Colonial Studies and Paradigms of Political-Economy: Transmodernity, Decolonial Thinking and Global Coloniality' (2011) 1 Transmodernity: Journal of Peripheral Cultural Production of the Luso-Hispanic World, 11.

16 Ruth Wilson Gilmore, *Golden Gulag: Prisons, Surplus, Crisis, and Opposition in Globalizing California* (University of California Press, 2007).

17 Thompson, Audrey Thompson, 'For: Anti-Racist Education' (1997) 27 (1) Curriculum Inquiry, 7–44, 14.

18 Ramon Grosfoguel, 'Decolonizing Post-Colonial Studies and Paradigms of Political-Economy: Transmodernity, Decolonial Thinking and Global Coloniality' (2011) 1 Transmodernity: Journal of Peripheral Cultural Production of the Luso-Hispanic World, 11.

19 Robbie Shilliam, *Race and the Undeserving Poor* (Agenda Publishing Limited 2018) 4.

90 *Foluke Ifejola Adebisi and Katie Bales*

the colour of one's skin (often not actually white). These meanings include innocence, competence, trustworthiness and financial fluidity; they place themselves in direct opposition to a particular articulation of Blackness. Whiteness, therefore, has a particular value, reserved meaning and specific place.[20] The meanings accompanying racialisation thus inexorably have material effect.

Regarding education, we use the term 'decoloniality' throughout this paper as opposed to 'decolonisation'. Decolonisation refers to a specific register and history which extends beyond academic agendas and education structures. Decolonisation specifically describes the overturning of colonisation and its afterlives by colonised and indigenous peoples. It would be presumptive and indeed arrogant to describe a decolonial praxis and ethics as the undoing of colonisation, especially considering our epistemological entanglement in higher education with the intellectual reproduction of coloniality. As Tuck and Yang tell us, decolonisation is not a substitute word to describe the good things we wish to do; for them, decolonisation 'requires the repatriation of Indigenous land and life'.[21] Thus, we also distinguish coloniality from colonisation. Coloniality here refers 'to patterns of power, that emerged as a result of colonialism... that now defines much of our culture, labour, social relations and knowledge production. Coloniality thus survives colonialism'.[22]

Thus, it is important here to explore the connections between racialisation, coloniality and decolonisation. The artificed production of 'race' was the main social technology that enabled the colonial endeavour; this includes marking African populations for enslavement and indigenous populations for the dispossession of their land.[23] Thus, colonisation proceeds on certain logics of hierarchisation of humanity that exceed the physical and political occupation of land. Those colonial logics of commodification and racialisation survive the formal end of occupation of land.[24] It is those afterlives and remnants of colonialism – coloniality – that provide the context for global decolonial discourse. Therefore, decolonial discourse and decolonial/antiracist education seek to imagine an after-colonial time-world where these logics and their harms do not reproduce themselves or govern our relationships with one another, or our relationship with nature.[25]

---

20 Zeus Leonardo, *Race, Whiteness, and Education* (Routledge, 2009) 92; Daniel Traber, *Whiteness, Otherness and the Individualism Paradox from Huck to Punk* (Springer, 2007) 13.

21 Eve Tuck and K. Wayne Yang, 'Decolonization Is Not a Metaphor' (2012) 1 (1) Decolonization: Indigeneity, Education & Society, 21.

22 Nelson Maldonado-Torres, 'On the Coloniality of Being' (2007) 21 Cultural Studies, 240.

23 Anibal Quijano and Michael Ennis, 'Coloniality of Power, Eurocentrism, and Latin America' (2000) 1 (3) Nepantla: Views from the South, 533–580, 533–535.

24 Nelson Maldonado-Torres, 'On the Coloniality of Being: Contributions to the Development of a Concept' (2007) 21 (2–3) Cultural Studies, 240–270, 243.

25 Walter D. Mignolo and Catherine E. Walsh, *On Decoloniality: Concepts, Analytics, Praxis* (Duke University Press, 2018) 7.

The harm at the nexus of law, coloniality, race and racialisation

> *In producing and maintaining global inequalities, extreme poverty, exploitation of labour, environmental degradation, torture, oppression and oppressions, physical destruction of lives and livelihoods, immediate or gradual death ... the law has not always been innocent.*[26]

The tenet that 'law is equal in operation' is a foundational concept taught to all first-year law students studying the 'Rule of Law'.[27] Yet in reality, this nod to equality does not survive scrutiny as history reveals that the creation and reproduction of social structures such as race, class and gender impact upon populations differently. The concept of equality also relies on the figure of the normative human to whom all are compared as equal. This figure is often characterised by features that are middle-class, male, property-owning, white and European (Eurocentric).[28] Dehumanisation below 'the line of the human' thus operates reciprocally, reliant on contingent veneration above the line.

Any discussion of the dehumanising impact of law needs to start from a discussion of colonial histories. Sylvia Wynter charts this, dating European imperial activity as beginning with the Portuguese invasion of Senegal West Africa in 1444.[29] The Portuguese legitimated their enslavement of non-Christians in both Africa and the Americas on grounds that the indigenous populations were 'enemies of Christ' and the expropriation of land on grounds that it was not owned by Christian Kings and therefore 'terra nullius' i.e. the lands of no one. During this time, in the British Isles, theories of 'improvement' of property were being developed and would be used to dispossess indigenous peoples of their land.[30] Locke's theorisation of improvement – the use of land for maximum value meant that: 'a settler could pre-empt land (i.e., appropriate it) and come to own it by mixing his labor with the land and cultivating it to a degree deemed sufficient by the colonial administration'.[31] Identifying peoples who were not using land in a degree deemed sufficient for coloniality was vital to the global expansion of Locke's philosophy. As impatience with the Pope and the Christian mission

---

26 Foluke Adebisi, 'Decolonising the Law School: Presences, Absences, Silences... and Hope' (2020) 54 The Law Teacher, 471.

27 Tom Bingham, *The Rule of Law* (Penguin Books 2011).

28 Costas Douzinas, *The End of Human Rights: Critical thought at the Turn of the Century* (Bloomsbury Publishing, 2000) 97.

29 Sylvia Wynter, 'Unsettling the Coloniality of Being/Power/Truth/Freedom: Towards the Human, After Man, Its Overrepresentation—An Argument' (2003) 3 CR: The New Centennial Review, 257.

30 Brenna Bhandar, *Colonial Lives of Property: Law, Land, and Racial Regimes of Ownership* (Duke University Press, 2018) 35.

31 Ibid, 59.

92 Foluke Ifejola Adebisi and Katie Bales

became more pressing with the Spanish sovereign, a new form of legitimacy arose which moved away from the 'enemies of Christ' classification to a more powerful and long-lasting social technology – 'race'.

> [The] indigenous peoples of the New World, together with the mass en-slaved peoples of Africa, were now to be reclassified as 'irrational'... 'savage' Indians, and as 'subrational' Negroes, in the terms of a formula based on an a-Christian premise of a by-nature difference between Spaniards and Indians, and by extrapolation, between Christian Euro-peans and Negroes.[32]

This purported irrationality, which applied to non-European customs, laws, politics and epistemologies, meant that these practices could be disregarded and the people who practiced them could be racialised 'below the line of the human'. Consequently, this enabled the mass use of Africans as kid-napped and coerced unfree labour as well as the imperial appropriation of indigenous land in Africa, Asia, Oceania and the Americas. Accordingly, artificed categorisations were used to justify the exploitation of particu-lar populations by European powers which allowed for the so called fruits of modernity. This exploitation required legal epistemologies such as ra-cially defining the 'slave' and land as disposable property coterminous with non-indigenous use.[33] It should be noted that the end of enslavement and formal colonisation was not accompanied by a termination of these legal epistemologies or the political and economic power structures that they helped to birth; both of which continue to be the main features of moder-nity. 'Modernity' in this sense refers to the transformation of societies from the supposedly premodern to the modern following a series of events (Re-naissance; French Revolution; and the Industrial Revolution) which facili-tated the age of Enlightenment, capitalism and democracy.[34] Erased from this narrative, however, is the emergence of the contemporary nation-state as a product of coloniality and the coerced labour integral to enslavement as facilitating the so called European 'miracle'.[35]

The entrenchment of capitalism as the dominant global economic system, which relied upon the dispossession of land and the redistribution of wealth from Global South and indigenous populations to countries in the Global

---

32 Sylvia Wynter, 'Unsettling the Coloniality of Being/Power/Truth/Freedom: Towards the Human, After Man, Its Overrepresentation—An Argument' (2003) 3 CR: The New Cen-tennial Review, 257.

33 Brenna Bhandar, 'Property, Law, and Race: Modes of Abstraction' (2014) 4 UC Irvine Law Review, 203.

34 Gurminder K Bhambra, *Rethinking Modernity: Postcolonialism and the Sociological Imag-ination* (Palgrave Macmillan 2009).

35 Walter D Mignolo, 'Delinking: The Rhetoric of Modernity, the Logic of Coloniality and the Grammar of De-Coloniality' (2007) 21 (2–3) Cultural Studies, 449–514.

Reinventing possibility 93

North, is one of the most damaging and primary aspects of the imperial project. This is coupled with centuries of use of unfree coerced African labour to underpin the slave economy from which capitalism emerged.[36] This is succinctly explained by Fields: the 'chief business of slavery [was] the production of cotton, sugar, rice, and tobacco' and not the production of 'white supremacy'.[37] In other words, material dispossession in perpetuity is the goal which racialisation and coloniality serve. Accordingly, the extraction of resources (e.g. gold, silver, sugar and cotton) and labour from colonial territories has had a significant impact on the environment and the economic health of countries located within the Global South. This is evidenced by Hickel who notes that in 1820, the income gap between the richest country and the poorest country was 3 to 1, by the end of formal colonialism in the middle of the nineteenth century this stood at 35 to 1.[38] By the end of 1913, Europe owned 'between one-third and one-half of the domestic capital of Asia and Africa, and more than three-quarters of their industrial capital'.[39] So, indigenous populations were disposed of land and their rights, which entrenched patterns of economic and political instability that, in the present, continue to compel people to leave their countries of origin in search of security. Forcing non-European populations into nation-states with arbitrary boundaries and compositions has also contributed to the contemporary global social condition and divide.[40] Consequently, ideas of human hierarchy based on race and 'civilisation', which were central to the colonial project, arguably, remain influential in the creation of law, policy and knowledge production today. This is perhaps most evident in the case of migration policy,[41] which distinguishes between desirable and undesirable migrants based on their country of origin.[42] Those unwanted remain subject to violent border control, destitution, detention and deportation, all facilitated and legitimated through law.[43] Laws governing the emergence of

36 Eric Williams, *Capitalism and Slavery* (UNC Press Books, 2014) 305–308.
37 Karen E Fields and Barbara Jeanne Fields, *Racecraft: The Soul of Inequality in American Life* (Verso Trade, 2014) 117.
38 Jason Hickel, *The Divide: A Brief Guide to Global Inequality and Its Solutions* (Windmill Books, 2017) 93 and 102.
39 Ibid, 99.
40 Makau wa Mutua, 'Why Redraw the Map of Africa: A Moral and Legal Inquiry' (1994) 16 Michigan Journal of International Law, 1113, 1120–1126.
41 Lucy Mayblin, *Asylum After Empire: Colonial Legacies in the Politics of Asylum Seeking* (Rowman & Littlefield, 2017); Lucy Mayblin, *Impoverishment and Asylum: Social Policy as Slow Violence* (Routledge, 2019).
42 Nikesh Shukla (ed), *The Good Immigrant* (Random House UK, 2017).
43 Ruben Andersson, *Illegality, Inc. : Clandestine Migration and the Business of Bordering Europe* (University of California Press, 2014); Katie Bales, 'The "Essential Living Needs" of Asylum Seekers: Lessons Learned from R (Refugee Action) v Secretary of State for the Home Department [2014] EWHC 1033' (2015) 37 Journal of Social Welfare and Family Law, 247; Katie Bales and Lucy Mayblin, 'Unfree Labour in Immigration Detention: Exploitation and Coercion of a Captive Immigrant Workforce' (2018) 47 Economy and

the contemporary state and the capture and retention of colonially appropriated non-European resources also remain integral to maintaining these geopolitical divides. As El-Enany explains, 'immigration law is the tool that ensures that dispossessed peoples have no claim over what was stolen from them',[44] and 'must therefore be understood as being on a continuum of colonialism'.[45] Thus, dispossession is not confined to the colonial era, but continues through the colonial, neo-colonial and neoliberal age. Violent dispossession fuels accumulation processes in every stage of capitalism – it is not a concept that should be treated as trapped in history.[46] Systems of imperialism continue to be reproduced as Global South countries are locked into World Bank and International Monetary Fund (IMF) loan conditions which replicate coercion and dependency rather than growth by charging exorbitant interest rates and imposing declining terms of trade through structural adjustment programmes – again legitimated through law. This is acknowledged by Harvey,[47] who asserts that credit systems are now the main lever for the extraction of wealth by finance capital.

Reflecting upon this history, it is important to draw out three issues. First, racialisation and dehumanisation legitimated the exploitation and expropriation of Global South populations which facilitated industrialisation and thereby capitalism. These processes have contributed to environmental degradation and climate emergencies. This is especially linked to theories of improvement which seek to maximise the use of land, space and labour to the detriment of the environment, human beings and human interactions with each other and with nature.[48] This has lasting consequences especially for the survival and opportunities of those living within former colonial states, the majority of whom are racialised as non-white. Those made most vulnerable remain exposed politically, environmentally, financially and socio-economically. But as acknowledged by Gilroy, even where individuals are not directly connected to colonial histories, they may nevertheless be caught up in a pattern of hostility, above and below the dividing line, because of its aftermath.[49]

Second, dehumanisation and negative stereotypes arising from racialisation continue to have resonance and power in terms of law and policymaking

---

Society, 191; Nicholas De Genova, 'Detention, Deportation, and Waiting: Toward a Theory of Migrant Detainability' (2019) 20 Gender a Výzkum, 92.

44 Nadine El-Enany, *(B) Ordering Britain: Law, Race and Empire* (Manchester University Press, 2020) 2.

45 Ibid, 5.

46 David Harvey, *The New Imperialism* (Oxford University Press, 2003).

47 David Harvey, *The Enigma of Capital and the Crises of Capitalism* (Profile Books Ltd, 2010).

48 Jeremy Bendik-Keymer, 'Facing Mass Extinction, It Is Prudent to Decolonise Lands and Laws: A Philosophical Essay on Respecting Jurisdiction' (2020) 29(4) *Griffith Law Review* 561–584.

49 Paul Gilroy, *After Empire: Melancholia or Convivial Culture?* (Routledge 2004).

as they remain entrenched within our economic systems, institutions and social interactions. This is borne out in the statistics for the UK: for example, job applicants with minoritised-sounding names are disadvantaged in the job market based on their names alone.[50] These findings are limited to not just the field of recruitment but also racial discrimination within employment[51] as well as discrimination and inequality across: education[52]; health (as evident in the death rate for Covid-19)[53]; housing (as evident in Grenfell)[54]; and application of the criminal law (as evident in the disproportionate rate of those designated under the nebulous 'BAME' who are searched, arrested and imprisoned).[55] Accordingly, racially minoritised students and people, despite their contributions, often suffer an identity crisis in a country that simultaneously tells them to assimilate into violence and 'go home' to a place they have never known, all because 'British society is one steeped in institutional legacies of slavery and oppression and... these legacies have yet to be properly acknowledged and addressed'.[56]

50 Valentina Di Stasio and Anthony Heath, 'Are Employers in Britain Discriminating against Ethnic Minorities?' (Growth, Equal Opportunities, Migration and Markets 2020) <http:// csi.nuff.ox.ac.uk/wp-content/uploads/2019/01/Are-employers-in-Britain-discriminating-against-ethnic-minorities_final.pdf> accessed 26 August 2021; Haroon Siddique and Matthew Hanrahan, 'What's in a Name? How "Mystery Shopping" Studies Show Bias' (*The Guardian*, 3 December 2018) <http://www.theguardian.com/uk-news/2018/dec/03/ whats-in-a-name-how-mystery-shopping-studies-show-bias> accessed 26 March 2021.

51 Nazia Parveen and Niamh McIntyre, '"Systemic Racism": Teachers Speak Out about Discrimination in UK Schools' (*The Guardian*, 24 March 2021) <http://www.theguardian. com/education/2021/mar/24/systemic-racism-teachers-speak-out-about-discrimination-in-uk-schools> accessed 26 March 2021; Trades Union Congress (TUC), 'Dying on the Job. Racism and Risk at Work' (2020) <https://www.tuc.org.uk/sites/default/files/2020-06/ Dying%20on%20the%20job%20final.pdf> accessed 15 November 2020.

52 David Gillborn, et al., 'Race, Racism and Education: Inequality, Resilience and Reform in Policy and Practice' (University of Birmingham 2016) <http://soc-for-ed-studies.org. uk/wp-content/uploads/2019/02/GillbornD-et-al_Race-Racism-and-Education.pdf> accessed 26 August 2021.

53 Foluke Adebisi, 'Numbers, Names, Bodies & COVID-19' (*Foluke's African Skies*, 30 March 2020) <https://folukeafrica.com/numbers-names-bodies-covid-19/> accessed 26 March 2021; Veena Raleigh and Jonathan Holmes, 'The Health of People from Ethnic Minority Groups in England' (*The King's Fund*, 17 February 2021) <https://www.kingsfund. org.uk/publications/health-people-ethnic-minority-groups-england> accessed 26 March 2021.

54 Dan Bulley, Jenny Edkins and Nadine El-Enany (eds), *After Grenfell: Violence, Resistance and Response* (Pluto Press 2019).

55 David Lammy, 'The Lammy Review' (2017) < https://assets.publishing.service.gov. uk/government/uploads/system/uploads/attachment_data/file/643001/lammy-review-final-report.pdf> accessed 26 August 2021; 'Stop and Search' <https://www.ethnicity-facts-figures.service.gov.uk/crime-justice-and-the-law/policing/stop-and-search/latest> accessed 28 March 2021.

56 Nick Cartwright and TO Cartwright, '"Why Is It My Problem If They Don't Take Part?" The (Non)Role of White Academics in Decolonising the Law School' (2020) 54 (4) The Law Teacher, 532.

Finally, it should be noted that the presence of law is intertwined throughout this narrative. It has legitimated the historical actions of state parties, but at the same time, the creation of law has been influenced by colonial histories, racialisation and dehumanisation. This is evident in the neoliberal policies governing our economy and trade regulations, our concept of private property, as well as the immigration laws and policies that govern our borders and the actions of immigrants within the state. As noted by Joel Modiri (drawing from the work of Robert A. Williams), in Western imagination, the law is regarded as a cherished and revered instrument of civilisation which served historically as the most vital and effective instrument of empire, authorising and imposing Europe's particular vision of truth upon indigenous communities.[57] This centring of enlightenment principles and thinking as the answer to many epistemological and ontological questions has meant that, to the detriment of other ways of knowing, certain European perspectives have been heightened to the status of irrefutable truths.[58] Consequently,

> Rationality was privileged over the emotional. The written record was privileged over the oral tradition. Jurists took Eurocentric ideas of right and just and reframed them as universal human rights. Autonomy was elevated above relational concerns. Kantian deontology became the dominant ideology. History was written, and rewritten, by the victors.[59]

Colonialism and imperialist thinking has thus influenced our higher education systems and the ways in which we teach and research law. By illuminating the existence of these histories and epistemologies, we allow students to step outside the doctrinal boundaries which operate on colonial logics of enclosure to reflect upon and critique the law. Decolonial/antiracist approaches in law thus acknowledge that the legal history which created our present realities has not always been kind or equally applied. If we want a legal profession able to influence, shape and understand the inequalities created and sustained by law, then this education is essential. In a world faced with the increasingly catastrophic effects of long histories of coloniality on humanity and on the environment, innovation is an urgent demand for a present and future world.

---

57 Foluke Adebisi, 'Decolonising the Law School: Presences, Absences, Silences... and Hope' (2020) 54 The Law Teacher, 471.

58 Emmanuel Chukwudi Eze (ed), *Race and the Enlightenment: A Reader* (Wiley-Blackwell, 1997).

59 Nick Cartwright and TO Cartwright, '"Why Is It My Problem If They Don't Take Part?" The (Non)Role of White Academics in Decolonising the Law School' (2020) 54 (4) The Law Teacher, 533.

Antiracist and decolonial approaches to legal education

As a teacher I believe that my role is to open up possibilities for students to reconnect with their personal, experiential knowledge and to develop a critique that reflects rather than conflicts with their experiences and characteristics.[60]

We would like to begin this section by reiterating that though we will be engaging with some reflection on pedagogical praxis, this chapter is not intended as a guide on how to 'decolonise' the law curriculum. To suggest that would be underestimate the amount of critical thinking necessitated by the task of decolonisation and decolonial praxis in education. There are copious resources on this already (either published or in the works),[61] and the criticality of the task cannot be restricted to a section of a short chapter such as this. The focus of this chapter, and the stated intention of the authors, is to revisit law schools and their functions considering the absence of 'race' from the curriculum. To this end, our suggestions here are meant to trigger critical reflection in ourselves and others that may lead to different innovations within and outside the academy. Therefore, we are also mindful that relying on pre-existing measures of success from within colonial structures for decolonial approaches may actually reify the logics of coloniality attempting to be dismantled. So, the desire to measure the 'effectiveness' of 'decolonisation' imbricates itself with the very structures that necessitate the urgency to decolonise. Furthermore, requests for how-to guides often deflect and restrict the collective task we all have as academics to continually rethink our curricula, often onto academics already marginalised within academia. Thus, antiracist/decolonial approaches are open-ended tasks that cannot be proceeded upon in a prescriptive manner but require us all to reinvent the

---

60 Kimberle Williams Crenshaw, 'Toward a Race-Conscious Pedagogy in Legal Education' (1988) 11 National Black Law Journal, 12 <https://escholarship.org/uc/item/0qp9p46c> accessed 22 March 2021.

61 Suhraiya Jivraj, 'Towards Anti-Racist Legal Pedagogy: A Resource' (2020) <https://research.kent.ac.uk/decolonising-law-schools/wp-content/uploads/sites/866/2020/09/Towards-Anti-racist-Legal-Pedagogy-A-Resource.pdf> accessed 15 May 2021; Foluke Adebisi, 'An Anti-Racism Reading List' (*Foluke's African Skies*, 11 May 2020) <https://folukeafrica.com/an-anti-racism-reading-list/> accessed 26 August 2021; Henna Masih, Victoria Brooks and Manvir Kaur Grewal, 'Students as Co-Creators: Decolonial Approaches to the Legal Curriculum' <http://cti.westminster.ac.uk/wp-content/uploads/sites/63/2021/05/Decolonial-approaches-to-the-legal-curriculum.pdf> accessed 26 August 2021; Sujith Xavier, Beverley Jacobs, Valarie Waboose, Jeffery G Hewitt and Amar Bhatia (eds), *Decolonizing Law: Indigenous, Third World and Settler Perspectives* (Routledge, 2021); Foluke Adebisi, 'Call for Papers: Decolonising Legal Pedagogy/Anti-Racist Legal Scholarship' (*Foluke's African Skies*, 1 March 2021) <https://folukeafrica.com/call-for-papers-decolonising-legal-pedagogy-anti-racist-legal-scholarship/> accessed 26 August 2021.

possibility of the law school and think within the complexities of the sector as well as the global ecosystems within which law schools find themselves.

The marketisation of higher education has placed more pressure on students to view the university as a vocational exercise where their role becomes one of passive consumers, conditioned to think that their voices and perspectives are irrelevant to their education[62]; however as law teachers, it is our collective responsibility to contest this. We can still inspire them to change the world. Thus, it should also be noted how the logics of improvement – extraction of maximum financial value – that facilitated colonisation of land and coercion of unfree labour replicate themselves in measures of success as well as the marketisation, massification, consumerisation and commodification of higher education. So, the subsummation of premodern global markets into the Euro-modern market as a logic of capitalism and coloniality also finds resonance in the standardisation and ranking of knowledge and education. Engaging with these structures marks the difference between diversity and transformative decoloniality. Consequently, though much of the call to 'decolonise' Universities rests upon greater racial diversity amongst staff members and students, students' 'disappointment is not simply over the lack of "colour" in the hallways',[63] but rather the dynamics and culture of the classroom, its impact upon minoritised students and more commonly the content and way they are taught. It is vital to also interrogate research agendas and processes in this discourse. This is especially vital for departments that describe their curricula as research-led, research-rich, research-informed or any variation thereof. To detect and address coloniality in knowledge transmission and formation is also to raise a disruptive teleological question. If legal epistemologies have been complicit in producing and reproducing coloniality – as we suggest here – can they be refashioned to contribute to building worlds that do not operate on colonial logics? As stated above, we do not think the answers are easy or absolute, but the questions invite us to enter into a cycle of immersing ourselves in relevant literature, questioning and reshaping our practices.

Legal epistemology provides us a rich starting point. Kimberle Crenshaw writes that the dominant form of legal teaching is that of 'perspectivelessness' which regards legal discourse as largely objective and in doing so discounts the relevance of particular cultural, political or class-based perspectives, serving to ignore the relevance of minoritised experiences when undertaking legal analysis.[64] Colonial histories fall outside the contrived

---

62 Nick Cartwright and TO Cartwright, '"Why Is It My Problem If They Don't Take Part?" The (Non)Role of White Academics in Decolonising the Law School' (2020) 54 (4) The Law Teacher, 532, 535.

63 Kimberle Williams Crenshaw, 'Toward a Race-Conscious Pedagogy in Legal Education' (1988) 11 National Black Law Journal, 2 <https://escholarship.org/uc/item/0qp9p46c> accessed 22 March 2021.

64 Ibid.

criteria of objectivity and 'perspectivelessness', this means they have been largely ignored within legal teaching.[65] Colonial histories have been removed from the narrative of the emergence of the modern world and law so as to produce perspectiveless standards of objectivity. The consequence is that students from minoritised backgrounds feel both emotionally and analytically disempowered and the student population more generally remain uneducated about the reality of law, its origin and its consequences. In this sense, perspectivelessness ignores that the ostensibly 'objective' viewpoint applied comes from a place of privilege, often a patriarchal, middle-class, white world view. Accordingly, 'the appearance of perspectivelessness is simply the illusion by which the dominant perspective is made to appear neutral, ordinary, and beyond question'.[66] Modiri draws upon the South African perspective of law to elucidate this issue when he notes that South African law today is mainly composed of Western traditions of liberal constitutionalism combined with the laws of the colonial settlers (the Dutch and English). Accordingly, the dominance of liberal constitutionalism in addition to the 'marginalization and denigration of indigenous African law', as well as the prominence of the white demographic in the legal academy and the Eurocentrism of South African jurisprudence scholars, renders South African law largely, 'white law', which marks indigenous perspectives in a civilisational narrative which conflicts with enlightenment ideas of 'progress, development and rights'.[67] Acknowledging that imperialism still governs legal epistemology is a significant factor in moving beyond this approach. However, it must also be supported through educating students about colonial histories and other perspectives on law and law-making.

The commodification of university education is another entry point into decolonial praxis. One of the key aspects here is to acknowledge and contest the paradigm of the neoliberal University which has adopted a 'decolonising' agenda as part of its profit-making enterprise. This involves great emphasis being placed upon Equality, Diversity, and Inclusivity agendas which centre statistics and data as well as utilising Black students and staff as a means of promoting 'diversity' within the institution, whilst at the same time still prioritising white epistemologies and ignoring wider structural and institutional racism. Though 'national rhetoric may have shifted to publicly disavow discrimination and injustice...the lack of shift in foundational values and design exposes the propagandized nature of "liberty and justice

---

65 Nick Cartwright and TO Cartwright, '"Why Is It My Problem If They Don't Take Part?" The (Non)Role of White Academics in Decolonising the Law School' (2020) 54 (4) The Law Teacher.

66 Kimberle Williams Crenshaw, 'Toward a Race-Conscious Pedagogy in Legal Education' (1988) 11 National Black Law Journal, 6 <https://escholarship.org/uc/item/0qp9p46c> accessed 22 March 2021.

67 Foluke Adebisi, 'Decolonising the Law School: Presences, Absences, Silences... and Hope' (2020) 54 The Law Teacher, 471.

100 *Foluke Ifejola Adebisi and Katie Bales*

for all"'.[68] A number of authors thus refer to universities' engagement with Black Lives Matter and decolonial agendas as 'plantation politics' – where Black bodies are appropriated as property and violent systems, such as Prevent,[69] continue to be implemented against the student population.[70] For these authors, bodies are still being racialised to extract unfree, coerced labour; racialised bodies are still placed subject to the 'slave patrol' and its afterlives. The consumerisation of the student class hides this underlying political logic, serving to perpetuate forms of structural and institutional racism. Accordingly, antiracist/decolonial approaches could start from a position of contesting the commodification of education and access to the Law School, which, through the imposition of fees, already shapes the composition of the legal profession through creating barriers to those from non-privileged backgrounds.[71]

The role of representation needs to be clarified here. As noted above, while statistics on staff and student numbers should not govern the debate on decoloniality, it is important for our students to feel represented within the classroom as this informs our understanding and experience of authoritative knowledge, which means that the career progression of non-white legal academics should be encouraged.[72] Trust is easier to foster in diverse schools where students feel valued by the academic staff teaching them and their perspectives and experiences are reflected in the literature provided. Where students are forced to assimilate whiteness and masculinity in relation to their learning, this shapes a different perspective on issues of knowledge, power and privilege that could otherwise be shaped by incorporating Blackness and femininity which forms part of the ways in which dominance and subordination continue to be reproduced in society.[73] Linked

---

68 T Elon Dancy II, Kirsten T Edwards and James Earl Davis, 'Historically White Universities and Plantation Politics: Anti-Blackness and Higher Education in the Black Lives Matter Era' (2018) 53 Urban Education, 176.

69 Katy Sian, 'Born Radicals? Prevent, Positivism, and "Race-Thinking"' (2017) 3 Palgrave Communications, 1; Katy Pal Sian, 'Spies, Surveillance and Stakeouts: Monitoring Muslim Moves in British State Schools' (2015) 18 Race Ethnicity and Education, 183.

70 T Elon Dancy II, Kirsten T Edwards and James Earl Davis, 'Historically White Universities and Plantation Politics: Anti-Blackness and Higher Education in the Black Lives Matter Era' (2018) 53 Urban Education, 176; Dian D Squire, Bianca C Williams and Franklin A Tuitt, 'Plantation Politics and Neoliberal Racism in Higher Education: A Framework for Reconstructing Anti-Racist Institutions' (2018) Teachers College Record, 120.

71 Owen Bowcott, 'Qualifying as a Barrister "May Cost New Students up to £127,000"' (*The Guardian*, 23 February 2016) <http://www.theguardian.com/law/2016/feb/23/qualifying-barrister-may-cost-new-students-127000> accessed 28 March 2021.

72 Ahmed Raza Memon and Suhraiya Jivraj, 'Trust, Courage and Silence: Carving Out Decolonial Spaces in Higher Education through Student–Staff Partnerships' (2020) 54 The Law Teacher, 475.

73 Nick Cartwright and TO Cartwright, '"Why Is It My Problem If They Don't Take Part?" The (Non)Role of White Academics in Decolonising the Law School' (2020) 54 (4) The Law Teacher.

Reinventing possibility 101

to this then are antiracist/decolonial approaches which seek to equally and comparatively juxtapose white imperialist epistemologies with other perspectives, utilising, for example, indigenous knowledge systems. So, these approaches, properly understood, are not focused on replacing white Global North scholars and their epistemologies with those from the Global South, but rather painting a complete picture by pushing forward content and epistemologies that remain silenced as part of the imperial hierarchical ordering of knowledge and tracing the impact of erasure in contemporary law and society. This also means revealing and centring colonial histories as part of the so-called development of Europe and our understanding of legal concepts such as 'property' and the rights of man, as outlined earlier in our chapter. So, the purpose of this is not just to have inclusive curricula. Decolonial approaches are about curating an epistemology and ethics of the past and present, for a newer and kinder future world.

Thus, Rutazibwa describes an overlapping triptych model for decolonising approaches in education which engage with the ontology, epistemology and normativity of a discipline.[74] First she asks us, as part of our teaching, to unpack what the discipline or field is, as well as the venerated myths the discipline has adopted.[75] This requires rethinking where we begin the story of a discipline in education. Here we could also ask ourselves what foundational teaching decolonial/antiracist approaches would require. Next, we must question the silence – as mentioned above, whose voices and what epistemologies are missing from our curriculum? Here we could look at our reading lists, but beyond that we also can consider the human experiences that we centre in our teaching and how we understand them. Finally, we must consider who our field does not serve and why. Adopting these foregoing approaches across law subjects and degrees requires a fundamental will to change our realities. Consequently, piecemeal approaches have proved easier to adopt and implement.

At the University of Bristol, for example, we, inter alia, attempt to educate our students on the imperial project and its connections with law through two optional third year programmes, 'Law and Race' and 'Rich Law, Poor Law'. Law and Race aims to, by examining the law through the evolving social construction of 'race', unsettle understanding of what law is and does. This aim is enabled by an interdisciplinary approach that examines the nexus of 'race' and 'law' through a framework that includes, history, philosophy, sociology, literature etc. The unit opens with an exploration of colonial history, with a specific focus on the development of race as a technology of material and psychic appropriation, accumulation and dispossession. The aim is to establish a solid knowledge base for understanding the

---

74 Olivia Rutazibwa, 'On Babies and Bathwater: Decolonizing International Development Studies' in Sara de Jong, Rosalba Icaza and Olivia U Rutazibwa (eds), *Decolonization and Feminisms in Global Teaching and Learning* (Routledge, 2018) 158–180.
75 Ibid, 163–167.

reproduction of colonial logics in our world, through the mechanism of the state, law and the seemingly race-neutral theories that underpin our knowledge structures. We thereafter explore epistemologies beyond the standard Western canon – postcolonial theory, indigenous knowledge systems, the Black Radical tradition and African philosophies, among others. Though Rich Law, Poor Law addresses the broader role of capitalism in creating and governing law and policy, race remains a key component of the module. Accordingly, we address the ways in which racism has enabled key moments of capitalist development, what Bhattacharyya terms 'racialised capitalism',[76] and the impact this has had on global wealth distribution, creating categories such as the 'new poor',[77] which at a global level includes refugees and economic migrants stranded outside of the gates of rich countries – the postcolonial variant of Fanon's 'zone of non-being'.[78] This also elucidates the contingent nature of the postcolonial condition. The wealth of those above the line is contingent on the poverty of those below the line and vice versa. In establishing students' understanding of the historical context, we then assess the law's response to those seeking asylum in the UK, specifically their treatment in accessing work and welfare. Drawing from a wide range of literature, we posit colonial histories and long trajectories of dehumanising theorisations as one means of understanding why law distinguishes between citizens and the asylum-seeking population. The feedback that we have received from students denotes shock at the treatment afforded to those seeking sanctuary in the UK but when situated within the context of colonial histories they understand this as part of a long historical narrative based on the exploitation and subjugation of Global South populations. Accordingly, rather than regarding the law as neutral, students in both units comprehend that law is politicised with capitalist gain as one of its prevailing functions. We argue that these pedagogical approaches 'work' in the sense that they provide voice for material that was previously absent from the curricula. However, we approach decolonial and antiracist praxis not as destination, but a desired constant part of law school practices, therefore these curricula additions are in perpetual development in response to student feedback and engagement.

Furthermore, a decolonial/antiracist approach cannot be achieved by containing the Law School's efforts to one or two specialised subjects, rather it needs to span across all subjects including those that are compulsory or foundational such as the law of obligations, land law, jurisprudence and human rights.[79] If we take the example of human rights (a staple of most

---

76 Gargi Bhattacharyya, *Rethinking Racial Capitalism: Questions of Reproduction and Survival* (Rowman & Littlefield International, Ltd 2018).

77 Zygmunt Bauman, *Work, Consumerism and the New Poor* (McGraw-Hill International, 2007).

78 Frantz Fanon, *Black Skin, White Masks* (Grove Press, 2008).

79 Sophie Rigney, 'Creating the Law School as a Meeting Place for Epistemologies: Decolonising the Teaching of Jurisprudence and Human Rights' (2020) 54 The Law Teacher, 503.

Reinventing possibility 103

compulsory public law modules) what is interesting in the context of colonial histories is that historically, they were both said to be universal, and were also restricted to white Europeans and European settler colonists.[80] It was only through the struggles of colonised peoples that human rights were expanded to cover all human beings. During the 1950s and early 1960s, for example, few international legal rules applied in the colonies to protect the rights of the 'natives'. With the help of several formerly colonised country delegates, the Universal Declaration of Human Rights was made applicable to member states and colonised peoples under their jurisdiction bringing them under the realm of international human rights law.[81] Similarly, while the Geneva Convention on the Status of Refugees was signed in 1951, it was not until 1967 that people outside of Europe could claim refugee status. Indeed, the colonial powers went to great lengths to exclude non-Europeans from human rights, including the right to asylum at the convention negotiations.[82] Chapter XI of the United Nations Charter, 'the Declaration regarding Non-Self-Governing Territories', also applied only to trust territories, not colonies.[83] Perhaps unsurprisingly, colonialism itself was also not regarded as a human rights issue until entry of numerous Third World States into the UN Commission on Human Rights, which began in 1967. In relation to universal rights then, not everybody was included in the category of 'human'. Though human rights purport that all people are born equal – on a historical level, these rights were never intended to be 'universal' nor are they enjoyed as such in practice. Immigration status, for example, continues to exclude migrants and asylum seekers from basic civil liberties and rights within state parties.[84] As acknowledged by Mignolo, 'the figure of the colonized did not qualify for the "rights of man and of the citizen" … The rights

---

80 AW Brian Simpson, *Human Rights and the End of Empire : Britain and the Genesis of the European Convention* (Oxford University Press 2004); Mark Mazower, *No Enchanted Palace: The End of Empire and the Ideological Origins of the United Nations : The End of Empire and the Ideological Origins of the United Nations* (Course Book, Princeton University Press 2010); Lucy Mayblin, 'Colonialism, Decolonisation, and the Right to Be Human: Britain and the 1951 Geneva Convention on the Status of Refugees' (2014) 27 Journal of Historical Sociology, 423; Lucy Mayblin, *Asylum after Empire : Colonial Legacies in the Politics of Asylum Seeking* (Roman & Littlefield International 2017).

81 Balakrishnan Rajagopal, *International Law from below: Development, Social Movements, and Third World Resistance* (Cambridge University Press 2003).

82 Lucy Mayblin, "Colonialism, Decolonisation, and the Right to Be Human: Britain and the 1951 Geneva Convention on the Status of Refugees" (2014) 27 (3) Journal of Historical Sociology, 423–441.

83 Balakrishnan Rajagopal, *International Law from below: Development, Social Movements, and Third World Resistance* (Cambridge University Press 2003).

84 Katie Bales and Lucy Mayblin, 'Unfree Labour in Immigration Detention: Exploitation and Coercion of a Captive Immigrant Workforce' (2018) 47 Economy and Society, 191; Katie Bales, 'Universal Credit: Not so Universal? Deconstructing the Impact of the Asylum Support System' (2013) 35 Journal of Social Welfare and Family Law, 427.

104   *Foluke Ifejola Adebisi and Katie Bales*

of man and of the citizen were not meant for black or enslaved people'.[85] These issues are however rarely highlighted or discussed in our teachings of public law. Instead, we focus on the universalist narrative following the Second World War without fully engaging with the exclusionary history from which human rights emerged.

Student participation is important in taking antiracist/decolonial approaches. As noted by Rigney, to be effective practitioners, students should attend to their personal and communal awareness of law, as well as their custodianship which includes 'being responsible for the law we are trained in'.[86] This means taking time to know what the law is, its structural conditions, where it comes from and why, the various harms enabled or caused by the very ontology of Eurocentric law, as well as an understanding that as 'Being responsible for one's law can be both an acknowledgement and a refusal: an acknowledgement of what has been done in the name of that law, and perhaps a refusal to accept this as appropriate'.[87] This process also includes both students and academics being self-reflexive about our individual positionality within the socio-legal sphere in a bid to 'decolonise oneself'. In decolonising the curriculum, self-decolonisation must start with an acceptance that the curriculum itself has indeed been colonised. Second, there must be a clear understanding of what 'colonisation' means in the context of higher education and note that academics must recognise their own role in creating and perpetuating this coloniality. As such, a true process of 'decolonisation', for Cartwright and Cartwright, is equally structural and individual. So, decolonial/antiracist approaches in legal knowledge and education take place in the context of staff-student collaborations, which open staff up to concerns that may go unnoticed otherwise. For example, in response to students' demands for 'decolonisation', Jivraj undertook a 'teaching enhancement innovation pilot'. The project that resulted, 'Decolonise UoK' sought to co-produce knowledge with students to inform pedagogy, policy and practice both in the law school and beyond as part of the optional third year module "Race, Religion and Law". However, the central purpose of the project was to get students to become 'researchers, knowledge producers and stakeholders in their own education'.[88] Accordingly, they provided students with training in research and ethics to become 'focus group leaders' able to conduct cafe style group discussions as well as one-on-one interviews with students anxious about being surveilled. The results of these

---

85 Walter Mignolo, *The Darker Side of Western Modernity: Global Futures, Decolonial Options* (Duke University Press 2011) 227.
86 Sophie Rigney, 'Creating the Law School as a Meeting Place for Epistemologies: Decolonising the Teaching of Jurisprudence and Human Rights' (2020) 54 *The Law Teacher*, 506.
87 Ibid.
88 Ahmed Raza Memon and Suhraiya Jivraj, 'Trust, Courage and Silence: Carving Out Decolonial Spaces in Higher Education through Student–Staff Partnerships' (2020) 54 The Law Teacher, 476.

sessions were published in the 'Decolonise UoK Manifesto'. The Manifesto itself made several demands echoing the common claims made as part of the decolonise agenda: to liberate the curriculum, diversify reading lists and tackle micro-aggressions experienced within and outside of the classroom. These experiences helped to unveil a number of additional issues, including the lack of culturally sensitive well-being services, the inadequacy of available channels for tackling racism and the increasing use of surveillance on campus as part of the Prevent Duty which tends to focus specifically on Muslims and Black men.[89] Jivraj and Memon write that within this context, the importance of staff-student connections in creating conditions for learning is essential: one means of achieving this is through the co-production of knowledge. Accordingly, they argue for "decolonial spaces" which can dismantle the mistrust in the relationship between students and the university.[90]

Consequently, decolonial/antiracist approaches should also reflect on the position of the westernised university in the international political economy of knowledge. It is important to remember that decolonisation is a repudiation of the global conditions introduced by coloniality and thus work to resist these conditions has existed since the dawn of coloniality. The westernised university has for most of this history been on the other side of this work. The neoliberal university, reliant as it is on colonial/modern/capitalist logics of commodification, financialisaton and maximisation of economic value of space and labour, is teleologically unable to take the lead in decolonisation. Thus, connecting decolonial/antiracist approaches in higher education with work done and being done by people at the coalface of confronting the most severe aspects of coloniality – people in the Global South and indigenous peoples – is vital to keeping decolonial work in westernised universities honest and humble.

Conclusion: antiracist and decolonial approaches in law for worlds otherwise

In this chapter we have, in revisiting the major concerns around the purposes of law schools, focused on the entanglements between law, coloniality and structural racism, with an understanding that our teaching and research in law can and should be antiracist and decolonial. However, the starting point for us is an appreciation of the role of racialisation in the emergence of the structural inequalities that have existed and continue to exist. This signals a need to look beyond the individual in our decolonial and antiracist work in higher education, understanding how this work fits in with wider activism that seeks to refuse colonial conditions of life. Any effort by law teachers to 'compartmentalise racial experiences present racism as a

89 Ibid.
90 Ibid.

106 *Foluke Ifejola Adebisi and Katie Bales*

series of individualized anomalous occurrences rather than systematically connected to larger institutional practices and values which are reflected in and reinforced by law'.[91] Antiracist/decolonial approaches seek to unveil the role of the law in racialisation, colonialism, and its afterlives. There is always more work to do and being done beyond the academy. Our work within the academy has the potential to significantly reposition how we view and teach the world and what the world may become beyond our teaching. Therefore, to use our scholarship to imagine and build fairer more equal worlds, we need to continually ask what world we want the law to produce beyond this necropolitical deathscape. Clark and Tsamenyi in Birks' collection state that though people see Western law as underpinned by moral values and authority, this can 'disintegrate when people see law merely as an instrument of repression'. Thus, legal education, and those teaching it, have a duty to ensure the law retains its moral force and is not trivialised or marginalised.[92] So, this chapter puts forth the urgent and audacious hope that, through our teaching and research, the death and destruction, oppression and dispossession that characterises the colonial logics and narratives that reproduce our world can be repudiated and reversed. This is still a work in progress, not only here but in law schools across the world. Yet as the conditions imposed by coloniality lead us to constantly live with the threat of irrevocable mass extinction, decolonial work remains necessary work.[93] In our case, students have responded well to the addition of this content across many units within the curriculum, both at undergraduate and postgraduate levels. Nevertheless, we understand that these responses need to be evidenced more empirically, so that we can track what the overall impact has been on student experience, knowledge and career choice. In fact, we do not know what futures our actions will bring about. But we are impelled by hope and only one assurance that our inaction will see the harms we describe here continue. This remains an uncertain and laborious task. Different jurisdictions have different colonial histories, which means that fitting in contextual decolonial approaches within wider geopolitical narratives requires significant scholarship from law teachers wishing to adopt a decolonial perspective. The consumerisation of higher education as well as the requirements of career progression may sometimes conflict with those of decolonial research – especially the learning and unlearning needed. Nevertheless, if, as we argue, the purposes of law schools should include teaching

---

91 Kimberle Williams Crenshaw, 'Toward a Race-Conscious Pedagogy in Legal Education' (1988) 11 National Black Law Journal <https://escholarship.org/uc/item/0qp9p46c> accessed 22 March 2021.

92 Eugene Clark and Martin Tsamenyi, 'Legal Education in the Twenty-First Century: A Time of Challenge' in Peter Birks (ed), *What Are Law Schools For?* (University Press 1996).

93 Jeremy Bendik-Keymer, 'Facing Mass Extinction, It Is Prudent to Decolonise Lands & Laws: A Philosophical Essay on Respecting Jurisdiction' (2020) 29(4) *Griffith Law Review* 561–584, 5.

our students to participate in and imagine a world where racial injustice, climate inequalities and extreme global poverty are no more, then legal education must continually reinvent possibility.

Bibliography

Adebisi F, 'An Anti-Racism Reading List' (*Foluke's African Skies*, 11 May 2020) <https://folukeafrica.com/an-anti-racism-reading-list/> accessed 26 August 2021.

Adebisi F, 'Call for Papers: Decolonising Legal Pedagogy/Anti-Racist Legal Scholarship' (*Foluke's African Skies*, 1 March 2021) <https://folukeafrica.com/call-for-papers-decolonising-legal-pedagogy-anti-racist-legal-scholarship/> accessed 26 August 2021.

Adebisi F, 'Decolonising the Law School: Presences, Absences, Silences ... and Hope' (2020) 54 *The Law Teacher* 471.

Adebisi F, 'Numbers, Names, Bodies & COVID-19' (*Foluke's African Skies*, 30 March 2020) <https://folukeafrica.com/numbers-names-bodies-covid-19/> accessed 26 March 2021.

Andersson R, *Illegality, Inc: Clandestine Migration and the Business of Bordering Europe* (University of California Press 2014).

Bales K, 'The "Essential Living Needs" of Asylum Seekers: Lessons Learned from R (Refugee Action) v Secretary of State for the Home Department (2014) EWHC 1033' (2015) 37 *Journal of Social Welfare and Family Law* 247.

Bales K, 'Universal Credit: Not so Universal? Deconstructing the Impact of the Asylum Support System' (2013) 35 *Journal of Social Welfare and Family Law* 427.

Bales K and Mayblin L, 'Unfree Labour in Immigration Detention: Exploitation and Coercion of a Captive Immigrant Workforce' (2018) 47 *Economy and Society* 191.

Barbot O, 'George Floyd and Our Collective Moral Injury' (2020) 110(9) *American Journal of Public Health* 1253–1253.

Bauman Z, *Work, Consumerism and the New Poor* (McGraw-Hill International 2007).

Bendik-Keymer J, 'Facing Mass Extinction, It Is Prudent to Decolonise Lands and Laws: A Philosophical Essay on Respecting Jurisdiction' (2020) 29(4) *Griffith Law Review* 561–584.

Bhambra GK, *Rethinking Modernity: Postcolonialism and the Sociological Imagination* (Palgrave Macmillan 2009).

Bhandar B, *Colonial Lives of Property: Law, Land, and Racial Regimes of Ownership* (Duke University Press 2018).

Bhandar B, 'Property, Law, and Race: Modes of Abstraction' (2014) 4 *UC Irvine Law Review* 203.

Bhattacharyya G, *Rethinking Racial Capitalism: Questions of Reproduction and Survival* (Rowman & Littlefield International Ltd 2018).

Bingham T, *The Rule of Law* (Penguin Books 2011).

Birks P, *What Are Law Schools For?* (University Press 1996).

Bowcott O, 'Qualifying as a Barrister "May Cost New Students up to £127,000"' (*The Guardian*, 23 February 2016) <http://www.theguardian.com/law/2016/feb/23/qualifying-barrister-may-cost-new-students-127000> accessed 28 March 2021.

Bulley D, Edkins J, and El-Enany N (eds), *After Grenfell: Violence, Resistance and Response* (Pluto Press 2019).

108 *Foluke Ifejola Adebisi and Katie Bales*

Cartwright N and Cartwright TO, '"Why Is It My Problem If They Don't Take Part?" The (Non) Role of White Academics in Decolonising the Law School' (2020) 54(4) *The Law Teacher* 532.

Clark E and Tsamenyi M, 'Legal Education in the Twenty-First Century: A Time of Challenge' in Peter Birks (ed) *What Are Law Schools For?* (University Press 1996).

Crenshaw KW, 'Toward a Race-Conscious Pedagogy in Legal Education' (1988) 11 *National Black Law Journal* < https://escholarship.org/uc/item/0qp9p46c> accessed 22 March 2021.

Dancy TE, Edwards KT, and Davis JE, 'Historically White Universities and Plantation Politics: Anti-Blackness and Higher Education in the Black Lives Matter Era' (2018) 53 *Urban Education* 176.

De Genova N, 'Detention, Deportation, and Waiting: Toward a Theory of Migrant Detainability' (2019) 20 *Gender a Výzkum* 92.

Di Stasio V and Heath A, 'Are Employers in Britain Discriminating Against Ethnic Minorities?' (*Growth, Equal Opportunities, Migration and Markets* 2020) <http://csi.nuff.ox.ac.uk/wp-content/uploads/2019/01/Are-employers-in-Britain-discriminating-against-ethnic-minorities_final.pdf> accessed 26 August 2021.

Douzinas C, *The End of Human Rights: Critical thought at the Turn of the Century* (Bloomsbury Publishing 2000).

El-Enany N, *(B) Ordering Britain: Law, Race and Empire* (Manchester University Press 2020).

Eze CE (ed), *Race and the Enlightenment: A Reader* (Wiley-Blackwell 1997).

Fanon F, *Black Skin, White Masks* (Grove Press 2008).

Fields KE and Fields BJ, *Racecraft: The Soul of Inequality in American Life* (Verso Trade 2014).

Gillborn D, 'Race, Racism and Education: Inequality, Resilience and Reform in Policy and Practice' (University of Birmingham 2016) <http://soc-for-ed-studies.org. uk/wp-content/uploads/2019/02/GillbornD-et-al_Race-Racism-and-Education. pdf> accessed 26 August 2021.

Gilmore RW, *Golden Gulag: Prisons, Surplus, Crisis, and Opposition in Globalizing California* (University of California Press 2007).

Gilroy P, *After Empire: Melancholia or Convivial Culture?* (Routledge 2004).

Goodrich P, 'Of Blackstone's Tower: Metaphors of Distance and Histories of the English Law School' in Peter Birks (ed) *What Are Law Schools For?* (Oxford University Press 1996).

Grosfoguel R, 'Decolonizing Post-Colonial Studies and Paradigms of Political-Economy: Transmodernity, Decolonial Thinking and Global Coloniality' (2011) 1(1) *Transmodernity: Journal of Peripheral Cultural Production of the Luso-Hispanic World.*

Grosfoguel R, 'What Is Racism?' (2016) 22 *Journal of World-Systems Research* 9–15.

Harvey D, *The Enigma of Capital and the Crises of Capitalism* (Profile Books Ltd 2010).

Harvey D, *The New Imperialism* (Oxford University Press 2003).

Hickel J, *The Divide: A Brief Guide to Global Inequality and Its Solutions* (Windmill Books 2017).

Jivraj S, 'Towards Anti-Racist Legal Pedagogy: A Resource' (2020) <https://research. kent.ac.uk/decolonising-law-schools/wp-content/uploads/sites/866/2020/09/ Towards-Anti-racist-Legal-Pedagogy-A-Resource.pdf> accessed 15 May 2021.

Lammy D, 'The Lammy Review' (2017) <https://assets.publishing.service.gov.uk/government/uploads/system/uploads/attachment_data/file/643001/lammy-review-final-report.pdf> accessed 26 August 2021.

Leonardo Z, *Race, Whiteness, and Education* (Routledge 2009).

Maldonado-Torres N, 'On the Coloniality of Being: Contributions to the Development of a Concept' (2007) 21(2–3) *Cultural Studies* 240–270.

Maqbool A, 'Black Lives Matter: From Social Media Post to Global Movement' (*BBC News*, 9 July 2020) <https://www.bbc.com/news/world-us-canada-53273381> accessed 23 March 2021.

Masih H, Brooks V, and Grewal MK, 'Students as Co-Creators: Decolonial Approaches to the Legal Curriculum' <http://cti.westminster.ac.uk/wp-content/uploads/sites/63/2021/05/Decolonial-approaches-to-the-legal-curriculum.pdf> accessed 26 August 2021.

Mayblin L, *Asylum after Empire: Colonial Legacies in the Politics of Asylum Seeking* (Roman & Littlefield International 2017).

Mayblin L, 'Colonialism, Decolonisation, and the Right to Be Human: Britain and the 1951 Geneva Convention on the Status of Refugees' (2014) 27(3) *Journal of Historical Sociology* 423–441.

Mayblin L, *Impoverishment and Asylum: Social Policy as Slow Violence* (Routledge 2019).

Mazower M, *No Enchanted Palace: The End of Empire and the Ideological Origins of the United Nations* (Course Book, Princeton University Press 2010).

McCann-Mortimer P, Augoustinos M, and LeCouteur A, 'Race'and the Human Genome Project: Constructions of Scientific Legitimacy' (2004) 15(4) *Discourse & Society* 409–432.

Memon AR and Jivraj S, 'Trust, Courage and Silence: Carving Out Decolonial Spaces in Higher Education through Student-Staff Partnerships' (2020) 54 *The Law Teacher* 475.

Mignolo WD, *The Darker Side of Western Modernity: Global Futures, Decolonial Options* (Duke University Press 2011).

Mignolo WD, 'Delinking: The Rhetoric of Modernity, the Logic of Coloniality and the Grammar of De-Coloniality' (2007) 21(2–3) *Cultural Studies* 449–514.

Mignolo WD and Walsh CE, *On Decoloniality: Concepts, Analytics, Praxis* (Duke University Press 2018).

Mills CW, *The Racial Contract* (Cornell University Press 2014).

Mutua MW, 'Why Redraw the Map of Africa: A Moral and Legal Inquiry' (1994) 16 *Michigan Journal of International Law* 1113.

Parveen N and McIntyre N, '"Systemic Racism": Teachers Speak Out about Discrimination in UK Schools' (*The Guardian* 24 March 2021) <http://www.theguardian.com/education/2021/mar/24/systemic-racism-teachers-speak-out-about-discrimination-in-uk-schools> accessed 26 March 2021.

Patel K, 'Race and a Decolonial Turn in Development Studies' (2020) 41(9) *Third World Quarterly* 1463–1475.

Quijano A and Ennis M, 'Coloniality of Power, Eurocentrism, and Latin America' (2000) 1(3) *Nepantla: Views from the South* 533–580.

Rajagopal B, *International Law from Below: Development, Social Movements, and Third World Resistance* (Cambridge University Press 2003).

Raleigh V and Holmes J, 'The Health of People from Ethnic Minority Groups in England' (*The King's Fund*, 17 February 2021) <https://www.kingsfund.org.

110   *Foluke Ifejola Adebisi and Katie Bales*

uk/publications/health-people-ethnic-minority-groups-england> accessed 26 March 2021.

Rigney S, 'Creating the Law School as a Meeting Place for Epistemologies: Decolonising the Teaching of Jurisprudence and Human Rights' (2020) 54 *The Law Teacher* 503.

Rutazibwa O, 'On Babies and Bathwater: Decolonizing International Development Studies' in Sara de Jong, Rosalba Icaza, and Olivia U. Rutazibwa (eds) *Decolonization and Feminisms in Global Teaching and Learning* (Routledge 2018).

Shilliam R, *Race and the Undeserving Poor* (Agenda Publishing Limited 2018).

Shukla N (ed), *The Good Immigrant* (Random House UK 2017).

Sian K, 'Born Radicals? Prevent, Positivism and "Race-Thinking"' (2017) 3 *Palgrave Communications* 1.

Sian K, 'Spies, Surveillance and Stakeouts: Monitoring Muslim Moves in British State Schools' (2015) 18 *Race, Ethnicity and Education* 183.

Siddique H and Hanrahan M, 'What's in a Name? How "Mystery Shopping" Studies Show Bias' (*The Guardian* 3 December 2018) <http://www.theguardian.com/uk-news/2018/dec/03/whats-in-a-name-how-mystery-shopping-studies-show-bias> accessed 26 March 2021.

Simpson AWB, *Human Rights and the End of Empire: Britain and the Genesis of the European Convention* (Oxford University Press 2004).

Squire DD, Williams BC, and Tuitt FA, 'Plantation Politics and Neoliberal Racism in Higher Education: A Framework for Reconstructing Anti-Racist Institutions' (2018) *Teachers College Record* 120.

Thompson A, 'For: Anti-Racist Education' (1997) 27(1) *Curriculum Inquiry* 7–44.

Traber D, *Whiteness, Otherness and the Individualism Paradox from Huck to Punk* (Springer 2007).

Trade Union Congress (TUC), 'Dying on the Job. Racism and Risk at Work' (*TUC*, 2020) <https://www.tuc.org.uk/sites/default/files/2020-06/Dying%20on%20the%20job%20final.pdf> accessed 15 November 2020.

Tuck E and Yang KW, 'Decolonization Is Not a Metaphor' (2012) 1(1) *Decolonization: Indigeneity, Education & Society* 1–40.

UK Government, 'Stop and Search' (*UK Government*, 22 February 2021) <https://www.ethnicity-facts-figures.service.gov.uk/crime-justice-and-the-law/policing/stop-and-search/latest> accessed 28 March 2021.

Williams E, *Capitalism and Slavery* (UNC Press Books 2014).

Wynter S, 'Unsettling the Coloniality of Being/Power/Truth/Freedom: Towards the Human, After Man, Its Overrepresentation – An Argument' (2003) 3 *CR: The New Centennial Review* 257–337.

Xavier S, Jacobs B, Waboose V, Hewitt JG, and Bhatia A (eds), *Decolonizing Law: Indigenous, Third World and Settler Perspectives* (Routledge 2021).

5 Who are law schools for? A story of class and gender

Jessica Guth and Doug Morrison

Introduction

Birks' collection[1] is striking in many ways, particularly in the fact that no women contributed to it and that the writing throughout comes from a particular place; a white, male, elitist place.[2] This evident gender bias, combined with the failure to acknowledge issues of class, race, and equality, is not isolated to law, nor to this time period[3] but Birks' collection not only serves to normalise it, by presenting law schools as seen from a narrowly drawn viewpoint, but also leaves the reader in little doubt as to who law schools are for: white men with interests in and links to the sort of things deemed important to the legal professions. This chapter takes the picture painted by Birks' collection as its starting point and begins by acknowledging that law schools are more than the offices and lecture halls that make up the physical space but are shaped by the people who inhabit them, staff at all levels and in all job roles, and of course students.[4] This sort of focus on the private life of law schools and questions of gender and class are under-researched in the context of modern legal education and therefore this

---

1 Peter Birks (ed), *What Are Law Schools For? Vol. 2 Pressing Problems in the Law* (Oxford University Press 1996).
2 See Peter Goodrich, 'Of Blackstone's Tower: Metaphors of Distance and Histories of the English Law School' in Peter Birks (ed), *What Are Law Schools For? Vol. 2 Pressing Problems in the Law* (Oxford University Press 1996). For other work exploring the particular masculine culture in law schools around the same time see Richard Collier, '"Nutty Professors", "Men in Suits", and "New Entrepreneurs": Corporeality, Subjectivity and Change in the Law School and Legal Practice' (1998) 7 (1) Social and Legal Studies, 27; Richard Collier, 'The Changing University and the (Legal) Academic Career – Rethinking the Relationship Between Women, Men and the "Private Life" of the Law School' (2002) 22 (1) Legal Studies.
3 See Joe R Feagin and Kimberley Ducey, *Elite White Men Ruling, Who, What, When, Where, and How*, (Routledge 2017).
4 Jean Lave and Etienne Wenger, *Situated Learning: Legitimate Peripheral Participation* (Cambridge University Press 1991).

DOI: 10.4324/9781003322092-5

112   *Jessica Guth and Doug Morrison*

chapter aims to re-start conversations had in the past[5] and bring conversations being had elsewhere[6] into our thinking. This chapter offers a pause to reflect on the inhabitants of law schools and submits that who inhabits law schools are intrinsically linked and determinate of what law schools are for. In considering whether the picture painted by Birks' collection was accurate then and remains accurate now we have reframed the original question from 'what' to 'who' because we believe that the who is important in understanding everything else. Birks points out that 'the chapters of this book, and this editorial preface no less, are personal insights into the life and purposes of law schools set out with the intention of enriching the debate'[7] and this chapter is exactly that too. Adopting to some degree an auto-ethnographical position, it provides personal insights, rooted in our lived experience, and based on our reflections, into our own place and the place of our peers and students in contemporary law schools. We hope to encourage others to reflect and join the conversation.[8]

The remainder of this chapter is structured as follows: the next section provides an insight into our reading of Birks' collection and the pictures we

---

5 See for example Pauline Anderson and Jenny Williams (ed), *Identity and Difference in Higher Education: Outsiders Within* (Ashgate 2001); Simon Anderson, Lorraine Murray and Paul Maharg, *Minority and Social Diversity in Legal Education in Scotland* (Scottish Executive 2003); Rosemary Auchmuty, 'Early Women Law Students at Cambridge and Oxford' (2008) 29 (1) Journal of Legal History, 63; Richard Collier, 'The Changing University and the (Legal) Academic Career -Rethinking the Relationship Between Women, Men and the "Private Life" of the Law School' (2002) 22 Legal Studies, 1–32; Fiona Cownie, *Legal Academics: Culture and Identities* (Hart Publishing 2004); Clare McGlynn, 'Women, Representation and the Legal Academy' (1999) 19 (1) Legal Studies, 68–92; Clare McGlynn, *The Woman Lawyer: Making the Difference* (Oxford University Press 1998); Celia Wells, 'Working Out Women in Law Schools' (2001) 21 (1) Legal Studies, 116–136.

6 For an overview see Ulrike Schultz, Gisela Shaw, Margaret Thornton and Rosemary Auchmuty, *Gender and Careers in the Legal Academy* (Hart 2001); Meera E Deo, *Unequal Profession: Race and Gender in Legal Academia* (Stanford University Press 2019); Elizabeth Mertz, Wamucii Njogu and Susan Gooding, 'What Difference Does Difference Make – The Challenge for Legal Education' (1998) 48 (1) Journal of Legal Education; Christina Möller, *Herkunft zählt fast immer. Soziale Ungleichheiten unter Universitätsprofessorinnen und -professoren* (Juventa 2015); Ulrike Schultz, Anja Böning, Ilka Peppmeier and Silke Schröder, *De jure und de facto: Professorinnen in der Rechtswissenschaft: geschlect und Wissenschaftskarriere im Rect* (Nomos 2018); Kathryne M Young, *How to Be Sort of Happy in Law School* (Stanford University Press 2018).

7 Peter Birks (ed), *What Are Law Schools For? Vol. 2 Pressing Problems in the Law* (Oxford University Press 1996) vi.

8 As such this chapter adds to the scholarship on women in law schools, working-class legal academics and diversity in law schools more generally which is often biographical, auto-biographical or small-scale in nature and provides a micro-level snapshot of the lived experience. See, for example, Celia Wells, *A Woman in Law: Reflections on Gender, Class and Politics* (Waterside Press 2019); Rosemary Auchmuty, 'Early Women Law Students at Cambridge and Oxford' (2008) 29 (1) Journal of Legal History, 63; Fiona Cownie, *Legal Academics: Culture and Identities* (Hart Publishing 2004); Clare McGlynn, 'Women, Representation and the Legal Academy' (1999).

have in our heads as we reflect on the reflections offered within it. We then consider our own biographies to critique the original Birks' collection and highlight that it never was a full picture of law schools in the 1990s. The final section briefly examines contemporary events such as the introduction of the Solicitors Qualifying Examination (SQE), Brexit, the Covid-19 pandemic, and the Black Lives Matter movement to further highlight how contemporary law schools may look different but the fundamental issues and debates around law schools and legal education have remained remarkably constant and who law schools are for has not changed.

Birks: who were law schools for then?

In Birks' collection, the contributions all seem to see a strong link between university law schools and the profession and make some, maybe counter intuitive assumptions about who therefore the academics inhabiting the law school and the students attending should be. Birks himself notes:

> A law school cannot hope to discharge its research function unless it can recruit from the top of the class. Whether a person has or has not got a First quickly becomes unimportant, but university lawyers have to come from the pool of those with that kind of ability.[9]

Writing of English legal education in the 1960s, Langbein notes that 'it was not meant to be closely practical',[10] but in essence 'a species of liberal arts education'.[11] Jumping forward to the 1990s, Langbein observes the distinction between English law schools as temples of scholarship and their more practical American counterparts which were more focused on training legal professionals no longer applied to the same extent, and that

> For a variety of reasons English University Law schools now occupy a more central role in the training of the professions... and in consequence, they do a better job than they used to in the advanced curriculum.[12]

This theme of law schools as Houses of Intellect for the Profession[13] is taken up by Savage and Watt who note 'we are now at a place where leading law schools and leading professionals are intimately involved with each

---

9 Peter Birks (ed), *What Are Law Schools For? Vol. 2 Pressing Problems in the Law* (Oxford University Press 1996) 1.
10 John H. Langbein, 'Chapter 1, Scholarly and Professional Objectives in Legal Education: American Trends and English Comparisons' in Peter Birks (ed), *What Are Law Schools For? Vol. 2 Pressing Problems in the Law* (Oxford University Press 1996) 1.
11 Ibid, 3.
12 Ibid, 3.
13 William Twining, *Blackstones's Tower: The English Law School* (Sweet and Maxwell 1994).

114   *Jessica Guth and Doug Morrison*

other's "creation".[14] Birks seems to suggest that perhaps there is still work to do in this regard though by noting that '[H]owever it comes about, more universities law schools, above all more of those with top-rated research rankings, must take on the vocational courses'.[15] While Birks, Savage and Watt, and Langbein appear to see the close links between law schools and the profession as a positive, Toddington is less convinced, at least in the context of legal skills. He states, 'A laudable but insufficiently theorised consensus on the need for curricular relevance has resulted in a narrowly professional understanding of legal skills',[16] when perhaps what is needed is the development of critical thinking skills and a focus on the critical autonomy required by any discipline. Birks and Langbein further comment on the requirement for doctoral degrees for law school staff 'creeping in' and neither seem convinced that this is a good thing although neither fully articulate why.[17] In spite of the lack of insistence on doctorates, research is seen as key to what university law schools do in many of the contributions in Birks' collection. It is seen as fundamental and as the core or heart of the law school. Some though seem concerned about the focus of that research with Langbein lamenting that in the context of American law schools 'national law schools seem ever less interested in law', or 'teaching law'.[18]

The views reflected in the collection are therefore missing an important voice in legal education: the voice of the teaching intensive institution. While their voice may be missing, commentary about them is perhaps not. Birks notes 'The Law School designed as a teaching machine would be a deplorable institution'[19] adding:

> A Law School which does nothing but teach is almost a contradiction in terms. It may look efficient and productive, but it will be free-riding on the work of other much more expensive institutions, and the knowledge which it imparts to its students will be second-hand, inert and unreliable. [20]

---

14 Nigel Savage and Gary Watt, 'Chapter 4, A House of Intellect for the Profession' in Peter Birks (ed), *What Are Law Schools For? Vol. 2 Pressing Problems in the Law* (Oxford University Press 1996) 47.

15 Peter Birks (ed), *What Are Law Schools For? Vol. 2 Pressing Problems in the Law* (Oxford University Press 1996) xi.

16 Stuart Toddington, 'Chapter 6 The Emperor's New Skills: The Academy, The Profession and the Idea of Legal Education' in Peter Birks (ed), *What Are Law Schools For? Vol. 2 Pressing Problems in the Law* (Oxford University Press 1996) 69.

17 Peter Birks (ed), *What Are Law Schools For? Vol. 2 Pressing Problems in the Law* (Oxford University Press 1996) ix; John H. Langbein, 'Chapter 1, Scholarly and Professional Objectives in Legal Education: American Trends and English Comparisons' in Peter Birks (ed), *What Are Law Schools For? Vol. 2 Pressing Problems in the Law* (Oxford University Press 1996) 6.

18 Ibid.

19 Peter Birks (ed), *What Are Law Schools For? Vol. 2 Pressing Problems in the Law* (Oxford University Press 1996) xi.

20 Ibid.

Who are law schools for? 115

For Birks, teaching and research are symbiotically linked, 'teaching at an advanced level stimulates and tests research and research vitalizes teaching at an advanced level',[21] contending that 'if university lawyers were asked which of the two mattered more, they would almost all object to the decoupling'.[22]

Overall, Birks' collection, through what it says and what it does not say, through who is included and who is not, suggests that law schools are all quite similar, that they are staffed by the best legal minds focused on a narrowly defined discipline whose key mission is to produce research about law (first and foremost) and teach the next generation of lawyers which probably means legal professionals. The picture we have in our heads as we read the contributions is one of lofty towers, yet dark corridors with scholars working behind closed doors poring over dusty law books; of white old men with posh English accents talking more to themselves than each other never mind anyone outside the academy who is not a Queens Council or a judge. It is not a picture of diversity or of debate amongst equals whatever our backgrounds. It does not look like women or ethnic minorities belong. It is not a picture of interdisciplinarity or even of collegiality. It feels doctrinal, research and legal practice focused, posh and not for us.

That picture although partially supported by Birks' collection is of course coloured by our experiences, knowledge, assumptions and prejudices and it is of course also embellished. We reflect on the reality of that picture in the next section. For now, it is worth noting that there are some themes in Birks' collection which feel oddly contemporary and familiar. On a basic level, Birks summarises what law schools did then and probably what they still do now, though the balance between those activities may have shifted for some or all institutions: 'Their current doing can be divided into three kinds. They facilitate research and publication, they teach, and they run themselves'.[23] The balance between those activities and who does what has always caused tension. Savage and Watt note those tensions in a way that certainly feels familiar 25 years later:

> The dilemmas multiply – legal science versus legal realism; liberal education against vocational education; education versus training; substance versus procedure; technical rationality versus reflective practice; education for the elite versus education for the majority; and then there is perhaps the most basic dilemma of all – the pragmatic versus the idyllic.[24]

---

21 Ibid, xi.
22 Ibid, vi.
23 Ibid, vi.
24 Nigel Savage and Gary Watt, 'Chapter 4, A House of Intellect for the Profession' in Peter Birks (ed), *What Are Law Schools For? Vol. 2 Pressing Problems in the Law* (Oxford University Press 1996) 45.

116   *Jessica Guth and Doug Morrison*

They continue to highlight some of the more personal or individual tensions many of us experience:

> We are simultaneously both legal professionals and academics: a combination of cultures which might be expected to produce persons for whom collaborative and cooperative exercise does not come naturally.[25]

All these tensions and how we individually and collectively choose to address them shape what sort of spaces law schools are as well as who they are for.

Our lives and Birks: do we belong here?

Our law school experience resonates with some of the reflections in Birks' collection but also paints a different picture. We use an auto-ethnographic approach to reflect on both our experiences and our practices, and while this of course only provides a small snapshot and is by definition subjective, we nonetheless believe it can provide valuable insights.[26] While we have not undertaken systematic auto-ethnographic research for this chapter, we have made use of many techniques inherent in that approach. Auto-ethnography as a method 'involves the describing and analysing personal experiences in order to understand cultural experiences'.[27] We have therefore written about our experiences based on our reflections and memories. Thus, offering a different, more personal way to think about Birks' collection and literature on contemporary law schools. Those reflections are explicitly set in the context of the literature, and we have sought to also compare our experiences to those of others to challenge our memories and reflections and better understand how they fit in. We have, for example, spent time talking about our time as students as we understand it in the context of the literature we now know; we have looked back at our earlier published writings as well as unpublished documents that help us reflect on our time as students as well as on our experiences as legal academics; and we have drawn on our private conversations (with each other and with others) to help us remember and acknowledge important events, insights and views that shaped who we were as students and who we are now as legal academics. Of course, we have made 'choices about which selves and experiences to share as a way of

---

25 Ibid, 57.

26 A useful introduction to auto-ethnography in legal education can be found in Elaine Gregersen, 'Exploring Autoethnography as a Method and Methodology in Legal Education Research' (2016) 3 (1) Asian Journal of Legal Education, 95–105.

27 Tony E Adams, Stacy Holamn Jones and Carolyn Ellis, *Autoethnography* (Oxford University Press 2015) Blurb.

Who are law schools for? 117

mitigating vulnerability and potential exposure to criticism'[28] but nonetheless the approach offers a deep and genuine reflection which goes beyond simply acknowledging our position as researchers[29] and thus offers a more personal insight into how we experience law schools and how our experience is shaped by and, in turn, shapes how others experience them. In this section, we therefore think about our own experience as law students around the time Birks' collection was published and as legal academics more recently. We recognise, of course, that our reflections are shaped by what has happened since we did our degrees and by our current experiences of legal academia. Nonetheless, we think that biography and reflection are useful tools to help us understand the themes of Birks' collection and the continuing relevance.

We studied law at roughly the same time, but our biographies are markedly different in many ways. Jess started her law degree at a pre-1992 institution in 1997 straight out of school having completed A-levels. Most of her schooling took place in Germany. She came from a single parent family, felt out of place at her German grammar school and much more at ease at her chosen English comprehensive school. The school she attended for GCSEs and A-Levels[30] was in a deprived and ethnically diverse area of West Yorkshire with a minority of pupils going on to sixth form and then university. Jess did not have any links to law, and it quickly became apparent that the vast majority of her peers at university did. Many had solicitors or barristers in the family with some coming from a long line of lawyers. Most had clear ideas of their intended career paths, and everyone wanted to enter the legal professions. However, with both parents involved in teaching at either secondary school or university level in Germany, Jess was well-placed to allow her to thrive in a higher education setting. She attended an old university. Women were in the majority on the degree programme, but men dominated the discussions, the student law society positions, and the extra-curricular competitions such as mooting, negotiating or client interviewing. The law school never felt like home. It always felt somewhat other with a different language and a different code that was inaccessible and alien and remained so until graduation and beyond. Legal concepts were fascinating and elusive at the same time and Jess hoped for more clarity when it came to the practicalities of the Legal Practice Course (LPC). That clarity came but with

---

28 Stacey Holman Jones, Tony Adams and Carolyn Ellis (ed), *Handbook of Autoethnography* (Routledge 2016).

29 Sarah Wall, 'An Autoethnography on Learning about Autoethnography' (2006) 5 (2) International Journal of Qualitative Methods, 146–160.

30 GCSEs refers to General Certificate of Secondary Education and is awarded to students in English, Welsh and Northern Irish schools in a specific subject after 2 years of study, usually in Years 10 and 11 of secondary school (age 16) and which are generally made up of a mixture of coursework and final exams. A-Levels are Advanced Levels and a school leaving qualification. They are usually taken after GCSEs and are also usually worked towards over two years and awarded in specific subjects based on coursework and exams.

118 *Jessica Guth and Doug Morrison*

it came boredom. That boredom continued once the excitement of having secured a training contract wore off. Legal practice, so it seemed to Jess, was nothing more than glorified form filling and occasionally some half-hearted performance in a court room, or more likely chambers, in front of a judge who had already decided that the male solicitor opposite was right or that her off-white shirt was the wrong colour. Two things were clear: law school, academic or vocational, had not prepared Jess for practice in any way at all and practicing law was far less interesting, exciting, or fun than thinking about law.

The route into legal academia was not quite as traditional as the initial route into practice. After a Master of Arts (MA) in Social Research, Jess was in the right place at the right time, and with the right language skills (the job required a German speaking researcher) to get a job as a research assistant on a large-funded project in a Russell Group institution. This job allowed her to tie in her doctoral research to the same project. The project was interdisciplinary drawing on sociology, geography and law and thus further shaping her approach to law as an academic discipline.[31] In 2007, Jess successfully applied for her first lectureship, was promoted to senior lecturer a few years later and eventually became Head of Law in 2014 before moving institutions in 2016. Academia felt less alien and more exciting than practice, but tensions were apparent from the start.[32] Working as a researcher in a research group that had very little to do with teaching, or students generally, highlighted the sometimes, stark distinctions between teaching and research and the way the two camps viewed each other. It removed the group and the researchers within it from the core of the university and into a self-important bubble isolated from the excitement and ideas learning and teaching activities can bring. Moving from that to a teaching intensive institution and programme highlighted the challenges in carrying out academic research without the backing of funded projects and dedicated research staff. Being an all-round academic is, and always has been, a balancing act. Being a female, openly gay all-round academic maybe even more so.

Doug commenced his law degree as a mature student[33] at a Russell Group university. Doug was already an established senior nurse, with his interest in law arising from practical events on the unit he ran. Doug's early education was disrupted by his parents' travel. His father was in the military, thus numerous schools followed. His career advice was rooted in the experience life in the 1980s in North England and the family military background. The advice was to enlist and going to university was not a blip on Doug's horizon

---

31 Jessica Guth, 'My Conversation Choices and Chances: Becoming a Law Lecturer in the 21st Century' (2008) 6 (1) Journal of Commonwealth Law and Legal Education, 41–54.

32 Jessica Guth, 'The Case for Time Turners – The Practicalities of Being a New Law Lecturer' (2009) 43 (2) The Law Teacher, 185–199.

33 A mature student is a person who has started their first undergraduate degree course aged 21 or over.

Who are law schools for? 119

at this point. When he commenced his undergraduate degree, it was out of curiosity rather than the desire to undertake legal practice. He did well, the modules were fascinating, the lecturers supportive. Doug continued his nursing job throughout this time and took on a work placement at a medium-sized law firm towards the end of the degree. Overall, his experience of legal practice was not positive, communication was replaced with expected deference or subservience. Whilst billable hours were the main drivers, it was clear that legal practice, albeit premised on this firm alone, was not for him. Doug applied for a PhD in 2002 and was offered a newly developed Graduate Teaching Assistant role. The role was interesting and allowed Doug a glimpse into academia. He enjoyed the debate and the curiosity of students and his own studies. He continued working part-time as a nurse and prior to completing his PhD, successfully obtained his first law lecturer's post. This was a busy but exciting time, completing a PhD, and settling into a new role. As a senior lecturer in a post-1992 institution, his experiences are now characterised by being too busy, being mostly unsupported, and with little or no mentoring available, particularly for a research-related activity. When Doug asked about research, he was told that 'research was something you do at elite universities'. Students were, and continue to be, viewed in the language of recruitment, in essence numbers and billable assets. These reflections sadly have not changed, and whilst Doug, like Jess, enjoys his job, there are times it leaves him asking critical questions such as who am I, what impact do I have, if any, and what am I doing here?

Are law schools for us? The question for us has two strands. First, was law school a place that had us in mind as students and second, do we belong here as staff? Both of those strands are complex and about what and who law schools are for and what it feels like to be there. The data from the 1995/1996 academic year shows that there were 55,226 law students studying in the UK.[34] The majority of those were undergraduates and the statistics suggest there were 752 full-time Post Graduate Research (PGR) and around 6,000 Post Graduate Taught (PGT) students and there was a relatively even gender split across all levels.[35] While data also shows that the number of working-class students was increasing, the gap between the percentage of lower social groups and higher social groups attending higher education did not really narrow.[36] Overall, the statistics available suggest that Twining's description

---

34 HESA, 'Students in Higher Education 1995/96' (*HESA*) <https://www.hesa.ac.uk/data-and-analysis/publications/students-1995-96> accessed 11 March 2021.
35 Ibid.
36 See Helen Connor and Sara Dewson with Claire Tylers, Judith Eccles, Jo Regan and Jane Aston, 'Social Class and Higher Education: Issues Affecting Decisions on Participation by Lower Social Class Groups' (*Institute for Employment Studies, Research Report No. 267*, 2001) <https://dera.ioe.ac.uk/4621/1/RR267.pdf> accessed 04 August 2021 where the distinction is made between higher social groups and lower social groups using the 1992 Standard Occupational Coding based on parents' (father's) occupation with professional,

120 Jessica Guth and Doug Morrison

of the fictional 'Law School Rutland' for the 1991–1992 academic year would paint a fairly accurate picture of the average law school in 1995-1996 too: '52 percent women; 20 percent from independent schools (UK), 15 percent mature (over 21); 12 percent from home ethnic minorities; 20 percent from overseas'.[37] Of course, those figures hide a huge variety[38] and while the gender split seems accurate, our recollection is of a lower number of ethnic minorities and mature students and some institutions will have had significantly higher numbers of students from independent schools.[39] The numbers suggest that law schools generally were indeed for Jess but perhaps did not really have Doug in mind as a mature student with a working-class background. As students, we were less aware of the schools our peers went to or what their parents did and more conscious of the ease with which some of them seemed to navigate the legal world, obtained work experience, and understood the sometimes confusing and always unwritten rules of networking and fitting in. We often felt we were on the outside looking in. We were also conscious of the focus most of our peers showed in pursuing careers in the professions and particularly in trying to secure training contracts in Magic Circle firms. We were less conscious, or perhaps just less concerned, with the make-up of the law school staff. Stereotypes of all-female administrative teams held true and all the professors we knew were male.[40] But as students, these things seemed unimportant, we judged our teachers by their ability to teach us and by how interesting we found their classes. We understood little of the hierarchies and politics of law schools and our future careers. 'Female representation in law schools has been strong for many decades'[41] and that visibility in the junior ranks for us hid the lack of senior women

---

intermediate and skilled non-manual making up the higher group and skilled manual, semi-skilled and unskilled making up the lower group.

37 William Twining, *Blackstones's Tower: The English Law School* (Sweet and Maxwell 1994) 73.

38 The variety was captured in surveys carried out by John Wilson, 'A Third Survey of University Legal Education in the United Kingdom' (1993) 13 (2) Legal Studies, 143; and by Phil Harris, Steven Bellerby and Patricia Leighton, *A Survey of Law Teaching* (Sweet and Maxwell 1993).

39 The Oxford admission statistics, for example, suggest that around half of the students attending Oxford came from independent schools which also consistently had higher acceptance rates than other schools. See Oxford University Gazette, 'Statistical Information on the University of Oxford' (*University of Oxford*) <https://gazette.web.ox.ac.uk/statistical-information-university-oxford> accessed 11 March 2021.

40 Given that in 1997 a survey carried out by Clare McGlynn showed only 4% of law professors were women it would not be unusual for law students in the 1990s to complete their studies without encountering a female professor. See Clare McGlynn, 'Women, Representation and the Legal Academy' (1999) 19 (1) Legal Studies, 68–92; Clare McGlynn, *The Woman Lawyer: Making the Difference* (Oxford University Press 1998).

41 Liz Duff and Lisa Webley, 'Gender and the Legal Academy in the UK: A Product of Proxies and Hiring and Promotion Practices' in Ulrike Schultz, Gisela Shaw, Margaret Thornton and Rosemary Auchmuty (eds), *Gender and Careers in the Legal Academy* (Hart 2001) 63–78, 71.

Who are law schools for? 121

which only became apparent and important at later stages of our careers.[42] And just as our accrued social capital, and in Doug's case, age and prior career, hid some of our non-traditional biographies that sometimes made us feel other but allowed us to fit in nonetheless, it also allowed us the luxury of not looking for working class role models or not interrogating our teachers' biographies to try and find how we might fit or who we might be. In any event, Jess did not want to be an academic, she wanted to be a lawyer and she wanted to be a lawyer 'back home' in a small northern high street where her accent would not matter.

Jess had the right vision for the law schools described in Birks' collection, she was interested in practice and a career as a lawyer yet interested enough in law to soak up and benefit from the socio-legal, contextual, and perhaps, liberal undertones of parts of the programme she studied. Female law students were not unusual and had Jess bothered to look; there were also plenty of academic role models albeit less visible the higher up the hierarchy one looked.[43] While Doug, as a white male, inherently appeared to fit, his background, the fact that he entered the degree programme as a mature student and without a clear intention to practice law also made him an outsider. In addition, his experience in a predominantly female profession allowed him to note things that were perhaps less obvious to others. For example, he noted that practical and academic opportunities arising via the law school were aimed predominantly at male students. Jess' experience supports this with law clinic, negotiation, mooting and client interviewing positions mostly being filled by her male peers with female participants being celebrated as the exception. Many male peers had secured vacation placements and training contracts, whereas many female peers had not. Of course, these memories may not be accurate, and we do not have the data to check them, but the memories are testament to what it felt like. While admission to law school might have been fairly even, in gender terms, by the time Birks' collection was published and we started studying, the experience of studying law was certainly gendered.[44] Doug further observed female students seeking to alter regional accents or eradicate them completely over the period

---

42 See Clare McGlynn, 'Women, Representation and the Legal Academy' (1999) 19 (1) Legal Studies, 68–92; Clare McGlynn, *The Woman Lawyer: Making the Difference* (Oxford University Press 1998).

43 Liz Duff and Lisa Webley, 'Gender and the Legal Academy in the UK: A Product of Proxies and Hiring and Promotion Practices' in Ulrike Schultz, Gisela Shaw, Margaret Thornton and Rosemary Auchmuty (eds), *Gender and Careers in the Legal Academy* (Hart 2001) highlight the steepness of the career pyramid in academia as well as the lack of women in the senior ranks.

44 Goodrich alludes to this. Peter Goodrich, 'Of Blackstone's Tower: Metaphors of Distance and Histories of the English Law School' in Peter Birks (ed), *What Are Law Schools For? Vol. 2 Pressing Problems in the Law* (Oxford University Press 1996); See Elizabeth Mertz, Wamucii Njogu and Susan Gooding, 'What Difference Does Difference Make – The Challenge for Legal Education' (1998) 48 (1) Journal of Legal Education.

of their studies. The rationale offered, was that certain firms or chambers would not consider applicants with regional accents and in fact Jess' experience of being told to 'tone down' her West Yorkshire accent during a Magic Circle firm recruitment dinner shows that this was not isolated to one institution.[45] This experience of being pressurised to fit in, can therefore be seen to have some common ground and indicates that whilst access to education is one thing, egalitarianism is another, and for those wanting to remain who they are, access to practice seems an increasingly distant promise.

A Lifelong Learning UK publication from 2005 suggests that in 1995-1996, there were 1,560 law staff but the publication does not provide a breakdown by gender or any other personal characteristics.[46] The available Higher Education Statistics Agency (HESA) data suggests that male staff far outnumbered female staff but that the number of women was rising slowly.[47] The statistics bear out our memories, and in doing so question the validity of the picture painted by Birks' collection. It seems more accurate to think about law schools of differing size, with increasing inclusivity, in terms of gender, social class, cultural, and ethnic diversity, as well as focus. Some schools boldly and successfully took a different approach to the mainstream one[48] and others focused much more explicitly on vocational and perhaps narrowly drawn curricula (predominantly new universities), whereas others encompassed a wider notion of what law is and what should be taught on law degrees (predominantly old universities). Law schools were beginning to be places for a much more diverse student body than Birks' collection suggests, or at least some law schools were. The same trend cannot be seen in legal practice causing a further problem for the diversification of law schools: those law schools seeing the majority of working class and ethnic minority students in their intake tend to be the more vocationally focused law schools but in spite of (or because of?) that focus, graduates from these law schools are also less likely to secure training contracts with the most prestigious firms.[49]

Access to the legal academy is an under-researched area and we know little about this at the micro or macro levels. For both of us, it was, in the

---

45 There is also more recent evidence that this issue has not gone away. See Melanie Reynolds, 'Working-Class Lecturers Should Come Out of the Closet' (*The Guardian*, 10 September 2018) <https://www.theguardian.com/commentisfree/2018/sep/10/university-working-class-divide-academics> accessed 13 March 2021.

46 Lifelong Learning UK, 'Higher Education Provision in the United Kingdom: An Analysis of HE Workforce Data' (2005) <https://dera.ioe.ac.uk/2340/1/he_report_05_12_22.pdf> accessed 11 March 2021.

47 HESA, 'Resources of Higher Education 2005/06' (HESA) < https://www.hesa.ac.uk/data-and-analysis/publications/resources-2005-06> accessed 04 August 2021.

48 See Celia Wells, *A Woman in Law: Reflections on Gender, Class and Politics* (Waterside Press 2019) who notes the radical approach taken by Warwick for example.

49 Jessica Guth and Kathryn Dutton, 'SQE-ezed Out: SRA, Status and Stasis' (2018) 52 (4) The Law Teacher, 425–438.

Who are law schools for? 123

end, relatively smooth. But for both of us, thriving in the academy has not been straightforward. Goodrich in Birks' collection notes that 'English Law Schools remain hierarchical, homosocial, ethnocentric and masculine domains'[50] and that goes some way to explaining the slight otherness we felt as students. We also believe that not that much has changed.[51] The HESA data shows us that in the 2018-2019 academic year, there were 6,140 academic staff working in law.[52] The gender balance has shifted with slightly more female than male staff (3,225 and 2,951 respectively) and most of us work full-time although a significant number (2,275) have part-time contracts. The statistics further suggest that we are also overwhelmingly white and not disabled.[53] While the number of female, openly LGBTQ+, ethnic minority, and disabled staff might have increased, it seems law school cultures are slower to change and embrace us all.[54] Not only do we sometimes wonder how a female average A-level student from a comprehensive school in an underprivileged area of West Yorkshire and a male mature student with a working-class background ended up with Russell Group PhDs and whether that would be possible now, but also our biographies force us to constantly ask who we are and whether our places of work really are for us. The answer is inevitably complex. We were appointed to our positions and therefore belong. We are part of the law school which we inhabit and thus take part in shaping it, but we are also other. We are academics in a vocationally focussed school, we are educators in a system of content delivery, we are focused on individual learning and journeys in a world of standardized metrics, and we are colleagues rather than competitors. We are researchers but perhaps researchers at the margins and we are teaching-focused with little interest in teaching for preparation for the professions. Our profiles clearly fit some institutions better than others but wherever we might see our fit, tensions remain. Goodrich's description of the trauma and insignificance

---

50 Peter Goodrich, 'Of Blackstone's Tower: Metaphors of Distance and Histories of the English Law School' in Peter Birks (ed), *What Are Law Schools For? Vol. 2 Pressing Problems in the Law* (Oxford University Press 1996) 68.
51 See Richard Collier, 'Rethinking Men, Masculinities and the Legal Academy: Or, Whatever Happened to the 'Nutty Professor?' in Ulrike Schultz, Gisela Shaw, Margaret Thornton and Rosemary Auchmuty, *Gender and Careers in the Legal Academy* (Hart 2001) 513; Hilary Sommerlad, 'Patriarchal Discourses in the UK Legal Academy: The Case of the Reasonable Man' in Ulrike Schultz, Gisela Shaw, Margaret Thornton and Rosemary Auchmuty (eds), *Gender and Careers in the Legal Academy* (Hart 2001) 531; See also Liz Duff and Lisa Webley, 'Gender and the Legal Academy in the UK: A Product of Proxies and Hiring and Promotion Practices' in Ulrike Schultz, Gisela Shaw, Margaret Thornton and Rosemary Auchmuty (eds), *Gender and Careers in the Legal Academy* (Hart 2001).
52 HESA, 'Higher Education Staff Data' (HESA) <https://www.hesa.ac.uk/data-and-analysis/staff> accessed 04 August 2021.
53 Ibid.
54 Liz Duff and Lisa Webley, 'Gender and the Legal Academy in the UK: A Product of Proxies and Hiring and Promotion Practices' in Ulrike Schultz, Gisela Shaw, Margaret Thornton and Rosemary Auchmuty (eds), *Gender and Careers in the Legal Academy* (Hart 2001).

124 *Jessica Guth and Doug Morrison*

of the law school experience goes some way to capturing the dissonance we, along with many other legal academics, sometimes feel as we seek to understand what law school is for and what our place within that mission might be: through elitism, isolation, relentless competitiveness and the maintenance of male hegemony, or homosociality, the law school reproduces the reasonable man, the black letter lawyer with the dull white face.[55] But that is not us. Law schools still do not really feel like they are for us, whether we inhabit them or not.[56]

Law schools in a time of crisis: who really matters?

The previous two sections have highlighted that, although Birks' collection was perhaps not an accurate picture of law schools when it was published, some of the issues arising from it suggest that law schools were and remain complex places. They seem to be for students who want to be lawyers, and by lawyers we usually mean solicitors and barristers; they seem to be for people, students, and staff alike, who have the social capital and crucially also the financial capital to access them and understand the complexities of different types of law schools and where they might best fit. Different law schools seem to be for different people, but that difference is one based on perceived quality rather than difference in purpose or approach. Overall, the key 'product' law schools offer is the undergraduate LLB which is held out to be very similar and equivalent across the sector. However, recent events and developments, perhaps even crisis points, have put into focus that law schools are still very much grappling with issues of diversity and who and what exactly they are for. The introduction of the SQE, Brexit, the Covid-19 pandemic, and perhaps also, the Black Lives Matter movement highlight how little we have moved on. Law schools might look different now but perhaps they do not feel much different, particularly to those of us who have always felt like we do not quite belong.

The introduction of the SQE has re-ignited the debates about what exactly the link between law schools and, in particular, undergraduate legal education and the professions should be. The reaction by the legal academy to the introduction of a centralised assessment for aspiring solicitors is interesting because in theory, the SQE has no impact on what undergraduate degrees include or the approach they take and because if anything the removal of requirements of a Qualifying Law Degree (QLD) provide more

---

55 Ibid.
56 What is striking of course is how many legal academics feel like this. Anecdotal conversations around fit and belonging as well as imposter syndrome as well as a mismatch between the values of individual academics and those espoused by our institutions suggest that many of us feel like outsiders in our law schools and our discipline at some point during our careers. The increasing well-being literature sheds some light on this but systematic research in this area is needed to fully understand these aspects of law school life.

freedom rather than less. Nonetheless, law schools across the country felt compelled to react to the SQE reinforcing the notion that law school and the professions are inextricably linked, and law schools are for aspiring legal practitioners. However, the way law schools are reacting differs widely with some predominantly research-intensive institutions simply explaining how what they already do can help prepare students for the SQE and most others incorporating elements of SQE preparation to a greater or lesser degree into their programme structures.[57] This has significant implications. Guth and Mason have noted the violence done to our discipline[58] and Mason explores how the SQE focuses on bivalent responses thus ushering in an impoverished vision of law, which he terms 'Bleak Legal Realism'.[59] This view of law ignores not only how legal truths are created or identified[60] but also the laws' socially constructed nature. It must be acknowledged that Mason's paper seeks to explore what it might mean to say 'a proposition of law is true correct or valid...and how we might test that ability to identify and construct such propositions'.[61] Mason views the Solicitors Regulation Authority's (SRA) shift to SQE as fervent evangelism, underpinned by the belief that they are the arbiter of legal knowledge and legal truth. On a macro level, this revelation simply reinforces earlier submissions, around power and lack of diversity. However, on a micro level, it reveals a profession seeking to ground its power premised on their own view of themselves and the skills required to do the job. This view of law, and by default who

---

57 Much of the information about the response to the SQE has been heavily guarded as commercially sensitive so it is difficult at this stage to know exactly who is doing what. However, the submission by the 4 Learned Associations to the Legal Services Board in January 2018 alludes to this: Association of Law Teachers, 'The SRA's Application to the LSB for Approval of the SQE: Submission to the LSB by the Four Law Subject Associations' (*Association of Law Teachers*, 2018) <http://lawteacher.ac.uk/wp-content/uploads/2020/04/Law_Subject_Associations_Submission_to_LSB.pdf> accessed 02 April 2021 and the following hint at the same point. Richard Bowyer, 'Regulatory Threats to the Law Degree: The Solicitors Qualifying Examination and the Purpose of Law Schools' (2019) 30 Law Critique, 117–121; Andrew Gilbert, 'Preparing for the Exam – Law School Websites and the SQE' (*Association of Law Teachers blog*, 9 October 2020) <http://lawteacher.ac.uk/sqe/preparing-for-the-exam-law-school-websites-and-the-sqe/> accessed 04 April 2021; Caroline Strevens, 'Implementing the SQE – Some Thoughts' (*Association of Law Teachers blog*, 1 December 2020) <http://lawteacher.ac.uk/sqe/implementing-the-sqe-some-thoughts/> accessed 04 April 2021.
58 See Luke Mason and Jessica Guth, 'Editorial Re-Claiming Our Discipline' (2018) 52 (4) The Law Teacher, 379–383, 383.
59 Luke Mason, 'SQEezing the Jurisprudence Out of the SRA's Super Exam: The SQE's Bleak Legal Realism and the Rejection of the Law's Multimodal Truth' (2018) 52 (4) The Law Teacher, 379–383, 410.
60 Ibid.
61 Luke Mason, 'SQEezing the Jurisprudence Out of the SRA's Super Exam: The SQE's Bleak Legal Realism and the Rejection of the Law's Multimodal Truth' (2018) 52 (4) The Law Teacher, 379–383, 411.

126 Jessica Guth and Doug Morrison

should practice law, reduces the practice to simple prognostication,[62] based on true or false,[63] a position more amenable to the application of an algorithm. In doing so, SQE 1 omits not only the laws' socially constructed nature but also the critical thinking[64] and soft skills[65] actually required of professional and client interaction. Law in the form of SQE 1 is reductionist at best and Pavlovian at worst and is in danger of creating a nightmare vision of legal worker drones excluded and unable to reference and 'recognise ambiguity and deal with uncertainty in the law'.[66] This analysis fits with the language of 'Bleak Legal Realism', and arguably extends further, in that what is taught is what the law is, rather than what the law ought to be, and is a view, cannot be countenanced. Law schools embracing the SQE reveal what they are – schools for practitioners of law with an interest in legal practice.[67] Paradoxically those schools will not be for people who want to enter the legal profession at the prestigious end, as they will still seek graduates who have been to law schools which have not pushed criticality or creativity out of their curriculum in favour of 'bleak legal realism'.[68] This view of law schools and legal practice is arguably not that far-fetched. Whilst the aim of

62 This view is echoed by Luke Mason, 'SQEezing the Jurisprudence Out of the SRA's Super Exam: The SQE's Bleak Legal Realism and the Rejection of the Law's Multimodal Truth' (2018) 52 (4) The Law Teacher, 379–383, 423, who submits it is an exercise in predicative justice.

63 Ibid, 411. This analysis reveals not only the failure of the profession to recall the role of the appellate courts in so called 'hard cases' but also some form of professional amnesia, as if all that was taught has been forgotten, whilst the so-called practice theory gap, seems inversely applied.

64 Luke Mason, 'SQEezing the Jurisprudence Out of the SRA's Super Exam: The SQE's Bleak Legal Realism and the Rejection of the Law's Multimodal Truth' (2018) 52 (4) The Law Teacher, 379–383; Jessica Guth and Kathryn Dutton, 'SQE-ezed Out: SRA, Status and Stasis' (2018) 52 (4) The Law Teacher, 425–438; Doug Morrison, 'The SQE and Creativity: A Race to the Bottom?' (2018) 52 (4) The Law Teacher, 476–477.

65 Stuart Toddington, 'Chapter 6 The Emperor's New Skills: The Academy, The Profession and the Idea of Legal Education' in Peter Birks (ed), *What Are Law Schools For? Vol. 2 Pressing Problems in the Law* (Oxford University Press 1996) 69–90, Arguably some of the soft skills are assessed through SQE 2 but this is doubtful. The skills tested in SQE 2 are practical legal skills and the interactions that are required can largely be scripted and rehearsed and will not necessarily capture genuine soft skills or people skills. Further research on the link between soft skills and the SQE 2 is required to understand this fully though.

66 Luke Mason, 'SQEezing the Jurisprudence Out of the SRA's Super Exam: the SQE's Bleak Legal Realism and the Rejection of the Law's Multimodal Truth' (2018) 52 (4) The Law Teacher, 379–383; QAA, 'Subject Benchmark Statement: Law (2019) <https://www.qaa. ac.uk/docs/qaa/subject-benchmark-statements/subject-benchmark-statement-law> accessed on 11 March 2021.

67 Ben Waters, 'The Solicitors Qualification Examination: Something for All? Some Challenges Facing Law Schools in England and Wales' (2018) 52 (4) The Law Teacher, 519.

68 Luke Mason, 'SQEezing the Jurisprudence Out of the SRA's Super Exam: The SQE's Bleak Legal Realism and the Rejection of the Law's Multimodal Truth' (2018) 52 (4) The Law Teacher, 379–383; Jessica Guth and Kathryn Dutton, 'SQE-ezed Out: SRA, Status

higher education in recent years may well be to increase access through the widening participation agenda, the reality is that it continues to be the domain of the higher socio-economic classes, especially in the context of elite or traditional universities.[69] Such conclusions resonate with the findings of Hussey and Smith, who note that

> whilst universities are reporting success in widening participation, there exists an apparent polarisation between those universities attracting working-class and minority ethnic students and those attracting the traditional university constituency.[70]

In the context of law, this lack of diversity is fatal. The importance of legal diversity is summed up by Guth and Dutton, for them and us, such diversity is crucial not only to the functioning of society but also to the furtherance of social justice.[71] Failure to achieve this means that widening participation, far from equating to equality of opportunity in higher education and law schools in particular,[72] can only be seen as a tool of obstruction and legal protectionism, in which diversity is both rhetorical and illusionary.[73] A conclusion which finds real-world support from the creation by students of [the] 93% Club,[74] whose name refers to the 93% of students who are state educated. It is seeking to raise awareness of what Guth and Dutton refer to as higher education and more specifically law's perpetuation of social dislocation, by failing to recruit into university and beyond already unrepresented social groups.[75]

---

and Stasis' (2018) 52 (4) The Law Teacher, 425–438; Doug Morrison, 'The SQE and Creativity: A Race to the Bottom?' (2018) 52 (4) The Law Teacher, 476–477.

69 Jessica Guth and Kathryn Dutton, 'SQE-ezed Out: SRA, Status and Stasis' (2018) 52 (4) The Law Teacher, 425–438, 429. See also Andrew Francis, 'Legal Education, Social Mobility, and Employability: Possible Selves, Curriculum Intervention, and the Role of Legal Work Experience' (2015) 42 (2) Journal of Law and Society, 173.

70 Trevor Hussey and Patrick Smith, *The Trouble with Higher Education: A Critical Examination of Our Universities* (Routledge 2010) 11.

71 Jessica Guth and Kathryn Dutton, 'SQE-ezed Out: SRA, Status and Stasis' (2018) 52 (4) The Law Teacher, 425–438, 426.

72 Ibid.

73 Ibid.

74 Ninety-Three Percent Club (LinkedIn) <https://www.linkedin.com/in/93clublaw/> accessed 5 March 2021, The club was originally formed by Sophie Pender at the University of Bristol. The 93% refers to those who undertake a state education. The 7% private education. The latter indicates wealth, social connections and parental as well as school networking. It is perhaps unsurprising that what is revealed is that 50% of doctors and 74% of judges are privately educated. For those disciplines, and in particular law, the concept of egalitarianism is clearly lacking.

75 Jessica Guth and Kathryn Dutton, 'SQE-ezed Out: SRA, Status and Stasis' (2018) 52 (4) The Law Teacher, 425–438, 426.

The impact of the UK's exit from the European Union is yet to be measured if it can ever be. If Langbein was correct that European integration 'has touched every field of English law, ... profoundly',[76] then the exit from the European Union is likely to have a similar impact and importantly that impact will be on law schools as well as the law itself. The Campaign for Social Science highlights clearly that if a significant proportion of EU nationals were to leave, UK law schools would face a significant drop in staff who offer experience of different legal systems and traditions as well as significant subject expertise.[77] That impact will not be the same across the sector. Guth and Hervey set out the potential threats Brexit brings and aptly summarise our concerns:

> Brexit represents a challenge to the values and identities that we express as law schools across the board in the UK: what we believe to be important about legal education, at least as a minimum level of agreement; and what that means for both what we do and who we are. [...]. Who we are again includes both a very mundane and practical sense of how the staff and students within each of our law schools understand their identities, but also the less mundane question of how we understand ourselves as communities of legal learners, scholars, and teachers. Brexit, over time, will force a greater diversification of legal education in the UK, where an internationalised curriculum (at least in the weaker sense of Europeanised legal education) is no longer part of what we all do, and who we all are.[78]

Just as Brexit is shining a light on the parochial and domestic nature of much of the law taught in our law schools,[79] the Black Lives Matter protests brought into sharp focus the extent to which they are colonial and often racist places. Following the murder of George Floyd in the United States on 25 May 2020 and the outpouring of grief and anger which followed across the world, some universities and individual university departments issued state-

---

76 John H Langbein, 'Chapter 1, Scholarly and Professional Objectives in Legal Education: American Trends and English Comparisons' in Peter Birks (ed), *What Are Law Schools For? Vol. 2 Pressing Problems in the Law* (Oxford University Press 1996) 3.

77 Ashley Lenihan and Sharon Witherspoon, 'A World of Talent: International Staff at UK Universities & The Future Migration System' (*Campaign for Social Science*, 2018) <https://campaignforsocialscience.org.uk/publications/a-world-of-talent/> accessed 1 February 2019; See also British Academy, 'Brexit Means...? The British Academy's Priorities for the Humanities and Social Sciences in the Current Negotiations' (British Academy, 2017) <https://www.thebritishacademy.ac.uk/sites/default/files/Brexit%20Means...TheBritishAcademy%27sPrioritiesForTheHumanitiesandSocialSciencesInTheCurrentNeogtiations.pdf> accessed 1 February 2019.

78 Jessica Guth and Tamara Hervey, 'Threats to Internationalised Legal Education in the Twenty-First Century UK' (2018) 52 (3) The Law Teacher, 350–370, 362.

79 Ibid.

Who are law schools for? 129

ments condemning racism and showing support for their black and ethnic minority students. Very few law schools made separate statements[80] and all institutions were arguably quite slow to react, something acknowledged in De Montfort University's statement posted on 5 June:

> Quite rightly, a significant number of people have been in touch this week to ask us why we have not released a statement. Please be assured, we have heard your voices and we hope our community will understand this delay was based on our desire to be authentic and not present a virtue-signalling statement.[81]

But in most cases, it is difficult to see how the statements made can be anything other than fairly cynical virtue-signalling which in some ways may be worse than not saying anything. Law schools on the whole failed to recognise the trauma caused to black and brown students in particular or offered support.[82] More fundamentally law school curricula remain colonial and predominantly white and dominated by discussions of law which do not acknowledge, never mind challenge, the contested nature of law, the violence that has been done and continues to be done by exporting legal concepts and ideas, or the alternative ways we could think about legal history, contemporary legal problems and who shapes those stories. While most university law schools are likely to have had some discussions about decolonising the curriculum or making the curriculum more inclusive generally, there is a

---

80 Some notable exceptions include: University of Oxford Faculty of Law, 'Anti-Racism Statement from the Law Faculty' (*University of Oxford*, 5 June 2020) <https://www.law.ox.ac.uk/news/2020-06-05-anti-racist-statement-law-faculty> accessed 13 March 2021; University College London Faculty of Law, 'UCL Laws Statement in Solidarity with Our Black Students, Staff and Alumni Around the World' (*University College London*) <https://www.ucl.ac.uk/laws/about/ucl-laws-statement-solidarity-our-black-students-staff-and-alumni-around-world> accessed 13 March 2021; University of Westminster Law School, 'Westminster Law School Supports the Black Lives Matter Movement: Stops the Silence Around Privilege, Racism and Decolonisation' (*University of Westminster*) <https://www.westminster.ac.uk/news/westminster-law-school-supports-the-black-lives-matter-movement-stops-the-silence-around-privilege > accessed 13 March 2021 which also held an event

81 De Montfort University, 'Black Lives Matter: De Montfort University Open Letter to Our Staff and Student Community' (*De Montfort University*, 5 June 2020) <https://www.dmu.ac.uk/about-dmu/news/2020/june/black-lives-matter-de-montfort-university-open-letter-to-our-staff-and-student-community.aspx> accessed 13 March 2021.

82 There were some exceptions with students being offered extensions for coursework or pointed to university support services such as seen in the examples in Jessica Guth and Tamara Hervey, 'Threats to Internationalised Legal Education in the Twenty-First Century UK' (2018) 52 (3) The Law Teacher, 350–370 and also in The University of Law, 'Black Lives Matter: Our Statement' (*The University of Law*) <https://www.law.ac.uk/resources/black-lives-matter/> accessed 06 August 2021; University of Warwick, 'WLS Statement: Racial Trauma' (*University of Warwick*) <https://warwick.ac.uk/fac/soc/law/aboutus/equality-diversity-inclusion/racialtrauma/> accessed 06 August 2021.

130   *Jessica Guth and Doug Morrison*

real risk that these are superficial, driven by needing to be seen to change rather than by a genuine desire to change.[83] Foluke Adebisi notes that 'decolonial thought in legal education [...] gives us an opportunity to look at our law schools and re-examine what is present, what is absent, what is silent and where our hope lies'.[84] Our concern is that for many law schools, decolonising simply means adding a few 'alternative' sources to the reading lists, changing a lecture to specifically consider indigenous rights or maybe having a seminar on slavery during black history month. In doing so, we reinforce the absences and silences rather than re-examining them, and in doing so, we remove all hope for our black and brown students and colleagues to see themselves reflected in the lives of our law schools. The hope is for us all to gain a richer (and more real) understanding of

> exactly how the past bleeds into the present, how we walk side by side with histories' ghosts, how we breathe coloniality every day, how our collective history is literally present in every single thing we do.[85]

The Covid-19 pandemic serves as a further reminder that law schools' white male, able-bodied and relatively financially privileged heritage impacts on who thrives in law schools today. Emerging research suggests that women in the academy have been hardest hit as they have juggled working with carer commitments,[86] whereas many men have been able to increase productivity by working from home.[87] What is most telling though are the assumptions many law schools appear to have made about who we are as staff and students. It was assumed that staff would have space at home to set up an office suitable for teaching, that we had the equipment or would purchase it ourselves, that our broadband was sufficiently powerful and stable and that we would be able to carry on business as usual but from a different place. The assumptions hardly hold true for academics, maybe particularly junior academics who are precariously employed, poorly paid and share space with others in similar positions. Similar assumptions were made about students. While the learning gap between poor and not poor children has been

---

83 For notable exceptions see the contributions to Foluke Adebisi (ed), *Special Issue: Decolonising the Law School* (2020) 54 (4) The Law Teacher.
84 Foluke Adebisi (ed), *Special Issue: Decolonising the Law School* (2020) 54 (4) The Law Teacher.
85 Ibid.
86 Chris Smith and Deirdre Watchorn, 'The Pandemic Is Making It Harder for Researchers but Women Are Hit the Hardest: 4 Findings from 80 Countries' (*London School of Economics and Political Science Impact Blog*, 17 September 2020) <https://blogs.lse.ac.uk/impactofsocialsciences/2020/09/17/the-pandemic-is-making-it-harder-for-researchers-but-women-are-hit-the-hardest-4-findings-from-80-countries/> accessed 15 March 2021.
87 Ibid.

Who are law schools for? 131

highlighted,[88] less attention has been paid to the impact Covid-19 has had on university students. The adoption of face-to-face on campus teaching during Covid-19, driven seemingly more by monetary concerns than student concerns, has simply reinforced, class, gender and racial discrimination, as evidenced by lack of thought for vulnerable groups, those shielding, those with carer responsibilities or those home schooling their own children.[89] Yes, they can log on to the recorded session, but if face-to-face is that important, this approach to these students is third class. As we write, the Covid-19 pandemic is not over. The issues raised here continue and the full impact will not become clear for some time yet. In order to learn from Covid-19 and make our law schools more inclusive places, the effects on students and staff will need to be fully researched in the future.

Law schools in 2020 and 2021 have been for students who can afford stable broadband, who can join online classes, have access to materials and equipment, and a safe, quiet, and suitable place to study. Law school has not been for those clinically vulnerable, disabled, poor or without a safe place to live and study. In other words, if progress had been made, the pandemic has returned many law schools to white male elitist places,[90] arguably because most of the decisions have also been made by them.

88 Children's Commissioner, 'Tackling the Disadvantage Gap During the Covid-19 Crisis' (*Children's Commissioner*, 22 April 2020) <https://www.childrenscommissioner.gov.uk/report/tackling-the-disadvantage-gap-during-the-covid-19-crisis/> accessed 15 March 2021; Education Endowment Foundation, 'Covid-19 Resources' (*Education Endowment Foundation*). <https://educationendowmentfoundation.org.uk/covid-19-resources/best-evidence-on-impact-of-school-closures-on-the-attainment-gap/> accessed 15 March 2021.

89 Anna Fazackerley, 'UK Universities 'Bullying' Junior Staff into Face-to-Face Teaching' (*The Guardian*, London, 25 September 2020) <https://www.theguardian.com/education/2020/sep/25/uk-universities-bullying-junior-staff-into-face-to-face-teaching> accessed 30 April 2021; Anna Fazackerley, "UK Universities Putting Finances above Student Safety, Expert Warns' (*The Guardian*, London, 1 August 2020) <https://www.theguardian.com/education/2020/aug/01/uk-universities-putting-finances-above-student-safety-expert-warns> accessed 30 April 2021; Anna Fazackerley, "UK Universities Wooing New Students with Upbeat Promises of a 'Totally Open Campus'" (*The Guardian*, London, 27 March 2020) <https://www.theguardian.com/education/2021/mar/27/uk-universities-new-students-upbeat-promises-totally-open-campus-covid> accessed 30 April 2021; Anna McKie, 'Covid: UK Union Calls for Teaching to Stay Online All Next Term' (*Times Higher Education*, 24 December 2020) <https://www.timeshighereducation.com/news/covid-uk-union-calls-teaching-stay-online-all-next-term> accessed 30 April 2021.

90 Research into the impact of the pandemic and actions taken to remedy that impact will have to take into account the differing impacts on different student groups and acknowledge that women, black and ethnic minority students, disabled students and those with working class backgrounds will have experienced the pandemic differently and will likely need more and different support in order to once again thrive in their chosen law school.

Conclusions: the more things change the more they stay the same

The proposition that the more things change the more they stay the same may be viewed merely as cynicism. However, Birks' collection read together with our own biographies and the literature on law schools supports the claim in various ways. The relationship between the professions and the academy continues to be a key theme which the SQE has brought into sharp focus. The vocational versus liberal legal education debate has been fuelled anew, this time with an increased risk of splitting the sector into those who say they prepare students for the SQE and thus offer students a 'bleak legal realism' and those elite institutions who will continue to offer a broader education and provide opportunities for their students to enter the elite ranks for the professions. The impact is likely to further decrease diversity, based on class, gender, and race and reduce opportunities for many by limiting access to some parts of the profession.[91] The picture serves to reflect the gloomy predication of Birk's collection of 'the professions ambition to marginalise (to professionalise) legal education'.[92]

The focus on research as key to what university law schools do has also not gone away. However, the assertion that teaching and research cannot be de-coupled perhaps no longer holds true. There are some institutions that are teaching only institutions, and in almost all institutions, there are legal academics on teaching contracts rather than teaching and research contracts.[93] While this might not in itself be problematic if the two academic tracks are seen as of equal value and rewarded as such, despite the rhetoric this is not the case. Generally, research intensive institutions are seen as more prestigious and elite and teaching only staff as lesser than their research active counterparts. A change from Birk's collection might be the focus on research which brings in grant funding and has demonstrable impact as the most valuable and important research. Law schools therefore value those who produce research outputs which impact the most. However,

---

91 Jessica Guth and Kathryn Dutton, 'SQE-ezed Out: SRA, Status and Stasis' (2018) 52 (4) The Law Teacher, 425–438.

92 Gareth Jones, 'Traditional Legal Scholarship: A Personal View' in Peter Birks (ed), *What Are Law Schools For? Vol. 2 Pressing Problems in the Law* (Oxford University Press 1996) 15.

93 Stefan Collini, 'Covid-19 Show Up UK Universities' Shameful Employment Practices' (*The Guardian*, London, 28 April 2020) <https://www.theguardian.com/education/2020/apr/28/covid-19-shows-up-uk-universities-shameful-employment-practices> accessed 04 May 2021; Simon Baker, 'Teaching-Only Contracts: 20,000 Moved on to Terms in Five Years' (*Times Higher Education*, 19 January 2021) <https://www.timeshighereducation.com/news/teaching-only-contracts-20000-moved-terms-five-years> accessed 04 May 2021; University and College Union, 'Second Class Academic Citizens: The Dehumanising Effects of Casualisation in Higher Education' (2020) <https://www.ucu.org.uk/media/10681/second_class_academic_citizens/pdf/secondclassacademiccitizens> accessed 04 May 2021.

there is other work to be done in law schools too and who does what work is gendered and impacts on different groups differently. As a result, women, black, ethnic minority and working-class staff often have far fewer opportunities and much less time to develop their research as they are taking on more pastoral and citizenship work.[94] Our reflections have shown that the unease we felt reading Birk's collection today is justified, that the concerns around a lack of diversity, implicit (at best) elitism and the nature of the relationship between the professions and the academy and the impact that has on the nature of law degrees all feel familiar because they are still important issues. While we can perhaps now say that law schools overall can be for everyone, not all law schools are for all of us and the implications of that are most keenly felt by those already underrepresented in what are perceived to be the most prestigious and the best elements of the academy and the professions. Birks was right when he said '[law schools] facilitate research and publication, they teach, and they run themselves'.[95] We now need to do more systematic research to capture issues around class and gender but also around race, disability, sexual orientation and any other markers of our identities and all of their intersections. We need to move the conversations on, to fully understand the different ways different groups experience those key activities in different settings, how we all negotiate them and how we can help all those working and studying in law schools to thrive.

Bibliography

Adams T, Jones S, and Ellis C, *Autoethnography* (Oxford University Press 2015).
Adebisi F (ed), Special Issue: Decolonising the Law School (2020) 54(4) *The Law Teacher* 471–474.
Anderson P and Williams J (ed), *Identity and Difference in Higher Education: Outsiders Within* (Ashgate 2001).
Anderson S, Murray L, and Maharg P, *Minority and Social Diversity in Legal Education in Scotland* (Scottish Executive 2003).
Association of Law Teachers, '*The SRA's Application to the LSB for Approval of the SQE: Submission to the LSB by the Four Law Subject Associations*' (*Association of Law Teachers*, 2018) <http://lawteacher.ac.uk/wp-content/uploads/2020/04/Law_Subject_Associations_Submission_to_LSB.pdf> accessed 2 April 2021.
Auchmuty R, 'Early Women Law Students at Cambridge and Oxford' (2008) 29(1) *Journal of Legal History* 63–97.
Baker S, 'Teaching-Only Contracts: 20,000 Moved on to Terms in Five Years' (*Times Higher Education*, 19 January 2021) <https://www.timeshighereducation.com/

---

94 Liz Duff and Lisa Webley, 'Gender and the Legal Academy in the UK: A Product of Proxies and Hiring and Promotion Practices' in Ulrike Schultz, Gisela Shaw, Margaret Thornton and Rosemary Auchmuty (eds), *Gender and Careers in the Legal Academy* (Hart 2001).
95 Peter Birks (ed), *What Are Law Schools For? Vol. 2 Pressing Problems in the Law* (Oxford University Press 1996) vi.

news/teaching-only-contracts-20000-moved-terms-five-years> accessed 4 May 2021.

Birks P (ed), *What Are Law Schools For? Vol. 2 Pressing Problems in the Law* (Oxford University Press 1996).

Bowyer R, 'Regulatory Threats to the Law Degree: The Solicitors Qualifying Examination and the Purpose of Law Schools' (2019) 30 *Law Critique* 117–121.

British Academy, 'Brexit Means...? The British Academy's Priorities for the Humanities and Social Sciences in the Current Negotiations' (British Academy, 2017) <https://www.thebritishacademy.ac.uk/sites/default/files/Brexit%20Means...TheBritishAcademy%27sPrioritiesForTheHumanitiesandSocialSciencesInThe-CurrentNeogtiations.pdf> accessed 1 February 2019.

Children's Commissioner, 'Tackling the Disadvantage Gap during the Covid-19 Crisis' (*Children's Commissioner,* 22 April 2020) <https://www.childrenscommissioner.gov.uk/report/tackling-the-disadvantage-gap-during-the-covid-19-crisis/> accessed 15 March 2021.

Collier R, '"Nutty Professors", "Men in Suits", and "New Entrepreneurs": Corporeality, Subjectivity and Change in the Law School and Legal Practice' (1998) 7(1) *Social and Legal Studies* 27–53.

Collier R, 'Rethinking Men, Masculinities and the Legal Academy: Or, Whatever Happened to the 'Nutty Professor?' in Ulrike Schultz, Gisela Shaw, Margaret Thornton, and Rosemary Auchmuty (eds), *Gender and Careers in the Legal Academy* (Hart 2001) 513.

Collier R, 'The Changing University and the (Legal) Academic Career – Rethinking the Relationship Between Women, Men and the "Private Life" of the Law School' (2002) 22(1) *Legal Studies* 1–32.

Collini S, 'Covid-19 Show Up UK Universities' Shameful Employment Practices' *(the Guardian,* London, 28 April 2020) <https://www.theguardian.com/education/2020/apr/28/covid-19-shows-up-uk-universities-shameful-employment-practices> accessed 4 May 2021.

Connor H and Dewson S with Tylers C, Eccles J, Regan J, and Aston J, 'Social Class and Higher Education: Issues Affecting Decisions on Participation by Lower Social Class Groups' (Institute for Employment Studies, Research Report No. 267, 2001) <https://dera.ioe.ac.uk/4621/1/RR267.pdf> accessed 4 August 2021.

Cownie F, *Legal Academics: Culture and Identities* (Hart Publishing 2004).

De Montfort University, 'Black Lives Matter: De Montfort University Open Letter to Our Staff and Student Community' *(De Montfort University,* 5 June 2020) <https://www.dmu.ac.uk/about-dmu/news/2020/june/black-lives-matter-de-montfort-university-open-letter-to-our-staff-and-student-community.aspx> accessed 13 March 2021.

Deo M, *Unequal Profession: Race and Gender in Legal Academia* (Stanford University Press 2019).

Duff L and Webley L, 'Gender and the Legal Academy in the UK: A Product of Proxies and Hiring and Promotion Practices' in Ulrike Schultz, Gisela Shaw, Margaret Thornton, and Rosemary Auchmuty (eds), *Gender and Careers in the Legal Academy* (Hart 2001).

Education Endowment Foundation, 'Covid-19 Resources' *(Education Endowment Foundation)* <https://educationendowmentfoundation.org.uk/covid-19-resources/best-evidence-on-impact-of-school-closures-on-the-attainment-gap/> accessed 15 March 2021.

Fazackerley A, 'UK Universities "Bullying" Junior Staff into Face-to-Face Teaching' *the Guardian* (London, 25 September 2020) <https://www.theguardian.com/education/2020/sep/25/uk-universities-bullying-junior-staff-into-face-to-face-teaching> accessed 30 April 2021.

Fazackerley A, "UK Universities Putting Finances above Student Safety, Expert Warns' *the Guardian* (London, 1 August 2020) <https://www.theguardian.com/education/2020/aug/01/uk-universities-putting-finances-above-student-safety-expert-warns> accessed 30 April 2021.

Fazackerley A, 'UK Universities Wooing New Students with Upbeat Promises of a "Totally Open Campus"' *The Guardian* (London, 27 March 2020) <https://www.theguardian.com/education/2021/mar/27/uk-universities-new-students-upbeat-promises-totally-open-campus-covid> accessed 30 April 2021.

Feagin J and Ducey K, *Elite White Men Ruling, Who, What, When, Where, and How,* (Routledge 2017).

Francis A, 'Legal Education, Social Mobility, and Employability: Possible Selves, Curriculum Intervention, and the Role of Legal Work Experience' (2015) 42(2) *Journal of Law and Society* 173–201.

Gilbert A, 'Preparing for the Exam – Law School Websites and the SQE' *(Association of Law Teachers* blog, 9 October 2020) <http://lawteacher.ac.uk/sqe/preparing-for-the-exam-law-school-websites-and-the-sqe/> accessed 4 April 2021.

Goodrich P, 'Of Blackstone's Tower: Metaphors of Distance and Histories of the English Law School' in Peter Birks (ed), *What Are Law Schools For? Vol. 2 Pressing Problems in the Law* (Oxford University Press 1996).

Gregersen E, 'Exploring Autoethnography as a Method and Methodology in Legal Education Research' (2016) 3(1) *Asian Journal of Legal Education* 95–105.

Guth J 'My Conversation Choices and Chances: Becoming a Law Lecturer in the 21st Century' (2008) 6(1) *Journal of Commonwealth Law and Legal Education* 41–54.

Guth J, 'The Case for Time Turners – the Practicalities of Being a New Law Lecturer' (2009) 43(2) *The Law Teacher* 185–199.

Guth J and Dutton K, 'SQE-ezed Out: SRA, Status and Stasis' (2018) 52(4) *The Law Teacher* 425–438.

Guth J and Hervey T, 'Threats to Internationalised Legal Education in the Twenty-First Century UK' (2018) 52(3) *The Law Teacher* 350–370.

Harris P, Steven Bellerby, and Patricia Leighton, *A Survey of Law Teaching* (Sweet and Maxwell 1993).

HESA, 'Higher Education Staff Data' (HESA) <https://www.hesa.ac.uk/data-and-analysis/staff> accessed 4 August 2021.

HESA, 'Resources of Higher Education 2005/06' (HESA) <https://www.hesa.ac.uk/data-and-analysis/publications/resources-2005-06> accessed 4 August 2021.

HESA, 'Students in Higher Education 1995/96' (HESA) <https://www.hesa.ac.uk/data-and-analysis/publications/students-1995-96> accessed 11 March 2021.

Hussey T and Smith P, The Trouble with Higher Education: *A Critical Examination of Our Universities* (Routledge 2010).

Jones G, 'Traditional Legal Scholarship: A Personal View' in Peter Birks (ed), *What Are Law Schools For? Vol. 2 Pressing Problems in the Law* (Oxford University Press 1996).

Jones S, Adams T, and Ellis C (ed) *Handbook of Autoethnography* (Routledge 2016).

Langbein J, 'Chapter 1, Scholarly and Professional Objectives in Legal Education: American Trends and English Comparisons,' in Peter Birks (ed), *What Are Law Schools For? Vol. 2 Pressing Problems in the Law* (Oxford University Press 1996).

Lave J and Wenger E, *Situated Learning: Legitimate Peripheral Participation* (Cambridge University Press 1991).

Lenihan A and Witherspoon S, A World of Talent: International Staff at UK Universities & the Future Migration System (Campaign for Social Science, 2018) <https://campaignforsocialscience.org.uk/publications/a-world-of-talent/> accessed 1 February 2019.

Lifelong Learning UK, "Higher Education Provision in the United Kingdom: An Analysis of HE Workforce Data' (2005) <https://dera.ioe.ac.uk/2340/1/he_report_05_12_22.pdf> accessed 11 March 2021.

Mason L, 'SQEezing the Jurisprudence Out of the SRA's Super Exam: The SQE's Bleak Legal Realism and the Rejection of the Law's Multimodal Truth' (2018) 52(4) *The Law Teacher* 379–383, 410.

Mason L, and Guth J, 'Editorial Re-claiming our Discipline' (2018) 52(4) *The Law Teacher,* 379–383.

McGlynn C, 'Women, Representation and the Legal Academy' (1999) 19(1) *Legal Studies* 68–92.

McGlynn C, *The Woman Lawyer: Making the Difference* (Oxford University Press 1998).

McKie A, 'Covid: UK Union Calls for Teaching to Stay Online All Next Term' *(Times Higher Education, 24 December 2020)* <https://www.timeshighereducation.com/news/covid-uk-union-calls-teaching-stay-online-all-next-term> accessed 30 April 2021.

Mertz E, Njogu W, and Gooding S, 'What Difference Does Difference Make – The Challenge for Legal Education' (1998) 48(1) *Journal of Legal Education* 1–87.

Möller C, *Herkunft zählt fast immer. Soziale Ungleichheiten unter Universitätsprofessorinnen und -professoren* (Juventa 2015).

Morrison D, 'The SQE and Creativity: A Race to the Bottom?' (2018) 52(4) *The Law Teacher* 476–477.

Ninety-Three Percent Club (LinkedIn) <https://www.linkedin.com/in/93clublaw/> accessed 5 March 2021.

Oxford University Gazette, 'Statistical Information on the University of Oxford' (University of Oxford) <https://gazette.web.ox.ac.uk/statistical-information-university-oxford> accessed 11 March 2021.

QAA, 'Subject Benchmark Statement: Law (2019) <https://www.qaa.ac.uk/docs/qaa/subject-benchmark-statements/subject-benchmark-statement-law> accessed on 11 March 2021.

Reynolds M, 'Working-Class Lecturers Should Come Out of the Closet' (*The Guardian,* 10 September 2018) <https://www.theguardian.com/commentisfree/2018/sep/10/university-working-class-divide-academics> accessed 13 March 2021.

Savage N and Watt G, 'Chapter 4, A House of Intellect for the Profession,' in Peter Birks (ed), *What Are Law Schools For? Vol. 2 Pressing Problems in the Law* (Oxford University Press 1996).

Schultz U, Böning A, Peppmeier I, and Schröder S, *De jure und de facto: Professorinnen in der Rechtswissenschaft: geschlect und Wissenschaftskarriere im Rect* (Nomos 2018).

Schultz U, Shaw G, Thornton M, and Auchmuty R, *Gender and Careers in the Legal Academy* (Hart 2001).

Smith C and Watchorn D, 'The Pandemic is Making it Harder for Researchers but Women are Hit the Hardest: 4 Findings From 80 Countries' *(London School of Economics and Political Science Impact Blog,* 17 September 2020) <https://blogs.lse.ac.uk/impactofsocialsciences/2020/09/17/the-pandemic-is-making-it-harder-for-researchers-but-women-are-hit-the-hardest-4-findings-from-80-countries/> accessed 15 March 2021.

Sommerlad H, 'Patriarchal Discourses in the UK Legal Academy: The Case of the Reasonable Man' in Ulrike Schultz, Gisela Shaw, Margaret Thornton, and Rosemary Auchmuty, *Gender and Careers in the Legal Academy* (Hart 2001).

Strevens C, 'Implementing the SQE – Some Thoughts' *(Association of Law Teachers blog,* 1 December 2020) <http://lawteacher.ac.uk/sqe/implementing-the-sqe-some-thoughts/> accessed 4 April 2021.

The University of Law, 'Black Lives Matter: Our Statement' *(The University of Law)* <https://www.law.ac.uk/resources/black-lives-matter/> accessed 6 August 2021.

Toddington S, 'Chapter 6 The Emperor's New Skills: The Academy, The Profession and the Idea of Legal Education,' in Peter Birks (ed), *What Are Law Schools For? Vol. 2 Pressing Problems in the Law* (Oxford University Press 1996).

Twining W, *Blackstones's Tower: The English Law School* (Sweet and Maxwell 1994).

University and College Union, 'Second Class Academic Citizens: the Dehumanising Effects of Casualisation in Higher Education' (2020) <https://www.ucu.org.uk/media/10681/second_class_academic_citizens/pdf/secondclassacademicciti-zens> accessed 4 May 2021.

University College London Faculty of Law, 'UCL Laws Statement in Solidarity with our Black Students, Staff and Alumni around the World' *(University College London)* <https://www.ucl.ac.uk/laws/about/ucl-laws-statement-solidarity-our-black-students-staff-and-alumni-around-world> accessed 13 March 2021.

University of Oxford Faculty of Law, 'Anti-Racism Statement from the Law Faculty' *(University of Oxford,* 5 June 2020) <https://www.law.ox.ac.uk/news/2020-06-05-anti-racist-statement-law-faculty> accessed 13 March 2021.

University of Warwick, 'WLS Statement: Racial Trauma' *(University of Warwick)* <https://warwick.ac.uk/fac/soc/law/aboutus/equality-diversity-inclusion/racial-trauma/> accessed 6 August 2021.

University of Westminster Law School, 'Westminster Law School Supports the Black Lives Matter Movement: Stops the Silence Around Privilege, Racism and Decolonisation' *(University of Westminster)* <https://www.westminster.ac.uk/news/westminster-law-school-supports-the-black-lives-matter-movement-stops-the-silence-around-privilege> accessed 13 March 2021.

Wall S, 'An Autoethnography on Learning about Autoethnography' (2006) 5(2) *International Journal of Qualitative Methods* 146–160.

Waters B, 'The Solicitors Qualification Examination: Something for All? Some Challenges Facing Law Schools in England and Wales' (2018) 52(4) *The Law Teacher* 519.

Wells C, *A Woman in Law: Reflections on Gender, Class and Politics* (Waterside Press 2019).

Wells C, 'Working out Women in Law Schools' (2001) 21(1) *Legal Studies* 116–136.

Wilson J, 'A Third Survey of University Legal Education in the United Kingdom' (1993) 13(2) *Legal Studies.*

Young K, *How to be Sort of Happy in Law School* (Stanford University Press 2018).

6 A change in outfit? Conceptualising legal skills in the contemporary law school

Emma Jones

Introduction

This chapter focuses on legal skills. In doing so, it draws inspiration from Stuart Toddington's chapter in Birks' collection titled 'The Emperor's New Skills: The Academy, The Profession and the Idea of Legal Education'.[1] The title makes an allusion to the Hans Christian Andersen folktale 'The Emperor's New Clothes', a story in which a vain Emperor is persuaded that only intelligent people, competent in their role, can see the (non-existent) clothes made by two supposed tailors. His courtiers, keen to be perceived as clever and able, all pretend to see the garments and it is only during a public procession that a child points out the Emperor is, in fact, not wearing any clothes, although the Emperor feels compelled to continue the parade despite this realisation. There are many interpretations of this folktale,[2] but for the purposes of this chapter, it is construed as a metaphor demonstrating the need to distinguish between, on the one hand, illusion and façade and, on the other hand, that which is authentic and real. The notion of 'authenticity' is complex, multi-faceted and contested even within the setting of education.[3] However, for the purpose of this chapter, it will be construed as meaning a set of skills which are either necessary or valuable in the pursuit of the normative ideal of legal education. Toddington's conception of the legal enterprise, and the skills it requires, will be explored further below.

Much of Toddington's chapter is focused upon identifying what constitutes an authentic 'legal' skill, as opposed to more generic academic, professional or entrepreneurial skills.[4] He is particularly critical of the conflation of the

---

1 Stuart Toddington, 'The Emperor's New Skills: The Academy, The Profession and the Idea of Legal Education' in Peter Birks (ed) *Pressing Problems in the Law: Volume 2: What Are Law Schools For?* (Oxford University Press, 1996) 69.
2 See, for example, Hollis Robbins, 'The Emperor's New Critique' (Autumn 2003) 34 (4) New Literary History, 670.
3 Joseph Petraglia, *Reality By Design: The Rhetoric and Technology of Authenticity in Education* (Routledge, 1998) 2.
4 Stuart Toddington, 'The Emperor's New Skills: The Academy, The Profession and the Idea of Legal Education' in Peter Birks (ed) *Pressing Problems in the Law: Volume 2: What Are Law Schools For?* (Oxford University Press, 1996) 87.

DOI: 10.4324/9781003322092-6

Conceptualising legal skills in the contemporary law school 139

term 'legal' with 'what Legal Professionals *do*' (original author's italics), arguing that this leads to a focus on 'managerial and organisational skills' which are not specifically legal in nature.[5] Instead, Toddington argues that there is a need to identify 'a rational concept of law' in which to ground a theory, and critical assessment, of legal skills.[6] For him, this is the notion that the normative ideal of law is to 'attempt to regulate and co-ordinate social life in a principled and rational fashion'.[7] In particular, he refers to the importance of legal skills 'where institutions must be designed to identify, inhibit and resolve disputes, co-ordinate policy, foster participation and inhibit conflict'.[8]

In essence, the 'Legal Profession'[9] seems to be the tailors of the folktale, weaving a notion of what comprises legal skills. This appears to provide legal education with an enticing outfit, consisting of the trappings required for a legal career. However, such an outfit is illusory because it equates the law with legal practice and fails to recognise the wider conception of the legal enterprise which should form the basis for identifying and developing (what Toddington terms as) authentic legal skills. Instead, the focus becomes upon skills 'required by any and every commercial enterprise' which do not capture 'the complexity and distinctiveness of legal phenomena'.[10]

This chapter will revisit Toddington's conceptualisation of legal skills to consider to what extent it can, and should, be applied within contemporary legal education. It will explore what constitutes a legal skill and to what extent legal skills form an integral part of the curriculum of law schools. In doing so, it will argue that legal education remains largely committed to a concept of legal skills created by the Legal Profession, in much the same way as Toddington identified in Birks' collection. The chapter will then move on to consider Toddington's normative ideal of law, which appears to be commensurate with the notion of legal education developing students' sense of citizenship, commonly identified as a key tenet of liberal legal education. Using this notion as a framework, I will argue that to meet such a normative ideal, it is necessary to expand Toddington's definition of legal skills,

---

5 Ibid, 76.

6 Ibid, 88.

7 Ibid, 77.

8 Ibid, 85.

9 Toddington capitalises the phrase Legal Profession when referring to the '*actual body of personnel and practices*' involved, to distinguish it from the normative ideal of a legal profession. The same practice has therefore been adopted within this chapter. Stuart Toddington, 'The Emperor's New Skills: The Academy, The Profession and the Idea of Legal Education' in Peter Birks (ed) *Pressing Problems in the Law: Volume 2: What Are Law Schools For?* (Oxford University Press, 1996) 69; Joseph Petraglia, *Reality By Design: The Rhetoric and Technology of Authenticity in Education* (Routledge, 1998).

10 Stuart Toddington, 'The Emperor's New Skills: The Academy, The Profession and the Idea of Legal Education' in Peter Birks (ed) *Pressing Problems in the Law: Volume 2: What Are Law Schools For?* (Oxford University Press, 1996) 7; see also Stuart Toddington, 'Skills, Quality and the Ideologies of Managerialism' (1994) 28 Law Teacher, 243.

140 *Emma Jones*

to recognise more generic academic skills, when applied specifically within the legal context, as a necessary component. The chapter will also suggest two further important ways of broadening out Toddington's categorisation of legal skills. The first is by incorporating digital skills[11] the second is to incorporate skills involving emotions. These are both vital parts of the law school experience. They are particularly relevant in the rapidly changing legal environment created by the COVID-19 global pandemic but also have long-term significance for both education and citizenship.[12]

Defining legal skills

The term 'skill' itself is often used in a loose and broad way, encompassing a wide range of attributes, abilities and competencies (terms which are themselves often used interchangeably with 'skills').[13] Recently writing in the context of English legal education, Guth captures this breadth well when she defines skills as 'how to do things rather than learning about things'.[14] She also notes that legal skills are difficult to define, choosing the wide definition of legal skills as 'those related to how to do things within the discipline of law broadly defined'.[15] Other recent literature suggests that the notion of a specifically legal skill is similarly vague in its use within legal education, with recent suggestions ranging from mindfulness[16] to cultural competence.[17] Despite Twining, as early as 1988, arguing both for the importance of legal skills and for the need for them to be more clearly theorised and practically developed, it appears that over 30 years later, difficulties still remain with conceptualising legal skills in a clear and defined manner.[18]

---

11 Ronald W Staudt and Marc Lauritsen, 'Justice, Lawyering and Legal Education in the Digital Age: Introduction' (2013) 88 Chicago-Kent Law Review, 687 <https://papers.ssrn.com/sol3/papers.cfm?abstract_id=2335470> accessed 15 August 2021.
12 See, for example, Jonathan Goldsmith, 'The Pandemic's Impact on Legal Education' (*The Law Society Gazette*, 15 December 2020) <https://www.lawgazette.co.uk/commentary-and-opinion/the-pandemics-impact-on-legal-education/5106805.article> accessed 3 March 2021.
13 Neville Bennett, Elisabeth Dunne, and Clive Carre, 'Patterns of Core and Generic Skill Provision in Higher Education' (1999) 37 (1) Higher Education, 71, 74; Cecilia KY Chan, Emily TY Fong, Lillian YY Luk and Robbie Ho, 'A Review of Literature on Challenges in the Development and Implementation of Generic Competencies in Higher Education Curriculum' (2017) 57 International Journal of Educational Development, 1, 4.
14 Jessica Guth, 'The Pasts and Futures of Legal Skills in English Law Schools' in Emma Jones and Fiona Cownie (eds), *Key Directions in Legal Education: National and International Perspectives* (Routledge, 2020) 161.
15 Jonathan Goldsmith, 'The Pandemic's Impact on Legal Education' (*The Law Society Gazette*, 15 December 2020) <https://www.lawgazette.co.uk/commentary-and-opinion/the-pandemics-impact-on-legal-education/5106805.article> accessed 3 March 2021, 162.
16 Katerina P Lewinbuk and Christy Gilbert, 'Law Student Heal Thy Self: Teaching Mindfulness as a Legal Skill' (2016) 41 Journal of Legal Professionals, 37.
17 Ederlina Co, 'Teaching Cultural Competence as a Fundamental Lawyering Skill' (2019) 23 Legal Writing: Journal of the Legal Writing Institute, 4.
18 William Twining, 'Legal Skills and Legal Education' (1988) 22 The Law Teacher, 4, 5.

Conceptualising legal skills in the contemporary law school 141

Toddington's discussion of legal skills makes it clear that they should be distinguished from generic academic, professional and entrepreneurial skills.[19] In terms of academic skills, he argues that skills such as 'logical reasoning, sifting information into the relevant and irrelevant, evaluating arguments' are generic academic skills.[20] In terms of professional skills, he divides these into 'Formal (generic) Professional Skills' and 'Substantive Professional Skills'.[21] The former are those general skills, for example, relating to management and administration, which a professional must master before going on to apply their specialist (substantive) skills. The latter is perhaps the most difficult to distinguish from legal skills as it covers 'Skills which must be developed in response to the nature of a substantive field of endeavour and its specific problems and tasks requiring full time attention'.[22] It can be surmised that, by differentiating it as a separate category from legal skills, Toddington was seeking to reinforce the idea that legal education, at undergraduate level in England and Wales, is not a vocational course focused on the production of professional attributes.

Interestingly, Toddington does not give any form of detailed definition of what constitutes a 'legal skill'. He simply states that they are 'skills required by, and specific to, the pursuit of the substantive goals of the legal enterprise rationally conceived'.[23] As discussed in the Introduction, for Toddington, these goals appear to be around the construction of civic society and the role that legal education can play in equipping its graduates to contribute to the development of institutions to regulate society in a 'principled and rational' manner.[24] Therefore, his notion of an authentic legal skill is one which will equip graduates in this fashion. However, the exact nature of these legal skills remains unclear as, overall, he focuses on what legal skills are not, rather than what they are.

The integration of skills within legal education

To explore whether Toddington's criticism of legal skills as largely determined by the Legal Profession remains relevant today, it is necessary to consider to what extent legal skills are now integrated into the curricula of law schools and which so-called legal skills are usually focused upon. In doing so, there is a need to take a somewhat broader view of what constitutes 'legal skills' than Toddington, drawing on existing discourse within the legal academy on the topic.

---

19 Stuart Toddington, 'The Emperor's New Skills: The Academy, The Profession and the Idea of Legal Education' in Peter Birks (ed) *Pressing Problems in the Law: Volume 2: What Are Law Schools For?* (Oxford University Press 1996) 87.
20 Ibid, 84.
21 Ibid, 86.
22 Ibid, 87.
23 Ibid, 87.
24 Ibid, 77.

142 *Emma Jones*

Toddington's chapter within Birks' collection begins by referring to the 'much current enthusiasm for skills provision' present throughout education generally and legal education in particular.[25] This implies that, at the time he was writing, there was already a strong interest in, and commitment to, the incorporation of skills within the undergraduate law degree. However, it should not be assumed that the inclusion of skills within the legal curriculum is, or ever was, wholly uncontentious. For Toddington to state that his focus is on 'the question of what role the academy... should play in this regard' is to imply that at the time of *Pressing Problems* the inclusion of skills was unsettled and in dispute. Indeed, several years earlier, Twining had referred to a 'considerable resistance to direct teaching of skills by many law teachers'.[26] In doing so, he noted that key objections included the notions that the teaching of skills was either 'illiberal, amoral, narrow, reactionary, anti-intellectual, impractical, or unnecessary'.[27]

In part, such opposition may well have stemmed from a reluctance to embrace change. Webb argues that, traditionally, undergraduate legal education within law schools had consisted of '3 years of doctrinal law-teaching, supported by research... and, perhaps, a dose of legal method to highlight the technicalities of legal problem-solving'.[28] This traditional focus on the transmission of legal knowledge, in the form of doctrinal rules and principles, prizes content in a way which renders skills at best as secondary and, at worst, as irrelevant. Wider conceptions of the role of legal education may well also have formed a part in such opposition. The original development of the doctrinal approach to legal education was intended to separate law as an academic discipline and carve out a niche which would ensure that 'From the tangles of the common law, the scholar could find the inner logic and principles required to guide practitioners, indoctrinate students in the tradition and move law forward'.[29] Once again, this implies a focus on content which seems to have been deeply embedded within the teaching of law.

However, Toddington was writing on the cusp of a more fundamental shift towards the inclusion of skills in both higher and legal education. Birks' collection was published in 1996, the year before the publication of the 1997 National Committee of Inquiry into Higher Education ('the Dearing Report') was tasked to take account of the principle that 'learning should be

---

25 Ibid, 69.
26 Jessica Guth, 'The Pasts and Futures of Legal Skills in English Law Schools' in Emma Jones and Fiona Cownie (eds), *Key Directions in Legal Education: National and International Perspectives* (Routledge, 2020) 8.
27 Stuart Toddington, 'The Emperor's New Skills: The Academy, The Profession and the Idea of Legal Education' in Peter Birks (ed), *Pressing Problems in the Law: Volume 2: What Are Law Schools For?* (Oxford University Press 1996).
28 Julian Webb, 'Where the Action Is: Developing Artistry in Legal Education' (1995) 2 International Journal of the Legal Profession, 187, 188.
29 Susan Bartie, 'The Lingering Core of Legal Scholarship' (2010) 30 (3) Legal Studies, 345, 348.

Conceptualising legal skills in the contemporary law school 143

increasingly responsive to employment needs and include the development of general skills, widely valued in employment'.[30] This principle, and the subsequent report and recommendations it generated, reflected the growth of a political-governmental ideology of neoliberalism, commonly associated with the 1980s Thatcher administration in the UK.[31] This emphasised the need for universities to produce 'commercially oriented professionals rather than public-interest professionals'.[32] As a result, there was an increased discourse around skills, with a particular focus on employability skills. In other words, on equipping students to be 'job ready', to enter the workforce upon graduation as productive members of the new knowledge economy.[33] Developments within the US also influenced this focus, including the neoliberal ideology of the 1980s Reagan administration, the academic skills revolution of the 1980s and (within legal education) pressure from the legal profession.[34] Toddington's statement precedes a long line of governmental reports which all emphasise the importance of skills, particularly those relating to employability. This includes the 2016 white paper 'Success as a Knowledge Economy: Teaching Excellence, Social Mobility & Student Choice' which refers to higher education as generating 'the know-how and skills that fuel our growth and provide the basis for our nation's intellectual and cultural success'.[35] This demonstrates that the focus upon skills, specifically employability skills, continues to be prevalent within higher education. It forms a part of the wider marketisation of higher education and consumerisation of students, although this remains a site of contention and (on occasion) resistance.[36]

30 National Committee of Inquiry into Higher Education, The Dearing Report: Higher Education in the Learning Society (*Education in England*, 1997) <http://www.educationengland.org.uk/documents/dearing1997/dearing1997.html> accessed 3 January 2021, 3.

31 Sophie EF Bessant, Zoe P Robinson and R Mark Ormerod, 'Neoliberalism, New Public Management and the Sustainable Development Agenda of Higher Education: History, Contradictions and Synergies' (2015) 21 (3) Environmental Education Research, 417–432.

32 Kathleen Lynch, 'Neoliberalism and Marketisation: The Implications for Higher Education' (2006) 5 (1) European Education Research Journal, 1.

33 Tim Moore and Janne Morton, 'The Myth of Job Readiness? Written Communication, Employability, and the 'Skills Gap' in Higher Education' (2017) 42 (3) Studies in Higher Education, 591, 591; see also Jo Frankham, 'Employability and Higher Education: The Follies of the 'Productivity Challenge' in the Teaching Excellence Framework' (2017) 32 (5) Journal of Education Policy, 628.

34 Robert Stevens, *Law School. Legal Education in America from the 1850s to the 1980s* (The University of North Carolina Press 1983).

35 Department for Business, Innovation and Skills, *Success as a Knowledge Economy: Teaching Excellent, Social Mobility and Student Choice* (2016) <https://assets.publishing.service.gov.uk/government/uploads/system/uploads/attachment_data/file/523546/bis-16-265-success-as-a-knowledge-economy-web.pdf> accessed 5 January 2021, 7.

36 See, for example, Fiona Cownie and Anthony Bradney, 'Gothic Horror? A Response to Margaret Thornton' (2005) 14 (2) Social & Legal Studies, 277; Kathleen Lynch, 'Neoliberalism and Marketisation: The Implications for Higher Education' (2006) 5 (1) European Education Research Journal, 1; Richard Collier, '"Love law, love life" Neoliberalism,

144   *Emma Jones*

The repercussions of this overall marketization agenda are widespread, diverse and often damaging throughout higher education. Law schools are certainly not immune from such repercussions, although the extent of resistance to them is disputed.[37] It is therefore unsurprising that there is evidence of skills, particularly employability skills, becoming a widely accepted part of the law school curriculum since 1996 at undergraduate level.[38] In a 1996 survey with responses from 76 law schools offering undergraduate and postgraduate courses in law, Harris and Jones found that a total of 43 included 'vocational skills' within their undergraduate provision, commonly via either discrete modules or their incorporation into the study of substantive legal topics (or both).[39] The majority of such provision was offered within 'new university' settings.[40] In the same year, the 'First Report on Legal Education and Training' by the Lord Chancellors' Advisory Committee on Legal Education and Conduct highlighted some deficiencies in skills within both academic and vocational legal education, citing legal research skills and the increasingly diverse range of more generic skills required within the legal profession.[41] A subsequent 2004 survey by Harris and Beinart with 58 responses to questions on skills found that around 25% had compulsory modules (or parts of modules) on 'lawyers' professional responsibilities', around 33% had included compulsory 'mooting' and 'courtroom skills' and around 66% had 'other practical skills' as compulsory components.[42] Since then, a steady stream of articles around skills development, often featuring law school-specific case studies, suggests that this provision has continued to expand.[43] This can perhaps be linked, at least in part, to the commensurate

---

Wellbeing and Gender in the Legal Profession – The Case of Law School' (2014) 17 (2) Legal Ethics, 202; Michael Tomlinson, 'The Impact of Market-Driven Higher Education on Student-University Relations: Investing, Consuming and Competing' (2016) 29 High Education Policy, 149.

37 Ronald W Staudt and Marc Lauritsen, 'Justice, Lawyering and Legal Education in the Digital Age: Introduction' (2013) 88 Chicago-Kent Law Review, 687 <https://papers.ssrn.com/sol3/papers.cfm?abstract_id=2335470> accessed 15 August 2021.

38 Jessica Guth, 'The Pasts and Futures of Legal Skills in English Law Schools' in Emma Jones and Fiona Cownie (eds) *Key Directions in Legal Education: National and International Perspectives* (Routledge 2020) 163.

39 Phil Harris and Martin Jones, 'A Survey of Law Schools in the United Kingdom' (1996) 31 (1) The Law Teacher, 38–126, 49–50.

40 Stuart Toddington, 'The Emperor's New Skills: The Academy, The Profession and the Idea of Legal Education' in Peter Birks (ed) *Pressing Problems in the Law: Volume 2: What Are Law Schools For?* (Oxford University Press 1996) 50.

41 The Lord Chancellors', *Advisory Committee on Legal Education and Conduct, First Report on Legal Education and Training* (London, 1996).

42 Phil Harris and Sarah Beinart, 'A Survey of Law Schools in the United Kingdom' (2004) 39 (3) The Law Teacher, 299.

43 See, for example, Juliet Turner, Alison Bone and Jeanette Ashton, 'Reasons Why Law Students Should Have Access to Learning Law through a Skills-Based Approach' (2018) 52 (1) The Law Teacher, 1; David Rigg, 'Embedding Employability in Assessment: Searching for the Balance between Academic Learning and Skills Development in Law:

Conceptualising legal skills in the contemporary law school 145

growth of clinical legal education provision in law schools.[44] Such provision is often viewed as playing an important role in developing students' skills, particularly those, such as client care, which are prized within legal practice.[45] Although the notion that students could become 'practice ready' as a result of this experience has been criticised,[46] the growth of clinical legal education within English law schools (and the commensurate focus upon skills) has continued.[47] There has also been speculation about whether the introduction of the Solicitors Qualifying Examination (SQE) will result in a greater focus upon legal skills, for law schools to prepare 'SQE-ready' graduates.[48] While the first part of the SQE focuses upon (what the Solicitor Regulation Authority) regards as 'functioning legal knowledge', the second part is focused upon legal skills, such as interviewing, advocacy, analysis, reading, writing and drafting.[49] If law schools decide to market their degree courses as preparing students to be 'SQE-ready', this could therefore result in a greater focus upon those practical skills required by the legal profession.

It is notable that the 1996 and 2004 surveys referred to above appear to equate legal skills to professional legal skills.[50] This is also a key focus within clinical legal education and would be at the heart of any adjustments

---

A Case Study' (2013) 47 (3) The Law Teacher, 404; Simon Brooman and Sarah Stirk, 'Who Am I?: Using Reflective Practice and Selfdetermination To Redefine 'Employability' in Legal Education' (2020) 41 Liverpool Law Review, 79.

44 James Marson, Adam Wilson and Mark Van Hoorebeek, 'The Necessity of Clinical Legal Education in University Law Schools: A UK Perspective' (2005) 7 International Journal of Clinical Legal Education, 29, 43.

45 Ann Thanaraj, 'Understanding How a Law Clinic Can Contribute towards Students' Development of Professional Responsibility' (2016) 23 International Journal of Clinical Legal Education, 89.

46 DJ Cantrell, 'Are Clinics a Magic Bullet?' (2014) 51 Alberta Law Review, 831; Margaret Martin Barry, 'Practice Ready: Are We There Yet?' (2012) 32 Boston College Journal of Law & Social Justice, 247; Robert J Condlin, '"Practice Ready Graduates": A Millennialist Fantasy' (2014–2015) 31 Touro Law Review 75.

47 James Sandbach and Richard Grimes, 'Law School Pro Bono and Clinic Report 2020: LawWorks and CLEO (Clinical Legal Education Organisation)' (2020) <https://www.lawworks.org.uk/sites/default/files/files/LawWorks%20Law%20Schools%20Report%202020_0.pdf> accessed 7 May 2021.

48 Dawn Jones, 'Legal Skills and the SQE: Confronting the Challenge Head on' (2018) 53 (1) The Law Teacher, 35; Ben Waters, 'The Solicitors Qualification Examination: Something for All? Some Challenges Facing Law Schools in England and Wales' 2018) 52 (4) The Law Teacher, 519.

49 Solicitor Regulation Authority, 'SQE1 and SQE2 Assessments' <https://www.sra.org.uk/students/sqe/sqe-assessments/> accessed 7 May 2021.

50 Robert Stevens, *Law School. Legal Education in America from the 1850s to the 1980s* (The University of North Carolina Press 1983); Fiona Cownie and Anthony Bradney, 'Gothic Horror? A Response to Margaret Thornton' (2005) 14 (2) Social & Legal Studies, 277; Kathleen Lynch, 'Neoliberalism and Marketisation: The Implications for Higher Education' (2006) 5 (1) European Education Research Journal, 1; Richard Collier, '"Love Law, Love Life" Neoliberalism, Wellbeing and Gender in the Legal Profession – The Case of Law School' (2014) 17 (2) Legal Ethics, 202; Michael Tomlinson, 'The Impact of

146 *Emma Jones*

to curricula as a result of the SQE.[51] However, this should not be taken to mean that skills which could be termed as academic legal skills have been ignored. Indeed, there is arguably an increased focus on these with the Quality Assurance Agency's 2019 Subject Benchmark Statement for law, which provides guidance on the academic standards expected from law graduates in the UK, emphasising that 'The study of law involves the acquisition of legal knowledge, general intellectual skills and certain skills that are specific to the study of law'.[52] Guth suggests that the broader widening participation agenda in higher education and the changes in how knowledge is conceived and accessed have both contributed to a 'consensus' that 'students should not be required to learn the basic skills... by osmosis as was previously expected'.[53] Such academic skills appear to have become largely integrated into the teaching of substantive law as an accepted part of the legal curriculum.[54]

Overall, what evidence there is on the integration of skills into the undergraduate legal curriculum suggests that there is an increasing focus on both academic and professional skills, with the latter mirroring the wider emphasis on employability within higher education overall. In terms of such employability skills, there is little (if any) indication that Toddington's assessment of the conceptualisation of legal skills has changed. It appears that much of what is termed as an employability or professional skill in law is still dictated by the practical needs of professional legal practice (e.g., the use of mooting skills).[55] Indeed, it has even been argued that this nexus with the legal profession is what 'ultimately guarantees its distinctive disciplinary identity'.[56] This continued adherence to the (perceived) wishes of the legal profession is somewhat surprising, given that figures demonstrate only a

---

Market-Driven Higher Education on Student-University Relations: Investing, Consuming and Competing' (2016) 29 High Education Policy, 149.

51 Jonathan Goldsmith, 'The Pandemic's Impact on Legal Education' (*The Law Society Gazette*, 15 December 2020) <https://www.lawgazette.co.uk/commentary-and-opinion/the-pandemics-impact-on-legal-education/5106805.article> accessed 3 March 2021; Phil Harris and Martin Jones, 'A Survey of Law Schools in the United Kingdom' (1996) 31 (1) The Law Teacher.

52 Quality Assurance Agency, 'Subject Benchmark Statement: Law' <https://www.qaa.ac.uk/docs/qaa/subject-benchmark-statements/subject-benchmark-statement-law.pdf?sfvrsn=b939c881_18> accessed 7 January 2021, 4.

53 Jessica Guth, 'The Pasts and Futures of Legal Skills in English Law Schools' in Emma Jones and Fiona Cownie (eds), *Key Directions in Legal Education: National and International Perspectives* (Routledge 2020) 163.

54 Ibid, 163.

55 For a discussion of how this is reflected in law schools' marketing see Graeme Broadbent and Pamela Sellman, 'Great Expectations? Law Schools, Websites and "The Student Experience"' (2013) 47 (1) The Law Teacher, 44.

56 Douglas W Vick, 'Interdisciplinarity and the Discipline of Law' (2004) 31 (2) Journal of Law and Society, 163.

Conceptualising legal skills in the contemporary law school   147

minority of law graduates will go on to enter the legal profession.[57] Indeed, the introduction of the SQE will remove the requirement for aspiring solicitors to have a qualifying law degree, simply requiring them to be graduates in any discipline (or have equivalent experience or qualifications).[58] Even if preparing students for professional legal practice was to be accepted to be a legitimate aim of the undergraduate law degree, the stratification of legal practice and the fast-paced development in areas such as technology and digital lawyering would suggest that this would be a Herculean undertaking.[59]

Much of what is integrated into the legal curriculum today seems to fall squarely outside Toddington's category of 'legal skills' and instead fall into his categorisation of generic academic skills and professional skills (both generic and specific). If his analysis is accepted, this means therefore that there remains a gap within undergraduate legal education – there must be legal skills that should be included and integrated into the law degree to achieve his conception of the legal enterprise, but currently are not. Even if his categorisation of skills is not accepted, it is necessary to consider what types of legal skills should be included within the law school curriculum. It is therefore necessary to consider Toddington's conception of the normative ideal of law, how this relates to his categorisation of legal skills and what this could mean in terms of identifying whether such a categorisation is both sufficient and appropriate.

Identifying the legal enterprise

Toddington's description of the normative ideal of law views it as a mechanism to appropriately guide and co-ordinate society.[60] He also takes great care to distinguish legal skills from vocational skills.[61] His approach to both of these points indicates an adherence to the tenets of a form of liberal legal

---

57 The Law Society of England and Wales, 'Entry Trends' (25 November 2020) <https://www.lawsociety.org.uk/en/career-advice/becoming-a-solicitor/entry-trends> accessed 26 February 2021; Lawyer Monthly, 'Law Graduate Opportunities Aren't Passing the Bar, Official Data Suggests' (January 2019) < https://www.lawyer-monthly.com/issues/2019/01/9/> accessed 26 February 2021.

58 Solicitors Regulation Authority, 'Solicitors Qualifying Examination ('SQE') (February 2021) <https://www.sra.org.uk/students/sqe/> accessed 26 February 2021.

59 In relation to the impact of technology on the legal profession, see Brian Simpson, 'Algorithms or Advocacy: Does the Legal Profession Have a Future in a Digital World?' (2016) 25 (1) Information & Communications Technology Law, 50.

60 Stuart Toddington, 'The Emperor's New Skills: The Academy, The Profession and the Idea of Legal Education' in Peter Birks (ed), *Pressing Problems in the Law: Volume 2: What Are Law Schools For?* (Oxford University Press 1996) 77.

61 Ibid, 77.

148 *Emma Jones*

education.[62] Although definitions of liberal legal education (and liberal education more generally) tend to be particularly diffuse,[63] a useful overall summary is that of Guth and Ashford who state:

> A liberal legal education is one which does not focus on education for a particular purpose other than education itself. It is not aimed at preparing students for a particular job or profession and is not concerned with notions such as employability. It is, however, concerned with pursuing knowledge for knowledge's sake and developing skills of knowledge acquisition through research, critical thought and debate.[64]

Such a form of liberal education could be viewed as a purely individual enterprise, one focused upon developing a 'better person'.[65] In other words, conceptualising learning as a means of personal development and growth, with the individual involved potentially choosing not to participate in, or contribute to, the life of the community and the development of the legal enterprise. However, there is a strong argument that such personal transformation is likely to lead to a sense of citizenship, often premised upon social justice, which will lead to many individuals wishing to contribute to the legal enterprise in some way.

Indeed, a number of writers on legal education have suggested that an appropriate end for a liberal approach to legal education is that of the 'good citizen'.[66] For example, Burridge and Webb suggest the product of a liberal legal education will be 'rational participants in the life of the community', once again reflecting Toddington's focus on contributions to civic society.[67] The normative ideal of what constitutes a such a citizen is potentially problematic, with Pue suggesting that appropriate citizenship is commonly

---

62 For a seminal discussion of liberal legal education, see Anthony Bradney, *Conversations Choices and Chances: The Liberal Law School in the Twenty-First Century* (Hart Publishing, 2003). For a discussion of the history of tensions between liberal and vocational forms of legal education see James Crook, 'A Brief History of Liberal Legal Education: The Battle Between Law as a Science and Law as a Liberal Art' (2017) 17 (2) Legal History, 30; and Susanna Menis, 'The Liberal, the Vocational and Legal Education: A Legal History Review – From Blackstone to a Law Degree (1972)' (2020) 54 (2) The Law Teacher, 285.

63 Sheldon Rothblatt, *Tradition and Change in English Legal Education. An Essay in History and Culture* (Faber and Faber 1976) 195.

64 Jessica Guth and Chris Ashford, 'The Legal Education and Training Review: Regulating Socio-Legal and Liberal Legal Education?' (2014) 48 (1) The Law Teacher, 5, 6, 5–19.

65 Roger Burridge and Julian Webb, 'The Values of Common Law Legal Education Reprised' (2009) 43 (2) The Law Teacher, 263, 264.

66 Roger Brownsword, "Law Schools for Lawyers, Citizens and People" in Fiona Cownie (ed), *The Law School: Global Issues, Local Questions* (Aldershot 1999).

67 Ibid; Stuart Toddington, 'The Emperor's New Skills: The Academy, The Profession and the Idea of Legal Education' in Peter Birks (ed), *Pressing Problems in the Law: Volume 2: What Are Law Schools For?* (Oxford University Press 1996) 77.

Conceptualising legal skills in the contemporary law school 149

equated to an individual with particular liberal values – 'Liberal states rest on the manufacture of liberal souls'.[68] Other writers on liberal legal education tend to focus more on the concept of the 'good people'.[69] However, Brownsword suggests that there is no dichotomy between the two, arguing:

> None of this presupposes that liberally-educated law graduates will be 'good citizens' in the sense that they will take a particular party-line in politico-legal debates, or even that they will be conscientious in supporting the ordinary democratic processes associated with representative government. However, it does presuppose that 'the law' will hold no mystery for these graduates and that they will be capable of making a rational assessment of the arguments relating to debates arising in and around the practice of law.[70]

It is worth noting the reference to a 'rational' assessment here, which mirrors Toddington's several references to rationality when discussing the normative ideal of law.[71]

Toddington only refers to his normative ideal of law relatively briefly. Therefore, it is not possible to precisely divine who he is envisaging as the product of his suggested focus on legal skills. However, it does appear to chime with the liberal notion of good citizenship, someone who will be able to contribute to the public debate around, and development of, law and legal institutions.

Viewing Toddington's conceptualisation of the legal enterprise and the normative ideal of law as focused upon good citizenship gives it enormous relevance and value for contemporary legal education. Particularly at a time where inequalities are increasingly pronounced, and new forms of authoritarianism are on the rise.[72] This gives the sense of authentic legal skills as those which both develop (and potentially transform) the individual but also contribute to a sense of citizenship and a contribution to society.

---

68 W Wesley Pue, 'Legal Education's Mission (2008) 42 (3) The Law Teacher, 270, 272; see also Kate Green and Hilary Limb, 'A Lib-Lib Pact: Silences in Legal Education' (1987) 21 (3) The Law Teacher, 256.
69 Douglas W Vick, 'Interdisciplinarity and the Discipline of Law' (2004) 31 (2) Journal of Law and Society.
70 Roger Brownsword, 'Law Schools for Citizens, Lawyers and People' in Fiona Cownie (ed), *The Law School – Global Issues, Local Questions* (Routledge 2018 reissue) 30.
71 Stuart Toddington, 'The Emperor's New Skills: The Academy, The Profession and the Idea of Legal Education' in Peter Birks (ed), *Pressing Problems in the Law: Volume 2: What Are Law Schools For?* (Oxford University Press 1996) 77, 88.
72 Michael Marmot and Jessica Allen, 'Covid-19: Exposing and Amplifying Inequalities' (2020) 74 (9) Community Health, 681–682; Jerzy J. Wiatr (ed), *New Authoritarianism: Challenges to Democracy in the 21st Century* (Barbara Budrich Publishers 2019).

150 *Emma Jones*

Authenticity and the legal enterprise

Focusing, then, on the liberal notion of good citizenship, what are the authentic legal skills required to achieve such a normative ideal? Perhaps Toddington was deliberately vague about this to facilitate further debate on the matter, or perhaps he simply did not have the space in Birks' collection to do this topic justice. Either way, it is arguably somewhat difficult to align the notion of citizenship with the narrow categorisation of legal skills he focuses upon.

Of course, there are potential benefits in such a narrow categorisation. In particular, it effectively ring-fences an area of skills which are discipline-specific, thus potentially lessening any 'fears for the future of law as a distinct discipline'.[73] At the same time, it clearly delineates the academic discipline of law from the professional practice of law and thus suggests the potential for evolution within the discipline. In other words, it carves out a specific niche for legal skills to occupy. There is a sense here of stripping away the illusion of finery bestowed by the legal profession and instead reverting to a form of pure, authentic legal skill.

References to authenticity in legal education have tended to focus upon the recreation or simulation of aspects of legal practice, implying that authenticity comes from absorbing those skills developed through legal practice.[74] If it is accepted that the relationship with the legal profession shapes laws' distinctive disciplinary contours, then eschewing professional legal skills could be seen as damaging. However, as noted above, it is difficult to divine the logic in continuing to harness law to the wishes of a profession which a dwindling number of law graduates actually enter.[75] Therefore, it can be argued that one strength of Toddington's categorisation lies in the way it recasts the notion of authenticity as one which is not reliant on the legal profession, nor is it reliant on other generic academic or professional skills (which, it can be surmised, he would view as effectively swapping one invisible garment for another). The notion of identifying authentic legal skills by their relationship to legal practice is no longer sustainable – it represents the new clothes of the eponymous fairy tale – perpetuating an illusion that law as an academic discipline should be focused upon professional

---

73 James Sandbach and Richard Grimes, 'Law School Pro Bono and Clinic Report 2020: LawWorks and CLEO (Clinical Legal Education Organisation)' (2020) <https://www.lawworks.org.uk/sites/default/files/files/LawWorks%20Law%20Schools%20Report%202020_0.pdf> accessed 7 May 2021, 188.

74 See, for example, Linda Kam, Michele Ruyters, Clare Coburn and Mary Toohey, 'Ger Real; A Case Study of Authentic Learning Activities in Legal Education' (2012) 19 Murdoch University Law Review, 17.

75 Dawn Jones, 'Legal Skills and the SQE: Confronting the Challenge Head on' (2018) 53 (1) The Law Teacher; Ben Waters, 'The Solicitors Qualification Examination: Something for All? Some Challenges Facing Law Schools in England and Wales' (2018) 52 (4) The Law Teacher.

Conceptualising legal skills in the contemporary law school 151

formation, whether in terms of more traditional professional lawyering skills or "SQE-readiness". Therefore, Toddington's work is important in upholding the intellectual value and strength of law as a discipline of study.

Toddington's approach also flies in the face of the wider employability agenda within higher education. Such an agenda has become increasingly significant in the marketised academy with Römgens *et al.* suggesting that 'the importance of employability is generally agreed-upon by policy makers and scholars alike'.[76] The ways in which the employability agenda are conceptualised and implemented in practice within universities are highly contested.[77] Nevertheless, references to authentic skills within higher education more generally tend to mirror this emphasis on employability, focusing on the notion that 'students demonstrate their knowledge and skills by performing real-world tasks'.[78] Whether eschewing this view of authenticity is seen as a benefit or disadvantage of Toddington's approach will once again depend upon the underpinning conceptualisation of the purpose of law and the law school. A number of proponents of liberal legal education have argued against employability being a key aim of undergraduate legal education, with Bradney stating:

> Both professional knowledge and technical information have value but in a liberal education they are acquired, if at all, not for the value that they have in their own terms but because they can facilitate the wider learning that constitutes a liberal education.[79]

The continued tensions between vocational (employability-focused) and liberal conceptions of legal education demonstrate that there is no single shared notion of what constitutes an authentic set of legal skills within legal education. Given Toddington's apparent sympathy with the liberal aims of legal education, and emphasis on citizenship, it seems likely he would characterise his own conception's rejection of the employability agenda as a benefit, despite it requiring resistance to wider policy agendas within institutions. His reference to generic professional skills and his concern that they focus on commercial and administrative functions also indicates his

---

76 Inge Römgens, Rémi Scoupe and Simon Beausaert, 'Unraveling the Concept of Employability, Bringing Together Research on Employability in Higher Education and the Workplace' (2020) 45 (12) Studies in Higher Education, 2588.

77 Mariana Alvio Gaio Alves and Michael Tomlinson, 'The Changing Value of Higher Education in England and Portugal: Massification, Marketization and Public Good' (2020) European Educational Research Journal, 1; Nickolas J James, 'More than Merely Work-Ready: Vocationalism Versus Professionalism in Legal Education' (2017) 40 (1) University of New South Wales Law Journal, 186.

78 Laura M. Greenstein, *Assessing 21st Century Skills: A Guide to Evaluating Mastery and Authentic Learning* (Corwin, 2012) 51.

79 Anthony Bradney, *Conversations Choices and Chances: The Liberal Law School in the Twenty-First Century* (Hart Publishing, 2003) 41.

152   *Emma Jones*

eschewing of a focus on employability.[80] This has a great value in challenging increasingly dominant narratives around employability and emphasising the intellectual worth of the law degree. It once again positions undergraduate legal education in a way which removes its dependence on the vagaries of neo-liberal agendas and restates the importance of both the legal enterprise, and the study of law as a part of that. In particular, it carves out the academic space to focus upon notions of citizenship and social justice, preventing such discussions from being 'crowded-out' of the curricula.

The above discussion demonstrates that Toddington's narrow categorisation of legal skills has appeal in the sense that it avoids the danger of donning the trappings of the employability agenda. However, it is arguably hard to support Toddington's approach when it comes to the distinction he draws between generic academic skills and legal skills.[81] While he acknowledges such academic skills as 'vitally important' within legal education, he suggests that these are the precursors to specifically legal skills.[82] Examples he gives of such generic skills include 'logical reasoning', 'sifting information into the relevant and irrelevant' and 'evaluating arguments'.[83] Returning to Toddington's normative ideal of law, it is difficult to see how these skills, when applied to legal rules and institutions, are not fundamental legal skills. Although they may be applied within other (if not all) academic disciplines, by applying them to legal subject-matter, it is credible to suggest that they therefore become authentically legal skills. To look at this point another way, what does a law student need in addition to these skills to succeed? It is difficult to pinpoint what could fall within the category of legal skills in the academic context which is not based on the application of these more generic skills. This is especially the case when wider professional and employability skills have already been excluded from this categorisation.

Even if legal skills were to be defined solely by reference to a doctrinal approach to law, which has sometimes been characterised as being at the very core of legal research and, by extension, legal education,[84] it is hard to see how legal and academic skills can be clearly delineated, for example, Hutchinson and Duncan's discussion of the definitions of doctrinal research refers to a range of skills which appear to be academic in nature, including finding and categorising relevant information (case law) and then applying critical analysis to legal issues (legal reasoning).[85] Indeed, the fact the gene-

---

80 Stuart Toddington, 'The Emperor's New Skills: The Academy, The Profession and the Idea of Legal Education' in Peter Birks (ed), *Pressing Problems in the Law: Volume 2: What Are Law Schools For?* (Oxford University Press 1996) 76, 86.

81 Ibid, 82.

82 Ibid, 82.

83 Ibid, 82.

84 Terry Hutchinson and Nigel Duncan, 'Defining and Describing What We Do: Doctrinal Legal Research' (2012) 17 Deakin Law Review, 83.

85 James Sandbach and Richard Grimes, 'Law School Pro Bono and Clinic Report 2020: LawWorks and CLEO (Clinical Legal Education Organisation)' (2020) <https://www.

sis of the doctrinal approach was largely based upon a desire to carve out a specific 'academic' niche for law and law schools, suggests a legal education based upon, and compatible with, a wider academic skillset.[86] It is possible that when Toddington refers to specifically legal skills he is thinking of the concept of 'thinking like a lawyer' in the sense it is sometimes applied within legal education, as 'a form of linear analysis in a constricted paradigm'.[87] However, this in itself is an amalgam of wider academic skills – such as synthesis and analysis, despite it being focused upon legal issues. It should also be noted that doctrinal approaches have commonly been associated with a focus on the Legal Profession and professional skills in a way which seems potentially incompatible with Toddington's normative ideal.[88]

Returning to the QAA Benchmark Statement for Law, the skills listed in this clearly demonstrate the way in which generic academic skills become legal skills when applied in a legal context. For example, it refers to

> [I]ntellectual independence, including the ability to ask and answer cogent questions about law and legal systems, identify gaps in their own knowledge and acquire new knowledge, and engage in critical analysis and evaluation.[89]

Each of these can be easily identified as generic academic skills, for example, a historian would be required to critically question and explore historical sources. Similarly, although an ability to 'recognise uncertainty and deal with ambiguity in law'[90] may at first glance appear to be a legal skill, this will also apply in other disciplines, for example, a historian dealing with differing accounts of an event given in a range of secondary sources. The reference to values and ethics within the statement is also not exclusive to law. Indeed, it is arguable that there is a more generic academic skill at the core of each academic legal skill. Therefore, rather than trying to make an artificial separation, it should be accepted that an authentic legal skill in the

---

lawworks.org.uk/sites/default/files/files/LawWorks%20Law%20Schools%20Report%20 2020_0.pdf> accessed 7 May 2021, 2011.

86 David Sugarman, 'Legal Theory, the Common Law Mind and the Making of the Textbook Tradition' in William Twining (ed), *Legal Theory and Common Law* (Basil Blackwell, 1986); Susan Bartie, 'The Lingering Core of Legal Scholarship' (2010) 30 (3) Legal Studies, 345.

87 Colin James, 'Lawyers'' Wellbeing and Professional Legal Education' (2008) 42 (1) The Law Teacher, 85, 91.

88 See, for example, Rita K Stropus, 'Mend It, Bend It, and Extend It: The Fate of Traditional Law School Methodology in the 21st Century' (1996) 27 (3) Loyola University of Chicago Law Journal, 449.

89 Quality Assurance Agency, 'Subject Benchmark Statement: Law' <https://www.qaa. ac.uk/docs/qaa/subject-benchmark-statements/subject-benchmark-statement-law.pdf?sfvrsn=b939c881_18> accessed 7 January 2021, 5.

90 Ibid.

154   *Emma Jones*

context of undergraduate legal education is, at its heart, an academic skill. This appears to be a logical conclusion given that law, in the form of the law degree, is an academic discipline. It also reflects both Toddington's normative ideal and the tenets of liberal legal education by assisting law students 'to inquire into, and to strive to understand, the regulatory practice that we identify as the practice of law'.[91] As such, it provides them with an insight and understanding necessary to contribute to society.

The above discussion on the categorisation of skills which flows from Toddington's normative ideal of law indicates that his definition of legal skills, whilst having significant benefits in preserving key tenets of liberal legal education, also has significant disadvantages when trying to determine a discrete class of legal skills which is separate from (what he terms as) generic academic skills. A broader, but more nuanced, approach is to identify the specific manifestations of such academic skills which are particular to the discipline of law and include these within the category of legal skills. This moves Toddington's category of legal skills into one which is more aligned with liberal legal education's conception of good citizenship, individuals who have the skills to make 'a rational assessment of the arguments relating to debates arising in and around the practice of law'[92] and to, as Toddington himself puts it, 'attempt to regulate and co-ordinate social life in a principled and rational fashion'.[93] An authentic legal skill therefore becomes one which assists in meeting legal education's normative ideal of the development of good citizenship. For proponents of liberal legal education, this is the genuine legal enterprise which lies below the flashier (and arguably more marketable) trappings of preparation for legal practice.

Within this new definition of authentic legal skills, there is a need to acknowledge and accept wider academic skills, in their application to legal issues, as an important movement towards an evolved version of Toddington's vision which can be applied within contemporary legal education. However, if we are to truly align the normative enterprise of legal education with the notion of fostering citizenship, simply incorporating these wider academic skills, as currently conceptualised, will not be sufficient on its own. The remainder of this chapter will illustrate this by exploring two areas of skill development which are largely viewed as non-academic or non-legal in nature, and have therefore largely been ignored or disregarded in more traditional conceptualisations of legal education, namely, digital skills and so-called

---

91 Roger Brownsword, 'Where Are All the Law Schools Going?' (1996) 30 (1) The Law Teacher, 1, 2.

92 Stuart Toddington, 'The Emperor's New Skills: The Academy, The Profession and the Idea of Legal Education' in Peter Birks (ed), *Pressing Problems in the Law: Volume 2: What Are Law Schools For?* (Oxford University Press 1996).

93 Ibid, 77.

Conceptualising legal skills in the contemporary law school 155

soft skills.[94] It is unsurprising that Toddington did not fully acknowledge these within Birks' collection as their future potential and impact was only nascent within the legal academy at the point. However, to provide a definition of authentic legal skills which is fit for the purpose of contemporary legal education, it is now necessary to build upon and broaden Toddington's original vision by exploring the value and importance of these.

Broadening the skills required of the 'good citizen'

It has already been argued that Toddington's normative ideal conforms to the liberal notion of a 'good citizen'.[95] He refers to the 'need for skills appropriate to the problems of institutional design in the modern state' and the need to focus upon 'rational and democratic administration'.[96] Whilst it is not possible within one chapter to tease out the myriad of skills that could be accommodated if this is translated into a broader category of legal skills, focusing upon the two areas of digital skills and skills involving emotions and applying these within the legal context is sufficient to highlight two sets of skills that are vital within this enterprise. Therefore, to meet Toddington's ideal, it is necessary to ensure that these two areas are incorporated within liberal education.

Digital skills

The reference to digital skills refers to the use of digital technologies, from word processing programmes to emails and internet search engines to Artificial Intelligence and Blockchain.[97] These skills are often equated with 'digital lawyering', in other words, the application of these technologies within legal practice.[98] This focus would suggest that digital skills fall within Toddington's conceptions of either professional or entrepreneurial skills.[99] However, the reach of digital skills goes far beyond those skills required for the world of legal practice or work more generally. Such skills are now

---

94 In relation to 'soft skills' and emotions see Emma Jones, *Emotions in the Law School: Transforming Legal Education Through the Passions* (Routledge 2019).

95 Douglas W Vick, 'Interdisciplinarity and the Discipline of Law' (2004) 31 (2) Journal of Law and Society.

96 Stuart Toddington, 'The Emperor's New Skills: The Academy, the Profession and the Idea of Legal Education' in Peter Birks (ed), *Pressing Problems in the Law: Volume 2: What Are Law Schools For?* (Oxford University Press 1996) 78.

97 Emma Jones, Francine Ryan, Ann Thanaraj and Terry Wong, *Digital Lawyering: Technology and Legal Practice in the 21st Century* (Routledge 2021).

98 Ann Thanaraj, 'Making the Case for a Digital Lawyering Framework in Legal Education' (2017) 2017 (3) International Review of Law.

99 Stuart Toddington, 'The Emperor's New Skills: The Academy, the Profession and the Idea of Legal Education' in Peter Birks (ed), *Pressing Problems in the Law: Volume 2: What Are Law Schools For?* (Oxford University Press, 1996) 87.

156 *Emma Jones*

essential for successful academic study generally, impacting upon academic performance and attainment.[100] Prior to the onset of Covid-19, there was a need for students (at a minimum) to be able to send and receive emails and undertake at least some forms of online information-gathering and research, with English universities increasingly focusing upon the development of digital competency frameworks.[101] The onset of Covid-19 has accelerated the emphasis on blended and remote learning within higher education with students now being required to access virtual learning environments, attend lectures and seminars online, conduct groupwork and undertake assessments virtually.[102] As well as having a generic academic application they also have discipline-specific implications, for example, within law schools, there are specific digital skills which are necessary from using online legal databases to find legislation and case law to formatting OSCOLA referencing. There are also a range of emerging digital skills which are becoming increasingly valued, from analysing digitally simulated legal scenarios to designing applications to promote access to justice.[103] Such skills also enable students to understand and explore the intersections between law and contemporary society, which is increasingly digital in nature. The impacts of digital literacy, digital poverty and the digital divide are all areas which impact upon issues such as access to justice in crucial ways. In future, citizenship will require individuals to engage with these issues to fully contribute to society and to ameliorate potentially detrimental impacts.[104]

Earlier in this chapter, it has been argued that Toddington's definition of a legal skill must be broadened to incorporate the legal manifestations of more general academic skills. At present, digital skills are not usually

---

100 Mahboobe Mehrvarz, Elham Heidari, Mohammadreza Farrokhnia and Omid Noroozi, 'The Mediating Role of Digital Informal Learning in the Relationship between Students' Digital Competency and Their Academic Performance' (2021) 167 Computers and Education; Laura Pagani, Gianluca Argentin, Marco Gui and Luca Stanca, 'The Impact of Digital Skills on Educational Outcomes: Evidence from Performance Tests' (2016) 42 (4) Educational Studies, 137.

101 Fiona JL Handley, 'Developing Digital Skills and Literacies in UK Higher Education: Recent Developments and a Case Study of the Digital Literacies Framework at the University of Brighton, UK' (2018) 48 (1) Publicaciones.

102 For an international overview of impacts see Amy W Thornberg, Robert J Ceglie and Dixie F Abernathy, *Handbook of Research on Lessons Learned from Transitioning to Virtual Classrooms During a Pandemic* (IGI Global, 2021).

103 See, for example, Hugh McFaul, Elizabeth FitzGerald, Francine Ryan and David Byrne, 'A Mobile App for Public Legal Education: A Case Study of Co-Designing with Students' (2020) 28 Research in Learning Technology, 2434; Emily Allbon, 'Too Cool for (Law) School? Using Technology to Engage Students in Legal Skills' (2013) 4 (1) European Journal of Law and Technology; Paul Maharg, 'Negotiating the Web: Legal Skills Learning in a Virtual Community' (2001) 15 (3) International Review of Law, Computers & Technology, 345.

104 For examples of these intersections see Christopher Lawless and Alex Faulkner (eds), *Material Worlds: Intersections of Law, Science, Technology, and Society* (Wiley-Blackwell 2012).

conceptualised as 'academic' in nature. However, they increasingly provide a vital foundation for students to be able to display and demonstrate their academic skills. They also have value in their own right in enabling students to navigate the intersections of law and today's digital society. To accept these into an enlarged definition of legal skills is to acknowledge the importance of digital technologies within society. In doing so, it is necessary to ensure that these do not simply become a form of professional skillset focused upon digital lawyering, but to emphasise their academic value and their necessity for contemporary citizenship.

Skills involving emotions

Another important set of skills which it is argued should be accepted as authentic legal skills are skills involving emotions, when applied within the legal context. A common short-hand for this type of skill is to refer to them as 'soft skills',[105] although this implies adherence to tenets of neo-liberal ideology,[106] as well as drawing a form of distinction from other key skills which is misleading. They are also sometimes encompassed by the terms 'emotional literacy' or 'emotional intelligence'.[107] Emotions can be defined as '...A particular, conscious event, high in intensity but short-lived and easily labelled and recalled'.[108] There is a large body of scientific evidence demonstrating that they are intertwined with all aspects of reasoning, judgment and decision-making.[109] However, despite this, higher education, and legal education in particular, has a history of ignoring emotion and affect or viewing it as a purely pastoral issue, unrelated to teaching and learning.[110] Although there are some notable exceptions, particularly within clinical

---

105 See, for example, Randall Kiser, *Soft Skills for the Effective Lawyer* (Cambridge University Press 2017).

106 Anne-Marie D'Aoust, 'Ties that Bind? Engaging Emotions, Governmentality and Neoliberalism: Introduction to the Special Issue' (2014) 28 (3) Global Society, 267.

107 Daniel Goleman, *Emotional Intelligence* (Bloomsbury 1996).

108 Brian H Bornstein and Richard L Wiener, 'Emotion and the Law: A Field Whose Time Has Come" in Brian H Bornstein and Richard L Wiener (eds), *Nebraska Symposium on Motivation. Emotion and the Law. Psychological Perspectives* (Springer 2010) 1, 1.

109 Amy W Thornberg, Robert J Ceglie and Dixie F Abernathy, *Handbook of Research on Lessons Learned from Transitioning to Virtual Classrooms During a Pandemic* (IGI Global 2021); Bandes and Blumenthal in discussing emotions observe that 'they influence the way we screen, categorize, and interpret information; influence our evaluations of the intentions or credibility of others; and help us decide what is important or valuable. Perhaps most important, they drive us to care about the outcome of our decision making and motivate us to take action, or refrain from taking action, on the situations we evaluate' (Susan A Bandes and Jeremy A Blumenthal, 'Emotion and the Law' (2012) 8 (1) Annual Review of Law and Social Science, 161).

110 Amy W Thornberg, Robert J Ceglie and Dixie F Abernathy, *Handbook of Research on Lessons Learned from Transitioning to Virtual Classrooms During a Pandemic* (IGI Global 2021).

158 *Emma Jones*

legal education where self-reflection is often encouraged, these are by no means the norm.[111]

There is a large body of evidence demonstrating that, in fact, emotions impact upon (and are impacted by) every aspect of a student's experience, including teaching and learning.[112] In other words, they are real and authentic elements of the law school experience. This means it is important for students to have the skills to enable them to study effectively, engage with the subject-matter and also look after their own well-being.[113] Law-related examples could include a student who finds the subject-matter of a particular case upsetting and has to be capable of interpreting their emotional response to understand the issue, a student who has had a previous experience with the law, or a group of students working together on a task requiring the social and emotional skills to navigate complex intra-personal relationship. As with the academic skills discussed above, these are not necessarily law-specific skills, for example, a historian may well have to deal with graphic accounts of disturbing events in history. However, they have specific manifestations when applied to legal study which appears to qualify them for inclusion within a broader category of authentic legal skills.

It was noted earlier that Toddington refers several times to rationality when discussing the normative ideal of law.[114] Law has often prized a certain form of rationality which positions itself as antithetical to emotions.[115] This is commonly reflected in the writings of proponents of liberal education, and liberal legal education, who largely focus on cognitive processes at

---

111 Kate Seear, Lisa Bliss, Paula Galowitz and Catherine F Klein, 'Exploring the Role of Emotions in Clinical Legal Education: Inquiry and Results from an International Workshop for Legal Educators' (2019) 53 (4) The Law Teacher, 487–499.

112 See, for example, Mary Helen Immordino-Yang, *Emotions, Learning and the Brain: Exploring the Educational Implications of Affective Neuroscience* (W. W. Norton & Co 2016); Chai M Tyng, Hafeez U Amin, Mohamad NM Saad and Aamir S Malik, 'The Influences of Emotion on Learning and Memory' (2017) 8 Frontiers in Psychology, 1454.

113 Craig Thorley, 'Not by Degrees: Improving Student Mental Health in the UK's Universities' (*Institute for Public Policy Research*, March 2017) Institute for Public Policy Research <https://www.ippr.org/files/2017-09/1504645674_not-by-degrees-170905.pdf> accessed 3 March 2021; Gareth Hughes and Leigh Spanner, 'The University Mental Health Charter' (*Student Minds*, 2019) <https://www.studentminds.org.uk/uploads/3/7/8/4/3784584/191208_umhc_artwork.pdf> accessed 3 March 2021; Jonathan Goldsmith, 'The Pandemic's Impact on Legal Education' (*The Law Society Gazette*, 15 December 2020) <https://www.lawgazette.co.uk/commentary-and-opinion/the-pandemics-impact-on-legal-education/5106805.article> accessed 3 March 2021; Aspasia I Tsaoussi, 'Using Soft Skills Courses to Inspire Law Teachers: A New Methodology for a More Humanistic Legal Education' (2020) 54 (1) The Law Teacher, 1.

114 Stuart Toddington, 'The Emperor's New Skills: The Academy, the Profession and the Idea of Legal Education' in Peter Birks (ed), *Pressing Problems in the Law: Volume 2: What Are Law Schools For?* (Oxford University Press 1996) 77, 88.

115 Terri A Maroney, 'Law and Emotion: A Proposed Taxonomy of an Emerging Field' (2006) 13 (2) Law and Human Behaviour, 119; Susan A Bandes and Jeremy Blumenthal, 'Emotion and the Law' (2012) 8 (1) Annual Review of Law and Social Science, 161.

Conceptualising legal skills in the contemporary law school 159

the expense of acknowledging emotions.[116] One interesting exception to this is Nussbaum who, writing about liberal education generally, argues that it should focus on developing a form of citizenship which requires 'narrative imagination', beginning by 'understanding the world from the point of view of the other'.[117] This suggests a form of empathy, which is generally understood to have both cognitive and affective components.[118]

Legal education still appears reluctant to incorporate emotions as integral component, meaning it is rarely expressly acknowledged, let alone emotional competencies being emphasised or taught.[119] However, it is arguable that this is gradually changing as legal educators begin to pioneer teaching methods which explicitly explore and validate emotional responses to topics and how students can regulate their reactions in healthy ways.[120] It also is likely that this process will be accelerated as a result of the Covid-19 global pandemic when the well-being of staff and students has come to the fore as a key issue for universities.[121] Although, understandably, much of the discussion on the pandemic within legal education to date has been on the need for law schools to shift to online delivery and assessment,[122] the massive

---

116 Emma Jones, *Emotions in the Law School: Transforming Legal Education through the Passions* (Routledge 2019) Chapter 1.

117 Martha Nussbaum, *Cultivating Humanity. A Classical Defence of Reform in Liberal Education* (Harvard University Press, 1997) 11.

118 Amy Coplan and Peter Goldie (eds), *Empathy. Philosophical and Psychological Perspectives* (Oxford University Press 2011) XXXIII–XXXIV.

119 Amy W Thornberg, Robert J Ceglie and Dixie F Abernathy, *Handbook of Research on Lessons Learned from Transitioning to Virtual Classrooms During a Pandemic* (IGI Global 2021); Paul Maharg and Caroline Maughan, 'Introduction' in Paul Maharg and Caroline Maughan (eds), *Affect and Legal Education: Emotion in Learning and Teaching the Law* (Ashgate Publishing 2011) 1–10.

120 For reference to affective skills, in particular, see Jessica Guth, 'The Pasts and Futures of Legal Skills in English Law Schools' in Emma Jones and Fiona Cownie (eds) *Key Directions in Legal Education: National and International Perspectives* (Routledge 2020). For interesting case studies which acknowledge the role of emotion see Sira Abenoza and César Arjona, 'Emotions and the Frontiers of Legal Education' (2017) 51 (4) The Law Teacher, 453–468; Senthorun Raj, 'Teaching Feeling: Bringing Emotion into the Law School' (2020) 55 (2) The Law Teacher.

121 See, for example, Matthew J Savage, Ruth James, Daniele Magistro, James Donaldson, Laura C Healy, Mary Nevill and Philip J Hennis, 'Mental Health and Movement Behaviour during the COVID-19 Pandemic in UK University Students: Prospective Cohort Study' (2020) 19 Mental Health and Physical Activity, 1; Richard Collier, 'Moving Across Silos: Legal Academic Wellbeing and the Legal Professions – Some Reflections on the UK Experience' in Janet Chan, Prue Vines and Michael Legg (eds), *Wellbeing in a Changing World: The Impact of Technology and Innovation on the Legal Profession* (Insentia 2020) 311–360; Richard Collier, 'Anxiety in the Legal Community – A Study of Junior Lawyers, Legal Practice and Legal Education' in Alex Davies (ed), *Lawyer Health and Wellbeing: How the Legal Profession Is Tackling Stress and Creating Resiliency* (Ark Publishing 2020).

122 See, for example, Yvonne Dutton and Seema Mohapatra, 'COVID-19 and Law Teaching: Guidance on Developing an Asynchronous Online Course for Law Students' (18

160 *Emma Jones*

implications for mental health and well-being amongst law students (and many other populations) will have to be acknowledged and processed.[123] This is arguably particularly the case in relation to law students, given the international evidence that their exposure to the discipline of law may render them particularly vulnerable to mental health and well-being issues.[124] The pandemic has demonstrated the interlinked nature of affect, emotion and well-being in a far more dramatic manner than the gradually building body of scientific evidence. Working out the implications of this for law schools and their students will require careful consideration of how so-called soft skills can and should be manifested within legal education, for example, via the incorporation of greater reflective practice, introducing law and emotions are a component of the curriculum and foregrounding well-being within all aspects of law school life.[125] The citizen of the future will also require an understanding, awareness and ability to apply 'soft skills' to enrich their relationship with society in the way heralded by Nussbaum.[126]

Conclusion

Since Toddington's chapter in Birks' collection, it may well be that the way in which some skills are demonstrated within legal education has changed. However, as discussed above, the types of skills required are still largely dictated by the (perceived) needs of the legal profession. This approach is neither justifiable nor sufficient. Toddington's categorisation of legal skills is effective in pointing out the illusory nature of reliance on these legal professional skills, and more generic professional skills. In contrast, his attempts to distinguish generic academic skills from legal skills are less convincing. It leaves a very narrow category of legal skills whilst at the same time failing to clearly identify what these could be. It seems unlikely such a vanishingly small category could assist in achieving Toddington's normative ideal of

---

 May 2020) St. Louis University Law Journal, 2021, Forthcoming, Indiana University Robert H. McKinney School of Law Research Paper No. 2020–7 <https://ssrn.com/abstract=3604331> accessed 3 March 2021.

123 Mental Health Foundation, 'Nine-Month Study Reveals Pandemic's Worsening Emotional Impacts on UK Adults' (*Mental Health Foundation*, 17 December 2020) <https://www.mentalhealth.org.uk/news/nine-month-study-reveals-pandemics-worsening-emotional-impacts-uk-adults> accessed 3 March 2021.

124 See, for example, Natalie K Skread and Shane L Rogers, 'Do Law Students Stand Apart from Other University Students in Their Quest for Mental Health: A Comparative Study on Wellbeing and Associated Behaviours in Law and Psychology Students' (2015) 42–43 International Journal of Law and Psychiatry, 81.

125 For the importance of a 'whole university' approach to wellbeing see Gareth Hughes and Leigh Spanner, 'The University Mental Health Charter' (*Student Minds*, 2019) <https://www.studentminds.org.uk/charter.html> accessed 21 April 2021.

126 Amy Coplan and Peter Goldie (eds), *Empathy. Philosophical and Psychological Perspectives* (Oxford University Press 2011).

law, which appears commensurate with good citizenship, a normative ideal commonly referred to as an end of liberal legal education.

Taking the development of good citizens as the appropriate end for legal education in English law schools means recasting the notion of an authentic legal skill as one which is required to develop students' understanding and engagement in citizenship, in other words, to shape individuals who will contribute to the positive development of society. While acknowledging the importance of the legal manifestations of general academic skills within this normative ideal, it is also necessary to encompass additional skills which are vital to the legal enterprise in contemporary society, namely, legal digital skills and skills involving emotions in a legal context. Both could, at least in part, be classed as integral to academic skills in contemporary legal education. However, they also go beyond these as crucial skillsets to ensure that the citizen of the future is one who can not only develop personally but also engage effectively with key issues facing society, issues which are likely to become even more pressing within a post-pandemic landscape. That is not to imply that these skillsets alone are required to achieve this normative ideal. There are undoubtedly a range of others whose contributions can and should be acknowledged and explored. However, the two chosen to consider within this chapter have a broad significance, from regulating emotions when dealing with complex legal issues to understanding the challenges posed by digital inequalities in ensuring access to justice.

Toddington's message that we must strive to identify authentic legal skills remains pertinent and important within today's law schools. By using the term 'authentic' to represent those skills which reflect the normative ideal of legal education and equating this to the development of the liberal notion of citizenship, this chapter has provided a framework to expand upon Toddington's original, narrow and somewhat nebulous conceptualisation of legal skills. At present, it seems the Emperor is still wearing his new clothes, and the need to find an authentic and real outfit and avoid equally glittering but diaphanous alternatives is as pressing as ever. It is hoped that this chapter will assist in developing the debate around legal skills by identifying two crucial skillsets to add to this concept and by providing a way to separate the authentic and real from the illusionary and false.

Bibliography

Abenoza S and Arjona C, 'Emotions and the Frontiers of Legal Education' (2017) 51(4) *The Law Teacher* 453–468.

Allbon E, 'Too Cool for (Law) School? Using Technology to Engage Students in Legal Skills' (2013) 4(1) *European Journal of Law and Technology*.

Alvio Gaio Alves M and Tomlinson M, 'The Changing Value of Higher Education in England and Portugal: Massification, Marketization and Public Good' (2020) *European Educational Research Journal* 1.

Bandes S and Blumenthal J, 'Emotion and the Law' (2012) 8(1) *Annual Review of Law and Social Science* 161.

162 *Emma Jones*

Bartie S, 'The Lingering Core of Legal Scholarship' (2010) 30(3) *Legal Studies* 345.

Bennett N, Dunne E, and Carre C, 'Patterns of Core and Generic Skill Provision in Higher Education' (1999) 37(1) *Higher Education* 71.

Bessant S, Robinson Z, and Ormerod R, 'Neoliberalism, New Public Management and the Sustainable Development Agenda of Higher Education: History, Contradictions and Synergies' (2015) 21(3) *Environmental Education Research* 417–432.

Bornstein B and Wiener R, 'Emotion and the Law: A Field Whose Time Has Come' in Brian H Bornstein and Richard L Wiener (eds), *Nebraska Symposium on Motivation. Emotion and the Law. Psychological Perspectives* (Springer 2010) 1.

Bradney A, *Conversations Choices and Chances: The Liberal Law School in the Twenty-First Century* (Hart Publishing 2003).

Broadbent G and Sellman P, 'Great Expectations? Law Schools, Websites and "The Student Experience"' (2013) 47(1) *The Law Teacher* 44.

Brooman S and Stirk S, 'Who Am I?: Using Reflective Practice and Self-Determination to Redefine 'Employability' in Legal Education' (2020) 41 *Liverpool Law Review* 79.

Brownsword R, 'Law Schools for Lawyers, Citizens and People' in Fiona Cownie (ed) *The Law School: Global Issues, Local Questions* (Aldershot 1999).

Brownsword R, 'Where Are All the Law Schools Going?' (1996) 30(1) *The Law Teacher* 1.

Burridge R and Webb J, 'The Values of Common Law Legal Education Reprised' (2009) 43(2) *The Law Teacher* 263, 264.

Cantrell D, 'Are Clinics a Magic Bullet?'(2014) 51 *Alberta Law Review* 831.

Chan C, Fong E, Luk L, and Ho R, 'A Review of Literature on Challenges in the Development and Implementation of Generic Competencies in Higher Education Curriculum' (2017) 57 *International Journal of Educational Development*, 1.

Co E, 'Teaching Cultural Competence as a Fundamental Lawyering Skill' (2019) 23 *Legal Writing: Journal of the Legal Writing Institute* 4.

Collier R, 'Anxiety in the Legal Community – A Study of Junior Lawyers, Legal Practice and Legal Education' in Alex Davies (ed) *Lawyer Health and Wellbeing: How the Legal Profession Is Tackling Stress and Creating Resiliency* (Ark Publishing 2020).

Collier R, '"Love Law, Love Life" Neoliberalism, Wellbeing and Gender in the Legal Profession – The Case of Law School' (2014) 17(2) *Legal Ethics* 202.

Collier R, 'Moving across Silos: Legal Academic Wellbeing and the Legal Professions – Some Reflections on the UK Experience' in Janet Chan, Prue Vines, and Michael Legg (eds) *Wellbeing in a Changing World: The Impact of Technology and Innovation on the Legal Profession* (Insentia 2020) 311–360.

Condlin R, '"Practice Ready Graduates": A Millennialist Fantasy' (2014–2015) 31 *Touro Law Review* 75.

Coplan A and Goldie P (eds), *Empathy. Philosophical and Psychological Perspectives* (Oxford University Press 2011).

Cownie F and Bradney A, 'Gothic Horror? A Response to Margaret Thornton' (2005) 14(2) *Social & Legal Studies* 277.

Crook J, 'A Brief History of Liberal Legal Education: The Battle between Law as a Science and Law as a Liberal Art' (2017) 17(2) *Legal History* 30.

D'Aoust A, 'Ties that Bind? Engaging Emotions, Governmentality and Neoliberalism: Introduction to the Special Issue' (2014) 28(3) *Global Society* 267.

Conceptualising legal skills in the contemporary law school 163

Department for Business, Innovation and Skills, *Success as a Knowledge Economy: Teaching Excellent, Social Mobility and Student Choice* (2016) <https://assets.publishing.service.gov.uk/government/uploads/system/uploads/attachment_data/file/523546/bis-16-265-success-as-a-knowledge-economy-web.pdf> accessed 5 January 2021.

Dutton Y and Mohapatra S, 'COVID-19 and Law Teaching: Guidance on Developing an Asynchronous Online Course for Law Students' (18 May 2020) *St. Louis University Law Journal*, 2021, Forthcoming, Indiana University Robert H. McKinney School of Law Research Paper No. 2020–7 <https://ssrn.com/abstract=3604331> accessed 3 March 2021.

Frankham J, 'Employability and Higher Education: The Follies of the 'Productivity Challenge' in the Teaching Excellence Framework' (2017) 32(5) *Journal of Education Policy* 628.

Goldsmith J, 'The Pandemic's Impact on Legal Education' (*The Law Society Gazette*, 15 December 2020) <https://www.lawgazette.co.uk/commentary-and-opinion/the-pandemics-impact-on-legal-education/5106805.article> accessed 3 March 2021.

Goleman D, *Emotional Intelligence* (Bloomsbury 1996).

Greenstein L, *Assessing 21st Century Skills: A Guide to Evaluating Mastery and Authentic Learning* (Corwin 2012) 51.

Guth J, 'The Pasts and Futures of Legal Skills in English Law Schools' in Emma Jones and Fiona Cownie (eds) *Key Directions in Legal Education: National and International Perspectives* (Routledge 2020).

Guth J and Ashford C, 'The Legal Education and Training Review: Regulating Socio-Legal and Liberal Legal Education?' (2014) 48(1) *The Law Teacher* 5.

Handley F, 'Developing Digital Skills and Literacies in UK Higher Education: Recent Developments and a Case Study of the Digital Literacies Framework at the University of Brighton, UK' (2018) 48(1) *Publicaciones.*

Harris P and Beinart S, 'A Survey of Law Schools in the United Kingdom' (2004) 39(3) *The Law Teacher* 299.

Harris P and Jones M, 'A Survey of Law Schools in the United Kingdom' (1996) 31(1) *The Law Teacher* 38–126.

Hughes G and Spanner L, 'The University Mental Health Charter' (*Student Minds*, 2019) <https://www.studentminds.org.uk/charter.html> accessed 21 April 2021.

Hutchinson T and Duncan N, 'Defining and Describing What We Do: Doctrinal Legal Research' (2012) 17 *Deakin Law Review* 83.

Immordino-Yang M, *Emotions, Learning and the Brain: Exploring the Educational Implications of Affective Neuroscience* (W. W. Norton & Co, 2016).

James C, 'Lawyers'' Wellbeing and Professional Legal Education' (2008) 42(1) *The Law Teacher* 85.

James N, 'More Than Merely Work-Ready: Vocationalism versus Professionalism in Legal Education' (2017) 40(1) *University of New South Wales Law Journal* 186.

Jones D, 'Legal Skills and the SQE: Confronting the Challenge Head on' (2018) 53(1) *The Law Teacher* 35.

Jones E, *Emotions in the Law School: Transforming Legal Education through the Passions* (Routledge 2019).

Jones E, Ryan F, Thanaraj A, and Wong T, *Digital Lawyering: Technology and Legal Practice in the 21st Century* (Routledge 2021).

164 *Emma Jones*

Kam L, Ruyters M, Coburn C, and Toohey M, 'Ger Real; A Case Study of Authentic Learning Activities in Legal Education' (2012) 19 *Murdoch University Law Review* 17.

Kiser R, *Soft Skills for the Effective Lawyer* (Cambridge University Press 2017).

Lawless C and Faulkner A (eds), *Material Worlds: Intersections of Law, Science, Technology, and Society* (Wiley-Blackwell 2012).

Lawyer Monthly, 'Law Graduate Opportunities Aren't Passing the Bar, Official Data Suggests' (January 2019) < https://www.lawyer-monthly.com/issues/2019/01/9/> accessed 26 February 2021.

Lewinbuk K and Gilbert C, 'Law Student Heal Thy Self: Teaching Mindfulness as a Legal Skill' (2016) 41 *Journal of Legal Professionals* 37.

Lynch K, 'Neoliberalism and Marketisation: The Implications for Higher Education' (2006) 5(1) *European Education Research Journal* 1.

Maharg P, 'Negotiating the Web: Legal Skills Learning in a Virtual Community' (2001) 15(3) *International Review of Law, Computers & Technology* 345.

Maharg P and Maughan C, 'Introduction' in Paul Maharg and Caroline Maughan (eds) *Affect and Legal Education: Emotion in Learning and Teaching the Law* (Ashgate Publishing 2011) 1–10.

Marmot M and Allen J, 'Covid-19: Exposing and Amplifying Inequalities' (2020) 74(9) *Community Health* 681–682.

Maroney T, 'Law and Emotion: A Proposed Taxonomy of an Emerging Field' (2006) 13(2) *Law and Human Behaviour* 119.

Marson J, Wilson A, and Van Hoorebeek M, 'The Necessity of Clinical Legal Education in University Law Schools: A UK Perspective' (2005) 7 *International Journal of Clinical Legal Education* 29.

Martin Barry M, 'Practice Ready: Are We There Yet?' (2012) 32 *Boston College Journal of Law & Social Justice* 247.

McFaul H, FitzGerald E, Ryan F, and Byrne D, 'A Mobile App for Public Legal Education: A Case Study of Co-Designing with Students' (2020) 28 *Research in Learning Technology* 2434.

Mehrvarz M, Heidari E, Farrokhnia M, and Noroozi O, 'The Mediating Role of Digital Informal Learning in the Relationship between Students' Digital Competency and Their Academic Performance' (2021) 167 *Computers and Education* 104184.

Menis S, 'The Liberal, the Vocational and Legal Education: A Legal History Review – From Blackstone to a Law Degree (1972)' (2020) 54(2) *The Law Teacher* 285.

Mental Health Foundation, 'Nine-Month Study Reveals Pandemic's Worsening Emotional Impacts on UK Adults' (*Mental Health Foundation*, 17 December 2020) <https://www.mentalhealth.org.uk/news/nine-month-study-reveals-pandemics-worsening-emotional-impacts-uk-adults> accessed 3 March 2021.

Moore T and Morton J, 'The Myth of Job Readiness? Written Communication, Employability, and the 'Skills Gap' in Higher Education' (2017) 42(3) *Studies in Higher Education* 591.

National Committee of Inquiry into Higher Education, The Dearing Report: Higher Education in the Learning Society (*Education in England*, 1997) <http://www.educationengland.org.uk/documents/dearing1997/dearing1997.html> accessed 3 January 2021.

Nussbaum M, *Cultivating Humanity. A Classical Defence of Reform in Liberal Education* (Harvard University Press 1997) 11.

Pagani L, Argentin G, Gui M, and Stanca L, 'The Impact of Digital Skills on Educational Outcomes: Evidence from Performance Tests' (2016) 42(4) *Educational Studies* 137.

Petraglia J, *Reality by Design: The Rhetoric and Technology of Authenticity in Education* (Routledge 1998).

Pue W, 'Legal Education's Mission (2008) 42(3) *The Law Teacher* 270, 272; see also Kate Green and Hilary Limb, 'A Lib-Lib Pact: Silences in Legal Education' (1987) 21(3) *The Law Teacher* 256.

Quality Assurance Agency, 'Subject Benchmark Statement: Law' <https://www.qaa.ac.uk/docs/qaa/subject-benchmark-statements/subject-benchmark-statement-law.pdf?sfvrsn=b939c881_18> accessed 7 January 2021.

Raj S, 'Teaching Feeling: Bringing Emotion into the Law School' (2020) 55(2) *The Law Teacher* 128.

Rigg D, 'Embedding Employability in Assessment: Searching for the Balance between Academic Learning and Skills Development in Law: A Case Study' (2013) 47(3) *The Law Teacher* 404.

Robbins H, 'The Emperor's New Critique' (Autumn 2003) 34(4) *New Literary History* 670.

Römgens I, Scoupe R, and Beausaert S, 'Unraveling the Concept of Employability, Bringing Together Research on Employability in Higher Education and the Workplace' (2020) 45(12) *Studies in Higher Education* 2588.

Rothblatt S, *Tradition and Change in English Legal Education. An Essay in History and Culture* (Faber and Faber 1976) 195.

Sandbach J and Grimes R, 'Law School Pro Bono and Clinic Report 2020: LawWorks and CLEO (Clinical Legal Education Organisation)' (2020) <https://www.lawworks.org.uk/sites/default/files/files/LawWorks%20Law%20Schools%20Report%202020_0.pdf> accessed 7 May 2021.

Savage M, James R, Magistro D, Donaldson J, Healy L, Nevill M, and Hennis P, 'Mental Health and Movement Behaviour during the COVID-19 Pandemic in UK University Students: Prospective Cohort Study' (2020) 19 *Mental Health and Physical Activity* 1.

Seear K, Bliss L, Galowitz P, and Klein C, 'Exploring the Role of Emotions in Clinical Legal Education: Inquiry and Results from an International Workshop for Legal Educators' (2019) 53(4) *The Law Teacher* 487–499.

Simpson B, 'Algorithms or Advocacy: Does the Legal Profession Have a Future in a Digital World?' (2016) 25(1) *Information & Communications Technology Law* 50.

Skread N and Rogers S, 'Do Law Students Stand Apart from Other University Students in Their Quest for Mental Health: A Comparative Study on Wellbeing and Associated Behaviours in Law and Psychology Students' (2015) 42–43 *International Journal of Law and Psychiatry* 81.

Solicitors Regulation Authority, 'Solicitors Qualifying Examination ('SQE') (February 2021) <https://www.sra.org.uk/students/sqe/> accessed 26 February 2021.

Solicitor Regulation Authority, 'SQE1 and SQE2 Assessments' <https://www.sra.org.uk/students/sqe/sqe-assessments/> accessed 7 May 2021.

Staudt R and Lauritsen M, 'Justice, Lawyering and Legal Education in the Digital Age: Introduction' (2013) 88 *Chicago-Kent Law Review* 687 <https://papers.ssrn.com/sol3/papers.cfm?abstract_id=2335470> accessed 15 August 2021.

Stevens R, *Law School. Legal Education in America from the 1850s to the 1980s* (The University of North Carolina Press 1983).

Stropus R, 'Mend It, Bend It, and Extend It: the Fate of Traditional Law School Methodology in the 21st Century' (1996) 27(3) *Loyola University of Chicago Law Journal* 449.

Sugarman D, 'Legal Theory, the Common Law Mind and the Making of the Textbook Tradition' in William Twining (ed) *Legal Theory and Common Law* (Basil Blackwell 1986).

Susan Bartie, 'The Lingering Core of Legal Scholarship' (2010) 30(3) *Legal Studies* 345.

Thanaraj A, 'Making the Case for a Digital Lawyering Framework in Legal Education' (2017) 2017(3) *International Review of Law* 17.

Thanaraj A, 'Understanding How a Law Clinic Can Contribute towards Students' Development of Professional Responsibility' (2016) 23 *International Journal of Clinical Legal Education* 89.

The Law Society of England and Wales, 'Entry Trends' (25 November 2020) <https://www.lawsociety.org.uk/en/career-advice/becoming-a-solicitor/entry-trends> accessed 26 February 2021.

The Lord Chancellors', *Advisory Committee on Legal Education and Conduct, First Report on Legal Education and Training* (London 1996).

Thorley C, 'Not by Degrees: Improving Student Mental Health in the UK's Universities' (*Institute for Public Policy Research*, March 2017) Institute for Public Policy Research <https://www.ippr.org/files/2017-09/1504645674_not-by-degrees-170905.pdf> accessed 3 March 2021.

Thornberg A, Ceglie R, and Abernathy D, *Handbook of Research on Lessons Learned from Transitioning to Virtual Classrooms during a Pandemic* (IGI Global 2021).

Toddington S, 'Skills, Quality and the Ideologies of Managerialism' (1994) 28 *Law Teacher* 243.

Toddington S, 'The Emperor's New Skills: The Academy, the Profession and the Idea of Legal Education' in Peter Birks (ed) *Pressing Problems in the Law: Volume 2: What Are Law Schools For?* (Oxford University Press 1996).

Tomlinson M, 'The Impact of Market-Driven Higher Education on Student-University Relations: Investing, Consuming and Competing' (2016) 29 *High Education Policy* 149.

Tsaoussi A, 'Using Soft Skills Courses to Inspire Law Teachers: A New Methodology for a More Humanistic Legal Education' (2020) 54(1) *The Law Teacher* 1.

Turner J, Bone A, and Ashton J, 'Reasons Why Law Students Should Have Access to Learning Law through a Skills-Based Approach' (2018) 52(1) *The Law Teacher* 1.

Twining W, 'Legal Skills and Legal Education' (1988) 22 *The Law Teacher* 4.

Tyng C, Amin H, Saad M, and Malik A, 'The Influences of Emotion on Learning and Memory' (2017) 8 *Frontiers in Psychology* 1454.

Vick D, 'Interdisciplinarity and the Discipline of Law' (2004) 31(2) *Journal of Law and Society* 163.

Waters B, 'The Solicitors Qualification Examination: Something for All? Some Challenges Facing Law Schools in England and Wales' (2018) 52(4) *The Law Teacher* 519.

Webb J, 'Where the Action Is: Developing Artistry in Legal Education' (1995) 2 *International Journal of the Legal Profession* 187, 188.

Wiatr J (ed), *New Authoritarianism: Challenges to Democracy in the 21st century* (Barbara Budrich Publishers 2019).

7 'Originary intimacy'

A thought experiment in jurisprudential legal education inquiry

Paul Maharg

Introduction

I studied law at Glasgow University 1990–1992 as a post-doctoral student (having studied undergraduate at Glasgow in Arts, majoring in literary theory and aesthetics, then completed a doctoral thesis at Edinburgh in the same areas); and after an Education degree, I taught adults for six years in a variety of outreach centres in areas of multiple deprivation in Glasgow. Four years later, then a law academic, I came across Birks' collection on the purpose of law schools in a second-hand bookshop in Glasgow called Voltaire & Rousseau. Picking it up, it looked like a curious publication: softback, monotone black binding, A4-sized pages, as if it were a report on legal education, or else the publisher wasn't giving much time and expense to the project.[1] And it was volume two of a series, the first being on substantive law, with no relation to the second. After studying on a law degree where private law dominated, where jurisprudence was an outlier and teaching quality was with significant exceptions poor, it was interesting to read the debates in Birks' collection. But coming from an Arts background, it was also frustrating, and the book read like a missed opportunity. Like the physical format of the book, it was an oddity. Reading it in Glasgow, in 1997, in a Scots culture and Scots legal culture background, it was remarkable that there was almost no discussion of any other jurisdiction in these isles except England, for example, and technology, digital or otherwise, appeared to be largely absent from the activities and the theory base of legal education.[2]

---

1 A prior volume on legal education was produced in 1994 and with identical binding; but as noted in Preface that volume had a different history, being the publication of papers arising from a seminar held at All Souls College, Oxford in May 1994 on the future of legal education. Peter BH Birks, *Reviewing Legal Education* (Oxford University Press 1994).
2 S.6 in Clark & Tsamenyi's chapter deals with it in overview. As we note in the chapter by Bleasdale, Maharg and Newbery-Jones, technology had been the topic of a chapter by Hugh Collins in the 1994 volume, *Reviewing Legal Education*. However even in that book there was little broad conception of technology and its effects on education, the law and society in general.

DOI: 10.4324/9781003322092-7

168 *Paul Maharg*

With the exception of the chapters by Toddington[3] and Goodrich,[4] the book had little to say to me unless it were of the state of English legal educational cultures and arguments: it seemed remote, marginal, curiously oppressive despite its wide-ranging topics.

This chapter is the second part of an exploration of the status of legal education as a jurisprudential activity.[5] In the first piece, I described how in the eleventh century, the newly discovered Justinianic codes and texts, voluminous, exotic, arcane, were collated, understood and put into practice, along with the ever-burgeoning, increasingly complex codes of canon law.[6] And how, to cope with the information overload brought about by this data, scholars developed interpretive methods and apparatuses over subsequent centuries that included glosses, commentaries, summaries and much else. Indeed, scholarly understanding of canon law and the reception of Roman law would not have been possible without the development of the textual grammars and technologies that were to become foundational to our understanding of law and legal method, its reception, structure and migration. In this sense, legal educational forms, cultures, technologies and genres on the one hand and legal jurisprudential methods on the other were closely allied in their early development. There was an 'originary intimacy' between legal method and educational method.[7]

In this chapter, I make the claim that the uneasy status of legal education stems not just from its multidisciplinary origins but also from it having

---

3 Stuart Toddington, 'The Emperor's New Skills: The Academy, The Profession and the Idea of Legal Education' in Peter Birks (ed), *Pressing Problems in the Law: Volume 2: What Are Law Schools For?* (Oxford University Press 1996).

4 Peter Goodrich, 'Of Blackstone's Tower: Metaphors of Distance and Histories of the English Law School' in Peter Birks (ed), *What Are Law Schools For?* (Oxford University Press 1996).

5 The first was Paul Maharg, 'Same as It Ever Was? Second Modernity, Technocracy, and the Design of Digital Legal Education' in Catrina Denvir (ed), *Modernising Legal Education* (Cambridge University Press 2020).

6 The medieval and renaissance background is detailed further in Paul Maharg, *Transforming Legal Education: Learning and Teaching the Law in the Early Twenty-First Century* (Routledge 2007) Chapter 5.

7 I borrow the phrase from studies on Heidegger's concept of Dasein. In *Sein und Zeit* Heidegger speaks of a '*Vertrautheit* or confident familiarity between *Dasein* and the world' (William Desmond). But others have noted that in Heidegger's numinous description of *Dasein*, there is a deep melancholy, a disjunct, a loss, borne of immersion in temporality and the world – see Agamben, Giorgio. 'The Use of the World.' In Giorgio Agamben, *The Use of Bodies* (Stanford University Press 2016) 38–48. In using the phrase, it may appear that I reify and make of early legal educations a nostalgic model that cannot be recreated or sustained in the modern period. Far from it: I recognize the serious difficulties inherent in those early beginnings in Paul Maharg, 'Same as It Ever Was? Second Modernity, Technocracy, and the Design of Digital Legal Education' in Catrina Denvir (ed), *Modernising Legal Education* (Cambridge University Press 2020); and as I describe at the end of this chapter, hold that it is still possible to create a new originary intimacy between legal educations and legal method.

'Originary intimacy' 169

no apparent place in the foundational methods and knowledge structures within the legal academy. This perennial anxiety, I argue, is a result of our loss of perspective brought about by modern amnesiac constructions of legal education: viewed from a different angle, the educative core of legal education has always been part of law's project, at least in the global north and west. That it has seemed of minor importance only in that project is itself a topic worthy of analysis and interrogation – in Lee Shulman's terms, legal education itself has become a shadow within northern and western jurisprudential traditions. Even within Birks' collection, we can see the traces of this subordination: empirical education research and links to education more generally, as well as other disciplines' forms of education and their history of education, which are surely part of a law school's intellectual context – all these are significantly absent from the volume. Here, therefore, I argue that now, a millennium after law's early educations, we need to return the 'originary intimacy' between education and method. I claim that within the modern period, such intimacy, of necessity always in tension, always critical, is essential for both law and its educations.

Indeed, for some time prior to Birks' collection, there had been strong arguments for *re*-claiming legal education as a core jurisprudential activity, and for the expansion of jurisprudence to include the educational theoretical challenges to law's project.[8] To demonstrate this, I have created a thought

---

8 The evidence for this lies less in English jurisprudential *oeuvres* and more in the traditions of other jurisdictions – Scotland's legal educational traditions are one example. See Francis Hutcheson's treatment of the status of emotion and rationality (distinguishing the roles played by impelling causes for conduct as opposed to justifications of behaviour in Francis Hutcheson, 'An Essay on the Nature and Conduct of the Passions and Affections' (first published in 1728) in Bernhard Fabian (ed), *Collected Works of Francis Hutcheson* (Facsimile edn, G Olms 1969–1990) vol II, 27–29; the Enlightenment reconsideration of education in Lord Henry Home Kames, *Introduction to the Art of Thinking. Enlarged with Additional Maxims and Illustrations* (Edinburgh 1764); Lord Henry Home Kames, *Loose Hints upon Education, Chiefly Concerning the Culture of the Heart* (Edinburgh 1781); Adam Smith, *Lectures on Jurisprudence* (Glasgow edn of the Works and Correspondence of Adam Smith, Liberty Fund Inc, New York, 1982) vol 5; John Cairns, 'The Influence of Smith's Jurisprudence on Legal Education in Scotland' in Peter Jones and Andrew S Skinner (eds), *Adam Smith Reviewed* (Edinburgh University Press 1992); James Lorimer, *The Institutes of Law: A Treatise of the Principles of Jurisprudence as Determined by Nature* (2nd edn, Edinburgh 1880); Neil MacCormick, Regius Professor of Law, Edinburgh University, took an interest in this tradition – e.g. Neil MacCormick, 'Law and Enlightenment' in RH Campbell and Andrew S Skinner (eds), *The Origins and Nature of the Scottish Enlightenment* (J Donald Publishers 1982).

The US tradition of pragmatist, neopragmatist, legal realist, New Legal Realist and European New Legal Realist traditions are more powerful examples. See for example the *oeuvres* of Karl Llewellyn, Roscoe Pound and the Columbia realists (comment on the last in Paul Maharg, *Transforming Legal Education: Learning and Teaching the Law in the Early Twenty-First Century* (Routledge 2007) Chapter 4; Elizabeth Mertz, *The Language of Law School: Learning to 'Think Like a Lawyer'* (Oxford University Press 2007).

170 *Paul Maharg*

experiment.[9] I reconstruct a jurisprudential argument from the materials and debates historically available to the Birks' collection authors that would offer an alternative position for legal education in its legal academic and professional contexts. There are two aims. First is to explore what I sensed even then, namely a deep disjunct between jurisprudential methodology and education, a disjunct that we can trace in Birks' collection. Second is to think myself back to the younger academic in the aptly-named Voltaire & Rousseau bookshop and to write the chapter that I might have written then.[10] Throughout my life as a legal academic I have researched and developed versions of legal realist thought within the field of legal education – what did I have to contribute in 1996? Since this is a case of historical thought experiment, in a reversal of the usual chronological end-point stated in the front matter of legal textbooks, I will begin by stating that in the following arguments, no resources are used that are later than the publication date of the Birks' collection – 7 November 1996.[11] My arguments are multidisciplinary in origin, but my approach is grounded in a particular mode of realist analysis, as will become evident.

---

9 For an introduction to the concept of a thought experiment, see Michael T Stuart, Yiftach Fehige and James Robert Brown (eds), *The Routledge Companion to Thought Experiments* (Routledge 2018). Their Introduction is an excellent overview of the literature and salient examples beyond science and technology, as well as the history of the philosophy of thought experiments. For a brief definition and an exploration of the literature on thought experiments, see Kimberley Brownlee and Zofia Stemplowska, 'Trapped in an Experience Machine with a Famous Violinist: Thought Experiments in Normative Theory' <www.academia.edu/371276/Trapped_in_an_Experience_Machine_with_a_Famous_Violinist_Thought_Experiments_in_Normative_Theory_with_Zofia_Stemplowska_> accessed 23 July 2021. I would claim that my thought experiment here conforms to two of their characteristics, in that I use it to 'demonstrate the consistency or coherence of a set of principles/ concepts' and 'reveal the scope of the application of a given principle' (ibid, 1).

It is interesting to note that for all the differences between the two Enlightenment figures, Voltaire and Rousseau, particularly on education, both used thought experiments – Voltaire most notably in his satirical novella, *Candide, ou l'Optimisme* (1759), Rousseau in his construction of an entire educational *ethos* in *Émile, ou De l'éducation* (1762). And both thought experiments were in different ways versions of *Bildungsroman*, the descriptive account of growing into maturity.

10 I do not, of course, claim that I would have written this chapter then. Rather, it is an exercise in counterfactuals that is typical of thought experiments – if I were to write then, which concepts and arguments was I aware of that I would use; and which ideas was I then exploring in which disciplines, that I would have used to construct the piece? How would I re-vision, rather than reverse, legal education?

11 Throughout I use footnotes to make comments on the situation in legal education pre-1996 and now in 2022.

The play of surfaces: Stanley Fish, anti-foundational pragmatism and legal education

The directions of neopragmatic theory are bewildering in their fecundity: Rorty's versions of irony, Derridean text-play and democracy; Stanley Fish's concept of the role of interpretive communities in shaping canons and professional practice; Cornel West's theory of prophetic pragmatism – these are only some of the more celebrated forms of the theory.[12] In a perceptive passage, Thomas Grey points out that

> from a certain philosophical perspective, Holmes' pragmatist theory of law is... essentially banal. At its most abstract level it concludes in truisms: Law is more a matter of experience than logic, and experience is tradition interpreted with one eye on coherence and another on policy.[13]

This passage is cited by Richard Rorty to illustrate what he terms the contemporary banality of pragmatism.[14] He claims that the lessons of pragmatism, now around a century old, have been well learned by jurists. As a result of this, for Rorty, only two issues in the new or neopragmatism are of interest: first, the replacement of the discourse of experience with that of language ('we new pragmatists talk about language instead of experience or mind or consciousness, as the old pragmatists did' [p. 91]); second, the abandonment of the search for a 'scientific method' in legal theory.[15] As Rorty points out, the two issues, though separate, are not unrelated: 'without the so-called "linguistic turn", the topic of "theory-neutral observation language" could not have been posed', and he cites Carnap, Hempel and Quine in defence of this view.[16]

His point is a perceptive one, but it is by no means all the story. Rorty's view of pragmatism could be interpreted to be what Harold Bloom has termed a *clinamen*, a creative swerve from the sources of his own discourse, a misreading of earlier pragmatists such as Dewey and others so as to distance them from his own pragmatist domain. Indeed, if we were to succumb to Rorty's beguiling tale of origins, we would be in danger of dismissing many of the most fruitful contemporary debates regarding the place of theory in legal studies and legal pedagogy. Central to these debates is the place of rhetoric in legal and humanist enquiry, and the extent to which enquiry in

---

12 For a summary of the connections between the early and latter-day pragmatisms, see Giles Gunn, *Thinking across the American Grain: Ideology, Intellect and the New Pragmatism* (University of Chicago Press 1992) 1–21.

13 Thomas Grey, 'Holmes and Legal Pragmatism' (1989) 41 (4) Stanford Law Review, 787, 814.

14 Richard Rorty, 'The Banality of Pragmatism and the Poetry of Justice' in Michael Brint and William Weaver (eds), *Pragmatism in Law and Society* (Westview Press 1991) 89.

15 Ibid, 91.

16 Ibid, 96.

172 *Paul Maharg*

rhetoric has powered the anti-foundational campaigns within legal theory and adjacent disciplines. As Cornel West put it, '[e]pistemic antifoundationalism... proceed[s] from taking seriously the impact of modern historical and rhetorical consciousness on truth and knowledge'.[17]

It is important, however, to define even within general terms, what is understood by 'rhetoric'. Most neopragmatists would react against a revival of the classical or Renaissance forms of rhetoric. Peter Goodrich made this point well in a review of Brian Vickers' lengthy *In Defence of Rhetoric* when he declared that 'the revival of rhetoric in legal studies runs the danger of archaism and worse of a blinkered refusal to accommodate theory to changing technologies of practice'.[18] His opposition to Vicker's foundational project is typical of the use to which neopragmatists put rhetoric. When neopragmatists employ the tools of rhetorical enquiry, they use rhetoric itself to signify epistemological concerns which are figured, pre-figured and retraced by the tropes of rhetorical delivery. The rhetorical turn is in fact an anti-foundational strategy, of which Stanley Fish probably provides the nearest thing to a definition we might find among the heterogenous neopragmatists:

> Anti-foundationalism teaches that questions of fact, truth, correctness, validity, and clarity can neither be posed nor answered in reference to some extracontextual, ahistorical, nonsituational reality, or rule, or law, or value; rather, anti-foundationalism asserts, all of these matters are intelligible and debatable only within the precincts of the contexts or situations or paradigms or communities that give them their local and changeable shape.[19]

We can see this at work in an essay by Fish, 'The Law Wishes to Have a Formal Existence'. The bland statement of the title, redolent of Wallace Stevens, is highly rhetorical, quietly provoking. It could read as ironic of law's desire, or as a neutral, objective statement of value. And if the essay's title is open to several interpretations, it signifies the status of what is about to come. Fish begins by adopting what appears to be an extreme pragmatist, indeed a typical Critical Legal Studies (CLS) approach: 'law is what you can get

---

17 Cornel West, 'Theory, Pragmatisms, and Politics' in Jonathan Arac and Barbara Johnson (eds), *Consequences of Theory* (Johns Hopkins University Press 1991) 36. For cross-disciplinary approaches to rhetoric, see H W Simons (ed), *The Rhetorical Turn: Invention and Persuasion in the Conduct of Inquiry* (University of Chicago Press, 1992); Richard H Roberts and James MM Good (eds), *The Recovery of Rhetoric: Persuasive Discourse and Disciplinarity in the Human Sciences* (Bristol Classical Press 1993).

18 Peter Goodrich, 'We Orators' (1990) 53 (4) Modern Law Review, 546, 563.

19 Stanley Fish, *Doing What Comes Naturally: Change, Rhetoric, and the Practice of Theory in Literary and Legal Studies* (Clarendon Press 1989) 344. At page 345, Fish provides a comprehensive cross-disciplinary list of antifoundationalist practitioners.

'Originary intimacy'   173

away with'.[20] But where CLS decries this, Fish holds it to be crucial to law's existence. The legal correctness of any decision is a function of the persuasiveness of the argument which led to that decision; and there is no escape from the necessity to persuade. Appeals beyond the immediate court and case to natural justice or public policy are simply other forms of rhetorical argument. In this sense, Fish's account of the practice of law is antifoundational, in that he denies there is a foundation or bedrock reality upon which the insubstantial pageant of rhetoric stands. Rhetoric is the real, and its supple contingency is vital to the working of law. The fact that 'law is at once thoroughly rhetorical and engaged in the effacing of its own rhetoricity' is not an elaborate way of denying that law *is* formalist in nature: Fish pushes this further to say that law's aspirations to a formal existence are a necessary disguise for its actual mode of existence, which is highly rhetorical.[21] In this way, law appears to allow of creativity in argument within bounded and discrete clearings. It appears to enable and disable argument according to what appear to be normative grounds, when in fact all that we have is, to adopt the title of another of Fish's essays, the play of surfaces, rhetorical creativity at work.[22]

Fish's accounts of the necessity of rhetoric to law spring from his own practice as a literary critic. Rhetoric is essential to Fish's method. He bases his critique of law not upon research founded in, say, discourse analysis, pragmatics or sociolinguistics, or the literature of professionalisation, but upon the neopragmatist recuperation of rhetoric. As a result, he is drawn into explanatory accounts of the ways in which rhetoric functions within law, and particularly within practice. His anti-foundationalist views on this have clashed, strongly at times, with those on more traditionalist wings of modern academic jurisprudence, including Dworkin and Posner. This has led some commentators to place Fish, if not in the company of New Historicists and CLS exponents, then at least by their side; but Fish, while admitting sympathy with some of their aims, has distanced himself from these groups. Indeed, Fish is curiously conventional in a number of his views, none more so than in those on legal education. In this respect, it is interesting to turn to the debate between Fish and Peter Goodrich on the subject of practice and theory.

Goodrich takes issue with Fish on the latter's assertion of the 'priority of practice over analysis and... the necessity of distinguishing separable and separate contexts of genre, specifically those of literary criticism or, rather

---

20 Stanley Fish, 'The Law Wishes to Have a Formal Existence' in Alan Norrie (ed), *Closure or Critique: New Directions in Legal Theory* (Edinburgh University Press 1993) 168.
21 Ibid, 170.
22 Stanley Fish, 'The Play of Surfaces: Theory and the Law' in Gregory Leyh (ed), *Legal Hermeneutics. History, Theory, and Practice* (University of California Press 1992).

174   Paul Maharg

improbably, philosophy and law'.[23] He quotes Fish's memorable observation that 'law is not philosophy, and it will not fade away because a few guys in Cambridge and Palo Alto are now able to deconstruct it'.[24] In the process of reaching this conclusion regarding the hermetic boundaries of those disciplines, Goodrich notes that Fish deliberately distances the realms of academic legal thought and legal practice, and that in Fish's account, practice becomes curiously inarticulate:

> the two are not simply and inexplicably deemed to be separate, as if teaching or discipline belonged somewhere topologically outside the real world of activity, but also hierarchically related, as if it were somehow better and more normal to act unthinkingly, to forget, to repress.[25]

Goodrich is not the first to criticise this aspect of Fish's neopragmatic approach to law's discipline. In a review of one of his essay collections, Ian Ward has revealed the extent to which Fish's view of practice departs from what actually happens in practice.[26] But Goodrich is perhaps the only critic to point out that Fish's account of the separation of the two domains contradicts Fish's own best insights into the rhetorical nature of legal practice.

Goodrich argues that this separation springs ineluctably from Fish's simultaneous argument that boundaries define a discipline, that a discipline, or for that matter a genre or a practice, cannot be defined without boundaries. He quotes Fish – 'every practice is... insulated and depends for its emergence as a practice – as an activity distinct from other activities – on a certain ignorance of its debts and complicities'.[27] Fish's point is an acute one: disciplines and practices do employ amnesiac strategies in order to create their own historical versions of themselves, and in this respect, his use of the word 'ignorance' must surely be ironic. After all, if practices forget, it is remembered for a least a time that something is in the process of being forgotten before that data entirely disappears. In this sense, practices never stop emerging: their strategies and their images constantly grow or fade, and amongst much else undergo paradigm shifts. And the very fact that such 'complicities' can, in the process of later historical, political and cultural analyses, be revealed and interpreted by those within the practice and others without it is also part of the continuous emergence of practice. Goodrich, though, reads Fish's observations on insulation as insularity:

---

23 Peter Goodrich, *Law in the Courts of Love: Literature and Other Minor Jurisprudences* (Routledge 1996) 115.
24 Ibid.
25 Ibid.
26 Ian Ward, 'The Educative Ambition of Law and Literature' (1993) 13 (3) Legal Studies, 323–331.
27 Stanley Fish, *There's No Such Thing as Free Speech and It's a Good Thing, Too* (Oxford University Press 1994) 174.

'*Originary intimacy*' 175

such a view of practice could only be true 'if we were prepared to distinguish rigidly practice from theory, activity from thought', which Goodrich clearly is not prepared to do.[28]

For Goodrich, it is precisely the rigidity, the lack of reflexivity he perceives in Fish's rhetoric that compels him to distance his own version of forgetting from that of Fish – 'just as critical historiography reads forgetting as a positive act, so a critical jurisprudence must confront... law's amnesia... and endeavour thereby to read the unconscious body of law'.[29] This involves re-membering the 'displacement and repression that make knowledge appear absolute in the theatre of law'.[30] Within Goodrich's own rhetorical intentions, therefore, Fish's conception of the relation of theory to practice is interpreted as complicity with an unsatisfactory *status quo*: 'Fish's *vita activa* or real world of practice is presented as being forever external to such merely rhetorical conceptions of knowledge as power'.[31]

Whether or not Goodrich's interpretation of Fish can be sustained (and I do think that at times Goodrich not only misses the anarchic playfulness with which Fish attacks crass interdisciplinary interpretations but also his genuine commitment to the anti-foundationalist cause), the point at issue in this debate is one that is central to the neopragmatist endeavour. It is also central to the theory and practice of contemporary legal education: namely, how relevant is theory to legal education? More specifically, can a theory of practice ever be useful to students learning the skills of practice, *any* practice, and to those engaged in the perilous enterprise of teaching these skills?

It should come as no surprise, given the Fish/Goodrich debate above, that Fish thinks not. He openly admits to being 'a card-carrying anti-foundationalist', but in the same essay, he insists that precisely because of the situatedness of practice, theory can have little effect on practice.[32] His argument, written with regard to the teaching of writing, goes something like this: anti-foundationalist rhetoric, with its emphasis on 'process over product, the replacement of a standard of correctness by the fluid and dynamic standard of effectiveness, the teaching of strategies rather than of rules and maxims', provides teachers of writing with the theory hope that if they change their epistemological assumptions, improvement in teaching and learning must follow.[33] For Fish, this is a false hope, and he demonstrates this by asking three questions of such theory hope. First,

---

28 Peter Goodrich, *Law in the Courts of Love: Literature and Other Minor Jurisprudences* (Routledge 1996) 118.
29 Ibid, 122.
30 Ibid, 122.
31 Ibid, 119.
32 Stanley Fish, 'Anti-Foundationalism, Theory Hope and the Teaching of Composition' in *Doing What Comes Naturally: Change, Rhetoric, and the Practice of Theory in Literary and Legal Studies* (Clarendon Press 1989) 347.
33 Ibid.

176   *Paul Maharg*

does anti-foundationalism as a model of epistemology provide us with directions for achieving the epistemological state it describes? Second, can an awareness of our own anti-foundationalism lead to more self-awareness of our situatedness; and third, can the teaching of anti-foundationalism make us better writers.

To all three Fish answers no, and principally because he argues that anti-foundationalism cannot be set apart from itself as a ground upon which to base awareness of itself, and that the attempt to do so is nothing less than the 'reinvention of foundationalism'.[34]

As he says later in the essay,

> teaching our students the lesson of anti-foundationalism, while it will put them in possession of a new philosophical perspective, will not give them a tool for operating in the world they already inhabit. Being told that you are in a situation will help you neither to dwell in it more perfectly nor to *write* within it more successfully.[35]

Fish's logic here is unimpeachable; but it is, to quote Dewey, the logic of the syllogism applied to the nature of situated experience.[36] Consciousness of our situation, like our use of rhetoric, proceeds by constant calling up of memory, constant anticipation and involves us in creating the very ground of our being even as we tread upon it. While it may not be possible to escape our situatedness, it is possible to move around within its constraints and to explore the nature of our situation and its constraints from within. Moreover, self-awareness is not a logic gate, an on/off switch, but a gradual and ever-changing environment, one in which the more we can, recursively, understand, recognise and predict patterns of understanding, recognition and prediction, the better we will be able to function within that environment.

Fish's rhetorical strength here, though, is the apparent simplicity with which he states grounds for his own understanding of the relation between theory and practice. As he observes, '[c]ompetent practitioners operate within a strong understanding of what the practice they are engaged in is *for*', which generates 'without the addition of further reflection a sense of what is and is not appropriate, useful or effective'.[37] For Fish, such a sense 'is not theoretical in any interestingly meaningful way'.[38] If it were, then 'a cyclist who would be able to explain the physics of balance would be, by virtue of that ability, a better cyclist'.[39]

---

34 Ibid, 349.
35 Ibid, 351.
36 Jo Ann Boydston (ed), *The Middle Works of John Dewey, 1899–1924* (Southern Illinois University Press 1976–1983) vol 15, 72.
37 Stanley Fish, *There's No Such Thing as Free Speech and It's a Good Thing, Too* (Oxford University Press 1994) 225.
38 Ibid, 225.
39 Ibid, 227.

'Originary intimacy'   177

It all seems so easy. Who could disagree with him on the subject of cycling, or – a similar analogy he makes – on the relevance of theory to baseball batting. But I suggest that we are compelled to disagree with him when we move to the subject of professional practice because he presents us with an impoverished account of professional practice theory. If we move to the adjacent field of educational research, we would find no lack of relevant theory for lawyers to choose from, particularly from cognitive educational fields. Michael Eraut, for instance, has pointed to the problematic relations between theory and praxis in professional education, while Klemp has adopted a more extreme position in declaring that content knowledge has little bearing on occupational performance.[40] Other professions, notably medicine, have developed sophisticated structures of professional practice courses to support the education of their own professionals, structures which have an effect on practice.[41] To encounter a truly enriched notion of practice, we could apply to the authoritative work of Donald Schön and other educational theorists which seeks to explain how we become practitioners in the first place. Schön is actually cited approvingly in *There's No Such Thing as Free Speech*, and in *Doing What Comes Naturally*.[42] His distinction between reflection-on-action (the *post mortem*, as it were, upon praxis) and reflection-in-action (the embedding of reflection within praxis) is highly relevant to Fish's concept of the determinacy of meaning with an

---

40 Michael Eraut, 'Knowledge Creation and Knowledge Use in Professional Contexts' (1985) 10 Studies in Higher Education, 117; George O Klemp, *Three Factors of Success in the World of Work: Implications for Curriculum Planning in Higher Education* (McBer 1977).

41 Brenda Barrett noted that in a conference paper William Twining observed in the debates on professional legal competency and training that 'almost none of the protagonists have any competence in educational theory'. Brenda Barrett, 'What Should We Be Learning about Legal Education?' (1990) 24 (4) Law Teacher, 3–15. As Barrett points out, 'debates on curriculum content have hitherto given relatively little consideration to the learning process as opposed to identifying the range of information to be imparted' (ibid, 6). See also Susan Bright, 'What, and How, Should We Be Teaching?' (1991) 25 (1) Law Teacher, 11. As she pointed out here, the 'traditional approach [to teaching and learning law] is coupled with, and may be explained by, the absence of serious epistemological debate on law teaching' (ibid, 11). Karl Mackie, in 'A strategy for legal education research' pointedly commented that 'there is wide agreement that legal education research has presented a fairly bleak picture in terms of its quantity or its impact on educational practice'. Karl Mackie, 'A Strategy for Legal Education Research' (1990) 24 (1) Law Teacher, 130, 132. As a result of the lack of interest of legal academics, students exhibit the same apathy: Peter Goodrich has pointed out that 'there are in all probability few topics of controversy that are of less interest to their recipients than the discussion of legal education is to the students of law. Education is a given'. Peter Goodrich, 'Psychoanalysis in Legal Education: Notes on the Violence of the Sign' in Roberta Kevelson (ed), *Law and Semiotics* (Plenum Press 1987) vol 1, 195. Even so, in the period between 1987 and 1996, it was observable that legal education had become much more prominent, thanks to increased syllabus and curriculum reform, the Funding Councils' Teaching Quality Assessments, the development of IT in legal pedagogy and other factors.

42 Stanley Fish, *There's No Such Thing as Free Speech and It's a Good Thing, Too* (Oxford University Press 1994) 242; Stanley Fish, *Doing What Comes Naturally: Change, Rhetoric, and the Practice of Theory in Literary and Legal Studies* (Clarendon Press 1989) 374–376.

178 *Paul Maharg*

interpretive community. Reflection-in-action can only come about when one is embedded within practice. Both he and Fish would agree entirely that '[the reader/practitioner] supplies *everything*', because he or she lives within 'a world that is produced by interpretive activity'.

The more one reviews the debates between neopragmatists and anti-foundationalists, the more the centrality of rhetoric in the relationship of theory vis-à-vis practice begins to be seen as a crucial cross-disciplinary educational dilemma. On occasion, it spills over into legal education. This can be seen if we briefly reference the debate between Neil MacCormick and Alan Hunt on the place of jurisprudence within the legal curriculum. The debate sprang from the publication of a report on the teaching of jurisprudence and legal theory in Britain.[43] MacCormick interpreted some of the report's findings as evidence that jurisprudence was becoming an optional subject in the curriculum. For MacCormick, this was 'a disturbing, indeed a deplorable trend'.[44] In his article, he mounts a defence of jurisprudence, basing his arguments on a foundationalist stance in which philosophy is privileged ('There are some questions which are specifically philosophical... and anyone who purports... to have a philosophy needs to have some considered and discursively statable view about them'), but which is also anti-foundationalist in part – e.g. at point 5: 'Answers can be put forward persuasively (rhetorically) and may be more or less plausible; never demonstrable with certainty'.[45] On these and other grounds, MacCormick argues for a special case for jurisprudence in the legal curriculum, in the second year (following the Scots model of the undergraduate LLB).

By contrast, Hunt is avowedly anti-foundationalist. He summarised his position in three statements: compulsory jurisprudence marginalised the subject; creating a special subject called 'jurisprudence' merely encouraged exclusion of theoretical considerations from the substantive law syllabi; and final year teaching of jurisprudence marginalised the domain by giving it the aura of a 'finishing school'.[46] He thus espouses theory over against jurisprudence, and, according to his version of the debate, where MacCormick sets out a neat rationalist and hierarchical stall, on his stall, the theories are in endless and open competition. The language he uses to contrast his jurisprudence course with MacCormick's is revealing. MacCormick's turns out to be teacher-centred, taking no account of learning styles, and is described in language such as 'ontologies', 'compare and contrast', 'standard measures', 'universal schemas'. It all sounds a little stuffy. Hunt's jurisprudence, you will not be surprised to hear, sounds much more engaging: theories 'voice... protest', and (quoting Goodrich), oppose the dominant paradigm's 'political and institutional academic superiority' and its 'repressive tolerance'. The

---

43 Hilaire Barnett and Dianna Yach, 'The Teaching of Jurisprudence and Legal Theory in British Universities and Polytechnics' (1985) 5 Legal Studies, 151.

44 Neil MacCormick, 'The Democratic Intellect and the Law' (1985) 5 Legal Studies, 172.

45 Quoted by Alan Hunt, 'The Role and Place of Theory in Legal Education: Reflections on Foundationalism' (1989) 9 (2) Legal Studies, 146.

46 Ibid, 147.

'Originary intimacy' 179

descriptions leave us in no doubt which would be the more exciting course to attend. And yet, as we know, Hunt's description, of course, content does not describe the course *process*, i.e. how the course is taught and learned. In this respect, Fish's point that E.D. Hirsch's change of position from a champion of 'a pedagogy based on normative notions of correctness, readability, and quantifiable effects', to one where he took into account the effects of 'particular cultural vocabularies' is apt:

> Does this mean that Hirsch wasn't doing a good job earlier or that he was teaching something beside cultural vocabularies before he came to recognize the impossibility of avoiding them? I would venture to guess that he was as good a teacher of composition before he saw the contextual light as he is now. Not only does being converted to anti-foundationalism bring with it no pedagogical payoff; being opposed to anti-foundationalism entails no pedagogical penalty.[47]

On a personal level, this is as true of Hirsch as it is of MacCormick; but it is highly doubtful, if Fish would assent to it being applied to, for example, Posner, whose work on the interface between law and literature he comprehensively dismisses in the essay 'Don't Know Much About the Middle Ages: Posner on Law and Literature'. In much the same way, he trashes – the word is not too strong – Dworkin's concept of chain interpretation.[48] There *is* a pedagogical payoff and a penalty, and it is a highly complex equation involving all aspects of the teaching and learning process.

But if there is a refutation of Fish's powerful occlusion of theory it lies, ironically enough, in rhetorical practice itself. In the next section, we shall take the case example of research into compositional skills as demonstration of a body of knowledge in which the relationship between theory and practice is complex and symbiotic, where the pragmatist and neopragmatist debates once again surface; and where profound issues of epistemology and meaning are never far from that surface.[49]

Legal education's rhetorical turns

As T.R. Donovan and B.W. McClelland pointed out, taking the long view of the research literature on rhetoric and composition, there was in the 1970s and 1980s a move, almost a Kuhnian paradigm shift, away from analysis of the product of writing alone, and towards investigation of the writing

---

47 Stanley Fish, *Doing What Comes Naturally: Change, Rhetoric, and the Practice of Theory in Literary and Legal Studies* (Clarendon Press 1989) 353.
48 Stanley Fish, 'Don't Know Much about the Middle Ages: Posner on Law and Literature' (1988) 97 Yale Law Journal, 777; Stanley Fish, 'Working on the Chain Gang: Interpretation in the Law and in Literary Criticism' (1982) 9 Critical Inquiry, 201.
49 Once again, I shall restrict myself to the literature that was available to the authors of Birks' collection.

180　*Paul Maharg*

process.[50] Barbara Couture makes the crucial point here, when discussing the ground-breaking work of Mina Shaughnessy. For Couture, Shaughnessy's work has inspired an attitude towards composition that is reflected in the best composition research: writing research should view the communication problems of writers as research questions 'whose answers lie in the processes and products of writing' and hold promise of explaining the varied ways we can mean in written discourse.[51] Such approaches give students access to the tools and concepts which will enable them to review and reflect upon their own writing processes, and which will help them to change these wherever they accept the need for change. They do so by foregrounding the process of writing as a valid subject for reflection.

If this is true of learners, it is even more applicable to researchers. Marton has pointed out the curious parallel here:

> If the learners segment the text into parts which are focused on without relation to each other, that is, if they adopt what Svensson calls an atomistic approach, they will fail to discover the basic structure of the text. If researchers segment data on the learners' performance and experience into parts which are focused on without relation to each other, that is, if they adopt an atomistic approach in their research, they will fail to see whether or not the learner discovered the basic structure of the text.[52]

There are clear methodological implications here which affect the ways in which we go about assessing and attempting to improve student writing. Interventionist programmes, according to Marton, would require to adopt a holistic approach to student writing by focusing on the process rather than the product. Other researchers working in different corners of the rhetoric and compositional field have agreed with him. For R.E. Young, process is crucial: what is *not* required is

> emphasis on the composed product rather than the composing process; the analysis of discourse into words, sentences, and paragraphs; the classification of discourse into description, narration, exposition, and

---

50 Timothy R Donovan and Ben W McClelland, *Eight Approaches to Teaching Composition* (National Council of Teachers of English 1980).

51 Barbara Couture, 'Bridging Epistemologies and Methodologies: Research in Written Language Function' in B Couture (ed), *Functional Approaches to Writing: Research Perspectives* (Ablex 1986) 6.

52 Ference Marton, 'Describing and Improving Learning' in RR Schmeck (ed), *Learning Strategies and Learning Styles* (Plenum Press 1988) 68, citing Lennart Svensson, 'Skill in Learning' in Ference Marton, Dai Hounsell and Noel Entwistle (eds), *The Experience of Learning* (Scottish Academic Press 1984).

'Originary intimacy' 181

argument; the strong concern with usage (syntax, spelling, punctuation) and with style (economy, clarity, emphasis).[53]

In order to understand how writers produce text, compositional researchers have constructed models of process. In these models, writing is seen not so much as a literary activity but as a problem-solving activity, one primarily concerned with design in words, where the process variables are almost infinite, and where the activities out of which formal writing evolves are seen as crucial to its communicative power. This process view of writing is in nature both descriptive and investigative of the processes writers adopt when generating text. It starts from what writers actually do, and attempts to analyse writing practices. In doing so, it investigates the interface between thought and writing, sometimes by means of verbal protocols or chronometrical studies.[54] In these investigations, writers are observed and monitored working in as near normal writing environments as possible, using writing habits they have developed over many years. Since the late 1960s, the amount and quality of research on the process view has increased significantly, and as a result, a number of partial process models have been predicated, most of which have implications for writing instruction.[55] Some of the more influential have been those of Flower and Hayes, Scardamalia and Bereiter, and Sharples.

For all of these researchers, writing is primarily problem-solving. They draw fundamental concepts to support this view from the extensive body of cognitive research into solvers' mental procedures or heuristics.[56] Their indebtedness to this literature is apparent in the concepts, methods and metaphors they use. Thus, van Dijk and Kintsch describe the goal-oriented production processes as being triggered by a 'flexible *mechanism*'; Brown and

---

53 Richard E Young, 'Paradigms and Problems: Needed Research in Rhetorical Invention' in Charles R Cooper and Lee C Odell (eds), *Research on Composing: Points of Departure* (National Council of Teachers of English 1978) 31.

54 See, for example, Linda Flower and JR Hayes, 'Identifying the Organisation of Writing Processes' in LW Gregg and ER Steinberg (eds), *Cognitive Processes in Writing* (Lawrence Erlbaum Associates 1980); A Matsuhashi and C Cooper, 'A Video Time-Monitored Observational Study: The Transcribing Behaviour and Composing Process of a Competent High School Writer' (American Educational Research Association Annual Meeting, Toronto, 1978) quoted by Carl Bereiter and Marlene Scardamalia, 'From Conversation to Composition: The Role of Instruction in a Developmental Process' (1982) 2 (1) Advances in Instructional Psychology, 60.

55 Eg Murray and Wason – Donald M Murray, 'Internal Revision: A Process of Discovery' in Charles R Cooper and Lee Odell (eds), *Research on Composing* (National Council of Teachers of English 1978); PC Wason, 'Specific Thoughts on the Writing Process' in LW Gregg and ER Steinberg (eds), *Cognitive Processes in Writing* (Lawrence Erlbaum Associates 1980).

56 Eg the classic work of Simon & Newell – see Linda Flower and JR Hayes, 'Identifying the Organisation of Writing Processes' in LW Gregg and ER Steinberg (eds), *Cognitive Processes in Writing* (Lawrence Erlbaum Associates 1980) 40.

182 Paul Maharg

Campione introduced the notion of 'self-regulatory mechanisms', that is, the processes of planning, monitoring, revising and evaluating; while Robert de Beaugrande analysed the relation between ideas and their expression in text in terms of 'conceptual and sequential *connectivity*'.[57] Sometimes researchers draw directly upon the discourse of artificial intelligence to represent their models. Scardamalia and Bereiter, for instance, describe Brown and Campione's mechanisms as 'subroutines that can be assembled along with other subroutines to constitute a program for accomplishing some task', while their flow diagrams of what they term the COMPARE, DIAGNOSE, OPERATE process in composition clearly reveal the influence of computer modelling.[58] Such influence is not limited to writing research, of course – in the 1970s and early 1980s, computer models and analogies heavily influenced the form and direction of research into human memory, for example.

One reason why researchers build models is that the writing process is highly individual and hidden from the researcher. Competence in writing does not derive directly from performance by writers, but from the constructions which the researcher derives from the data obtained through observation; or from the model which he or she imposes on the data in order to rationalise and explain it. The models, therefore, are in themselves highly rhetorical: they set out to persuade us, the readers of the research literature, that the researcher can illuminate or make sense of, or otherwise uncover aspects of writing process.

Moreover, and almost by default, compositional and rhetorical research considers the relationship between reading and writing to be vital. In this area, the speech-act theories of J.L. Austin and their development by J.R. Searle, J. Sadock, and K. Bach and R.M. Harnish are a common philosophical ancestry to the research in composition and rhetoric.[59] All these theories are concerned to include the reader in the speech act. For these theorists, the reader's or listener's interpretations of the speaker's utterances and intentions are a crucial part of communication.

---

57 Robert de Beaugrande, *Text, Discourse and Process: Toward a Multidisciplinary Science of Texts* (Ablex 1980); Ann L Brown and Joseph C Campione, 'Inducing Flexible Thinking: A Problem of Access' in Morton Friedman, JP Das and Neil O'Conner (eds), *Intelligence and Learning* (Plenum Press 1981); Teun A van Dijk and Walter Kintsch, *Strategies of Discourse Comprehension* (Academic Press 1983) 264.

58 Marlene Scardamalia and Carl Bereiter, 'Cognitive Coping Strategies and the Problem of "Inert Knowledge"' in Susan F Chipman, Robert Glaser and Judith W Segal (eds), *Thinking and Learning Skills. Volume 2: Research and Open Questions* (Lawrence Erlbaum Associates 1985) 568.

59 JL Austin, *How To Do Things with Words* (Oxford 1962); John R Searle, *Speech Acts: An Essay in the Philosophy of Language* (Cambridge University Press 1969); Jerrold Sadock, *Toward a Linguistic Theory of Speech Acts* (Academic Press 1974); John R Searle, *Expression and Meaning: Studies in the Theory of Speech Acts* (Cambridge University Press 1979); Kent Bach and Robert M Harnish, *Linguistic Communication and Speech Acts* (MIT Press 1979).

'Originary intimacy'   183

The models of Flower and Hayes are a typical example of this. They treated the composing process as comprising four types of activities – *planning*, where writers set goals, recall items from memory and begin to organise ideas and goal; *translating*, where goals, ideas and knowledge are rendered into clauses, sentences and paragraphs; *reviewing*, where writers test their text against their intentions and alter text or articulate new ideas stimulated by their re-reading; and *monitoring*, where metacognitive processes link and coordinate planning, translating and reviewing.[60] In addition, Flower and Hayes viewed writing as an activity involving multiple constraints – of time, purpose, awareness of audience, grammatical and orthographic forms, amongst many. If this approach appears to reproduce traditional rhetorical didactics, it is far from being the case. Flower and Hayes emphasised and researched cognitive strategies, sub-routines, automatized production strategies, social context and many other variables in the processes of text production and interpretation.

They summarised three implications that their view of writing has for writing instruction. First, writing is a thinking process, one of problem-solving, where there are no correct ways to write, 'only alternative approaches to the endless series of problems and decisions' involved in composing. Some of these approaches are more effective in a given context than others, and therefore – their second implication – one goal of instruction is to 'give writers increased awareness of alternatives as they work through the problem of writing'[61] so that – the third implication – they come to a knowledge of '*how to write*, not just what good writing looks like'.[62] This view of the writing process is echoed by many others – Ann Matsuhashi, for example, quotes Frank Smith's acute observation that writing 'covers its own traces'.[63] Smith is referring, of course, to the effect a text has on a reader; but it is also true in many respects of the effect that his or her writing has upon the writer.

In all three points, as throughout their work, Flower and Hayes adhere to a view of writing instruction which is innately optimistic. It is a view that is taken by their problem-solving models and could not be further from behaviourist instructional methods: 'writers' faulty or inadequate understanding of the writing process actually prevents them from doing what they could do. It is not that they lack the skills to write, but that they do not know how or when to use them'.[64] If this is the case, it becomes the central task of

---

60 Linda Flower and JR Hayes, 'Identifying the Organisation of Writing Processes' in LW Gregg and ER Steinberg (eds), *Cognitive Processes in Writing* (Lawrence Erlbaum Associates 1980) 41.

61 Ibid, 56.

62 Ibid.

63 Ann Matsuhashi, *Writing in Real Time: Modeling Production Processes* (Ablex 1987) 198.

64 Linda Flower and JR Hayes, 'Identifying the Organisation of Writing Processes' in LW Gregg and ER Steinberg (eds), *Cognitive Processes in Writing* (Lawrence Erlbaum Associates 1980) 67.

184   *Paul Maharg*

writing instruction both to help writers understand the writing process and to create tools which will support that process.

Many other researchers and theorists confirm this view of writing instruction, though they might disagree about process models or classroom approaches.[65] Collins and Gentner, for example, describe a process of compositional 'downsliding' as being one where the writer is drawn away from high-level aims to lower and lower levels of task processing, such as correcting spelling and grammatical errors.[66] They treat this process as one which inhibits a writer's compositional flow. Scardamalia and Bereiter, however, take a more nuanced view, asserting that attention given to the mechanics of writing 'creates the need for a greater amount of reconstructive activity at higher levels of text representation' which produces 'benefits in terms of coherence, [and] disadvantages in terms of richness of content'.[67] Scardamalia and Bereiter's analyses of their experimental results lead them to conclude that at any one moment, a writer will have a number of different possible representations of a text which he or she juggles to the limit of short-term memory. These are constructed as they are needed according to the writers' immediate purpose and can be vague and fragmentary or clear and detailed.[68] Given the complexity of these production factors in composition, Scardamalia and Bereiter focus on the need for writing instruction to provide 'facilitative intervention' for writers, that is, ways to intervene in the writing process so as to facilitate it. These include – in the domain of children's writing – scaffolding the direction and topics of writing by providing opening words in a sentence to stimulate writing strategies, or final sentences towards which goals the children wrote. Conjecturing that children's reviewing and evaluative processes were unformed because they lacked an 'internal feedback system',[69] they facilitated review by asking children to compare each sentence of their texts to cards on which were written evaluative phrases (e.g. 'People may not understand what I mean here'),[70] and directive phrases ('I'd better say more'). In another article, they refined their concept of facilitative intervention further by describing two constitutive aspects: '*procedural* facilitation', defined as 'any reduction in the executive demands of a task that permits learners to make fuller use of the knowledge

---

65 Marlene Scardamalia, Carl Bereiter and Hillel Goelman, 'The Role of Production Factors in Writing Ability' in Martin Nystrand (eds), *What Writers Know: The Language, Process, and Structure of Written Discourse* (Academic Press 1982).

66 Allan Collins and Dedre Gentner, 'A Framework for a Cognitive Theory of Writing' in LW Gregg and ER Steinberg (eds), *Cognitive Processes in Writing* (Lawrence Erlbaum Associates 1980).

67 Marlene Scardamalia, Carl Bereiter and Hillel Goelman, 'The Role of Production Factors in Writing Ability' in Martin Nystrand (eds), *What Writers Know: The Language, Process, and Structure of Written Discourse* (Academic Press 1982) 207.

68 Ibid, 203–204.

69 Ibid, 37.

70 Ibid, 38.

'Originary intimacy' 185

and skills they already have',[71] and *'substantive* facilitation', where a teacher is an active partner or collaborator in the process of writing.

Scardamalia and Bereiter summarised their approach to procedural facilitation in children's writing in seven principles. These principles are an interesting example of, to use Fish's terms, the pedagogical payoff offered by situational research:

1   minimise the attention that must be devoted to running executive routines;
2   make potentially infinite sets of choices finite;
3   structure procedures so as to bye-pass rather than support immature tendencies;
4   foster metacognition by making normally covert processes overt[72];
5   provide labels to make tacit knowledge more accessible; and
6   use procedures that can be scaled upward or downward in complexity.[73]

Despite all the differences of terminology and opinion, all cognitive researchers make one identical claim and disclaimer. They claim that their research has direct implications for writing instruction, but they admit that their models of the writing process are incomplete and require further research. Nevertheless, their models are useful because they illuminate areas of the writing process that can be scaffolded by teachers.

Other researchers have drawn upon research from more overtly educational sources. In this respect, the research of Gordon Pask has been influential.[74] Pask defined a *learning strategy* as the particular ways that students solved problems. He categorised two strategies: '*holist*, preferring global predicates and relations of topics, and *serialists*, preferring not to use such relations and learning step-by-step'.[75] Pask elaborates the categories further, but concludes that 'successful learning does involve innovation or discovery but also the *integration* of both local and global rules. Both serial and holistic strategies are needed to achieve understanding'.[76] Pask is describing here the process of learning, but the same strategic categories have been applied to the process of writing. Biggs found similarities between approaches to

---

71 Ibid, 52.
72 Such metacognition research could also be taken as an example of the sort of self-awareness that Fish says cannot happen.
73 Marlene Scardamalia, Carl Bereiter and Hillel Goelman, 'The Role of Production Factors in Writing Ability' in Martin Nystrand (eds), *What Writers Know: The Language, Process, and Structure of Written Discourse* (Academic Press 1982) 55–58.
74 See, eg, Gordon Pask, 'Learning Strategies, Teaching Strategies, and Conceptual or Learning Styles' in Ronald R Schmeck (ed), *Learning Strategies and Learning Styles* (Plenum Press 1988).
75 Ibid, 87.
76 Ibid, 87.

186   *Paul Maharg*

learning and to writing.[77] He reviewed three analyses of the writing process – the distinction Flower makes between 'writer-based' and 'reader-based' prose,[78] Hounsell's investigations into the 'conceptions' of writing held by students,[79] and the contrast of 'knowledge-telling' and 'reflective writing' proposed by Scardamalia and Bereiter.[80]

Based on his readings of these analyses, Biggs discerned a pattern in this research that paralleled the distinction made by Marton in his description of deep and surface approaches to learning, and which derived from 'the level at which the writer's attention is focused; a surface level consisting of the words and sentences used, or a deep level consisting of the discourse itself'.[81] Marton's categories rely partly on Svensson's earlier research into comprehension and learning, where Svensson distinguished between a 'holistic' approach (readers moving 'toward understanding the text as a whole'), and an 'atomistic' approach (readers focusing on reading micro-tasks and lacking 'orientation towards the message as a whole').[82]

Biggs' parallel is an intriguing one, but the comparison should be treated with caution, for a number of reasons. One basic methodological caveat must be that the studies conducted by Svensson, Marton and Pask are all based on data that derives from experiments on reading comprehension, with evaluation instruments such as predictive and recall questions. None of them directly involve evaluation of writing skills. The processes of reading and writing overlap in many areas, but they are self-evidently different skills domains, and what constitutes 'deep' and 'surface' approaches to writing are quite different from 'deep' and 'surface' reading skills. A good example of this is the research carried out by Scardamalia, Bereiter and Goelman into the role of production factors in the composing process.[83] They analysed in particular the mental representation of a text, and how attention given over to generation of text at a low level – puzzling over the correct spelling of 'necessary' for example – could affect the high-level representation of the text – what the writer might want to identify as the main

---

77 John Biggs, 'Approaches to Learning and to Essay Writing' in Ronald R Schmeck (ed), *Learning Strategies and Learning Styles* (Plenum Press 1988) 189–192.

78 Linda Flower and JR Hayes, 'Identifying the Organisation of Writing Processes' in LW Gregg and ER Steinberg (eds), *Cognitive Processes in Writing* (Lawrence Erlbaum Associates 1980).

79 Ference Marton, Dai Hounsell and Noel James Entwistle, *The Experience of Learning. Implications for Teaching and Studying in Higher Education* (Edinburgh, Scottish Academic Press 1997).

80 Marlene Scardamalia, Carl Bereiter and Hillel Goelman, 'The Role of Production Factors in Writing Ability' in Martin Nystrand (ed), *What Writers Know: The Language, Process, and Structure of Written Discourse* (Academic Press 1982).

81 John Biggs, 'Approaches to Learning and to Essay Writing' in Ronald R Schmeck (ed), *Learning Strategies and Learning Styles* (Plenum Press 1988) 191.

82 Lennart Svensson, *Study Skill and Learning* (Acta Universitatis Gothoburgensis 1976).

83 Marlene Scardamalia, Carl Bereiter and Hillel Goelman, 'The Role of Production Factors in Writing Ability' in Martin Nystrand (ed), *What Writers Know: The Language, Process, and Structure of Written Discourse* (Academic Press 1982).

idea in a developing paragraph. The quality of attention given to high-level aims in writing would appear to parallel Svensson's 'holistic', Pask's 'holist' categories, in that such attention tends towards the global, creates relations between topics and would appear to play an executive role in composing. Downsliding – the derogatory tone is illuminating – echoes the 'atomistic' and the 'serialist'; it is marked by a tendency to move step-by-step, in fragments, and with its emphasis on micro-tasks, works against the defined creativity of the high-level aims. Scardamalia et al. questioned the conventional wisdom that 'having to attend to low-level considerations such as spelling and punctuation interferes with attention to higher-level concerns of composition'.[84] For them, the high-level aims are not static, performing an executive function during composing, from which writers stray into downsliding. Rather, they stress the fluid, iterative nature of the composing process, one where mental representations of text are constantly being generated, then decaying, then being renewed as the situation warrants. Where Flower, for instance, sees memory loss induced by downsliding as an obstruction to composing, Scardamalia et al. see a reconstructive activity operating at all levels of the composing process. They postulate that the

> important production factor is... reconstructive activity that influences the writer's ability to plan at all levels of composition from the lowest levels of mechanics to the highest levels of rhetorical intent. We no longer view attention to mechanics as interfering with higher-level processes. Rather, it creates the need for a greater amount of reconstructive activity at higher levels of text representation, and this can have benefits as well as disadvantages as far as the production of extended discourse is concerned – benefits in terms of coherence, disadvantages in terms of richness of content.[85]

The language here is that of situatedness; but implicit in it is a recognition that it is important to articulate as far as possible what happens in the writing process. And as the approach to procedural facilitation outlined above by Scardamalia and Bereiter reveals, the link between research and pedagogy is a fruitful one.

The link to the pragmatist approach could not be more apparent. Writing research presupposes epistemological models; writing is situational in every sense for both reader and writer; novice strategies evolve from practice but can be more successful if research on successful writing processes is learned and applied; writing is pattern-recognition; writing consists of dialogues, internalised protocols and multiple and complex levels of decision-making.

---

84 Marlene Scardamalia and Carl Bereiter, *The Psychology of Written Composition* (Lawrence Erlbaum Associates 1987) 105.
85 Ibid, 207.

188   *Paul Maharg*

Moreover, writing research such as this requires application to specific genres and narratives. The Flower & Hayes model, for instance, has specific effects when employed in legal education, bearing in mind the discipline's cognitive load of primary legal resources and legal reasoning upon both novice and professional compositional practices.[86] Under these conditions, specific strategies for working memory are required if it is not to be overloaded when problem-solving. Finally, writing is also social cognition: Fish's anti-foundationalist interpretive communities are key to how writing is produced, how a reading is interpreted, how disciplinary norms are created and altered.

These are only some of the links. There are many others, but they are rarely taken up either in educational or jurisprudential theory and practice, certainly in UK law schools. The jurisprudential and the rhetorical remain isolated and as a result, both are impoverished in legal studies.

Conclusion

In his history of American legal education, Robert Stevens points out that many of the post-1945 experiments in legal education and especially in legal skills have their origin in the experiments of the 1920s and 1930s.[87] It is no coincidence that both Karl Llewellyn and Jerome Franks wrote in favour of clinical legal skills.[88] This interest stretches back to the pragmatist re-evaluation by Dewey of the nature of the logics actually in use by lawyers. Both Llewellyn and Frank, like Dewey, rejected Langdellian case method educational approaches and advocated versions of clinical legal skills methods based upon the primacy of experience and – to use a favourite word of the later anti-foundationalists – situatedness. Founded on a pragmatism that stems from a philosophical tradition in Dewey, Pierce and others, this is a more sophisticated approach than the relatively simple equation of pragmatism with managerialist skills education described by Toddington in the Birks' collection.[89] Since Birks' collection, movements such as the New Legal Realism have developed this line of juristic thinking.[90]

---

86 See eg Marilyn L Turner and Randall W Engle, 'Is Working Memory Capacity Task Dependent?' (1989) 28 Journal of Memory and Language, 127; Marecel A Just and Patricia A Carpenter, 'A Capacity Theory of Comprehension: Individual Differences in Working Memory' (1992) 99 Psychological Review, 122.

87 Robert Stevens, *Law School: Legal Education in America from the 1850s to the 1980s* (University of North Carolina Press 1983) 210.

88 Karl Llewellyn, 'The Place of Skills in Legal Education' *AALS Handbook* (American Association of Law Schools 1944); Jerome Frank, 'Why Not a Clinical Lawyer School?' (1933) 81 University of Pennsylvania Law Review, 907.

89 Stuart Toddington, 'The Emperor's New Skills: The Academy, The Profession and the Idea of Legal Education' in Peter Birks (ed), *Pressing Problems in the Law: Volume 2: What Are Law Schools For?* (Oxford University Press 1996).

90 See in particular the work of Beth Mertz and her colleagues, eg Elizabeth Mertz, *The Language of Law School: Learning to 'Think Like a Lawyer'* (Oxford University Press 2007); Mindie Lazarus-Black, Meera Deo and Elizabeth Mertz (eds), *Power, Legal Education,*

'Originary intimacy' 189

Dewey's writings on law were acutely relevant to the Columbia experiments in legal education.[91] In much the same way, the critical debate over the place of anti-foundationalism in law, and the place of rhetoric in legal education today, is still of central importance to us. Whether or not legal educational theories or any other kind of theory can enable our law students to be better professionals, better persons, is a central debate that legal academics themselves need to engage in. Such a debate must be cross-disciplinary in nature for – as Dewey recognised very early in his career – many educational issues can only be debated seriously if the issues are related to theories of learning, cognition, society and the theoretical bases of the subject discipline. As we can see from the debates of the neopragmatists, the issue belongs not just to the 'finishing school' class of jurisprudence but has ramifications for the methodology of all legal pedagogy. In particular, it is relevant to the philosophical and cognitive bases of the clinical legal skills movement, in which rhetoric plays a prominent part. The parallel with early curriculum reforms at Columbia is apt: we require to enter this debate and engage with the issues which Dewey and others realised were so fundamental to legal pedagogy, if we want our attempts to improve teaching and learning to succeed.

What has this chapter's thought experiment proven? There are three points that it reveals. It reminds us, first, that education always and everywhere presupposes epistemology. If this is so, we need to ask ourselves which epistemologies we enact, and which practices we adopt as a consequence. Here, I argue for an applied epistemology of theoretically laden educational practice that also is a theory of meaning. Academics need to become the 'practical epistemologists' referred to by Ronald Barnett, for whom the task of securing the university as 'a special site of knowing, of knowing about knowing' takes place through the integration of 'the three epistemological elements of openness, responsiveness and action in the world'.[92] Legal academics are by no means unaware of this, but the implications of findings from educational research have still to be widely understood and enacted in legal education.

Second, and continuing from point one, the family relations between jurisprudence, education and areas of applied research such as technology-related and rhetorical discourses remain unrecognised and underdeveloped. In particular, the dynamic critical force of interdisciplinary thinking and practice, demonstrated in the thought experiment here through analysis of

---

and Law School Cultures (Emerging Legal Education Series, Routledge 2019); Shauhin Talesh, Elizabeth Mertz and Heinz Klug, Research Handbook on Modern Legal Realism (Research Handbooks in Legal Theory Series, Edward Elgar Publishing 2021).

91 See Paul Maharg, 'Same as It Ever Was? Second Modernity, Technocracy, and the Design of Digital Legal Education' in C Denvir (ed), Modernising Legal Education (Cambridge University Press 2020) Chapter 6.

92 Ronald Barnett, 'A Knowledge Strategy for Universities' in Ronald Barnett and Anne Griffin (eds), The End of Knowledge in Higher Education (Cassell 1997) 17.

190   *Paul Maharg*

the anti-foundational debates and their relationship to rhetorical theory and practice, has still not been made visible within the curricula of many of our legal educations. Perhaps the only author in the Birks' collection to recognise the radical nature of such thinking with any clarity was Peter Goodrich who understood the hegemonic control exercised by the master narrative that is constructed around liberal law schools:

> Even in its liberal variant, the history of the English law school is an exercise in a profoundly disciplinary or normalising control in which the ideal of professional persona is 'the great man', the ideal of relation is one of estrangement, the model of legal system is exclusively that of English common law, and the acme of reason is an ill-considered casuistry.[93]

Third, whatever the methodology of Birks' collection – who was chosen to write and why, for example, and the process of chapter selection and editing – in our own research, we need to ask the meta-questions of our legal educational theory and practice that Birks' collection attempted to address: why do we do this? What is our purpose?

Thought experiments can assist us in all this. They help us to make the phenomenological distinction between an experiential anticipation and an experiential expectation. In the formulation of Harald Wiltsche, when I flip a light switch, my anticipation of the appearance of light is not 'consciously experienced in the normal course of events' but if I have just repaired the light switch and I flip it, then anticipation becomes expectation – 'an act in its own right and [with] the status of an explicit prognosis of future events'.[94] Much of education takes place within the bracket of anticipation, not least because habit and routine make our lives liveable. Thought experiments, though, can help us break the carapace of mundane anticipation that occludes the real nature of an educational experience and help us to transform anticipation into experimental expectation that is the hallmark of innovation in education. As in the exploration of historical episodes in interdisciplinary research represented by the section on rhetoric above, they can illuminate radicalism in the root, *radix*, of our current educational practices. They can return us to an originary intimacy with the roots of our own jurisprudential practices. And finally, they can also help us to create a new grammar of jurisprudence.

---

93 Peter Goodrich, "Of Blackstone's Tower: Metaphors of Distance and Histories of the English Law School" in Peter Birks (ed), *What Are Law Schools For?* (Oxford University Press 1996) 68.

94 Harald Wiltsche, 'Phenomenology and Thought Experiments. Thought Experiments as Anticipation Pumps' in Michael T Stuart, Yiftach Fehige and James Robert Brown (eds), *The Routledge Companion to Thought Experiments* (Routledge 2017) 357.

Standing amidst the dim book stacks of Voltaire & Rousseau and leafing through Birks' collection, I *sensed* the book was unsatisfactory. Quarter of a century later, I would argue that our purposes in law schools are now much more diverse, but that the foundations need renewal. Along with radical education that is open, diverse, critical and socially situated, we need to reclaim our forgotten and invisible intellectual heritages, their originary intimacies, grounded in interdisciplinary jurisprudential inquiry.

Bibliography

Agamben G, *The Use of Bodies* (Stanford University Press 2016).

Austin J, *How To Do Things with Words* (Oxford 1962).

Bach K and Harnish R, *Linguistic Communication and Speech Acts* (MIT Press 1979).

Barnett H and Yach D, 'The Teaching of Jurisprudence and Legal Theory in British Universities and Polytechnics' (1985) 5(2) *Legal Studies* 151–171.

Barnett R, 'A Knowledge Strategy for Universities' in Ronald Barnett and Anne Griffin (eds) *The End of Knowledge in Higher Education* (Cassell 1997).

Barrett B, 'What Should We Be Learning about Legal Education?' (1990) 24(4) *Law Teacher* 3–15.

de Beaugrande R, *Text, Discourse and Process: Toward a Multidisciplinary Science of Texts* (Ablex 1980).

Bereiter C and Scardamalia M, 'From Conversation to Composition: The Role of Instruction in a Developmental Process' (1982) 2(1–64) *Advances in Instructional Psychology* 1–64.

Biggs J, 'Approaches to Learning and to Essay Writing' in Ronald R Schmeck (ed) *Learning Strategies and Learning Styles* (Plenum Press 1988).

Birks P, *Reviewing Legal Education* (Oxford University Press 1994).

Boydston J (ed), *The Middle Works of John Dewey, 1899–1924* (Southern Illinois University Press 1976–1983).

Bright S, 'What, and How, Should We Be Teaching?' (1991) 25(1) *Law Teacher* 11–25.

Brown A and Campione J, 'Inducing Flexible Thinking: A Problem of Access' in Morton Friedman, JP Das, and Neil O'Conner (eds) *Intelligence and Learning* (Plenum Press 1981).

Brownlee K and Stemplowska Z, 'Trapped in an Experience Machine with a Famous Violinist: Thought Experiments in Normative Theory' <www.academia.edu/371276/Trapped_in_an_Experience_Machine_with_a_Famous_Violinist_Thought_Experiments_in_Normative_Theory_with_Zofia_Stemplowska_> accessed 23 July 2021.

Cairns J, 'The Influence of Smith's Jurisprudence on Legal Education in Scotland' in Peter Jones and Andrew S Skinner (eds) *Adam Smith Reviewed* (Edinburgh University Press 1992).

Collins A and Gentner D, 'A Framework for a Cognitive Theory of Writing' in LW Gregg and ER Steinberg (eds) *Cognitive Processes in Writing* (Lawrence Erlbaum Associates 1980).

Couture B, 'Bridging Epistemologies and Methodologies: Research in Written Language Function' in B Couture (ed) *Functional Approaches to Writing: Research Perspectives* (Ablex 1986).

192 Paul Maharg

van Dijk T and Kintsch W, *Strategies of Discourse Comprehension* (Academic Press 1983).

Donovan T and McClelland B, *Eight Approaches to Teaching Composition* (National Council of Teachers of English 1980).

Eraut M, 'Knowledge Creation and Knowledge Use in Professional Contexts' (1985) 10 *Studies in Higher Education* 117–133.

Fish S, 'Anti-Foundationalism, Theory Hope and the Teaching of Composition' in *Doing What Comes Naturally: Change, Rhetoric, and the Practice of Theory in Literary and Legal Studies* (Clarendon Press 1989).

Fish S, *Doing What Comes Naturally: Change, Rhetoric, and the Practice of Theory in Literary and Legal Studies* (Clarendon Press 1989).

Fish S, 'Don't Know Much about the Middle Ages: Posner on Law and Literature' (1988) 97(5) *Yale Law Journal* 777–797.

Fish S, 'The Law Wishes to Have a Formal Existence' in Alan Norrie (ed) *Closure or Critique: New Directions in Legal Theory* (Edinburgh University Press 1993).

Fish S, 'The Play of Surfaces: Theory and the Law' in Gregory Leyh (ed) *Legal Hermeneutics. History, Theory, and Practice* (University of California Press 1992).

Fish S, *There's No Such Thing as Free Speech and It's a Good Thing, Too* (Oxford University Press 1994).

Fish S, 'Working on the Chain Gang: Interpretation in the Law and in Literary Criticism' (1982) 9(1) *Critical Inquiry* 201–216.

Flower L and Hayes J, 'Identifying the Organisation of Writing Processes' in LW Gregg and ER Steinberg (eds) *Cognitive Processes in Writing* (Lawrence Erlbaum Associates 1980).

Frank J, 'Why Not a Clinical Lawyer School?' (1933) 81(8) *University of Pennsylvania Law Review* 907–923.

Goodrich P, *Law in the Courts of Love: Literature and Other Minor Jurisprudences* (Routledge 1996).

Goodrich P, 'Of Blackstone's Tower: Metaphors of Distance and Histories of the English Law School' in Peter Birks (ed) *What Are Law Schools For?* (Oxford University Press 1996).

Goodrich P, 'Psychoanalysis in Legal Education: Notes on the Violence of the Sign' in Roberta Kevelson (ed) *Law and Semiotics* (Plenum Press 1987).

Goodrich P, 'We Orators' (1990) 53(4) *Modern Law Review* 546–567.

Grey T, 'Holmes and Legal Pragmatism' (1989) 41(4) *Stanford Law Review* 787–834.

Gunn G, *Thinking across the American Grain: Ideology, Intellect and the New Pragmatism* (University of Chicago Press 1992).

Hunt A, 'The Role and Place of Theory in Legal Education: Reflections on Foundationalism' (1989) 9(2) *Legal Studies* 146–164.

Hutcheson F, 'An Essay on the Nature and Conduct of the Passions and Affections' (first published in 1728) in Bernhard Fabian (ed) *Collected Works of Francis Hutcheson* (Facsimile edn, G Olms 1969–1990).

Just M and Carpenter P, 'A Capacity Theory of Comprehension: Individual Differences in Working Memory' (1992) 99 *Psychological Review* 122–137.

Kames H, *Introduction to the Art of Thinking. Enlarged with Additional Maxims and Illustrations* (Edinburgh 1764).

Kames H, *Loose Hints upon Education, Chiefly Concerning the Culture of the Heart* (Edinburgh 1781).

Klemp G, *Three Factors of Success in the World of Work: Implications for Curriculum Planning in Higher Education* (McBer 1977).

Lazarus-Black M, Deo M, and Mertz E (eds), *Power, Legal Education, and Law School Cultures* (Emerging Legal Education Series, Routledge 2019).

Llewellyn K, 'The Place of Skills in Legal Education' in *AALS Handbook* (American Association of Law Schools 1944).

Lorimer J, *The Institutes of Law: A Treatise of the Principles of Jurisprudence as Determined by Nature* (2nd edn, Edinburgh 1880).

MacCormick N, 'Law and Enlightenment' in RH Campbell and Andrew S Skinner (eds) *The Origins and Nature of the Scottish Enlightenment* (J Donald Publishers 1982).

MacCormick N, 'The Democratic Intellect and the Law' (1985) 5(2) *Legal Studies* 172–182.

Mackie K, 'A Strategy for Legal Education Research' (1990) 24(1) *Law Teacher* 130–143.

Maharg P, 'Same as It Ever Was? Second Modernity, Technocracy, and the Design of Digital Legal Education' in Catrina Denvir (ed) *Modernising Legal Education* (Cambridge University Press 2020).

Maharg P, *Transforming Legal Education: Learning and Teaching the Law in the Early Twenty-First Century* (Routledge 2007).

Marton F, 'Describing and Improving Learning' in RR Schmeck (ed) *Learning Strategies and Learning Styles* (Plenum Press 1988).

Marton F, Hounsell D, and Entwistle N, *The Experience of Learning. Implications for Teaching and Studying in Higher Education* (Edinburgh, Scottish Academic Press 1997).

Matsuhashi A, *Writing in Real Time: Modeling Production Processes* (Ablex 1987).

Matsuhashi A and Cooper C, 'A Video Time-Monitored Observational Study: The Transcribing Behaviour and Composing Process of a Competent High School Writer' (American Educational Research Association Annual Meeting, Toronto 1978).

Mertz E, *The Language of Law School: Learning to 'Think Like a Lawyer'* (Oxford University Press 2007).

Murray D, 'Internal Revision: A Process of Discovery' in Charles R Cooper and Lee Odell (eds) *Research on Composing* (National Council of Teachers of English 1978).

Pask G, 'Learning Strategies, Teaching Strategies, and Conceptual or Learning Styles' in Ronald R Schmeck (ed) *Learning Strategies and Learning Styles* (Plenum Press 1988).

Roberts R and Good J (eds), *The Recovery of Rhetoric: Persuasive Discourse and Disciplinarity in the Human Sciences* (Bristol Classical Press 1993).

Rorty R, 'The Banality of Pragmatism and the Poetry of Justice' in Michael Brint and William Weaver (eds) *Pragmatism in Law and Society* (Westview Press 1991).

Sadock J, *Toward a Linguistic Theory of Speech Acts* (Academic Press 1974).

Scardamalia M and Bereiter C, 'Cognitive Coping Strategies and the Problem of "Inert Knowledge"' in Susan F Chipman, Robert Glaser, and Judith W Segal (eds) *Thinking and Learning Skills: Volume 2: Research and Open Questions* (Lawrence Erlbaum Associates 1985).

Scardamalia M and Bereiter C, *The Psychology of Written Composition* (Lawrence Erlbaum Associates 1987).

Scardamalia M, Bereiter C, and Goelman H, 'The Role of Production Factors in Writing Ability' in Martin Nystrand (ed) *What Writers Know: The Language, Process, and Structure of Written Discourse* (Academic Press 1982).

194   *Paul Maharg*

Searle J, *Expression and Meaning: Studies in the Theory of Speech Acts* (Cambridge University Press 1979).

Searle J, *Speech Acts: An Essay in the Philosophy of Language* (Cambridge University Press 1969).

Simons H (ed), *The Rhetorical Turn: Invention and Persuasion in the Conduct of Inquiry* (University of Chicago Press, 1992).

Smith A, *Lectures on Jurisprudence* (Glasgow edn of the Works and Correspondence of Adam Smith, Liberty Fund Inc, New York 1982).

Stevens R, *Law School: Legal Education in America from the 1850s to the 1980s* (University of North Carolina Press 1983).

Stuart M, Yiftach Fehige, and James Robert Brown (eds), *The Routledge Companion to Thought Experiments* (Routledge 2018).

Svensson L, 'Skill in Learning' in Ference Marton, Dai Hounsell, and Noel Entwistle (eds) *The Experience of Learning* (Scottish Academic Press 1984).

Svensson L, *Study Skill and Learning* (Acta Universitatis Gothoburgensis 1976).

Talesh S, Mertz E, and Klug H, *Research Handbook on Modern Legal Realism* (Research Handbooks in Legal Theory Series, Edward Elgar Publishing 2021).

Toddington S, 'The Emperor's New Skills: The Academy, the Profession and the Idea of Legal Education' in Peter Birks (ed) *Pressing Problems in the Law: Volume 2: What Are Law Schools For?* (Oxford University Press 1996).

Turner M and Engle R, 'Is Working Memory Capacity Task Dependent?' (1989) 28 *Journal of Memory and Language* 127–154.

Ward I, 'The Educative Ambition of Law and Literature' (1993) 13(3) *Legal Studies* 323–131

Wason P, 'Specific Thoughts on the Writing Process' in LW Gregg and ER Steinberg (eds) *Cognitive Processes in Writing* (Lawrence Erlbaum Associates 1980).

West C, 'Theory, Pragmatisms, and Politics' in Jonathan Arac and Barbara Johnson (eds) *Consequences of Theory* (Johns Hopkins University Press 1991).

Wiltsche H, 'Phenomenology and Thought Experiments. Thought Experiments as Anticipation Pumps' in Michael T Stuart, Yiftach Fehige, and James Robert Brown (eds) *The Routledge Companion to Thought Experiments* (Routledge 2017).

Young R, 'Paradigms and Problems: Needed Research in Rhetorical Invention' in Charles R Cooper and Lee C Odell (eds) *Research on Composing: Points of Departure* (National Council of Teachers of English 1978).

8 Three authors in search of phenomenologies of learning and technology

Lydia Bleasdale, Paul Maharg and Craig Newbery-Jones

The situation of action is ... an inexhaustibly rich resource.[1]

Introduction

It is a modernist trope to turn art's gaze upon itself, and make that self-conscious, self-reflexive, and make it new and unfamiliar. For the reader, viewer or listener even today, a century later, it is still an activity that disquiets and disorients conventional forms of the production and experience of art. The fragmented poetic narratives of Pound and Eliot, the sculptures of Henri Gaudier-Brzeska, the fictions of Joyce and Woolf, Picasso's cubist art and Russian Formalists' *ostranenie* are celebrated examples. Luigi Pirandello's characters in *Six Characters in Search of an Author* similarly inhabited a dramatic space where they usurped the conventional relationships of dramatist and the characters on stage.[2] They questioned their existence as fictions, railed against the incompleteness of the author's representation of them and their motives, argued and discussed the nature of their formal existences, and tried to escape the instrumental, neutralised nature of their lives on the stage.

In this chapter, we three authors similarly question our roles as critics and practitioners in the fields of learning and technology. Who are the authors of this chapter – technology or we three humans, or some kind of cyber-entities? What are the effects on our educational theories and practices of using digital technology, in the early twenty-first century? What is the place of Birks' collection, composed in the mid-1990s, and does he have anything valuable to say to us several decades later on these subjects? Certainly, at first glance in Birks' collection, there is little treatment of technology,

---

1 Lucy Suchman, *Plans and Situated Actions: The Problem of Human-Machine Communication* (Cambridge University Press 1987) 33.
2 The play was first staged in Rome, May 1921, exactly a century ago, at which the audience rioted in protest. At a later staging that year, in Milan, the play was received rapturously.

DOI: 10.4324/9781003322092-8

196   *Lydia Bleasdale et al.*

technological or design theory or the substantial interdisciplinary body of information theory that was already gathering around the digital revolution by the mid-1990s.

Moreover, we speak as a collective, and individually; and our chapter comprises explorations of three quite different yet intersecting issues that are essential to technology and legal education. In the first section, Craig treats of interdisciplinary theory and considers how the Bakhtinian chronotope can help us analyse and understand the nature and context of digital legal educational interventions. In the second section, Lydia explores the necessity for some kind of community, and the effects that digital education has upon the formation of such identity. In the third section, Paul explores examples of the educational form discussed throughout the chapter by Craig and Lydia, namely, the academic lecture, and how the digital rendering of this affects learning. In the conclusion, the authors discuss the implications for a phenomenological approach to learning and technology, and comment on the curious technological lacuna in Birks' collection.

Rethinking the space and time of the lecture: exploring the chronotopes of legal education

In a time of pandemic, the challenges faced by learners and educators are inevitably numerous, but the foremost challenges are resultant from the paradigm shifts around the space and consequential spatiality of education, while also posing significant challenges to our understandings of the time and temporality of learning. Although space and time exist as two distinct and separate observable dimensions, they are inherently interconnected. Legal pedagogy focuses overwhelmingly on the space around which learning is centred[3] while failing to fully consider spatiality,[4] whereas the influence of time[5] and temporality has not been convincingly examined. It goes without saying that the interconnectedness between the spatial and temporal in legal pedagogy has not been studied.

---

3 Nicholas P Terry, 'Bricks Plus Bytes: How Click-and-Brick Will Define Legal Education Space' (2001) 46 Villanova Law Review, 95; Debra D Burke, 'Scale-Up! Classroom Design and Use Can Facilitate Learning' (2015) 49 Law Teacher, 189; Norma Martin Clement, 'The Use and Impact of the Collaborative Lecture Theatres: Digging up the Foundations of the Lecture Theatre' (Teaching Enhancement Project Report Leeds Institute for Teaching Excellence 2018); Jason James Turner, Puteri Sofia Amirnuddin and Harmahinder Singh Iqbal Singh, 'University Legal Learning Spaces Effectiveness in Developing Employability Skills of Future Law Graduates' (2019) 16 Malaysian Journal of Learning and Instruction, 49.

4 Carolyn Wooley and S Beattie, 'Communal Reflections on the Workplace: Locating Learning for the Legal Professional' (2011) 12 International Journal of Work-Integrated Learning, 19.

5 Joel M Modiri, 'The Time and Space of Critical Legal Pedagogy' (2016) 27 Stellenbosch Law Review, 507.

However, it is worth noting here that the spatiotemporal challenges to legal education should be an important consideration for the continued integration of technology into existing learning modalities beyond the pandemic context. Over the past two decades, there have been major changes in pedagogy led by technology and digital transformation. For example, the growth and developing sophistication of virtual learning environments,[6] the widespread use of online databases and digital resources,[7] increasing deployment of digital collaborative spaces within the educational context,[8] and the influence of Twitter and social networking has seen traditional learning spaces augmented by the digital.[9] As technological developments accelerate and engagement with digital platforms deepens, a spatiotemporal understanding of engagement with a multitude of learning spaces becomes more fundamental to pedagogy. It is the connectedness between the spatial and temporal that will dictate the relationship between technology and the student learner, and an understanding of such interconnectedness will become fundamental to the development of future curricula, educational innovation, and the evolving landscape of legal education.

Legal education has always had to incorporate and adapt to technological changes, changes which have undoubtedly changed modalities of learning. But it is argued here that the influence of technology has been felt, in varying degrees, across all strata of legal education in the past two decades more than it has in any period before it. As a consequence, there needs to be consideration of the implementation and deployment of technology alongside the broader experience of student learning, to understand these changes through a spatiotemporal lens, thinking about space and time as interconnected dimensions. In the context of this chapter, space refers to the locative, a place where things happen (be it a physical space, digital space, or hybrid space), but also a more dynamic dimension.[10] A space is enriched by the multiplicity of such relational connectedness[11] and is 'a product of

---

6 Sefton Bloxham, Paul Maharg and Patricia McKellar, 'Summary Report on the UKCLE/BILETA VLE Project' (2007) Journal of Information Law and Technology <https://warwick.ac.uk/fac/soc/law/elj/jilt/2007_1/vle_report> accessed 4 August 2021.

7 Richard A Matasar and Rosemary Shiels, 'Electronic Law Students: Repercussions on Legal Education' (1994) 29 The Valparaiso University Law Review, 909; Sefton Bloxham, 'Widening Access and the Use of ICT in Legal Education' (2005) 39 Law Teacher, 93.

8 Craig John Newbery-Jones, 'Trying to Do the Right Thing: Experiential Learning, E-Learning and Employability Skills in Modern Legal Education' (2015) 6 European Journal of Law and Technology <https://ejlt.org/index.php/ejlt/article/view/389/545> accessed 4 August 2021; Lisa Bugden, P Redmond and J Greaney, 'Online Collaboration as a Pedagogical Approach to Learning and Teaching Undergraduate Legal Education' (2018) 52 Law Teacher, 85.

9 Marcus Smith, 'Integrating Technology in Contemporary Legal Education' (2020) 54 Law Teacher, 209.

10 Doreen Massey, *For Space* (Sage 2005).

11 Andreas Philippopoulos-Mihalopoulos, 'And for Law: Why Space Cannot Be Understood Without Law' (2018) Law, Culture and the Humanities <https://doi.org/10.1177/1743872118765708> accessed 4 August 2021.

198 Lydia Bleasdale et al.

interrelations and embedded practices, a sphere of multiple possibilities.'[12] Spatiality by consequence is the product of such interrelations, particularly the product of interconnecting communal relations, where space and time are interconnected.[13] McGregor states that 'thinking in this way produces a dynamic and politicised understanding of space, it challenges the view of places as pre-existing and bounded, replacing it with an open conception of place as hybrid, provisional and porous.'[14] Time, in contrast, has been widely understood to be a measurement through which we can measure change or duration and 'is usually measured as progression into the future while present events are continuously relegated to the past.'[15] In contrast, temporality is the experience or construction of time that is inherently linked to the subjective context of those who experience it.[16] Therefore, space cannot be understood without the consideration of time, and space can be considered to be continuously in a process of unfolding, is never complete and endlessly reshaped and reformed by the passage of time.[17] This interconnection between space and time exists in an 'inherently dynamic simultaneity.'[18]

Drawing upon the work of Valverde,[19] the interconnectedness between space and time can be explored through the concept of the chronotope. The chronotope is a device conceived by Mikhail Bakhtin to analyse how configurations of the spatiotemporal are characterised in literature.[20] Specifically, he outlined how in 'the literary artistic chronotope, spatial and temporal indicators are fused into one carefully thought-out, concrete whole.'[21] Valverde explains Bakhtin's conceptions of the chronotope as 'the intrinsic connectedness of spatial and temporal relationships that are artistically expressed in literature. *Time as it were, thickens, takes on flesh, becomes artistically visible; likewise, space becomes charged and responsive to the movements*

---

12 Andreas Philippopoulos-Mihalopoulos, 'Law's Spatial Turn: Geography, Justice and a Certain Fear of Space' (2011) 7 Law, Culture and the Humanities, 187, 194.
13 Doreen Massey, *Space, Place and Gender* (Polity Press 1994).
14 Jane McGregor, 'Studying Spatiality' (British Educational Research Association Annual Conference, Manchester, September 2004).
15 Fae Garland and Mitchell Travis, 'Temporal Bodies: Emergencies, Emergence, and Intersex Embodiment' in Chris Dietz, Mitchell Travis and Michael Thompson (eds), *A Jurisprudence of the Body* (Palgrave Macmillan 2020) 120.
16 Anna Bennett and Penny Jane Burke, 'Re/Conceptualising Time and Temporality: An Exploration of Time in Higher Education' (2018) 39 Discourse: Studies in the Cultural Politics of Education, 913.
17 Doreen Massey, *For Space* (Sage 2005).
18 Doreen Massey, *Space, Place and Gender* (Polity Press 1994) 2–3.
19 Mariana Valverde, *Chronotopes of Law: Jurisdiction, Scale and Governance* (Routledge 2015).
20 Mikhail M Bakhtin, *The Dialogic Imagination: Four Essays* (Michael Holquist ed & tr, Caryl Emerson tr, University of Texas Press 1981).
21 Ibid, 84.

Three authors in search of phenomenologies 199

of time, plot, and history.'[22] Valverde continues that '"time" and "space" are thus *not* taken as separate dimension to be considered one after the other'[23] but instead needs to be analysed as a configured whole.

Valverde illustrates the chronotope in a legal context by drawing upon the example of the courtroom.[24] The courtroom exists as a different space at different times. Prior to the judge or magistrate taking their seats on the bench or calling the court to session, the courtroom is merely an architectural display of law's majesty, a symbol of state authority or simply, a room. It is an understanding of the spatiotemporal configurations that makes it a courtroom; a space of legal authority and legal record that is documented under the authority of the judge. Even when the room is filled with those carrying out their duties, those appearing before the court, and those observing the proceedings, the courtroom is not recognised as a courtroom until an appointed hour and proceedings are commenced by the presence and will of the judge. Yet, before and after such time, it is still a legally significant space and the time of law within this legal space does not follow a linear progression as we would recognise it. Legal time can be broken through adjournment or disruption and is resumed upon recommencement by the legal authority. This is often recorded as one spatiotemporal event and presented through one record. But this fails to reflect the true passage of time and excludes events occurring outside this official record. These can enrich our understanding of law, the legal process and the sites of power, authority and inequality in legal procedure.

Valverde argues that 'like literary genres, different legal processes are shaped and given meaning by particular spacetimes.'[25] However, Valverde also issues a warning about the use of the chronotope in legal research; explaining how 'chronotopes do not simply exist somewhere but instead... this idea can lead a re-visioning of legal and governance mechanisms.'[26] It is argued here that the law school, particularly the lecture, can be examined through the chronotopic device. Legal education has specific spatial and temporal spheres that have been deepened through the blending of analogue and digital spaces for learning and learning community. (Legal) education is a phenomenon drawing upon the individual lived experiences of students within the analogue and digital space and within an ever-expanding temporal dimension. This experience is ever changing, and to understand the student experience, we need to ruminate upon the shifting, evolving and malleable chronotopes of legal education. It is argued here that assessing such experiences with reference to their spatiotemporal characteristics will

22 Mariana Valverde, *Chronotopes of Law: Jurisdiction, Scale and Governance* (Routledge 2015) 9–10.
23 Ibid, 10.
24 Ibid, 17.
25 Ibid, 11.
26 Ibid, 180.

200   *Lydia Bleasdale et al.*

deepen theoretical discourse around the use of technology, specifically the analogue and digital space in legal education, and as a consequence prompt more critical engagement with curriculum development. By thinking about the multitude of different interrelationships within spaces of legal education, we can more wholly understand the learner experience and truly evaluate meaningful engagement with educative spaces. By re-envisioning student interaction within specific traditional and non-traditional, direct and indirect, analogue and digital learning spaces, alongside a dynamic appraisal of the temporality of such interactions, we can reflect more holistically on the complete phenomenon of legal education. The usage of this concept is particularly relevant to legal education due to its shifting modes of space and time and the multifaceted approach to utilisation of space, particularly in reference to tech-facilitation.

While Covid-19 has disrupted multiple spheres of legal education, the most noticeable space that has been upended is the traditional, didactic lecture. Based on government guidance, most, if not all, law schools in England and Wales have replaced large lectures with synchronous or asynchronous online delivery. Like the courtroom, the lecture theatre is a dynamic space, a site of multiple interrelationships in multiple temporalities. While formal learning begins with an opening address and ends with closing remarks, this is merely the formal learning opportunity that the majority of pedagogy recognises. However, it is within the physical space of the lecture theatre and outside (before and after entering the room), while preparing for or consolidating the 'formal' lecture material and travelling to and from the physical lecture space, that informal learning and community building occurs, experiences that shape student and social citizenship transpire, and co-curricular and non-curricular learning and personal development takes place and crosses academic, non-academic, and professional spaces.

There are also examples of multiple interactions occurring within different temporalities. While a student in a lecture may have one eye and ear on the lecture material, they may also be engaged in a dialogue with another student through the exchange of handwritten notes or even conversing with another student within that class, a friend outside of this space via an instantaneous message. The student in question may physically be in one spacetime while engaging within another spacetime. It is therefore inevitable that changing the paradigm to remote, recorded or content captured lecture material removes multiple relational processes within this space, particularly around co-curricular or non-curricular learning and community building.

The chronotopic view of a lecture is paralleled to the chronotopic analysis in other educational settings. Brown and Renshaw describe the concept of the chronotope as providing a

> way of viewing a student's participation in the classroom as being a situated, dynamic process constituted through the interaction of past experience, ongoing involvement, and yet-to-be-accomplished goals.

Neither the product of learning, as coming to know, nor the process of learning, as ways of coming to know, is viewed as fixed or stable. Viewed as relational and transformative, classroom contexts become creative spaces in which identities, both personal and collective, may be imagined, enacted, and contested.[27]

Higher education, specifically the lecture, is no different. The concept of the chronotope can be used to revise the spatiality and temporality of legal education, taking us beyond limited understandings of physical and digital space and decentralising the university's arbitrary conceptions of time and the academic timetable. As discussed earlier, the impact on learning in a time of pandemic has been substantial, yet it is the impact on communities of learning, cohesion and a sense of belonging within cohorts, alongside issues with time management and motivation that have been most pertinent for our students and, as a result, us as educators.[28]

If we take the lecture theatre as a site of multiple spatiotemporalities, then this shift to recorded, online delivery creates a decentralisation of time and working practice; inevitably rendering the timetable, as traditionally understood, meaningless. This is the first disruptive act in the disentanglement of such individual, subjective space and time from our conceptions of space and time in the physical law school. The pre-recorded nature of digital lectures removes students not just from the physical space of the lecture theatre but also from their individual spatiality. While lecture theatres are traditionally understood as places of learning and knowledge, they provide opportunity much beyond this in terms of community building, fostering a sense of belonging, peer support and social interaction. It is inevitable that such disruption leads to detachment of cohorts from this physical space and such spatiality. Thinking beyond the physical lecture space can encourage us to rethink both the community space and the cohort's experience of time. The nature of pre-recorded lectures also decentres the learning experience of students in regard to their temporality. This is more than just 'choosing' when to engage with such learning materials, but also the manner through which they engage with lecture materials and construct their own self-curated learning experiences. The fact that pre-recorded, online lectures exist outside of the formal university timetable and that time can be manipulated by the student viewing the recording means that students are able to engage with such content in a manner and at a time most conducive to their

---

27 Raymond Brown and Peter Renshaw, 'Positioning Students as Actors and Authors: A Chronotopic Analysis of Collaborative Learning Activities' (2006) 13 Mind, Culture, and Activity, 247, 249.

28 Rosie Hunnam and Jim Dickinson, 'How to Build Back Student Community and Opportunity Between Now and the New Year' (*WONKHE*, 31 March 2021) <https://wonkhe.com/blogs/how-to-build-back-student-community-and-opportunity-between-now-and-the-new-year/> accessed 5 August 2021.

learning. However, this can also have profound issues for those students who struggle to engage[29] and require the structure of in-person and timetabled learning activities to guide them. The decentring of the lecture from the timetable or university time also raises issues for a range of students and demographics as learning is subject to the individual's temporality in other spaces (be it home, study space, coffee shop, etc.). This transplantation of such a learning activity places the lecture in another space-time, be it a positive or negative experience.

In models of hybrid delivery, there is usually opportunity to mitigate broader issues through small group teaching and chances for broader engagement and interaction with the law school community in other varied law school spaces. However, in a time of pandemic, this is not possible. Where schools and universities have offered face-to-face (f2f), in-person delivery, these are often still isolated, socially distant experiences and limited in number. A possible exception to this is distance learning which, when designed well, looks specifically to developing cohort cohesion and a community of learning. Yet, there is still a broader influence of expectation or choice in distance learning with a resultant or curriculum-embedded preparedness that assist students in mitigating some of these feelings of detachment or fostering belonging in alternative ways.

While we have focused here on the lecture as a universal example, as the influence and reliance of technology continues to deepen, there will be further challenges to the experience of students that will facilitate a deeper understanding of the relationships between space and time in the learning experience. Across the globe, university leaders will be looking at the lessons learnt from Covid-19 with a view to increase (or at least finesse) digital engagement and look towards more significant and central approaches to digital transformation. Physical learning spaces will inevitably be replaced with digital platforms of convenience. Both the space and time of learning will exist in multiple interrelationships and individual temporalities. The integration of instantaneous, all-encompassing virtual spaces to deal with queries, discussions and engagement with academic subject matter will be provided for but such instantaneous engagement will decentre the law school time and official communication channels will get subsumed within informal, peer communications. Again, this is not new and the law school as an educational environment has been in flux for a number of years. Specifically, the more central use of virtual learning environments and digital resources, the influence of social networking and instantaneous communications, and shifting modes of engagement have seen traditional learning spaces be augmented by the digital, and a transfer of peer support into informal (often

---

29 Rebecca Montacute and Carl Cullinane, 'Learning in Lockdown' (*Sutton Trust*, January 2021) <www.suttontrust.com/wp-content/uploads/2021/01/Learning-in-Lockdown.pdf> accessed 5 August 2021.

digital) channels and platforms. Generally, the lived experience of this generation of digital natives in higher education means that students already seek out peer support in informal ways via remote engagement with unverified, support networks. The ease of engagement (particularly on platforms already used by students) and elements of anonymity can lead to an erosion of aspects of traditional community and potentially vital support sites (e.g. personal tutoring) replaced by tech-facilitated platforms. This is another example of the decentralisation of support as a result of engagement with a broader range of formal and informal support structures across multiple space-times.

This chapter is not arguing that tech-facilitation and hybrid modalities of learning are worrisome, dangerous or not desired. They are fundamental to the future of legal education. And regardless of the context of this pandemic, such tech migration, whether we like it or not, is leading to more constructivist learning modalities. We need to draw upon the chronotopic device to understand all aspects of legal education. Legal pedagogy needs to look beyond the formal learning experience, disconnect from university time and acknowledge the open conception of space, in order to understand the interrelationships that occur in the multitude of law school spaces and reconsider our understanding of temporality in the context of the twenty-first-century law school. Only by truly understanding the interconnectedness between space and time in legal education can we make meaningful and significant interventions.

Community, identity and the individual: social identity and identity formation

The move to solely online or hybrid forms of teaching during the pandemic, and the potential retention of some form of hybrid learning beyond the 2020/2021 academic year, has implications for many aspects of Higher Education – particularly for traditionally 'face-to-face' institutions. The pedagogical implications of hybrid or solely online learning have been explored to a greater extent than their implications for the development and transformation of student identity.

Identity is defined by Ibarra as entailing the attachment of 'various meanings ... to a person by self and others ... based on people's social roles and group memberships (social identities) as well as the personal and character traits they display and others attribute to them based on their conduct (personal identities).'[30] This 'social identity' approach

---

30 Herminia Ibarra, 'Provisional Selves: Experimenting with Image and Identity in Professional Adaptation' (1999) 44 Administrative Science Quarterly, 764, 766.

204 *Lydia Bleasdale et al.*

means we can define and understand ourselves in terms of our personal identity – seeing ourselves in terms of interests, attitudes and behaviours that differ in important ways from those of other *individuals*. On the other hand, there are also a range of contexts in which we define and understand ourselves in terms of one or more *social* identities – seeing our interests, attitudes and behaviours as aligned with those of other members of the groups to which we belong (i.e. in-groups) but as different from those of groups to which we do not belong (out-groups)...social relationships ... have a fundamental bearing on a person's understanding of *who* they are and, as a result, on *what they are able to* do (emphasis in original).[31]

Identity is therefore formed not only through our own sense of self and what is important to us but also through social interaction with individuals and groups.

Furthermore, identity is multi-dimensional. Students, for example, might have identities as a student, as well as a family member, friend, future professional, fan of a particular hobby, someone who is 'academically gifted' and so on.[32] These identities will, for some, continue in their transition into and through university, although most will experience challenges and transformations to at least some of their identities. Previous educational identities, for example, might not be reflective of their experiences in this different educational context.[33] Former identities as an excellent student who is well-regarded within a small school setting might be challenged by the early experience of receiving disappointing marks, or of comparing oneself to others and feeling academically deficient, particularly within a much larger academic setting.[34] In this way, we can understand identity as

---

31 Tegan Cruwys, S Alexander Haslam, Genevieve A Dingle, et al., 'Depression and Social Identity: An Integrative Review' (2014) 18 Personality and Social Psychology Review, 215, 218.
32 Marjatta Lairio, Sauli Puukari and Anne Kouvo, 'Studying at University as Part of Student Life and Identity Construction' (2013) 57 Scandinavian Journal of Educational Research, 115.
33 Hazel Christie, Lyn Tett, Vivienne E Cree, Jenny Hounsell and Velda McCune, '"A Real Rollercoaster of Confidence and Emotions:" Learning to Be a University Student' (2008) 33 Studies in Higher Education, 567; Michelle Samura, 'Remaking Selves, Repositioning Selves, or Remaking Space: An Examination of Asian American College Students' Processes of "Belonging"' (2016) 57 Journal of College Student Development, 135.
34 Marjatta Lairio, Sauli Puukari and Anne Kouvo, 'Studying at University as Part of Student Life and Identity Construction' (2013) 57 Scandinavian Journal of Educational Research, 115; Dorthe Hoj Jensen and Jolanda Jetten, 'The Importance of Developing Students' Academic and Professional Identities in Higher Education' (2016) 57 Journal of College Student Development, 1027; Lydia Bleasdale and Sarah Humphreys, 'Undergraduate Resilience Research Project: Project Report' (Leeds Institute for Teaching Excellence 2018) <https://teachingexcellence.leeds.ac.uk/wp-content/uploads/sites/89/2018/01/LITEbleasdalehumphreys_fullreport_online.pdf> accessed 5 August 2021.

Three authors in search of phenomenologies 205

neither singular nor fixed, and as developed not in isolation but in response to interactions.[35]

Seeing identity as crystals in a kaleidoscope, changing in response to individual and societal influences and pressures, reinforces universities as social institutions: they are not only sites for academic development, ordinarily they are also sites in which 'students construct a sense of self that situates them in a particular social location with a set of corresponding social roles.'[36] Literature concerning the identity formation of university students has predominantly focused upon university as a site in which academic / educational identity and professional identity are developed. Academic / educational identity is described as a

> social structure that is located in the individual and is based on the meanings formed in the context of education. First, educational identity consists of self-identity, the 'I' in the language of symbolic interactionalism, and secondly, it includes reflections from other people, the 'me' or the objective self ... 'me' refers to social identity, the way people understand themselves in relation to others.[37]

Learner identities are therefore fluid and constructed not only by instructional work but also by the learner's previous identity, their prior learning and their interactions with staff and students.[38]

Professional identity is how an individual perceives themselves in whichever professional role they have adopted or are considering adopting. According to Ibarra, professional identity can be formed prior to entry into the desired profession:

---

35 John Goldie, 'The Formation of Professional Identity in Medical Students: Considerations for Educators' (2012) 34 Medical Teacher, e641.

36 Peter Kaufman, 'The Sociology of College Students' Identity Formation' (2014) New Directions for Higher Education, 35, 37.

37 Erja Moore, 'Educational Identities of Adult University Graduates' (2006) 50 Scandinavian Journal of Educational Research, 149, 150.

38 Lesley Scanlon, Louise Rowling and Zita Weber, '"You Don't Have Like an Identity... You are Just Lost in a Crowd:" Forming a Student Identity in the First-Year Transition to University' (2007) 10 Journal of Youth Studies, 223; Tracy Levett-Jones, Judith Lathlean, Isabel Higgins and Margaret McMillan, 'Staff–Student Relationships and Their Impact on Nursing Students' Belongingness and Learning' (2009) 65 Journal of Advanced Nursing, 316; Jacqueline Aundree Baxter, 'Who Am I and What Keeps Me Going? Profiling the Distance Learning Student in Higher Education' (2012) 13 International Review Research in Open and Distance Learning, 107; Liz Thomas, 'Building Student Engagement and Belonging in Higher Education at a Time of Change: Final Report from the What Works? Student Retention & Success Programme' (2012) <www.heacademy.ac.uk/system/files/what_works_final_report_0.pdf> accessed 5 August 2021; Rowaida Jaber and Eileen Kennedy, '"Not the Same Person Anymore:" Groupwork, Identity and Social Learning Online' (2017) 38 Distance Education, 216.

206   *Lydia Bleasdale et al.*

people adapt to new professional roles by experimenting with images that serve as trials for possible but not yet fully elaborated professional identities. These 'provisional selves' are temporary solutions people use to bridge the gap between their current capacities and self-conceptions and the representations they hold about what attitudes and behaviors are expected in the new role.[39]

Professional identity formation has been considered in the context of health-care students such as doctors, nurses, pharmacists and dentists[40]; distance learners[41]; social work students[42]; as well as law students.[43] Although the

39 Herminia Ibarra, 'Provisional Selves: Experimenting with Image and Identity in Professional Adaptation' (1999) 44 Administrative Science Quarterly, 764, 765. See also Hazel Rose Markus and Paula Nurius, 'Possible Selves' (1986) 41 American Psychologist, 954.

40 Lynn V Monrouxe, 'Identity, Identification and Medical Education: Why Should We Care?' (2010) 44 Medical Education, 40; Ian Wilson, Leanne S Cowin, Maree Johnson and Helen Young, 'Professional Identity in Medical Students: Pedagogical Challenges to Medical Education' (2013) 25 Teaching and Learning in Medicine, 369; Richard L Cruess, Sylvia R Cruess, J Donald Boudreau, Linda Snell and Yvonne Steinert, 'Reframing Medical Education to Support Professional Identity Formation' (2014) 89 Academic Medicine, 1446; Anne Wong and Karen Trollope-Kumar, 'Reflections: An Inquiry into Medical Students' Professional Identity Formation' (2014) 48 Medical Education, 489; Richard L Cruess, Sylvia R Cruess, J Donald Boudreau, Linda Snell and Yvonne Steinert, 'A Schematic Representation of the Professional Identity Formation and Socialization of Medical Students and Residents: A Guide for Medical Educators' (2015) 90 Academic Medicine, 718; Selma Sabancıogullari and Selma Dogan, 'Effects of the Professional Identity Development Programme on the Professional Identity, Job Satisfaction and Burnout Levels of Nurses: A Pilot Study' (2015) 21 International Journal of Nursing Practice, 847; Pirashanthie Vivekananda-Schmidt, James Crossley and Deborah Murdoch-Eaton, 'A Model of Professional Self-Identity Formation in Student Doctors and Dentists: A Mixed Method Study' (2015) 15 BMC Medical Education Art, 83; Gemma Quinn, Beverly Lucas and Jonathan Silcock, 'Professional Identity Formation in Pharmacy Students During an Early Preregistration Training Placement' (2020) 84 American Journal of Pharmaceutical Education, 1132; Diane O'Doherty, Aidan Culhane, Jane O'Doherty, Sarah Harney, Liam Glynn, Helena McKeague and Dervla Kelly, 'Medical Students and Clinical Placements – A Qualitative Study of the Continuum of Professional Identity Formation' (2021) 32 Education for Primary Care, 202.

41 Jacqueline Aundree Baxter, 'Who Am I and What Keeps Me Going? Profiling the Distance Learning Student in Higher Education' (2012) 13 International Review Research in Open and Distance Learning, 107; Lorraine Delaney and Margaret Farren, 'No "Self" Left Behind? Part-Time Distance Learning University Graduates: Social Class, Graduate Identity and Employability' (2016) 31 Open Learning: Journal of Open, Distance and E-Learning, 194.

42 Shelley L Craig, Gio Iacono, Megan S Paceley, Michael P Dentato and Kerrie EH Boyle, 'Intersecting Sexual, Gender, and Professional Identities Among Social Work Students: The Importance of Identity Integration' (2017) 53 Journal of Social Work Education, 466.

43 Kath Hall, Molly T O'Brien and Stephen Tang, 'Developing a Professional Identity in Law School: A View from Australia' (2010) 4 Phoenix Law Review, 19; Lydia Bleasdale and Sarah Humphreys, 'Identity, Well-Being and Law Students' in Caroline Strevens and Rachael Fielding (eds), *Educating for Well-Being in Law: Positive Professional Identities and Practice* (Routledge 2020); Emma Jones, 'Connectivity, Socialisation and Identity

educational context for undergraduate law students in England and Wales means that they will not necessarily develop a specific professional identity as a lawyer in the same way as, for example, a North American law student might, professional identity formation can occur for those students who are intent on entering a particular profession. For law students, socialisation resulting in a better understanding of their own future professional selves can occur through, for example, work experience or pro bono opportunities. Through the exposure to professionals working within a field which the student aspires to enter (law, working for a council, working within the charity sector, or working within a school for example), the student can begin to form a sense of what their future professional identity and future professional self will be.[44]

There is a wealth of literature covering the importance of identity development to university students. Participants in Høj Jensen and Jetten's study of Danish and Australian university students regarded both academic and personal identity as 'necessary right from entering university to achieve good learning, to feel confident, and to stay motivated.'[45] Participants also highlighted the importance of educators in the development of their professional identity, reflecting upon issues such as how interesting they made certain areas seem as future disciplines to work in. Overall, 'academic identity supported feelings of belonging in higher education, and professional identity supported feelings of adequacy in understanding how to do their future jobs and the purpose of the learning.'[46]

Adopting the social identity approach to identity formation, it is clear how academic and professional identity can be informed not only through personal beliefs about one's own capabilities and potential but also through interactions – including in and around the lecture theatre space. The communal experience of physically travelling to the learning space; waiting to enter and to find a seat; leaving together; having discussions about understanding of topics; likes or dislikes of particular modules; getting anticipated and desired marks; getting the marks necessary to achieve desired future professional goals; following the steps necessary to reach those goals and steps already taken to do so; being introduced to future professional

---

Formation: Exploring Mental Well-Being in Online Distance Learning Law Students' in Caroline Strevens and Rachael Fielding (eds), *Educating for Well-Being in Law: Positive Professional Identities and Practice* (Routledge 2020).

44 Andrew Francis, 'Legal Education, Social Mobility, and Employability: Possible Selves, Curriculum Intervention, and the Role of Legal Work Experience' (2015) 42 Journal of Law & Society, 173.

45 Dorthe Hoj Jensen and Jolanda Jetten, 'The Importance of Developing Students' Academic and Professional Identities in Higher Education' (2016) 57 Journal of College Student Development, 1034.

46 Ibid, 1038. See also Pirashanthie Vivekananda-Schmidt and John Sandars, 'Belongingness and Its Implications for Undergraduate Health Professions Education: A Scoping Review' (2018) 29 Education for Primary Care, 268.

role models through guest lectures; asking and having answered questions by the lecturer before and after class; and of physically seeing the diverse (or not) student body of which each student is part are all factors which can and do inform the development of the student's identity during their time at university, as well as help them to form friendships (particularly critical to identity in the first year of study[47]), increase their motivation, enhance their learning gains and help them to develop 'generic capabilities' such as critical thinking, self-managed learning and group work.[48] The removal of the lecture as a site in which such interactions can happen, in combination with the removal or scaling back of other opportunities in which to have identity-forming experiences (e.g. in-person seminars, volunteering opportunities and work experience),[49] has implications for how all students, but particularly those who began university as undergraduates in 2020, have constructed their identity over the past year.

Many students are, of course, accustomed to online interactions, including forming and maintaining friendships online,[50] and opportunities for identity formation exist within those online spaces. The lecture as one space in which such opportunities for interaction between students and their fellow students, and students and staff, ordinarily arise has been replaced by,

47 Lisa Thomas, Elizabeth Orme and Finola Kerrigan, 'Student Loneliness: The Role of Social Media Through Life Transitions' (2020) 146 Computers & Education Art, 103754.
48 Maureen Tam, 'University Impact on Student Growth: A Quality Measure?' (2002) 24 Journal of Higher Education Policy and Management, 211; David Kember and Doris YP Leung, 'The Influence of the Teaching and Learning Environment on the Development of Generic Capabilities Needed For a Knowledge-Based Society' (2005) 8 Learning Environments Research, 245; Vanessa M Buote, S Mark Pancer, Michael W Pratt, et al., 'The Importance of Friends Friendship and Adjustment Among 1st-Year University Students' (2007) 22 Journal of Adolescent Research, 665; Tierra M Freeman, Lynley H Anderman and Jane M Jensen, 'Sense of Belonging in College Freshmen at the Classroom and Campus Levels' (2007) 75 Journal of Experimental Education, 203; Tracy Levett-Jones and Judith Lathlean, 'Belongingness: A Prerequisite for Nursing Students' Clinical Learning' (2008) 8 Nurse Education in Practice 103; Lyanda Vermeulen and Henk G Schmidt, 'Learning Environment, Learning Process, Academic Outcomes and Career Success of University Graduates' (2008) 33 Studies in Higher Education, 431; Peter Kaufman, 'The Sociology of College Students' Identity Formation' (2014) New Directions for Higher Education.
49 Rebecca Montacute and Erica Holt-White, 'Covid-19 and the University Experience' (Sutton Trust, February 2021) <www.suttontrust.com/wp-content/uploads/2021/02/Covid-19-and-the-University-Experience.pdf> accessed 5 August 2021; Rosie Hunnam and Jim Dickinson, 'How to Build Back Student Community and Opportunity Between Now and the New Year' (WONKHE, 31 March 2021) <https://wonkhe.com/blogs/how-to-build-back-student-community-and-opportunity-between-now-and-the-new-year/> accessed 5 August 2021.
50 Jacqueline Aundree Baxter and Jo Haycock, 'Roles and Student Identities in Online Large Course Forums: Implications for Practice' (2014) 15 International Review of Research in Open and Distance Learning, 20; Lisa Thomas, Elizabeth Orme and Finola Kerrigan, 'Student Loneliness: The Role of Social Media Through Life Transitions' (2020) 146 Computers & Education Art, 103754.

Three authors in search of phenomenologies 209

for example, online support hours, online teaching and online volunteering opportunities. However, the experience of higher education institutions is that the formation and maintenance of meaningful connections has been one of the primary challenges of student education during the pandemic.[51] Even in institutions that primarily operate online outside of the context of a pandemic, the development of student connections is a perennial challenge.[52] It should also be noted that students who elect to attend university remotely have made that prior choice and, according to Baxter's study of Open University students, do not expect a great deal of social interaction, if any.[53] The same is not true of students attending what would ordinarily have been a f2f institution in 2020/2021, when both students and institutions were grappling with adjustments, including those necessitated by regularly changing government regulations and guidance. Furthermore, Baxter found that distance learners' identity was partly affected by their expectations of distance learning, and how they felt they would cope with it, particularly in terms of group work and engagement with fellow students. This is pertinent when considering students electing to study at an ordinarily f2f institution in 2020/2021: these students were not entering university as distance learners, with those prior expectations, but were instead having to regularly adjust both their identities (including as a student vis-à-vis other students), alongside their learning habits.

A (slim) majority of students report being satisfied with online learning,[54] which comes with the added benefit of offering flexibility for example, commuter students, and those with caring responsibilities and/or part-time jobs. Identity formation opportunities were nonetheless lost through, for

---

51 Office for National Statistics, 'Coronavirus and the Impact on Students in Higher Education in England: September to December 2020' (*Office for National Statistics* 21 December 2020) <www.ons.gov.uk/peoplepopulationandcommunity/educationandchildcare/articles/coronavirusandtheimpactonstudentsinhighereducationinenglandseptembertodecember2020/2020-12-21> accessed 5 August 2021.

52 Moira Dunworth, 'What a Difference a Day Makes: The Positive Outcomes of Early Face-to-Face Opportunities to Establish a Student Identity in Distance Learning Students New to Higher Education' (2012) 18 Journal of Adult and Continuing Education, 3; Association of Law Teachers, 'Connecting Legal Education: Wellbeing of Online Distance Learning Students' (*ALT Blog*, 9 June 2020) <http://lawteacher.ac.uk/connecting-legal-education/connecting-legal-education-wellbeing-of-online-distance-learning-students/> accessed 5 August 2021.

53 Jacqueline Aundree Baxter, 'Who Am I and What Keeps Me Going? Profiling the Distance Learning Student in Higher Education' (2012) 13 International Review Research in Open and Distance Learning.

54 Rachel Hewitt, 'HEPI Policy Note 29: Students' Views on the Impact of Coronavirus on Their Higher Education Experience in 2021' (*Higher Education Policy Institute*, April 2021) <www.hepi.ac.uk/2021/04/01/students-views-on-the-impact-of-coronavirus-on-their-higher-education-experience-in-2021/> accessed 5 August 2021.

210 *Lydia Bleasdale et al.*

example, the majority of learning taking place in isolation from other students,[55] as well as some students not being on campus and remaining at the family home (whether from the start of the academic year, or in response to local and subsequently national lockdowns). Even for those students who had planned to live at home, ordinarily they would have come onto campus and been physically amongst other students, feeling part of the student and university community through that presence – that sense of belonging, and the changes to identity which can come with that, has been profoundly different during the 2020/2021 academic year as compared with previous years. These opportunities have been limited by Covid-19 regulations, despite institutional efforts to create online social activities and, as a result, conversations which would usually take place within the lecture theatre, for example, are less regular, less impromptu, subject to more technological disruption and overall are more stifled.

The formation and transformation of identity is notably vulnerable to power dynamics and the greater potential for some individuals and institutions to exert power over others.[56] The move to an online setting could remove the opportunity for some of those power dynamics to be at play: Christie's study of 'widening participation' of students receiving in-person teaching, for example, found that they were differentiated from middle-class students on the grounds of finances, clothing, cars and work which they were doing, factors which might be less obvious in a more remote setting.[57] However, these power dynamics have potentially been replaced by others. Phirangee and Malec, in their study of online students at two Canadian universities, found that students were 'othered' on the grounds of their professional identity (having a job), academic identity and ethnic identity.[58] Furthermore, the online setting is not an equal platform: some students will have access to more advanced technology, better internet connection and spaces more conducive both to independent study and to contributions to online classes.[59] This has implications both for the potential opportunities

---

55 Office for National Statistics, 'Coronavirus and the Impact on Students in Higher Education in England: September to December 2020' (*Office for National Statistics*, 21 December 2020) <www.ons.gov.uk/peoplepopulationandcommunity/educationandchildcare/articles/coronavirusandtheimpactonstudentsinhighereducationinenglandseptembertodecember2020/2020-12-21> accessed 5 August 2021.
56 John Goldie, 'The Formation of Professional Identity in Medical Students: Considerations for Educators' (2012) 34 Medical Teacher, e641; Michelle Samura, 'Remaking Selves, Repositioning Selves, or Remaking Space: An Examination of Asian American College Students' Processes of "Belonging"' (2016) 57 Journal of College Student Development, 135.
57 Hazel Christie, 'Emotional Journeys: Young People and Transitions to University' (2009) 30 British Journal of Sociology of Education, 123.
58 Krystle Phirangee and Alesia Malec, 'Othering in Online Learning: An Examination of Social Presence, Identity, and Sense of Community' (2017) 38 Distance Education, 160.
59 Rebecca Montacute and Carl Cullinane, 'Learning in Lockdown' (*Sutton Trust*, January 2021) <www.suttontrust.com/wp-content/uploads/2021/01/Learning-in-Lockdown.pdf>

Three authors in search of phenomenologies 211

for a student's identity to develop (it is hard to develop social interaction on an unstable Wi-Fi connection) and the existing sense of anonymity students report feeling even when learning f2f will be exacerbated for some through the online setting,[60] but also for their ability to preserve with seeing themselves as a student whose future professional identity is attainable.[61]

Opportunities to develop a rounded, informed academic and professional identity will therefore have changed and most likely reduced in 2020/2021.[62] This chapter is not suggesting that technological advances are worrisome but, as institutions begin to consider the 'post-pandemic' university landscape and the role of hybrid learning within that, urges caution in assuming every aspect of the student experience, and of the development of student identity specifically, can automatically be achieved through a hybrid model. The informal learning opportunities through which communities and identity develop, which have traditionally occurred in and around the lecture (as well as other educational spaces), must be replaced by similar opportunities elsewhere within and outside of the student timetable. Although not every student will take advantage of such opportunities, their facilitation is nevertheless important for those who do wish to do so (and conveys a message that the institution takes seriously opportunities for community development). Those institutions which would previously have primarily offered f2f instruction but which are now intending to deliver (or are considering delivering) hybrid instruction, must (in the event that it is safe to do so) re-energise efforts to build programme and student communities[63] through, for example, in-person, regular personal tutoring sessions, including on a one-to-one and group basis,[64] peer mentoring,[65] social activities (including

---

accessed 5 August 2021; Rebecca Montacute and Erica Holt-White, 'Covid-19 and the University Experience' (*Sutton Trust*, February 2021) <www.suttontrust.com/wp-content/uploads/2021/02/Covid-19-and-the-University-Experience.pdf> accessed 5 August 2021.

60 Lesley Scanlon, Louise Rowling and Zita Weber, '"You Don't Have Like an Identity... You are Just Lost in a Crowd:" Forming a Student Identity in the First-Year Transition to University' (2007) 10 Journal of Youth Studies, 223; Rowaida Jaber and Eileen Kennedy, '"Not the Same Person Anymore:" Groupwork, Identity and Social Learning Online' (2017) 38 Distance Education, 216.

61 G Cavallaro Johnson and G Watson, '"Oh Gawd, How Am I Going to Fit Into This?": Producing [Mature] First-Year Student Identity' (2004) 18 Language and Education, 474.

62 Rosie Hunnam and Jim Dickinson, 'How to Build Back Student Community and Opportunity Between Now and the New Year' (*WONKHE*, 31 March 2021) <https://wonkhe.com/blogs/how-to-build-back-student-community-and-opportunity-between-now-and-the-new-year/> accessed 5 August 2021.

63 Lisa Thomas, Elizabeth Orme and Finola Kerrigan, 'Student Loneliness: The Role of Social Media Through Life Transitions' (2020) 146 Computers & Education Art, 103754.

64 Lydia Bleasdale and Sarah Humphreys, 'Undergraduate Resilience Research Project: Project Report' (Leeds Institute for Teaching Excellence 2018) <https://teachingexcellence.leeds.ac.uk/wp-content/uploads/sites/89/2018/01/LITEbleasdalehumphreys_fullreport_online.pdf> accessed 5 August 2021.

65 Liz Thomas, 'Building Student Engagement and Belonging in Higher Education at a Time of Change: Final Report from the What Works? Student Retention & Success Programme'

212 *Lydia Bleasdale et al.*

between students and between staff and students) and other in-person teaching provision, so as to ensure students who have elected to attend an institution now offering hybrid provision continue to have a multitude of opportunities to develop their identities.

The lecture as cyber-event

In the light of Craig's adaptation of the chronotope and Lydia's critique of the landscape of the post-pandemic university, Paul now analyses a case study that provides two contrasting examples of chronotopes in two lecture series and discusses detailed methods of facilitating legal learning online. The first lecture series was first written around 2002 on civil procedure in Scots law and delivered by an Advocate. The duration of a typical lecture in this series was around 120 minutes – around 2 hours with a break in the middle. It was delivered as a conventional lecture in a f2f lecture room at Strathclyde University. The lecturer spoke to the audience, who listened and took notes synchronously. This activity is *au fond* as true of the University of Bologna medieval lecture rooms that still survive, as much as a contemporary lecture theatre equipped with digital technologies. In all historical types, the lecturer is framed by space between audience and speaker, which may include dais, podium, book support, and the black/whiteboard or projector screen behind. The architecture and furniture signify social position in the knowledge hierarchy and function in the room. At front and possibly to the sides, depending upon the design of the audience space, students generally sit, listen, take notes and talk with each other. Entering and exiting the physical lecture theatre becomes its own social theatre for students, as Lydia discussed above; but the chronology of the event between entering and leaving is determined by the speaker, who controls duration and pace as well as content and much else such as affective tone. All this contributes to Craig's definition of the lecture chronotope.

Around four years on, the whole analogue lecture series had been transformed in the course of one year into a digital lecture series; and let's analyse briefly one lecture in the series, on enforcement of decrees.[66] Its duration is not 100 minutes or a proportion thereof: rather what might be termed its

---

(2012) <www.heacademy.ac.uk/system/files/what_works_final_report_0.pdf> accessed 5 August 2021.

66 See Patricia McKellar and Paul Maharg, 'Virtual Learning Environments: The Alternative to the Box Under the Bed' (2005) 39 Law Teacher, 43; Paul Maharg, 'Multimedia and the Docuverse of Law: Learning and the Representation of Knowledge' in Paul Maharg (ed) *Transforming Legal Education: Learning and Teaching the Law in the Early Twenty-First Century* (Ashgate Publishing 2007). This chapter describes extensively the context, background, research and research methodologies of our experiments in webcasting and a brief research literature review of the prior studies on webcasting.

The designer and coder of the digital environment was David Sams of the GGSL's Learning Technologies Development Unit. His work and his background in photography

Three authors in search of phenomenologies 213

Figure 8.1 Digital lecture, Civil Procedure, Glasgow Graduate School of Law, c. 2004.

Bergsonian *durée réelle* was around 20 minutes; and in no sense can that *durée* be understood as a conventional lecture. To describe it, we are compelled to describe not the physical environment but the graphical design, for that is the meta-narrative of the digital event. Here (see Figure 8.1), it comprises the presence of a speaker, surrounded by multiple forms of hypertext links, animations and textual information. She speaks directly, quietly, to the camera lens and therefore to the viewer. The sense of intimacy and social presence is thus strong.[67] So too is that of architecture – emphatically not a physical architecture, but a graphical and symbolic architecture, comprising cues, information links and texts.[68]

That graphical design is built around the guiding concept of 'framing.'[69] Within the overall window of the app in Figure 8.1, there are at least three

---

and design was critical to the success of the webcast environments used in the GGSL and Strathclyde Law School.
67 Evidenced by student responses in our research.
68 The speaker, Patricia McKellar, is not actually in the space she seems to occupy – the image is green-screened, and the frames and texts were of course added in post-production.
69 The concept of the frame, deriving from the discourse of art and cartography, is used in many disciplines. See Gale MacLachlan and Ian Reid, *Framing and Interpretation* (Melbourne University Press 1994); Paul Duro (ed), *Rhetoric of the Frame: Essays on the Boundaries of the Artwork* (Cambridge University Press 1996). For a useful application of the concept to law, and one directly applicable here, see Ronald KL Collins and David M Skover, 'Paratexts' (1992) 44 Stanford Law Review, 509:

Any technique that reproduces reality enframes or shapes reality. ... Enframing, therefore, is a quality of any mode of representation, and varies according to the selected mode. Different modes of representation, with their different types of enframing, will set

214 *Lydia Bleasdale et al.*

Figure 8.2 Identity frame.

frames that compose the graphical interface, all of them as carefully rehearsed and planned as the gloss in a glossed Justinianic manuscript or the frontispiece of a Renaissance legal text. They can be specified as follows:

1 *Identity frame*: who produced this, on behalf of whom, titles, origins, foundations. Note that this frame sites the viewer within the identity of the institution, as a member of that community of knowledge. Colour cuing links the legal substance (civil litigation) with the educational and technological developers (Learning Technologies Development Unit) (Figure 8.2).

---

different boundaries ... oral, written, print, and paratextual modes of representation enframe reality in radically different ways. Thus, a shift from one mode of representation to another produces far-reaching consequences for law, which currently is highly dependent on texts of one sort or another.

(510, fn 5)

This concept has a number of similarities with Heidegger's concept of 'enframing' (*das Gestell*), by which representation of the object world is not just a re-presentation, but a rupturing as well as a capturing. See Martin Heidegger, *The Question Concerning Technology and Other Essays* (William Lovitt tr, Harper & Row 1977) 19–20. Very often this 'enframing' goes unnoticed because it must be so in order to work its effect – 'what has produced and manipulated the frame puts everything to work in order to efface the frame effect,' Jacques Derrida, *The Truth in Painting* (Geoff Bennington and Ian McLeod trs, University of Chicago Press 1987) 73. There are points of similarity here between Derrida's concept of the frame, and Bernard Jackson's exploration of the ways in which the pragmatics of courtroom discourse operate at deep levels within court narratives; and, of course, the same is true of the pragmatics of legal educational praxis. Bernard Jackson, 'Towards an Interdisciplinary Model of Legal Communication' in Bernard Jackson (ed), *Legal Semiotics and the Sociology of Law* (Oñati Institute 1994); Bernard Jackson, 'Thematization and the Narrative Typifications of the Law' in David Nelkin (ed), *Law as Communication* (Aldershot 1996).

Three authors in search of phenomenologies 215

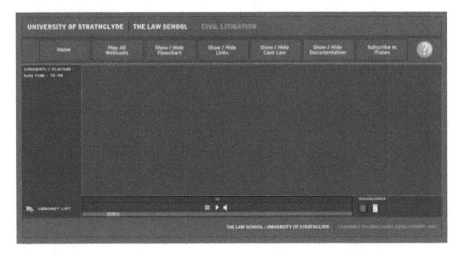

Figure 8.3 Navigation frame.

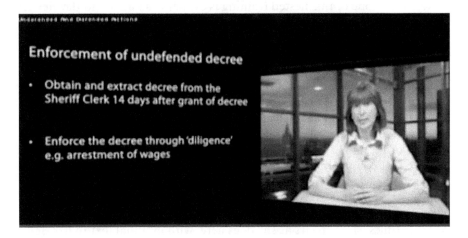

Figure 8.4 Knowledge frame.

2 *Navigation frame*: how to move within the whole lecture series, how to hover over the whole series by calling up a flowchart of nodes, links to cases, legislation, documentation and functionalities such as downloads to iTunes, as well as general questions (Figure 8.3).
3 *Knowledge frame*. This comprises the video, bullet point slides and where relevant animations that summarise or anticipate what the speaker says (Figure 8.4).

216   *Lydia Bleasdale et al.*

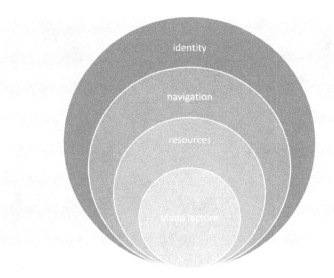

Figure 8.5 Layers of engagement.

Note that none of this nested framing is explicitly signalled to the viewer: it is subtle and implicit and helps guide a viewer's attention. It is grounded in the principles of good HCI (human-computer interaction) or UX (user experience), in particular those of Richard Meyer, and draws learners into the docuverse of law it represents (Figure 8.5).[70]

Also note the visual elements of this frame. The speaker is speaking in front of a 'green screen' upon which was superimposed the photograph of a sunset over central Glasgow taken from an office. The corner post of the office window to her left and behind is the perspectival point. Note how the text of the bullet points is angled so that the text becomes part of the perspectival composition *within* the frame while in tension with the video window. The whole frame is composed as a performance that is *not* performance. At times, the speaker reduces to a postage stamp in the top right-hand corner if we want viewers to focus more on information in the frame. At other times, she appears as she does here, with minimal text to her right.

If we were to contrast the analogue with the digital lecture, however, perhaps the most striking difference lies in the chronologies of the two events. Three points are worth noting:

1   The whole digital lecture series on civil procedure was significantly shorter than the f2f series – around half the total length in duration.[71]

---

70   See, for example, Richard E Mayer (ed), *Cambridge Handbook of Multimedia Learning* (Cambridge University Press 2005).
71   Strathclyde University Law School's Learning Technologies Development Unit was involved in designing, filming and producing webcasts for a broad range of other subjects such as Evidence and Domestic Relations; and in each project, it proved to be the case

Three authors in search of phenomenologies 217

There are several reasons for this. F2f lecturers frequently repeat information, not just by preview and review, but within the body of the lecture to ensure that the audience has understood the content of the lecture – the intellectual pace of the lecture tends to be slow. In addition, lecturers tend to speak more slowly, and some use more formal syntax than they would in conversation. In the digital series, the speaker spoke at normal, steady, conversational pace and volume, with no repetitions, but still with emphases in her tone of voice and gesture.

2   The individual digital 'lectures' or webcasts within the series are much shorter than a conventional 50-minute lecture: in fact, all the lectures in the series rarely extended beyond 20 minutes, sometimes less than 10 minutes. The result of this is an increased focus less on the fixed 50-minute time envelope, and more on the intellectual structure of the knowledge object(s) that are core to the lecture or webcast. Time is no longer a structuring element: intellectual and educational structure is the main framing device for the viewer.

3   Point 2 has further consequences. The digital series is designed so that power lies not with the speaker but with the viewer. The viewer can stop the speaker, rewind her, pause, restart, follow links away from her, read texts, think, go for a coffee, resume viewing, communicate with others about content and much else. Indeed, part of the immersive quality of the digital event lies in its ability to empower viewers to learn much more on their own terms: they are given agency, and given the intellectual resources to think around, research and contextualise the words of the speaker. Above all, control of time is more in their hands.

Temporality, as Lydia noted in the second section of this chapter, has rarely been analysed with reference to spatiality in legal education; and we would hold that the sophistication of digital learning object design rests in part on a sophisticated understanding of how time and space can be created anew within cyberspace. Indeed, the root of this word, from the Greek κυβερνήτης meaning helmsman, indicates the sense of agency, dynamic control, movement and purpose based upon action on and reaction to the world around one.[72]

Of course, we have been describing only one form of digital lecture or webcast. Compare what is described above with another type of digital lecture, where the live f2f lecture to an audience is recorded digitally. It is significantly different from the digital lecture we have described above. The digital object becomes the equivalent of a film of a play, or a TV live event with a live audience. Watching it, we are aware we are *not* there, aware of

---

that the total length of the digital webcast series was considerably less than the f2f lecture series, sometimes by as much as 40–50%.

72 The prefix cyber- is cognate with our word 'gover-' as in governor, government. (The Greek /k/ became /g/ in Latin, and the plosive /b/ became a fricative /v/ as the word developed from Latin into French. See Oxford English Dictionary <https://www.oed.com/view/Entry/273740#eid139487349> accessed 5 August 2021.

the audience that the speaker addresses even if there are no cutaway shots to the audience, largely because of the style of speech and gesture adopted by the speaker, and because of the cues provided by the speaker's physical environment. In this recorded f2f lecture, the lecturer and listeners exist paradoxically in a digitised analogue chronotope and is one of the reasons why recorded lectures tend to be awkward renderings of knowledge: we watch an event that has been filmed but which was not designed as a digital chronotope. Instead, we view an event composed for and performed to the audience in the lecture room. Digital viewers are thereby doubly viewers, outside the f2f chronotope and its narrative cues, and very much set apart from the community within the lecture room.

By contrast, in the digital civil procedure lecture chronotope described above, the lecture is designed uniquely as a digital object. There were several important design differences, all significantly aesthetic, and all of them affecting the time and space of learning:

1   The speaker addresses the viewer personally, directly, not an audience largely off-camera. The result is a conversational intimacy that is much more social, and more powerful for being a frame of social presence. It includes factors such as the speaker's direct gaze that drifts and returns to the lens; the subtle drama of her lit face with its poise, tilt, angles, expressions, gestures; the inflected voice; the depth of lens space; and the psychology of pose and repose (leaning forward to the lens, resting back, neutral position, poise of head, open shoulders becoming three-quarter profile, and the like).
2   Just as the standard 50-minute lecture was broken up, and the intellectual structures of the course were recast into knowledge objects of varying length, so too were the ways that knowledge could be accessed by the viewer:

  • Full length feature – watch every webcast object in sequence from start to finish.
  • Helicopter over the sequencing and select which objects to view and interact with.
  • Watch sequences and interact with objects repeatedly and/or out of sequence.
  • Helicopter by nodes or by a topical list.

These navigational aids are not simply helpful aids such as page numbers in a book. They are critical to the ways in which knowledge is processed by learners, and they fundamentally change the nature of knowledge acquisition by the learner.

So far, I have described the result of many hours of planning and design around the environment that we wanted to create. But we also planned future interactions of the environment, based upon analysis of copious student

Three authors in search of phenomenologies   219

Table 8.1 Threefold views of knowledge acquisition[73]

	Presentational view	Structural view	Transactional view
Functionality	1 Video lectures 2 Resource base, including PPT slides, documentation, cases, statutes and MCQs	1 Flowchart 2 Rollover on each node, containing summary of node information 3 Links to Presentation and Transactional views	1 To include multimedia units and document workflow, with drafting tools, videos, etc. 2 Links to Presentation and Structural views
Typical user purposes	1 Initial familiarisation with concepts and rules 2 Highly structured and teacher-centred learning 3 Use of resources to create learning objects	1 Gain an overview of the structure of legal procedure 2 Identify possible options or directions in procedure 3 Taken notes that can be attached to the flowchart	1 Prepare for written pleadings 2 Prepare for advocacy 3 Prepare for actual drafting or court appearance 4 Liaise with virtual firm or others in a transaction
Supports	1 Broad chronology of Sheriff Court procedure in Scotland 2 Detailed knowledge of concepts and rules 3 Global set of resources	1 . Overview of legal process based upon a flowchart 2 Quick access to forms of hearings 3 Commentaries 4 Global set of resources	1 Detailed understanding and analysis of specific forms of procedure 2 Quick access to forms for court events 3 Commentaries and practice notes 4 Global set of resources attached to a multimedia unit or document workflow
Personalised functionalities	1 Bookmarking 2 Notetaking	1 Bookmarking 2 Notetaking 3 Extracting	1 Bookmarking 2 Notetaking 3 Extracting 4 Mash-ups 5 Collaborative sharing and co-creation

73 This is described in more detail by Maharg: 'Multimedia and the Docuverse of Law: Learning and the Representation of Knowledge' in Paul Maharg (ed) *Transforming Legal Education: Learning and Teaching the Law in the Early Twenty-First Century* (Ashgate Publishing 2007). It goes without saying that the amount of planning and design involved in creating digital resources such as these is considerable. But viewed long-term, the return on investment (ROI) is actually more persuasive than might at first appear. The spike of costs and time commitment to create the initial resources pays back over time. In an unpublished paper Maharg itemised the ROI of a set of multimedia skills-based resources created for a professional course in Scotland that consisted of seven units, approximately —five to seven hours in learner duration online. The total cost of the initial build in 2002 was around £40,000 (and this at a time where there was little in the way of middleware to mitigate production costs). When learner hours were multiplied by use of student cohorts between the period 2002 and 2018, that amounted to 20,850 hours of tuition, which would have cost the programme around £145,000 had the multimedia units not been created and used over that period. There were, of course, other positives: students used the resources during the whole programme and later, e.g. in their traineeships; and the development of the resources involved partnerships with other centres, e.g. Oxford Institute for Legal Practice and the WS Society in Edinburgh.

220 *Lydia Bleasdale et al.*

feedback on how they interacted with the environment, as well as listening to academic comment on the experience of filming and production, and what academic staff wanted the digital environment to do for them.[74] We drew up our plans for a threefold knowledge-view which we defined below (Table 8.1). This is not a taxonomy but rather an array of views that support methods of acquiring and practising knowledge:

Too often digital design is described as if it is an impoverished environment by comparison to the f2f lecture – the assumption being that f2f is more human, and digital somehow less than human. Yet it is created by humans and is no less an affordance than a book – only different.

That difference is critical. Experiencing the digital flow through a variety of views, students can *extemporize* on their understandings. We use the word in its strict sense, namely, to compose or perform without prior preparation – literally, out of or beyond time. They can do so because they are no longer bound to the timescale of the lecturer's narrative. They can view, listen, stop to link, stop entirely and do something else, return, review, move backward or forward in the narrative. They often have the transcript of the lecture but having it in various channels allows for different modes of interaction. The script of the lecture is much more flexibly a 'knowledge object,' in the terms of Entwistle and other phenomenographic researchers, to be shaped by students.[75] In doing so, students engage in four types of activities (and this is borne out by our research)[76]:

1 *Excerpt and understand*: identify what they don't know, and focus on what they want to learn
2 *Memorise and rehearse*: what needs to be remembered, memorise, recall, link with previous knowledge
3 *Extemporise and explore*: move knowledge around 'what if' questions and fact/procedure patterns; link up to older knowledge; become aware of or anticipate gaps in knowledge that require more excerpting and understanding
4 *Apply in a community of purpose and activity*: for example in a revision group, or better still in the context of a simulation of a legal activity.

---

74 Described in more detail in McKellar and Maharg. Patricia McKellar and Paul Maharg, 'Virtual Learning Environments: The Alternative to the Box Under the Bed' (2005) 39 Law Teacher, 43.
75 Noel Entwistle and Ference Marton, 'Knowledge Objects: Understandings Constituted Through Intensive Academic Study' (1994) 64 British Journal of Educational Psychology, 161; Noel Entwistle and Dorothy Entwistle, 'Preparing for Examinations: The Interplay of Memorising and Understanding, and the Development of Knowledge Objects' (2003) 22 Higher Education Research and Development, 19.
76 Paul Maharg, 'Multimedia and the Docuverse of Law: Learning and the Representation of Knowledge' in Paul Maharg (ed) *Transforming Legal Education: Learning and Teaching the Law in the Early Twenty-First Century* (Ashgate Publishing 2007).

Three authors in search of phenomenologies 221

As before, this is not in any sense a Bloomian taxonomy. These cognitive activities can take place in any order or be nested one within the other (e.g. students can collaborate in a simulation (4) and move between 1 and 3 in order to achieve 4). What is important is that the student moves amongst the four stages in order to form what Entwistle calls the 'knowledge object' of domain knowledge, here civil procedure.[77] In this sense, students develop their identity of themselves as legal thinkers. It is also an engaging way to converge skills both academic and professional; and bodies of knowledge, both substantive and procedural.[78]

Some of these were implemented (e.g. the production of multimedia modules). The final development, which was to allow students to mix, mash, dub and redub the video granules, and thus create a community of sharing, never took place. In a paradoxical sense, it was both the most important, in the sense of giving students authority over digital resources and autonomy in learning; but also, the least important for us, because our programme of study was largely f2f and therefore the collaborative element was there in physical meetings between students. And this point is critical in any consideration of Lydia's argument about identity formation in the post-pandemic university for, regardless of how learning is facilitated by digital designs and constructed by students, such formation is as essential for the online context as it is for the f2f context.

Conclusion: phenomenologies of learning and technology

We have been in search of answers to four questions, all of which deal with what might be termed the phenomenologies of learning with technology: who is the author of this chapter – technology or we three humans, or some kind of cyber entity? What are the effects on our educational theories and practices of using digital technology, in the early twenty-first century? What is the place of Birks' collection, composed in the mid-1990s? And does he have anything valuable to say to us several decades later on these subjects?

In answer to these questions, we would hold that our thinking is ineluctably stained with cyber. We cannot escape it and in that sense, technology

---

77 Noel Entwistle and Ference Marton, 'Knowledge Objects: Understandings Constituted Through Intensive Academic Study' (1994) 64 British Journal of Educational Psychology, 161; Noel Entwistle and Dorothy Entwistle, 'Preparing for Examinations: The Interplay of Memorising and Understanding, and the Development of Knowledge Objects' (2003) 22 Higher Education Research and Development, 19.

78 This applies to both in-person simulations with simulated clients (SCs) and digital simulation environments. Across 14 centres internationally, the results are universally positive. For example, at Osgoode Hall Law School the use of SCs on a first year, first term course was rated by 99.6% of the students as a worthwhile learning experience. Use of the digital simulation environment has been similarly praised by students for engaging them in transactional learning and making the assessment of that learning much more realistic and rigorous.

222 *Lydia Bleasdale et al.*

speaks through us, while we mediate, intermediate and disintermediate its power. As Craig has pointed out, the complexities of interdisciplinary theory can enrich our understanding as designers of digital contexts; and as Lydia observes, even our fundamental social being, our identities and communities are profoundly affected by it. In these senses, digital technology is opening up the very ground of educational theory and practice in legal education.

What did Birks' collection say about technology? As pointed out in the introduction, there is almost no discussion of technology or technology theory in the volume. And yet there was at the time considerable technology available to students and staff in law schools: photocopiers, screen projection, word processing programs, computers, email, hypertext programmes, early web applications, the emergence of digital access to primary resources, expert legal systems, the UK-wide government-funded Teaching Learning and Technology Programme with the Law programme based at Strathclyde and Warwick University Law Schools, the annual BILETA conferences (which started in the mid-1980s), the theoretical understandings of networked societies (e.g. see the work of Manuel Castells), the substantial constructivist research base around Jerome Bruner, Seymour Papert, Lucy Suchman, to cite only a fraction of the considerable research – all this and much else were available before the mid-1990s.[79]

In this, Birks was of his generation and background. Indeed, we would argue that the discussion of technology-theory has been impoverished in legal education until relatively recently. There are three reasons for this, all of them still relevant to us today and in the future:

1   Educational technology, *any* technology, was not yet a mode of legal educational discourse that was recognised as research worthy of being a legal education topic. This was the case because the view of technology in legal education was largely instrumental, with little awareness of the multi-disciplinary theories and debates surrounding the development and use of educational technologies and their effects on society. Indeed, this is true of the material culture of legal learning in all jurisdictions. Histories of law schools rarely mention technology except in passing as a facilitation for other forms of change. This is still the case: material culture is poorly researched, little regarded and largely historyless. Following Suchman's acute comment in the chapter epigraph, we have ignored the inexhaustible richness of the situation of action. We need to change that.

---

79 Jerome Bruner, *The Process of Education* (Harvard University Press 1960); Seymour Papert, *Mindstorms: Children, Computers and Powerful Ideas* (Basic Books 1980); Lucy Suchman, *Plans and Situated Actions: The Problem of Human-Machine Communication* (Cambridge University Press 1987)

Three authors in search of phenomenologies   223

2   The representation of knowledge and the learning that results from it is rarely raised as a point for consideration. The Birks' collection elides the issue that, over the last half century or so, has become a cornerstone of New Rhetoric and New Media critique, namely that *the form of any educational intervention powerfully determines the effects of its content.* Consider a lecture composed as a glossed manuscript, or printed in a book, or delivered as a f2f lecture, or recorded as a televisual lecture, or published as a digital lecture as described above. Across these and many other media (podcast, twitter feed, etc.), the lecture would never have identical content or time scales; and it would have a significantly different effects upon learners depending on channels and forms of communication. In that sense, the evolution of the lecture in our chapter becomes an origami unicorn – a shifting, protean, narrative device that leads us to question the cybernature of our knowledge and renders more uncertain the phenomenological digitalising of our identities as humans.[80]

3   Birks' collection, for all its critiques of the purpose of law schools, takes a conservative view of change, particularly technological change. This is symptomatic of a deeper elision about education in the volume (Goodrich's chapter apart): namely that pedagogies-in-use become the received truth, a hegemonic framework that precedes and concludes our understandings of educational innovation.[81] Birks' collection ignores the technological situation of action and as a result the technology-in-use at the time becomes hegemonic, unquestioned, the *de facto* quality standard to which future technologies are disruptors. It might be argued that, when Birks' collection authors were writing, the state of theory in legal educational technology was still relatively immature. But this merely describes the book's legal education culture and cannot explain the lack of wider vision. Technology, design and their effects had long been discussed in educational literatures, and the social effects of

---

80   We refer of course to the film *Bladerunner*, Director's Cut. The main character Deckard, who is a human hunter of replicants, dreams of a unicorn. The origami unicorn left outside his rooms by another character, Gaff, suggests that Gaff has access to Deckard's dreams or has implanted the dream, and therefore that Deckard is not a human but himself is a replicant. But the evidence is not straightforward in the narrative; and, in a fascinatingly unresolved debate, opinion as to the existential nature of Deckard was split even amongst those involved in the making of the film: the actors, the author (Philip K. Dick), the director, the screen writer and the visualisers. See Marilyn Gwaltney, 'Androids as a Device for Reflection on Personhood' in Judith Kerman (ed), *Retrofitting Blade Runner: Issues in Ridley Scott's Blade Runner and Philip K. Dick's Do Androids Dream of Electric Sheep* (Popular Press 1991).

81   This is nothing new. Educationalists such as Henry Giroux, Henry Jenkins and Lee Shulman have made similar arguments. See Lee Shulman, 'Signature Pedagogies in the Professions' (2005) 134 Daedalus 52; Henry Jenkins, *Convergence Culture: Where Old and New Media Collide* (New York University Press 2006); Henry A Giroux, *On Critical Pedagogy* (2nd edn, Bloomsbury Publishing 2020).

224   *Lydia Bleasdale et al.*

digital were already being discussed.[82] Birks' collection is often cited as a source of ideas on the liberal law school, and yet the world view of the volume is itself illiberal on technology: he and his authors do nothing to shape the relations between humans and technology which, in the Anthropocene we inhabit, has become, since Heidegger's seminal essay on 'The Question Concerning Technology' if not before, one of the most pressing existential questions facing us.

One of the hidden engines of the hegemonic frameworks we inhabit is time – an essential element in both narrative devices such as chronotopes, and in identity formation itself. As Heidegger observed of technology-use in his essay 'all distances in time and space are shrinking.' But the result of this will not be what we think it will be, for 'the hasty setting aside of all distances brings no nearness; for nearness does not consist in a small amount of distance.' Published in 1954, the essay is a remarkably acute description of our condition in 2021, at what is after all still the start of the digital age, where space and time are transformed and vast quantities of data overwhelm our attention. Nearness, intimacy, community, identity, learning, work patterns, economics, democracy, responsibility and ethics – all are changed and were changing at the time of Birks' collection.

And now, quarter of a century later, we need to give much more attention to these. The issues and questions concerning technology speak through us, in the same way that language speaks through us. If as Craig avers above quoting Valverde, chronotopes 'can lead to a re-visioning of legal and governance mechanisms'; if as Lydia urges the sophistication of informal learning in community and identity formation requires better opportunities than we currently have; if as Paul argues the genres of learning such as the digital lecture need radical re-design, then it is clear, we need a more porous concept of what law schools are for than we have had either historically or in our present moment.

---

82 See Martin Heidegger, *The Question Concerning Technology and Other Essays* (William Lovitt tr, Harper & Row 1977); Sherry Turkle, *The Second Self: Computers and the Human Spirit* (MIT Press 1984); Hubert Dreyfus and Stuart Dreyfus, *Mind over Machine: The Power of Human Intuition and Expertise in the Era of the Computer* (Blackwell Publishers 1986); Ronald Staudt, 'The Electronic Law School: A 1992 Snapshot of the Centre for Law and Computers at Chicago-Kent College of Law' (1993) 3 (6) Computers & Law, 33; David Jacobson, 'Contexts and Cues in Cyberspace: The Pragmatics of Naming in Text-Based Virtual Realities' (1996) 52 Journal of Anthropological Research, 461; Sherry Turkle, *Life on the Screen: Identity in the Age of the Internet* (Simon & Schuster 1997); Sherry Turkle *The Second Self: Computers and the Human Spirit* (2nd edn, MIT Press 2005); Manuel Castells *The Rise of the Network Society: The Information Age: Economy, Society and Culture* (John Wiley & Sons 1996). In addition, the first decade of the British and Irish Law Education Technology (BILETA) conferences provided ample proof of the growing interest in and use of digital technologies in law schools in the UK – see British and Irish Law Education and Technology Association, 'Conference Papers' (*BILETA*, 2021) < https://www.bileta.org.uk/conference-papers/> accessed 28 September 2021.

Bibliography

Association of Law Teachers, 'Connecting Legal Education: Wellbeing of Online Distance Learning Students' (*ALT Blog*, 9 June 2020) <http://lawteacher.ac.uk/connecting-legal-education/connecting-legal-education-wellbeing-of-online-distance-learning-students/> accessed 5 August 2021.

Baxter J, 'Who Am I and What Keeps Me Going? Profiling the Distance Learning Student in Higher Education' (2012) 13 *The International Review of in Open and Distance Learning* 107.

Baxter J and Haycock J, 'Roles and Student Identities in Online Large Course Forums: Implications for Practice' (2014) 15 *The International Review of in Open and Distance Learning* 20.

Bennett A and Burke PJ, 'Re/Conceptualising Time and Temporality: An Exploration of Time in Higher Education' (2018) 39 *Discourse: Studies in the Cultural Politics of Education* 913.

Bleasdale L and Humphreys S, 'Identity, Well-Being and Law Students' in C Strevens and R Fielding (eds) *Educating for Well-Being in Law: Positive Professional Identities and Practice* (Routledge 2020).

Bleasdale L and Humphreys S, 'Undergraduate Resilience Research Project: Project Report' (*Leeds Institute for Teaching Excellence* 2018) <https://teachingexcellence.leeds.ac.uk/wp-content/uploads/sites/89/2018/01/LITEbleasdalehumphreys_full-report_online.pdf> accessed 5 August 2021.

Bloxham S, 'Widening Access and the Use of ICT in Legal Education' (2005) 39 *The Law Teacher* 93.

Bloxham S, Maharg P, and McKellar P, 'Summary Report on the UKCLE/BILETA VLE Project' (*JILT*, 2007) <https://warwick.ac.uk/fac/soc/law/elj/jilt/2007_1/vle_report> accessed 4 August 2021.

Brown R and Renshaw P, 'Positioning Students as Actors and Authors: A Chronotopic Analysis of Collaborative Learning Activities' (2006) 13 *Mind, Culture, and Activity* 247.

Bruner J, *The Process of Education* (Harvard University Press 1960).

Bugden L, Redmond P, and Greaney J, 'Online Collaboration as a Pedagogical Approach to Learning and Teaching Undergraduate Legal Education' (2018) 52 *The Law Teacher* 85.

Buote VM and others, 'The Importance of Friends Friendship and Adjustment among 1st-Year University Students' (2007) 22 *Journal of Adolescent Research* 665.

Burke DD, 'Scale-Up! Classroom Design and Use Can Facilitate Learning' (2015) 49 *The Law Teacher* 189.

Castells, M. *The Rise of the Network Society: The Information Age: Economy, Society and Culture* (John Wiley & Sons 1996).

Cavallaro Johnson G and Watson G, '"Oh Gawd, How am I Going to Fit into This?:" Producing [Mature] First-Year Student Identity' (2004) 18 *Language and Education* 474.

Christie H, 'Emotional Journeys: Young People and Transitions to University' (2009) 30 *British Journal of Sociology of Education* 123.

Christie H and others, '"A Real Rollercoaster of Confidence and Emotions:" Learning to Be a University Student' (2008) 33 *Studies in Higher Education* 567.

Collins R KL and Skover DM, 'Paratexts' (1992) 44 *Stanford Law Review* 509.

226 *Lydia Bleasdale et al.*

Craig SL and others, 'Intersecting Sexual, Gender, and Professional Identities among Social Work Students: The Importance of Identity Integration' (2017) 53 *Journal of Social Work Education* 466.

Cruess RL and others, 'A Schematic Representation of the Professional Identity Formation and Socialization of Medical Students and Residents: A Guide for Medical Educators' (2015) 90 *Academic Medicine* 718.

Cruess RL and others, 'Reframing Medical Education to Support Professional Identity Formation' (2014) 89 *Academic Medicine* 1446.

Cruwys T and others, 'Depression and Social Identity: An Integrative Review' (2014) 18 *Personality and Social Psychology Review* 215.

Delaney L and Farren M, 'No "Self" Left Behind? Part-Time Distance Learning University Graduates: Social Class, Graduate Identity and Employability' (2016) 31 *Opening Learning: Journal of Open, Distance and E-Learning* 194.

Derrida J, *The Truth in Painting* (G Bennington and I McLeod trs, University of Chicago Press 1987).

Dreyfus H and Dreyfus S, *Mind over Machine: The Power of Human Intuition and Expertise in the Era of the Computer* (Blackwell Publishers 1986).

Dunworth M, 'What a Difference a Day Makes: The Positive Outcomes of Early Face-to-Face Opportunities to Establish a Student Identity in Distance Learning Students New to Higher Education' (2012) 18 *Journal of Adult and Continuing Education* 3.

Duro P (ed), *Rhetoric of the Frame: Essays on the Boundaries of the Artwork* (Cambridge University Press 1996).

Entwistle N and Entwistle D, 'Preparing for Examinations: The Interplay of Memorising and Understanding, and the Development of Knowledge Objects' (2003) 22 *Higher Education Research and Development* 19.

Entwistle N and Marton F, 'Knowledge Objects: Understandings Constituted Through Intensive Academic Study' (1994) 64 *British Journal of Educational Psychology* 161.

Francis A, 'Legal Education, Social Mobility, and Employability: Possible Selves, Curriculum Intervention, and the Role of Legal Work Experience' (2015) 42 *Journal of Law and Society* 173.

Freeman TM, Anderman LH, and Jensen JM, 'Sense of Belonging in College Freshmen at the Classroom and Campus Levels' (2007) 75 *Journal of Experimental Education* 203.

Garland F and Travis M, 'Temporal Bodies: Emergencies, Emergence, and Intersex Embodiment' in C Dietz, M Travis, and M Thompson (eds) *A Jurisprudence of the Body* (Palgrave Macmillan 2020).

Giroux HA, *On Critical Pedagogy* (2nd edn, Bloomsbury Publishing 2020).

Goldie J, 'The Formation of Professional Identity in Medical Students: Considerations for Educators' (2012) 34 *Medical Teacher* e641.

Gwaltney M, 'Androids as a Device for Reflection on Personhood' in J Kerman (ed) *Retrofitting Blade Runner: Issues in Ridley Scott's Blade Runner and Philip K. Dick's Do Androids Dream of Electric Sheep* (Popular Press 1991).

Hall K, O'Brien MT, and Tang S, 'Developing a Professional Identity in Law School: A View from Australia' (2010) 4 *Phoenix Law Review* 19.

Heidegger M, *The Question Concerning Technology and Other Essays* (W Lovitt tr, Harper & Row 1977).

Hewitt R, 'HEPI Policy Note 29: Students' Views on the Impact of Coronavirus on Their Higher Education Experience in 2021' (*Higher Education Policy Institute*, April 2021) <www.hepi.ac.uk/2021/04/01/students-views-on-the-impact-of-coronavirus-on-their-higher-education-experience-in-2021/> accessed 5 August 2021.

Høj Jensen D and Jetten J, 'The Importance of Developing Students' Academic and Professional Identities in Higher Education' (2016) 57 *Journal of College Student Development* 1027.

Holquist M, Carlyle E, and Bakhtin MM, *The Dialogic Imagination: Four Essays* (University of Texas Press 1981).

Hunnam R and Dickinson J, 'How to Build Back Student Community and Opportunity Between Now and the New Year' (*WONKHE*, 31 March 2021) <https://wonkhe.com/blogs/how-to-build-back-student-community-and-opportunity-between-now-and-the-new-year/> accessed 5 August 2021.

Ibarra H, 'Provisional Selves: Experimenting with Image and Identity in Professional Adaptation' (1999) 44 *Administrative Science Quarterly* 764.

Jaber R and Kennedy E, '"Not the Same Person Anymore:" Groupwork, Identity and Social Learning Online' (2017) 38 *Distance Education* 216.

Jackson B, 'Thematization and the Narrative Typifications of the Law' in D Nelkin (ed) *Law as Communication* (Aldershot 1996).

Jackson B, 'Towards an Interdisciplinary Model of Legal Communication' in B Jackson (ed) *Legal Semiotics and the Sociology of Law* (Oñati Institute 1994).

Jacobson D, 'Contexts and Cues in Cyberspace: The Pragmatics of Naming in Text-Based Virtual Realities' (1996) 52 *Journal of Anthropological Research* 461.

Jenkins H, *Convergence Culture: Where Old and New Media Collide* (New York University Press 2006).

Jones E, 'Connectivity, Socialisation and Identity Formation: Exploring Mental Well-Being in Online Distance Learning Law Students' in C Strevens and R Fielding (eds) *Educating for Well-Being in Law: Positive Professional Identities and Practice* (Routledge 2020).

Kaufman P, 'The Sociology of College Students' Identity Formation' (2014) 2014 *New Directions for Higher Education* 35.

Kember D and Leung DYP, 'The Influence of the Teaching and Learning Environment on the Development of Generic Capabilities Needed for a Knowledge-Based Society' (2005) 8 *Learning Environments Research* 245.

Lairio M, Sauli Puukari S, and Kouvo A, 'Studying at University as Part of Student Life and Identity Construction' (2013) 57 *Scandinavian Journal of Educational Research* 115.

Levett-Jones T and Lathlean J, 'Belongingness: A Prerequisite for Nursing Students' Clinical Learning' (2008) 8 *Nurse Education in Practice* 103.

Levett-Jones T and others, 'Staff –Student Relationships and Their Impact on Nursing Students' Belongingness and Learning' (2009) 65 *Journal of Advanced Nursing* 316.

MacLachlan G and Reid I, *Framing and Interpretation* (Melbourne University Press 1994).

Maharg P, 'Multimedia and the Docuverse of Law: Learning and the Representation of Knowledge' in P Maharg (ed) *Transforming Legal Education: Learning and Teaching the Law in the Early Twenty-First Century* (Ashgate Publishing 2007).

228 *Lydia Bleasdale et al.*

Markus H and Nurius P, 'Possible Selves' (1986) 41 *American Psychologist* 954.

Martin Clement N, 'The Use and Impact of the Collaborative Lecture Theatres: Digging up the Foundations of the Lecture Theatre' (Teaching Enhancement Project Report Leeds Institute for Teaching Excellence 2018).

Massey D, *For Space* (Sage 2005).

Massey D, *Space, Place and Gender* (Polity Press 1994).

Matasar RA and Shiels R, 'Electronic Law Students: Repercussions on Legal Education' (1994) 29 *The Valparaiso University Law Review* 909.

Mayer RE (ed), *Cambridge Handbook of Multimedia Learning* (Cambridge University Press 2005).

McGregor J, 'Studying Spatiality' (British Educational Research Association Annual Conference, Manchester, September 2004).

McKellar P and Maharg P, 'Virtual Learning Environments: The Alternative to the Box under the Bed' (2005) 39 *The Law Teacher* 43.

Modiri J, 'The Time and Space of Critical Legal Pedagogy' (2016) 27 *Stellenbosch Law Review* 507.

Monrouxe LV, 'Identity, Identification and Medical Education: Why Should We Care?' (2010) 44 *Medical Education* 40.

Montacute R and Cullinane C, 'Learning in Lockdown' (*Sutton Trust*, January 2021) <www.suttontrust.com/wp-content/uploads/2021/01/Learning-in-Lockdown.pdf> accessed 5 August 2021.

Montacute R and Holt-White E, 'Covid-19 and the University Experience' (*Sutton Trust*, February 2021) <www.suttontrust.com/wp-content/uploads/2021/02/Covid-19-and-the-University-Experience.pdf> accessed 5 August 2021.

Moore E, 'Educational Identities of Adult University Graduates' (2006) 50 *Scandinavian Journal of Educational Research* 149.

Newbery-Jones CJ, 'Trying to Do the Right Thing: Experiential Learning, E-Learning and Employability Skills in Modern Legal Education' (2015) 6 *EJLT* <https://ejlt.org/index.php/ejlt/article/view/389/545> accessed 4 August 2021.

O'Doherty D and others, 'Medical Students and Clinical Placements – A Qualitative Study of the Continuum of Professional Identity Formation' (2021) 32 *Education for Primary Care* 202.

Office for National Statistics, 'Coronavirus and the Impact on Students in Higher Education in England: September to December 2020' (*Office for National Statistics*, 21 December 2020) <www.ons.gov.uk/peoplepopulationandcommunity/educationandchildcare/articles/coronavirusandtheimpactonstudentsinhighereducationinenglandseptembertodecember2020/2020-12-21> accessed 5 August 2021.

Papert S, *Mindstorms: Children, Computers and Powerful Ideas* (Basic Books 1980).

Philippopoulos-Mihalopoulos A, 'And for Law: Why Space Cannot Be Understood Without Law' (2018) *Law Culture and the Humanities* <https://doi.org/10.1177/1743872118765708> accessed 4 August 2021.

Philippopoulos-Mihalopoulos A, 'Law's Spatial Turn: Geography, Justice and a Certain Fear of Space' (2011) 7 *Law Culture and the Humanities* 187.

Phirangee K and Malec A, 'Othering in Online Learning: An Examination of Social Presence, Identity, and Sense of Community' (2017) 38 *Distance Education* 160.

Quinn G, Lucas B, and Silcock J, 'Professional Identity Formation in Pharmacy Students during an Early Preregistration Training Placement' (2020) 84 *American Journal of Pharmaceutical Education* 1132.

Sabancıogullari S and Dogan S, 'Effects of the Professional Identity Development Programme on the Professional Identity, Job Satisfaction and Burnout Levels of Nurses: A Pilot Study' (2015) 21 *International Journal of Nursing Practice* 847.

Samura M, 'Remaking Selves, Repositioning Selves, or Remaking Space: An Examination of Asian American College Students' Processes of "Belonging"' (2016) 57 *Journal of College Student Development* 135.

Scanlon L, Rowling L, and Weber Z, '"You Don't Have Like an Identity…You Are Just Lost in a Crowd:" Forming a Student Identity in the First-Year Transition to University' (2007) 10 *Journal of Youth Studies* 223.

Shulman L, 'Signature Pedagogies in the Professions' (2005) 134 *Daedalus* 52.

Smith M, 'Integrating Technology in Contemporary Legal Education' (2020) 54 *The Law Teacher* 209.

Staudt R, 'The Electronic Law School: A 1992 Snapshot of the Centre for Law and Computers at Chicago-Kent College of Law' (1993) 3(6) *Computers & Law* 33.

Suchman L, *Plans and Situated Actions: The Problem of Human-Machine Communication* (Cambridge University Press 1987).

Tam M, 'University Impact on Student Growth: A Quality Measure?' (2002) 24 *Journal of Higher Education Policy and Management* 211.

Terry NP, 'Bricks Plus Bytes: How Click-and-Brick Will Define Legal Education Space' (2001) 46 *Villanova Law Review* 95.

Thomas L, 'Building Student Engagement and Belonging in Higher Education at a Time of Change: Final Report from the What Works? Student Retention & Success Programme' (2012) <www.heacademy.ac.uk/system/files/what_works_final_report_0.pdf> accessed 5 August 2021.

Thomas L, Orme E, and Kerrigan F, 'Student Loneliness: The Role of Social Media through Life Transitions' (2020) 146 *Computers & Education Art* 103754.

Turkle S, *Life on the Screen: Identity in the Age of the Internet* (Simon & Schuster 1997).

Turkle S, *The Second Self: Computers and the Human Spirit* (MIT Press 1984).

Turkle S, *The Second Self: Computers and the Human Spirit* (2nd edn, MIT Press 2005).

Turner JJ, Amirnuddin PS, and Singh HSI, 'University Legal Learning Spaces Effectiveness in Developing Employability Skills of Future Law Graduates' (2019) 16 *Malaysian Journal of Learning and Instruction* 49.

Valverde M, *Chronotopes of Law: Jurisdiction, Scale and Governance* (Routledge 2015).

Vermeulen L and Schmidt HG, 'Learning Environment, Learning Process, Academic Outcomes and Career Success of University Graduates' (2008) 33 *Studies in Higher Education* 431.

Vivekananda-Schmidt P, Crossley J, and Murdoch-Eaton D, 'A Model of Professional Self-Identity Formation in Student Doctors and Dentists: A Mixed Method Study' (2015) 15 *BMC Medical Education Art* 83.

Vivekananda-Schmidt P and Sandars J, 'Belongingness and Its Implications for Undergraduate Health Professions Education: A Scoping Review' (2018) 29 *Education for Primary Care* 268.

230 *Lydia Bleasdale et al.*

Wilson I and others, 'Professional Identity in Medical Students: Pedagogical Challenges to Medical Education' (2013) 25 *Teaching and Learning in Medicine* 369.

Wong A and Trollope-Kumar KD, 'Reflections: An Inquiry into Medical Students' Professional Identity Formation' (2014) 48 *Medical Education* 489.

Woodley C and Beattie S, 'Communal Reflections on the Workplace: Locating Learning for the Legal Professional' (2011) 12 *International Journal of Work-Integrated Learning* 19.

9 What is the law school for in a post-pandemic world?[1]

Margaret Thornton[2]

Introduction: The Neoliberal Embrace

The question posed in the long title of Birks' collection: *What Are Law Schools For?*[3] elicited no definitive answer when posed at the cusp of the millennial turn and is one that continues to elude us today. Indeed, the question has been a provocation ever since university law schools were first established in the nineteenth century when, like Janus, they were positioned to look simultaneously in two directions: with one face fixed in the direction of the university and intellectual freedom, and the other facing legal practice. Indeed, the belief that law schools were constrained by the presuppositions of legal practice prevailed and informed the opposition to their establishment.[4] Thorsten Veblen wrote in 1918 that 'law schools belong in the modern university no more than a school of fencing or dancing'[5] Nevertheless, however much law wanted to be accepted as a university discipline, it continued to defer to legal practice. As a result, law schools were beset with a sense of schizophrenia,[6] but I suggest that the historic debate has more

---

1 An earlier version of this paper was presented as a keynote address at 'Revisiting "Pressing Problems in the Law: What is Law School for?" 20 Years On', Faculty of Business and Law, University of Northumbria, 17 June 2019. I thank Rachel Dunn and Victoria Roper for organising the conference and inviting me to speak. I also thank the Modern Law Review for financial support.

2 Emerita Professor, ANU College of Law, Australian National University, Canberra, margaret.thornton@anu.edu.au.

3 Peter Birks (ed), *Pressing Problems in the Law: What Are Law Schools For?* (Oxford University Press 1996).

4 Linda Martin, 'From Apprenticeship to Law School: A Social History of Legal Education in Nineteenth Century New South Wales' (1986) 9 UNSW Law Journal, 111–143.

5 Thorsten Veblen, *The Higher Learning in America: The Annotated Edition: A Memorandum on the Conduct of Universities by Business Men* (first published 1918, Richard F Teichgraeber III ed, annotated edn, Johns Hopkins University Press 2015) 182.

6 Nigel Savage and Gary Watt, 'A "House of Intellect" for the Profession' in Peter Birks (ed), *Pressing Problems in the Law: What Are Law Schools For?* (Oxford University Press 1996) 45–57.

DOI: 10.4324/9781003322092-9

232 *Margaret Thornton*

recently been overshadowed by the neoliberalisation of higher education, rendering an unequivocal response to Birks' question even more recondite.

Birks' collection contains no more than a hint of what was to come with the millennial turn, although Birks himself alludes to the experience of a decade of hostile government policy,[7] and Clark and Tsamenyi's essay refers to the phenomenon of 'creeping corporatism' that was beginning to impact Australian law schools.[8] The catalyst was state disinvestment in public education, which had the effect of transforming universities and law schools into sites of income generation. The last 25 years have seen a dramatic increase in the number of law schools and law students, while academics have been pressured to be more productive in terms of research, despite having to teach more students and generally do more with less. While referring to law schools as 'profit centres' might be better suited to private law schools,[9] my focus is directed to the public university, which is the norm in the Anglo-Australian tradition, albeit increasingly subjected to a process of 'submerged privatization'.[10]

In an endeavour to understand how capital accumulation rapidly moved to centre-stage in universities and significantly affected the lives of students and legal academics, I first address the neoliberal turn. Although of intense academic interest,[11] neoliberalism is a highly contested term and might better be described as a political practice than a coherent theory. Indeed, its multifarious meanings have led to neoliberalism increasingly functioning as a rhetorical device.[12] As will be seen, its amorphous character has enabled it to thrive in the university sector.[13] Under Keynesianism, or social liberalism, higher education, like health and welfare, was regarded as a public good. It was free or virtually free and funded from the public purse through

---

7 Peter Birks, 'Editor's Preface' in Peter Birks (ed), *Pressing Problems in the Law: What Are Law Schools For?* (Oxford University Press 1996) v–xviii, x.

8 Eugene Clark and Martin Tsamenyi, 'Legal Education in the Twenty-First Century: A Time of Challenge' in Peter Birks (ed), *Pressing Problems in the Law: What Are Law Schools For?* (Oxford University Press 1996) 17–44, 43.

9 A Michael Froomkin, 'The Virtual Law School, 2.0' (2020) University of Miami Legal Studies Research Paper No. 3728114.

10 Kanishka Jayasuriya, 'COVID-19, Markets and the Crisis of the Higher Education Regulatory State: The Case of Australia' (2020) 18 (4) Globalizations, 26 <https://www.tandfonline.com/doi/pdf/10.1080/14747731.2020.1815461> accessed 01 September 2021; Margaret Thornton, *Privatising the Public University: The Case of Law* (Routledge 2012).

11 Ben Whitham, 'Post-Crash Neoliberalism in Theory and Practice' (2018) 16 (4) Political Studies Association, 252–264; Paul Michael Garrett, 'Revisiting "The Birth of Biopolitics": Foucault's Account of Neoliberalism and the Remaking of Social Policy' (2018) 48 (3) International Journal Politics, Culture & Society, 1–19.

12 Terry Flew, 'Michel Foucault's *The Birth of Biopolitics* and Contemporary Neo-Liberalism Debates' (2012) 108 (1) Thesis Eleven, 44–65, 45.

13 Jean Parker and Damien Cahill, 'The Retreat from Neoliberalism That Was Not: Australia's Building the Education Revolution' (2017) 52 (2) Australian Journal of Political Science, 257–271, 258.

What is the law school for in a post-pandemic world? 233

progressive taxation. Under neoliberalism, the transformation of aspects of human life not formerly thought to be appropriate for commercialisation occurred in conjunction with regressive taxation. However, the market embrace does not mean that the state has moved away from the market, but the market has moved into the state, with government itself becoming a market actor.[14] As a result, the 'public' in the public university is now only nominal.

Some commentators thought that the global financial crisis (GFC) (2008–2009) should have brought about an end to neoliberalism,[15] or at least restricted it,[16] while a few thought that the GFC left the hegemony of neoliberalism undiminished.[17] Paul Krugman suggests that the fact that neoliberalism continues to flourish reveals its 'zombie quality', that is, while 'it should have died, it keeps on coming'.[18] Hence, the hope that there might be a return to free higher education, such as that expressed by former UK Labour leader, Jeremy Corbyn,[19] appears fanciful in light of the financial benefits flowing from what has become the 'higher education industry'.

Although neoliberalism draws on the work of political economists, such as Friedrich Hayek[20] and Milton Friedman,[21] it has never been committed solely to free market fundamentalism or laissez-faire, nor does it share the conservative belief in deregulation or small government. Ironically, as the state has disinvested in higher education, it has increased regulation through auditing, evaluation and other forms of accountability to produce a pool of skilled job-ready human capital in order to enhance international

---

14 Wendy Brown, *Undoing the Demos: Neoliberalism's Stealth Revolution* (MIT Press 2015) 20.

15 Kevin Rudd, 'The Global Financial Crisis' (*The Monthly*, Melbourne, February 2009) 20–29.

16 John Comaroff, 'The End of Neoliberalism? What Is Left of the Left' (2011) 637 Annals, AAPS 141–147.

17 Luca Mavelli, 'Governing the Resilience of Neoliberalism through Biopolitics' (2017) 23 (3) European Journal of International Relations, 489–451.

18 Paul Krugman, 'All the President's Zombies' (*The New York Times*, NYC, 24 August 2009) <https://www.nytimes.com/2009/08/24/opinion/24krugman.html> accessed 22 July 2021.

19 Rowena Mason, 'Labour Pledges to Abolish Tuition Fees as early as Autumn 2017' (*The Guardian*, London, 30 July 2017) <https://www.theguardian.com/education/2017/may/21/labour-abolish-university-tuition-fees-jeremy-corbyn-eu-uk-europe> accessed 22 July 2021; US Presidential candidate, Bernie Sanders, made a similar proposal in 2019. See Tara Golshan, 'Bernie Sanders's Free College Proposal Just Got a Whole Lot Bigger' (*Vox*, Washington DC, 23 June 2019) <https://www.vox.com/policy-and-politics/2019/6/23/18714615/bernie-sanders-free-college-for-all-2020-student-loan-debt> accessed 22 July 2021.

20 Friedrich A von Hayek, *The Road to Serfdom* (Routledge & Kegan Paul 1976).

21 Milton Friedman and Rose D Friedman, *Capitalism and Freedom* (University of Chicago Press 1962); Milton Friedman and Rose Friedman, *Free to Choose: A Personal Statement* (Harcourt Brace Jovanovich 1980) 25.

234 *Margaret Thornton*

competitiveness.[22] Hence, Foucault's concept of governmentality[23] encapsulates the diffused form of governance that now pervades all aspects of society, including the university where it is affected through the ideology of managerialism. A new class of managers, pithily dubbed the 'manageriat' by Rob Watts,[24] determines the direction of the university and has replaced the professoriate as the university elite. All too often, the manageriat is dismissive of consultation, collegiality and academic expertise.[25]

Prior to Covid-19, higher education was extraordinarily lucrative, adding approximately AUD 140 billion per annum to the Australian economy in 2019, and was the third-largest export earner behind coal and iron ore.[26] This profitability led to the sector being resourced by the state at a low level.[27] While disaggregated figures for the proportion of the higher education budget contributed by law are not available, the commodification of legal education has clearly become one of the reasons for 'what law schools are for' in the twenty-first century, an issue that was only just beginning to crystallise at the time of Birks' collection in the 1990s.

There are two interconnected facets of neoliberalism to which I draw attention, both of which are significant in responding to Birks' question: they are capital accumulation and human capital. The first, capital accumulation, relates to the generation of income, which includes passing on to consumers the cost of higher education through a user-pays system that is designed to encompass not only the costs associated with tuition but also the generation of additional funding in a context of competition and globalisation. The second facet, human capital, relates to the way individuals who are the beneficiaries of this commitment can shape their futures. Foucault's prescient study of neoliberalism, *The Birth of Biopolitics*, based on lectures delivered in 1979, shows how the theory of human capital is a way of being and thinking that transcends the economic sphere.[28] The distinctive aspect of Foucault's theory that illuminates the answer to our question is the conceptualisation of the self as a sort of enterprise, in which the individual

---

22 Mark Purcell, *Recapturing Democracy: Neoliberalization and the Struggle for Alternative Urban Futures* (Routledge 2008).

23 Michel Foucault, 'Governmentality' in Graham Burchell, Colin Gordon and Peter Miller (eds), *The Foucault Effect: Studies in Governmentality, with Two Lectures by and an Interview with Michel Foucault* (University of Chicago Press 1991).

24 Rob Watts, *Public Universities, Managerialism and the Value of Higher Education* (Palgrave Macmillan 2017).

25 Richard Joseph, 'The Cost of Managerialism in the University: An Autoethnographical Account of an Academic Redundancy Process' (2015) 33 (2) Prometheus, 1–25.

26 Universities Australia, 'Data Snapshot 2019' (2019) 4.

27 Like the UK, Australia scores highly in terms of output, but poorly in terms of resourcing of higher education. Australia is ranked 34th out of 50 countries in the resourcing of higher education as a percentage of GDP. See Universities Australia, '2020 Higher Education Facts and Figures' (2020) 84.

28 Michel Foucault, *The Birth of Biopolitics: Lectures at the Collège de France, 1978–1979*, (Michel Senellart ed, Graham Burchell tr, Palgrave Macmillan 2008) 226–228.

What is the law school for in a post-pandemic world? 235

seeks to produce [his] own capital by making meaningful choices and decisions.[29] I suggest that this theory is very pertinent in understanding the contemporary role of both law students and legal academics. This is despite the advent of Covid-19. Although universities received a sharp jolt as a result of the collapse of the international student market due to the pandemic, I will nevertheless suggest that the state has been unable to let go of the idea of higher education as a source of income generation and job-ready human capital.

Capital Accumulation

Higher education has long been regarded as a public good, but Lyotard observed at the cusp of the neoliberal turn that knowledge had become the revolutionary trading commodity, replacing land, raw materials and cheap labour.[30] A key impetus on the part of the Dawkins reform of higher education in Australia in 1988 was to make higher education available to more young people with the aim of enhancing the calibre of the workforce and increasing Australia's competitiveness on the world stage.[31] All colleges of advanced education, which were comparable to polytechnics in the UK, became universities overnight, but the funding of higher education was not proportionately increased.[32] The twin aims of educating more job-ready students while reducing the cost to the public purse underscores the way higher education has been neoliberalised.

Initially, the government was neutral regarding the disciplines that universities chose to offer (apart from medicine which could affect the cost of health care). Vice-chancellors were nevertheless keen to establish law schools as law was viewed as a prestigious discipline that would attract well-credentialed students.[33] More pragmatically, it was believed that law could

---

29 Ibid.
30 Jean L Lyotard, *The Post Modern Condition: A Report on Knowledge* (Manchester University Press 1984).
31 Australia Department of Employment, Education and Training, *Higher Education: A Policy Statement* (Cmd 202, 1988); Hon J S Dawkins' aims were subsequently affirmed in the Bradley Report. Australia Department of Education, Employment and Workplace Relations, *Review of Australian Higher Education: Final Report* (2008).
32 Simon Marginson and Mark Considine, *The Enterprise University: Power, Governance and Reinvention in Australia* (Cambridge University Press 2000) 30–33, 56.
33 E Eugene Clark and Martin Tsamenyi, 'Legal Education in the Twenty-First Century: A Time of Challenge' in Peter Birks (ed), *What Are Law Schools For?* (Oxford University Press 1996) 32.

be taught 'on the cheap' through a 'chalk and talk' large lecture format,[34] despite the pedagogical superiority of small group interactive teaching.[35]

The popularity of law as a course of study and its comparatively low cost quickly led to it becoming something of a milch cow for universities.[36] If substantial numbers of law students were admitted, it made economic sense to use the income to cross-subsidise laboratory-based Science, Technology, Engineering, and Math (STEM) disciplines that were expensive to support. This led to a rapid proliferation of law schools and the 12 Australian law schools of 1988 quickly climbed to 40,[37] an increase also replicated in the UK.[38]

The legal profession was not enthusiastic about the increasing numbers of law graduates and from time-to-time concern was expressed that the profession would be unable to accommodate them.[39] The profession may also have felt that numerosity detracted from the exclusiveness traditionally associated with professionalism, but its opposition became less vociferous over time. The profession's desire that law schools focus on preparing students for legal practice dovetailed with the government's aim that universities focus on preparing job-ready graduates. Although all graduates could not be absorbed into traditional legal practice, the versatility of the Law degree

34 Ibid. The attraction of the law degree for VCs in the UK as the cheapest form of mass tertiary education was noted by Hepple. See Bob Hepple, 'Some Concluding Reflections' in Peter Birks (ed), *Reviewing Legal Education* (Oxford University Press 1994) 119; E Eugene Clark and Martin Tsamenyi, 'Legal Education in the Twenty-First Century: A Time of Challenge' in Peter Birks (ed), *What Are Law Schools For?* (Oxford University Press 1996) 32.

35 Marlene Le Brun and Richard Johnstone, *The Quiet (R)evolution: Improving Student Learning in Law* (Law Book Company 1994).

36 Brian Z Tamanaha, *Failing Law Schools* (Chicago University Press 2012) 29.

37 This includes the first for-profit law school, Sydney City School of Law, TOP Education Institute, established in 2016.

38 There were reported to be 23 university law schools in the UK in 1966. See John Wilson, 'A Survey of Legal Education in the United Kingdom' (1966) 9 (1) Journal of the Society of Public Teachers of Law, 29, 30. This figure has expanded to approximately 110 according to figures in *Wikipedia*. Wikipedia, 'Legal Education in the United Kingdom' <https://en.wikipedia.org/wiki/Legal_education_in_the_United_Kingdom> accessed 21 July 2021. The number proliferated following passage of the *Further and Higher Education Act 1992* when polytechnics became universities. It is notable that two of the private for-profit providers, BPP and the University of Law had the highest number of students (9,485 and 9,060 respectively) among alternative providers in 2018–2019. Higher Education Statistics Agency, 'Higher Education Student Statistics: UK, 2018/19' <https://www.hesa.ac.uk/news/16-01-2020/sb255-higher-education-student-statistics > accessed online 21 July 2021.

39 Edmund Tadros and Katie Walsh, 'Too Many Law Graduates and Not Enough Jobs', Financial Review (22 October 2015) <www.afr.com/business/legal/too-many-law-graduates-and-not-enough-jobs-20151020-gkdbyx> accessed 21 July 2021.

Deference to the legal profession lingered on, however, and in 1992, the Law Admissions Consultative Committee (LACC) determined that graduates seeking admission to legal practice needed to demonstrate competence in core areas of knowledge. Known as the 'Priestley 11',[41] the standardised areas of knowledge focused on doctrinal and technical competence, with a commercial bias.[42] It is notable that the Priestley 11 has barely changed since 1992, despite being revised in 2019.[43] There was suspicion about any new law school that adopted an overtly theoretical or critical stance rather than one that was conservatively focused on the traditional and applied knowledge deemed appropriate for private practice.[44] However, the elevation of applied knowledge above theory and critique was not peculiar to law as the Organisation for Economic Co-operation and Development (OECD) also noted the shift in higher education from 'know what' to 'know how' in the 1990s.[45] This orientation was internalised by the student consumer in the pressure to prioritise vocationalism over professionalism.[46]

Capital accumulation in the university sector was most graphically illustrated by the introduction of fees. Tuition was free for Australian students prior to 1989, after which undergraduate fees were set at a modest AUD 1,800 per annum across all disciplines. Rather than using the term 'fees', however, an innovative deferred repayment scheme was devised that euphemistically referred to a 'contribution' (the Higher Education Contribution Scheme (HECS), now the Higher Education Loan Program (HELP)).[47] The scheme did not require students to begin repayment until they attained a

40 Edmund Tadros, 'Law Degree the New Arts Degree, Students Warned' (*Financial Review*, 14 February 2014).

41 After Justice Priestley who chaired the Law Admissions Consultative Committee of State and Territory Law Admitting Authorities in 1992.

42 The specified areas of knowledge are: Criminal Law and Procedure, Torts, Contracts, Property, Equity (including Trusts), Company Law, Administrative Law, Federal and State Constitutional Law, Civil Procedure, Evidence, Ethics and Professional Responsibility.

43 Law Council of Australia, Law Admissions Consultative Committee, *Prescribed Areas of Knowledge* (Australia\SDCL\657475579.01, 2019).

44 Mary Keyes and Richard Johnstone, 'Changing Legal Education: Rhetoric, Reality and Prospects for the Future' (2004) 26 (4) Sydney Law Review, 537–564, 557.

45 Organisation for Economic Cooperation and Development, 'The Knowledge-Based Economy' (1996) <https://www.basicknowledge101.com/pdf/KNOWLEDGE-BASED%20 ECONOMY.pdf#:~:text=The%20term%20%E2%80%9Cknowledge-based%20 economy%E2%80%9D%20stems%20from%20this%20fuller,traditional%20 economics%2C%20as%20reflected%20in%20%E2%80%9Cnew%20growth%20 theory%E2%80%9D> accessed 26 August 2021.

46 Nickolas J James, 'More than Merely Word-Ready: Vocationalism Versus Professionalism in Legal Education' (2017) 4 (1) *UNSW Law Journal*, 186–209.

47 The architect of the scheme was Professor Bruce Chapman, an economist at the Australian National University. See Bruce Chapman, Timothy Higgins and Joseph E Stiglitz

238 *Margaret Thornton*

certain income level, whereupon repayment was effected through the taxation system. This deferred repayment scheme lies at the heart of the success of the corporatisation of Australian higher education and has since been emulated in many other parts of the world, including the UK.[48] The initiative enabled the cost of higher education to be passed on to students without the need for a substantial up-front payment. As a result of this insidious process of 'submerged privatization',[49] the user pays system was quickly normalised and once accepted, fees began to be increased, with law in a cluster of professional disciplines charged at the highest rate.[50] This accorded with the argument put forward by key neoliberal economist, Milton Friedman, that students in professional disciplines should pay more for their education as they could expect to be the recipients of high incomes on graduation.[51]

The privatising imperative that was taking place in Australian higher education was occurring in lockstep with the UK, although political and funding complexities prevent a direct comparison.[52] After undergraduate fees were raised from £3,000 to £9,000 a year in 2012/2013 in England and Wales, and government support for teaching was removed,[53] the (conservative) Australian Coalition Government (Liberal and Country Parties) proposed going a step further by deregulating fees altogether, but the proposal

---

(eds), *Income Contingent Loans: Theory, Practice and Prospects* (International Economics Association, Palgrave Macmillan 2014).

48 Jill Rowbotham, 'HELP for Nations Looking at Income-Contingent Loans' (*The Australian*, New South Wales, 2 July 2019).

49 Kanishka Jayasuriya, 'COVID-19, Markets and the Crisis of the Higher Education Regulatory State: The Case of Australia' (2020) 18 (4) Globalizations <https://www.tandfonline.com/doi/pdf/10.1080/14747731.2020.1815461> accessed 01 September 2021, 26.

50 Along with Medicine, Dentistry and Veterinary Science. Kim Jackson, 'The Higher Education Contribution Scheme' (*e-brief, Parliament of Australia*, December 2000, updated March 2001, July 2003, August 2003) <http://www.aph.gov.au/About_Parliament/Parliamentary_Departments/Parliamentary_Library/Publications_Archive/archive/hecs> accessed 21 July 2021.

51 Milton Friedman, *Capitalism and Freedom* (University of Chicago Press 1962) 105.

52 The allusion to 'the UK' is something of a misnomer in view of the policy of decentralisation and devolution that has been developing in the last 30 years. While England is by far the largest higher education sector in the UK, Scotland, Wales and Ireland display some marked differences arising from their distinctive political cultures. The most striking is that of Scotland, which does not charge fees to Scottish students. For a valuable analysis of the governance of UK higher education, see Michael Shattock and Aniko Horvath, 'The Decentralisation of the Governance of UK Higher Education: The Effects of Devolution to Scotland, Wales and Northern Ireland, and on England' (2020) 2 (2) Policy Reviews in Higher Education, 164–178; see also, Sheila Riddell, 'Widening Access to Scottish Higher Education: Unresolved Issues and Future Challenges' (2016) 48 (1) Scottish Educational Review, 3–12.

53 The fee cap was increased by inflation (2.8%) to £9,250 in 2017/2018 for institutions with a Teaching Excellence Framework (TEF) rating of Meets Expectation. See Paul Bolton, 'Tuition Fee Statistics' (briefing paper no.917, UK House of Commons Library, 19 February 2018) <https://researchbriefings.files.parliament.uk/documents/SN00917/SN00917.pdf> accessed 21 July 2021.

What is the law school for in a post-pandemic world? 239

was dropped because of strong opposition from the electorate at the prospect of undergraduate fees of AUD 100,000 or more.[54] New and regional universities also could have found themselves in the invidious situation of struggling to compete for students with well-established metropolitan institutions, a scenario that was politically unacceptable. The American experience of deregulation shows that once prestigious law schools set fees at a high level, non-élite schools believe that they must follow suit in order to remain competitive.[55] This engenders an upward spiral with the perverse result that students with the lowest income potential are confronted with the highest fees,[56] a scenario that was disastrous for many American law graduates at the time of the GFC. However, the allure of increased income in a corporatised climate outweighs issues of equity. Wendy Brown cites the example of the University of California, Los Angeles (UCLA) Business School that chose to forego USD 8 million a year in state funds in exchange for the flexibility to raise tuition and spurn restrictions on salary caps.[57]

Although the deregulation of fees was rejected by the Australian electorate, the conservative Coalition Government remained committed to reducing the cost of higher education to the public purse and periodic budgetary cuts were made. The shortfalls induced universities to place pressure on their law schools to increase enrolments.[58] The simultaneous cutting of law school budgets led not only to further austerity measures, but compelled law schools to devise various entrepreneurial responses.

Coursework master's degrees quickly became the most popular income-generating initiative. This is because the Australian Government initially prohibited the charging of full fees for undergraduate degrees, other than for international students, but postgraduate courses were not so constrained.[59] To maximise enrolments, master's degrees were commonly offered in block mode, or intensively, such as over one or two weeks to appeal to employed graduates who wished to upgrade their qualifications. The attractiveness of these courses was enhanced by bringing in international 'stars' to teach them. Masters' courses proved to be lucrative for law schools, particularly

---

54 Margaret Thornton, 'Deregulation, Debt and the Disciplines of Law' (2014) 39 Alternative Law Journal, 213–216.

55 Brian Z Tamanaha, *Failing Law Schools* (University of Chicago Press 2012) 132.

56 Ibid.

57 The UCLA Business School, the Anderson School of Management, was privatised in 2012. See Wendy Brown, *Undoing the Demos* (Zone Books 2015) 199.

58 Dawn Oliver, 'Teaching and Learning Law: The Pressures on the Liberal Law Degree' in Peter Birks (ed), *Reviewing Legal Education* (Oxford University Press 1994) 80.

59 E Eugene Clark and Martin Tsamenyi, 'Legal Education in the Twenty-First Century: A Time of Challenge' in Peter Birks (ed), *What Are Law Schools For?* (Oxford University Press 1996) 33.

240 *Margaret Thornton*

the research-intensive Group of Eight (Go8) universities,[60] but competition policy invariably posed a problem for regional and new universities.

The LLB (Bachelor of Laws) has traditionally been the basic Law degree in Australia, commonly offered in conjunction with another degree, such as Arts or Commerce over five years. More recently, the Juris Doctor (JD) has become a popular alternative for many law schools because of its income-generating potential. Its postgraduate classification enabled law schools to circumvent the prohibition on charging full fees for undergraduate courses,[61] although there are now some government-funded JD places.[62] The JD has therefore become a valuable source of funding, designed to compensate for the reduction in government funding. It is normally offered over three years like its American counterpart, and the nomenclature is also believed to have greater international currency than the LLB, thereby appealing to the international student market.

The attraction of the JD is borne out by an initiative developed by Bond University, a private not-for-profit university, which has taken advantage of Canada's cap on law school places by offering a bespoke course (the Bond Canadian Law Program) that satisfies Canadian admission requirements. Bond's location on the Queensland Gold Coast with a sub-tropical climate and ready access to beaches attracts annual cohorts of full fee-paying Canadian students,[63] with well over 2,000 having graduated with a Bond JD to date.[64]

The Bond example highlights the increased importance of marketing, a key plank of capital accumulation. The creation of a unique 'brand' is central to competition policy through which the market metanarrative seeks to capture the idealised futures imagined for prospective law students.[65] In the competition for market share, the language used is redolent of that found in a tourist brochure where the focus is on the aesthetic of pleasure, which includes the proximity of the law school to beaches, sporting facilities and night life, as in the Bond example. The advertising generally accords short

---

60 Australian National University, Monash University, University of Adelaide, University of Melbourne, University of Queensland, University of Sydney, University of New South Wales, and University of Western Australia.

61 Donna Cooper, Sheryl Jackson, Rosalind Mason and Mary Toohey, 'The Emergence of the JD in the Australian Legal Education Marketplace and its Impact on Academic Standards' (2011) 21 Legal Education Review, 23–48.

62 This includes all students enrolled in the University of Western Australia Law School JD.

63 Bond University, 'Bond Canadian Law Program' (*Bond University*, 2021) <https://bond. edu.au/intl/future-students/study-bond/search-program/law/information-students-canada> accessed 26 August 2021.

64 The programme has been operating for 20 years and over 100 Canadians graduate every year with a Bond JD or LLB. Legal Line, 'Bond University, Australia' (Legal Line, 2021) <https://www.legalline.ca/legal-answers/bond-university/> accessed 26 August 2021.

65 Margaret Thornton and Lucinda Shannon, '"Selling the Dream": Law School Branding and the Illusion of Choice' (2013) 23 *Legal Education Review* 2, 249–271.

What is the law school for in a post-pandemic world? 241

shrift to the more prosaic elements associated with studying law, such as reading lengthy judgments. Similarly, no reference is made to the ballooning number of graduates competing for positions, or the increasing levels of stress suffered by young lawyers.[66] The suggestion that law students can expect a glamorous and fun-filled career as a high-flying legal practitioner leads directly to the idea of the student as human capital.

Human Capital

Students

Foucault elaborates on the human capital aspect of neoliberalism in which individuals are encouraged to view their lives and identities as a kind of enterprise.[67] The individual is the subject of personal enterprise because [he] earns '[his] own wages, administers [his] own consumption and produces [his] own satisfaction, but also embodies [his] own assets and productivity'.[68] Foucault's conceptualisation of *homo oeconomicus* as an entrepreneur of [him]self[69] is well illustrated in the case of the law student. The theory shows how education is a valuable means of enhancing human capital; it is not just a source of capital accumulation for the state, but the two conceptualisations are closely imbricated. Foucault locates the competence-machine within a comprehensive neoliberal 'environmental analysis' of human capital.[70]

Foucault's theory resonates with public choice theory in which students are identified as 'rational egoists' and 'utility maximisers' who set out to

---

66 Kate Allman, 'The Burnout Profession' (2019) Law Society Journal Online <https://lsj.com.au/articles/the-burnout-profession/> accessed 21 July 2021; Richard Collier, 'Anxiety and Wellbeing Amongst Junior Lawyers: A Research Study' (Presentation at 'Mind your Head', *Anxiety UK*, London 2019) <https://www.lawcare.org.uk/files/Junior-Lawyer-Collier-Anxiety-UK-Briefing-Report.pdf> accessed 27 August 2021.
67 Michael Foucault, *The Birth of Biopolitics* (Macmillan USA 2010) 225–226. For analysis, see Lois McNay, 'Self as Enterprise: Dilemmas of Control and Resistance in Foucault's *The Birth of Biopolitics*' (2009) 26 (6) Theory, Culture & Society, 55–77.
68 Michael Foucault, *The Birth of Biopolitics* (Macmillan USA 2010) 225–227; Marius Gudmand-Høyer and Thomas Lopdrup Hjorth, 'Liberal Biopolitics Reborn' (2009) 7 Foucault Studies, 99–130, 121.
69 Michael Foucault, *The Birth of Biopolitics* (Macmillan USA 2010) 226. McNay, 'Self as Enterprise' 61. I agree with Wendy Brown (*Undoing the Demos*, 99–107) that the gender of *homo oeconomicus* is problematic. This is particularly the case in respect of law students when they are overwhelmingly female. For the most part, however, there is probably little difference in the gender of law students in respect of enterprise, unless a female student has children, in which case she is likely to face the typical dilemmas and choices of women in the workforce who are still expected to assume primary responsibility for caring and face high costs for childcare, which has become another site of privatisation.
70 Marius Gudmand-Høyer and Thomas Lopdrup Hjorth, 'Liberal Biopolitics Reborn' (2009) 7 Foucault Studies, 99–130, 121.

242 *Margaret Thornton*

maximise their return on the expenditure they outlay.[71] Not only does this encourage them to aim for the best paying jobs, but it also influences their experience while at law school. The focus on enterprise sees students exercising their consumer power to shape the curriculum in a way that is instrumentally beneficial. They may agitate for a more applied orientation to satisfy job readiness, arguing that theoretical perspectives such as legal history, jurisprudence and feminist legal theory do not accord with the job ready paradigm.[72] Indeed, it is not the role of higher education in a neoliberal climate to produce critically aware graduates but a pool of job-ready skilled human capital to enhance competitiveness in the market.[73] We can see how the individual aims of the law student as entrepreneur dovetail with the broader aims of the neoliberal state directed towards capital accumulation, particularly the way that 'know how' is privileged over 'know what' in the new knowledge economy.[74] Given the dynamism of contemporary society and the radically new ways of practising law,[75] there is nevertheless value in a liberal legal education that equips law graduates to cope with an ever-changing social and legal landscape, but a liberal legal education directed to an uncertain future does not accord with job readiness in the here and now.

Student consumers seek to influence the mode of delivery, as well as the substance of what is taught in order to accommodate the competing dimensions of their lives, including the need, or the perceived need, to engage in paid work. The evidence shows that the proportion of students engaging in paid work, usually on a casual or part-time basis, has been increasing over a number of years, although it may include working on a full-time basis, even when enrolled in a full-time degree.[76] While I do not have disaggregated

---

71 Peter Self, *Government by the Market: The Politics of Public Choice* (Macmillan 1993) 4–11.

72 Margaret Thornton, *Privatising the Public University: The Case of Law* (Routledge 2012) 67–70, *et passim.*

73 Mark Purcell, *Recapturing Democracy* (Routledge 2008).

74 Organisation for Economic Cooperation and Development, 'The Knowledge-Based Economy' (1996) <https://www.basicknowledge101.com/pdf/KNOWLEDGE-BASED%20 ECONOMY.pdf#:~:text=The%20term%20%E2%80%9Cknowledge-based%20 economy%E2%80%9D%20stems%20from%20this%20fuller,traditional%20 economics%2C%20as%20reflected%20in%20%E2%80%9Cnew%20growth%20theory-%E2%80%9D.> accessed 26 August 2021.

75 Lisa Webley, John Flood, Julian Webb, Francesca Bartlett, Kate Galloway and Kieran Tranter, 'The Profession(s)' Engagements with LawTech: Narratives and Archetypes of Future Law' (2019) 1 (1) Law, Technology and Humans, 6–26 <https://lthj.qut.edu.au/ article/view/1314/841> accessed 26 July 2021; Margaret Thornton, 'Towards the Uberisation of Legal Practice' (2019) 1 (1) Law, Technology and Humans, 46–63 <https://doi. org/10.5204/lthj.v1i1.1277> accessed 26 July 2021.

76 Thomas Le Barbanchon, Diego Ubfae and Fedeerico Araya, 'The Effects of Working While in School' (*VOX. CEPR Policy Portal*, 16 December 2019) <https://voxeu.org/ article/effects-working-while-school> accessed 26 July 2021; Albert Sanchez-Gelaberi,

What is the law school for in a post-pandemic world? 243

figures for law students, a position as a paralegal, or even an unpaid intern, is regarded as desirable to assist in quick starting a career in a highly competitive legal labour market. Prior to Covid-19, the trend to spend more time in paid work significantly impacted on class attendance and small group interaction. As consumers, students expect their needs to be accommodated through flexible offerings such as recorded lectures and ready access to online resources, which does not guarantee their attendance at classes.[77]

The consumerist pressure from students has also resulted in attempts to make law courses easier and more palatable. Credentialism is the order of the day even if it is at the expense of intellectual growth. Enterprising students complain if a lecturer has set an assignment that they believe to be too taxing. They claim to be so time-poor due to work, social and sporting commitments that they must be strategic in their use of time. Hence, rather than persevering with the reading of lengthy cases, they commonly buy ready-made summaries, such as those available from an internet site such as *LawSkool.com* or from previous students.[78]

Human capital theory is not restricted to law students' power over curricula and pedagogy, for they are also able to exert power over academics and institutions through completion of student experience surveys.[79] In 2018, the Australian Government imposed an 'efficiency dividend' on the Commonwealth Grant Scheme based on a university's rates of completion, attrition, and student satisfaction. Such mechanisms compel universities to manage proactively the cost and value of what they do, that is, secure 'effectiveness, efficiency and value for money'.[80] The efficiency dividend allowed course satisfaction surveys to be considered in promotion applications. Such measures ensure a high degree of deference by universities towards student/customers, which has the potential to contribute not only to the 'dumbing down' of content that students consider 'too hard', but it may also lead to grade inflation

---

Mijail Figueroa and Marina Elias, 'Working While Studying in Higher Education: The Impact of the Economic Crisis on Academic and Labour Market Success' (2017) 52 European Journal of Education, 231–244; Natalie Gil, 'One in Seven Students Work Full-Time While They Study' (*The Guardian*, London, 12 August 2014) <https://www.theguardian.com/education/2014/aug/11/students-work-part-time-employability> accessed 26 July 2021.

77 Natalie Skead, Liam Elphick, Fiona McGaughey, Murray Wesson, Kate Offer and Michael Montalto, 'If You Record, They Will Not Come – But Does It Really Matter? Student Attendance and Lecture Recording at an Australian Law School' (2020) 54 (3) The Law Teacher, 349–367.

78 Margaret Thornton, 'The Challenge for Law Schools of Satisfying Multiple Masters' (2020) 62 (2) Australian Universities Review, 5–13.

79 The Higher Education Student Experience, *2019 Student Experience Survey* (Department of Education and Training, Canberra, 2020).

80 Universities UK, 'Efficiency and Effectiveness in Higher Education: A Report by the Universities UK Efficiency and Modernisation Task Group' (*Universities UK*, 2011) <https://www.universitiesuk.ac.uk/policy-and-analysis/reports/Pages/report-by-efficiency-and-modernisation-task-group.aspx> accessed 26 July 2021.

244 *Margaret Thornton*

when lecturers are held responsible by students for their lacklustre performance.[81] A law school might capitulate to a student who appeals a grade in order to avoid a complaint being lodged with an external body, such as an ombudsman, which could result in adverse publicity and damage the brand name of the institution.

The incidental role of a university education, such as producing an educated citizenry, has become passé in a neoliberal climate, for what is required is technically skilled human capital, 'not educated participants in public life'.[82] Rote learning and regurgitation, famously referred to by Freire as the 'banking method' of knowledge acquisition,[83] have therefore come to be preferred over deep learning.[84] The seeds of invidiousness associated with the applied approach were already discernible at the time of the Birks' collection. Dawn Oliver, for example, warned about the dangers of consumerism producing a lowest common denominator approach.[85]

It is notable that the leaning towards applied knowledge and 'know how' over the theoretical and critical is apparent in the turning away from a law school education in favour of a reversion to apprenticeships in the UK,[86] where 80% of the apprentice's time is spent in practice. The apprenticeship is advertised as a 'cost-free' alternative to admission to legal practice and all costs of training and assessment are paid for through the apprenticeship levy fund.[87] As apprentices receive a salary from the outset, apprenticeships are likely to appeal to those who are keen to maximise their personal capital quickly without undertaking a lengthy period of study at a university.

The student as enterprise has little interest in a liberal legal education that is interdisciplinary, comparative or sociolegal, although there are always a few students who are interested in legal theory, law reform and social justice. For the most part, however, enterprising students want to be assured that

---

81 Margaret Thornton, *Privatising the Public University: The Case of Law* (Routledge 2012) 104–107.

82 Wendy Brown, *Undoing the Demos: Neoliberalism's Stealth Revolution* (Zone Books 2015) 177.

83 Paulo Freire, *Pedagogy of the Oppressed: 30th Anniversary Edition* (Continuum Press 2005).

84 Bob Hepple, 'Some Concluding Reflections' in Peter Birks (ed), *Reviewing Legal Education* (Oxford University Press 1994) 109.

85 Dawn Oliver, 'Teaching and Learning Law: The Pressures on the Liberal Law Degree' in Peter Birks (ed), *Reviewing Legal Education* (Oxford University Press 1994) 82.

86 Jemma Smith (ed), 'Law Apprenticeships' (*Prospects*, May 2021) <https://www.prospects.ac.uk/jobs-and-work-experience/job-sectors/law-sector/law-apprenticeships> accessed 26 July 2021; See also Solicitors Regulation Authority 'Solicitor Apprenticeships' (*SRA*, April 2021) <SRA | Solicitor apprenticeships | Solicitors Regulation Authority> accessed 26 July 2021.

87 Ibid.

What is the law school for in a post-pandemic world? 245

what they are taught is *relevant*[88]; if this means only basic 'know how', that will suffice.

Legal Academics

As neoliberal subjects, legal academics are also engaged in a kind of enterprise. While there has always been an element of self-promotion associated with ascending the academic ladder, entrepreneurialism has become a desirable 'third stream activity',[89] along with teaching and research. This is most clearly discernible in the way that competition within a marketised economy has compelled law schools to prioritise research over teaching,[90] but it is the entrepreneurial value of the research, not the pursuit of knowledge for its own sake, à la Newman,[91] that is most highly valued. This inversion of the way research is valued has fostered a substantial body of interdisciplinary literature termed 'critical university studies' (CUS).[92]

Excellence in research is rendered calculable through auditing schemes such as the Excellence in Research for Australia (ERA)[93] and the Research Excellence Framework (REF) in the UK.[94] A high ranking in these metrics not only enhances the reputation of the university but also secures the future of individual academics. As Burrows shows, a myriad of different metrics is invoked to measure what is now deemed to possess financial value in the marketised academy.[95] Even though a law school hopes that a high ranking will attract international students, metrics are invariably based on research achievements rather than teaching excellence. As a result, scholarship is increasingly the coin of the realm.[96] Rankings are also bound to

---

88 Cris Shore and Laura McLauchlan, '"Third Mission" Activities, Commercialisation and Academic Entrepreneurs' (2012) 20 Social Anthropology, 267–286.

89 Ibid.

90 Liz Morrish, 'Academic Identities in the Managed University: Neoliberalism and Resistance at Newcastle University, UK' (2017) 59 (2) Australian Universities Review, 23–25.

91 John Henry Newman, *The Idea of a University* (1st published 1852, Ian T Ker (ed), Oxford University Press 1976).

92 For discussion, see Richard Collier, '"Left Pessimists" in "Rose Coloured Glasses"? Reflections on the Political Economy of Socio-Legal Studies and (Legal) Academic Well-Being' (2020) 47 (52) Journal of Law and Society, S244–S261.

93 Australian Government and Australian Research Council, 'Excellence in Research for Australia' <https://www.arc.gov.au/excellence-research-australia> accessed 26 July 2021.

94 Research Excellence Framework, 'Research Excellence Framework' <https://www.ref. ac.uk/> accessed 26 July 2021.

95 Roger Burrows, 'Living with the H-Index? Metric Assemblages in the Contemporary Academy' (2012) 60 (2) The Sociological Review <https://onlinelibrary.wiley.com/doi/abs/10.1111/j.1467-954X.2012.02077.x> accessed 26 July 2021.

96 Nora V Demleitner, 'Colliding or Coalescing: Leading a Faculty and an Administration in the Academic Enterprise' (2010/2011) 42 University of Toledo Law Review, 605–617.

246 *Margaret Thornton*

be influenced by the age and wealth of an institution,[97] although new and regional law schools are ranked as though they were on a level playing field with Oxbridge and the Ivy League.

The commercialisation of research is prominent in the assessment of entrepreneurialism, although law does not score highly in knowledge transfer, which is dominated by STEM subjects. Nevertheless, research outcomes in the form of publications are central to the computation of rankings in law schools. The flexibilisation of academic staff has been the response by management to teaching expanding numbers of students.[98] This means that while research-active faculty are likely to occupy continuing positions, teaching has been increasingly casualised.[99] Successful grant recipients are encouraged to buy out their teaching obligations by engaging cheaper casual staff so that they can focus on their research, all of which has contributed to the undervaluation of teaching and a movement away from what the law school once was for.

While academia might downplay the extent of casualisation that has emerged as a corollary of corporatisation, Australian universities have been described as 'the most avid employers of precarious labour since the 1990s',[100] which further downplays the importance of teaching. Instead of hiring legal academics thought to be the best teachers, scholarly potential takes precedence as the primary criterion for recruitment. When it became apparent that the ever-expanding precariat faced an uncertain future in the academy with little hope of realising their own capital, a new category of employment, the Scholarly Teaching Fellow, was created with greater security of tenure and the possibility of eventually transferring to a balanced teaching/research position.[101] However, interviews conducted by Goodman et al. suggest that this new position is no less exploitative than casual teaching, with respondents reporting that they felt 'chained to the desk' or were

---

97 Richard W Bourne, 'The Coming Crash in Legal Education: How We Got Here, and Where We Go Now' (2011/2012) 45 Creighton Law Review, 690–691.

98 James Goodman et al., *Scholarly Teaching Fellows as a New Category of Employment in Australian Universities: Impacts and Prospects for Teaching and Learning: Goodman Report* (Department of Education, Skills and Employment, Australian Government, Canberra, 2020) 1.

99 Wendy Brown, *Undoing the Demos: Neoliberalism's Stealth Revolution* (Zone Books 2015) 197.

100 Calculated at 59.3% of the Australian academic workforce in 2018. See James Goodman et al., *Scholarly Teaching Fellows as a New Category of Employment in Australian Universities: Impacts and Prospects for Teaching and Learning: Goodman Report* (Department of Education, Skills and Employment, Australian Government, Canberra, 2020) 4; Kanishka Jayasuriya, 'COVID-19, Markets and the Crisis of the Higher Education Regulatory State: The Case of Australia' (2020) 18 (4) Globalizations.

101 James Goodman et al., *Scholarly Teaching Fellows as a New Category of Employment in Australian Universities: Impacts and Prospects for Teaching and Learning: Goodman Report* (Department of Education, Skills and Employment, Australian Government, Canberra, 2020).

What is the law school for in a post-pandemic world?   247

compelled to 'clock up 90 to 110 hours a week'.[102] Like casual academics, the new fellows are subject to the whims of management in terms of what they teach, how much they teach and whether they will have a contract for the next semester or not.

Human capital, like academic capitalism generally, is always haunted by risk.[103] Albeit occupying a more secure status than that of the casualised precariat, the future of full-time legal academics in continuing positions is also fraught in a neoliberal climate. Falling below par in terms of research productivity, for example, as demonstrated by ERA assessments and league tables, can be fatal. While tenure has disappeared in many law schools, the possibility of redundancy is always present, even for the most talented legal academics. The instability in the higher education sector arising from frequent cuts and austerity measures has contributed to uncertainty and stress. Consequently, the issue of well-being among law teachers (as well as students) has become a major topic of research within the context of CUS.[104]

As Bradney and Cownie demonstrate, the position of legal academics has become increasingly ambivalent. While the legal academy has been professionalised through a focus on research and publication, it has been simultaneously proletarianised as a result of managerialism.[105] Bradney and Cownie nevertheless argue that professionalism has exerted a radical and more lasting effect on law schools than proletarianisation.[106] Indeed, the growth of sociolegal scholarship in recent decades has been profound.[107] While academics still retain a modicum of autonomy in terms of how they spend their time, where they do so and what they choose to research, they are increasingly subject to the vagaries of managerialism in a volatile climate involving constant scrutiny and accountability. Those in new and regional law schools, where there is likely to be little discretionary money, may face impossibly heavy teaching loads. Their position is invidious when excellence in scholarly productivity rather than teaching excellence has

---

102 Ibid, 28.

103 Ulrich Beck, *Risk Society: Towards a New Modernity* (Mark Ritter tr, Sage 1992).

104 Richard Collier, 'Reflections on the UK Experience of Legal Academic Wellbeing and the Legal Profession: Moving Across Silos' in Michael Legg, Prue Vines and Janet Chan (eds), *The Impact of Technology and Innovation on the Wellbeing of the Legal Profession* (Intersentia 2020); Colin James, Caroline Strevens and Rachael Field, 'Law Teachers Speak Out: What Do Law Schools Need to Change?' in Michael Legg, Prue Vines and Janet Chan (eds), *The Impact of Technology and Innovation on the Wellbeing of the Legal Profession* (Intersentia 2020).

105 Anthony Bradney and Fiona Cownie, 'The Changing Position of Legal Academics in the United Kingdom: Professionalization or Proletarianization?' (2020) Journal of Law and Society, S227–S243.

106 Ibid, 243.

107 Richard Collier, '"Left Pessimists" in 'Rose Coloured Glasses'? Reflections on the Political Economy of Socio-Legal Studies and (Legal) Academic Well-Being' (2020) 47 (S2) Journal of Law and Society, S244–S261.

248 *Margaret Thornton*

become the 'coin of the realm'. This is apparent with the widespread redundancies that occurred in the wake of Covid-19, to which I turn.

Covid-19: The First Cut

The impact of Covid-19 on higher education has been profound as it emerged in the aftermath of a growing fiscal crisis in Australian higher education.[108] The financial impact arising from the loss of international students because of border closures has been the major focus of concern and reliance on this source of income reveals the fragility of the political economy of higher education.

The closure of the Australian border to foreign nationals (without permanent residency) from February 2020 began to send shock waves throughout the higher education sector, particularly the Go8 where there had been a concentration of international students, whose fees subsidised research. It has been estimated that AUD 16 billion will be lost from the sector between 2020 and 2023, based on the drop in international student revenue, which is likely to impact all institutions.[109] The loss is acutely felt as the sector was AUD 2.3 billion in surplus in 2019.[110] The decline in international students elsewhere, particularly in the US[111] and the UK,[112] has been similarly disastrous.[113]

---

108 Kanishka Jayasuriya, 'COVID-19, Markets and the Crisis of the Higher Education Regulatory State: The Case of Australia' (2020) 18 (4) Globalizations, 26 <https://www.tandfonline.com/doi/pdf/10.1080/14747731.2020.1815461> accessed 01 September 2021.

109 Hazel Ferguson and Susan Love, 'The Impact of COVID-19 on Australian Higher Education and Overseas Students – What Do the Numbers Say?' (*Parliamentary Library, Parliament of Australia*, 12 August 2020) <https://www.aph.gov.au/About_Parliament/Parliamentary_Departments/Parliamentary_Library/FlagPost/2020/August/Universities_and_COVID> accessed 26 July 2021.

110 Lisa Visentin, 'Universities Facing $2 Billion Loss as Job Cuts Total More Than 17,000' (*Sydney Morning Herald*, Sydney, 3 February 2021) <https://www.smh.com.au/politics/federal/universities-facing-2-billion-loss-as-job-cuts-total-more-than-17-000-20210202-p56yqc.html> accessed 26 July 2021.

111 In the US, a dramatic decline in international students has been reported. See Mary Beth Marklein, 'New International Student Enrolments Drop by 43% in US' (*University World News*, 23 November 2020) <https://www.universityworldnews.com/post.php?story=20201116050900954> accessed 26 July 2021. For a comprehensive overview of the impact on the EU and OECD member states, see European Migration Network, European Commission, 'Inform #2: Impact of COVID-19 on International Students in EU and OECD Member States' (2020) <https://www.oecd.org/migration/mig/00_eu_inform5_return_en.pdf> accessed 26 July 2021. Uncertainties in the legal labour market may also affect the enrolment of domestic students. See Andrew Smalley, 'Higher Education Responses to Coronavirus (COVID-19)' (*National Conference of State Legislatures*, 28 December 2020) <https://www.ncsl.org/research/education/higher-education-responses-to-coronavirus-covid-19.aspx> accessed 26 July 2021.

112 Paul Bolton and Sue Hubble, 'Coronavirus: Financial Impact on Higher Education' (Briefing Paper, House of Commons Library, UK Parliament, London, 2020) <https://commonslibrary.parliament.uk/research-briefings/cbp-8954/> accessed 26 July 2021.

113 The graphic impact on research and the cross-subsidisation of STEM teaching as a result will leave what Bolton and Hubble describe as a 'black hole of hundreds of millions of

What is the law school for in a post-pandemic world? 249

It is notable that many international students themselves have suffered significantly as a result of losing their paid employment in Australia, for they found themselves ineligible for government stimulus moneys, along with academics who had lost their jobs.[114] Whereas the Australian Government provided generous stimulus packages under its Job Seeker and Job Keeper programmes to businesses and workers deleteriously affected by Covid-19, academics, students and universities were all deemed ineligible for these programmes, thereby once again underscoring the contemporary ambivalence about higher education as a public good. At least 17,300 academics lost their jobs in 2020 and more losses are predicted for 2021 in light of the revenue shortfalls.[115] Judith Brett has suggested that Covid-19 has turned 'an incremental decline into an existential crisis'.[116]

Instead of assisting the sector at a time of crisis, the Australian Government has ramped up pressure on universities to do more. It has enacted legislation designed to compensate for the collapse of the international student market by reducing further the cost of higher education to the public purse by selectively increasing student fees and providing incentives to encourage universities to produce more 'job-ready graduates'.[117] There is nothing subtle about this as the phrase is included in the title of the Act: Higher Education Support Amendment (JobReady Graduates and Supporting Regional and Remote Students) Act 2020. The Act provides incentives to increase enrolments in areas designated as national priorities, namely, STEM, together with Nursing and Teaching. The financial contributions by students in these areas will be reduced while government contributions will be increased. In contrast, students in areas such as law and the humanities will be charged more, and the government contribution reduced.

A brief look at the different clusters clearly illustrates the point. The maximum student contribution for a government-supported place in Law, Accounting, Economics, Commerce, Communication, Society and Culture from 1 January 2021 was increased to AUD 14,500 per annum, while the Commonwealth contribution was reduced to AUD1,200 (7%). This contrasts with a government-supported place in Education, Clinical Psychology, English, Mathematics or Statistics, where the cost to the student is AUD 3,950

---

pounds in tuition fees'. See A Michael Froomkin, 'The Virtual Law School, 2.0' (2020) University of Miami Legal Studies Research Paper No. 3728114.

114 John Ross, 'Foreign Students "Disproportionately Impoverished" by Pandemic' (*Times Higher Education*, 10 August 2020). The plight of international students in Canada has also been noted. See David Firang, 'The Impact of COVID-19 Pandemic on International Students in Canada' (2020) 63 (6) International Social Work, 820–824.

115 Lisa Visentin, 'Universities Facing $2 Billion Loss as Job Cuts Total More Than 17,000' (*The Sydney Morning Herald*, Sydney, 3 February 2021) <https://www.smh.com.au/politics/federal/universities-facing-2-billion-loss-as-job-cuts-total-more-than-17-000-20210202-p56yqc.html> accessed 26 July 2021.

116 Judith Brett, 'The Bin Fire of the Humanities'(*The Monthly*, March 2021) 20–27, 26.

117 Paul Kniest, 'Students Pay More; Staff Do More; Universities Get Less' (November 2020) 27 (3) Advocate, 25–27, 26.

250 *Margaret Thornton*

and the Commonwealth contribution is AUD 13,250 (77%).[118] We can therefore see how government is engineering the focus on job readiness according to discipline. However, it remains to be seen what effect this intervention will have on student choice, as HECS-HELP still exists with its 'submerged privatization' of fees.[119] While the fee differential may not be sufficient to deter students from enrolling in law rather than in, say, a cheaper STEM subject, an increase in unpaid HECS-HELP loans may well occur as a result of economic pressure, if Covid-19 persists.[120]

The Australian National Tertiary Education Union's analysis of the tuition data reveals that the selective increase in fees will not offset the reduction in state funding, for there will be an overall loss in resourcing from government of approximately 6%.[121] The outcome will undoubtedly be larger classes and heavier workloads. In fact, as a result of the financial loss to higher education in 2020, most Australian law schools were compelled to resort to redundancies together with a range of austerity measures, such as dispensing with casual staff and cutting research and discretionary spending. While the casualisation of the academic workforce pre-Covid-19 (estimated by the National Tertiary Education Union to amount to approximately 45%)[122] had been regarded as a rational response to cuts in university operating costs, a substantial proportion of casual staff have since failed to have their contracts renewed. It is also notable that Covid-19 exposed extensive wage theft perpetrated against casual staff, amounting to millions of dollars, which many universities have since had to repay.[123] The underpayment arose from a range of factors, including the sleight of hand in classifying work in such a way that it attracted a lower rate of pay, such as treating tutorials as 'demonstrations' or 'information sessions', and not paying for work such as the time expended in consultation with students or

---

118 For details regarding other funding clusters, see Parliament of Australia 'Schedule 2 of the Higher Education Support Amendment (Job-Ready Graduates and Supporting Regional and Remote Students) Act 2020 and the Explanatory Memorandum to the Act' <https://www.legislation.gov.au/Details/C2020A00093> accessed 01 September 2021.
119 Kanishka Jayasuriya, 'COVID-19, Markets and the Crisis of the Higher Education Regulatory State: The Case of Australia' (2020) 18 (4) Globalizations, 26 <https://www.tandfonline.com/doi/pdf/10.1080/14747731.2020.1815461> accessed 01 September 2021.
120 Ibid.
121 Paul Kniest, 'Students Pay More; Staff Do More; Universities Get Less' (November 2020) 27 (3) Advocate, 25–27, 27.
122 Damien Cahill, 'Wage Theft and Casual Work Are Built into University Business Models' (*The Conversation*, Sydney, 27 October 2020) <https://theconversation.com/wage-theft-and-casual-work-are-built-into-university-business-models-147555> accessed 26 July 2021.
123 Ibid; Damien Cahill, 'Wage Theft Is Core University Business' (November 2020) 27 (3) Advocate, 28–29; Ellen Smith, 'Casual Wage Theft Par for the Course' (*Saturday Paper*, Melbourne 30 January 2021) 7.

What is the law school for in a post-pandemic world? 251

class preparation.[124] As Cahill argues, underpayment was 'built into university business models'.[125]

One of the objectives of the new Job Ready Graduates Act is to increase the number of student places without the need for additional investment from the public purse,[126] leaving it to universities themselves to work out how to manage their straitened budgets. One hope is to regain the lost international student market, in respect of which some universities have proposed charter flights in order to bring to Australia international students unable to secure commercial flights.[127]

While the attraction of law as a discipline has not diminished, prospective students are not being lured by financial inducements under the Job Ready Graduates Act. However, as the government focus is on increasing the proportion of domestic students to counteract the loss of international students, universities have offered their own inducements by lowering their cut-off scores for domestic students. The increased number of students in conjunction with limited resources is likely to exacerbate the pressure on academics. In addition to heavy teaching loads, they will still be expected to demonstrate heightened research productivity, including pressure to commercialise their research in order to augment the weakened research budgets of universities.

Once lockdown occurred as a result of Covid-19, law schools were compelled to move rapidly to on-line delivery, which proved to be a challenge in terms of both the expertise of staff and the availability of appropriate technology. However, as the costs of online teaching are generally believed to be lower than those associated with face-to-face teaching (although this is disputed),[128] we are likely to see more of it, despite the suggestive evidence from the US that online learning is less pedagogically effective.[129] Hence, it is notable that students at multiple US colleges and universities have instituted class actions in an attempt to obtain refunds after the move

---

124 Damien Cahill, 'Wage Theft and Casual Work Are Built into University Business Models' (*The Conversation*, Sydney, 27 October 2020) <https://theconversation.com/wage-theft-and-casual-work-are-built-into-university-business-models-147555> accessed 26 July 2021.

125 Ibid.

126 Paul Kniest, 'Students Pay More; Staff Do More; Universities Get Less' (November 2020) 27 (3) Advocate, 25–27, 27.

127 Wade Zaglas, 'Student Accommodation Providers Prepared to Charter Flights and Quarantine Students' (*Campus Review*, 18 January 2021) <https://www.campusreview.com.au/2021/01/student-accommodation-providers-prepared-to-charter-flights-and-quarantine-students/> accessed 26 July 2021.

128 SMYTHSYS, 'Online Classes Should NOT Be Cheaper Than Face to Face Classes' (*Teachers Madrid*, 20 October 2020) <https://teachersmadrid.es/10238/online-classes-should-not-be-cheaper-than-face-to-face-classes/> accessed 26 July 2021.

129 A. Michael Froomkin, 'The Virtual Law School 2.0', University of Miami Legal Studies Research paper No. 3728114, 56; Vanya Agarwal, 'COVID-19: The Push towards Online Legal Education' (*Legal Bites Law & Beyond*, 30 July 2020) <https://www.legalbites.in/covid-19-online-legal-education> accessed 26 July 2021.

252 *Margaret Thornton*

to on-line teaching in 2020.[130] A Harvard law student, for example, initiated suit against the university because tuition prices remained the same despite classes moving to remote learning.[131] A class action instituted against the University of San Diego stated that the students had 'contracted and paid for an education, not course credits...They paid for the robust education and full experience of academic life on USD's campus; remote online learning cannot provide the same value as in-person education'.[132] Nevertheless, no action has succeeded to date, and few have passed the initial stage of hearing.[133] The litigation is nevertheless a clear example of student as entrepreneur seeking to determine how a course should be delivered. In contrast to the US position, Marginson notes that UK institutions were unwilling to move to online teaching for fear of losing market share.[134]

Conclusion

I have sought to identify the contradictions at the heart of contemporary legal education in an endeavour to answer Birks' question 'what is the law school for?' It is apparent that the law school now serves multiple purposes. It can no longer be said to be in a state of 'infeudation' to the legal profession where its primary role is to prepare students for practice.[135] The centrality of a core curriculum such as the Priestley 11 nevertheless makes clear that preparing students for practice continues to be one of the reasons for what the law school is for, but the neoliberal aim of preparing job-ready new

---

130 Ibid, 40–41. I am unaware of comparable litigation in Australia.
131 Lauren Lantry, 'Harvard Law Student Sues University over Tuition Prices as Classes Remain Online' (ABC News Exclusive, 23 June 2020) <https://abcnews.go.com/US/abc-news-exclusive-harvard-law-student-sues-university/story?id=71345292> accessed 26 July 2021; David Owens, 'Yale Student Sues University Claiming Online Courses Were Inferior, Seeks Tuition Refund, Class Action Status' (*Hartford Courant*, 4 August 2020) <https://www.courant.com/coronavirus/hc-news-coronavirus-student-sues-yale-20200804-eyr4lbjs2nhz7lapjgvrtnyyea-story.htmlhttps://www.courant.com/coronavirus/hc-news-coronavirus-student-sues-yale-20200804-eyr4lbjs2nhz7lapjgvrtnyyea-story.html> accessed 26 July 2021.
132 Kristina Davis, 'A Federal Lawsuit against the University of San Diego Is the Latest Asking for Prorated Tuition and Fees to Reflect the Switch to Online Learning' (*The San Diego Union-Tribune*, 18 October 2020) <https://www.sandiegouniontribune.com/news/courts/story/2020-10-18/lawsuits-refunds-coronavirus-universities-san-diego> accessed 26 July 2021.
133 Ibid.
134 Simon Marginson, 'Covid-19 and the Market Model of Higher Education: Something Has to Give, and It Won't Be the Pandemic' (*Centre for Global Higher Education Blog*, 17 July 2020) <https://www.researchcghe.org/blog/2020-07-20-covid-19-and-the-market-model-of-higher-education-something-has-to-give-and-it-wont-be-the-pandemic/> accessed 26 July 2021.
135 Claude Thomasset and René Laperrière, 'Faculties under Influence: The Infeudation of Law Schools to the Legal Professions' in Fiona Cownie (ed), *The Law School: Global Issues, Local Questions* (Ashgate 1999).

knowledge workers for the labour market cannot be ignored. Similarly, the idea of the law school as a source of financialisation for the state cannot be disregarded either, together with the consumerist ramifications that arise from law students having to pay high fees.

In addition to pursuing instrumental aims, the neoliberalisation of higher education has inadvertently produced positive effects, particularly in respect of the democratisation of access to law schools through the deferred repayment system, HECS-HELP, so that a legal education is no longer the preserve of the privileged few. Democratisation has also challenged the historically masculinised and raced character of both the legal academy and legal practice. Nevertheless, the seemingly positive aspects of heterogeneity are downplayed by the contradictions and inconsistencies of neoliberalism as the degendering, decolonising and diversifying project is disrupted by frequent fee hikes and ever more creative means of control devised by the manageriat in the interests of capital accumulation.

The historical debates about whether a law school belonged in the university or not revolved around the question of whether teaching law for practice would involve an undiluted focus on applied knowledge and the presuppositions of legal practice. The neoliberal aim of producing job-ready human capital is blatantly instrumental in serving the economy and making Australia competitive on the world stage. However, the project is replete with contradictions, such as those arising from the focus on legal research, which carries unexpected benefits with it. In becoming an important aim of the corporatised legal academy, scholarly research has transformed the nature of the legal academy and its modus operandi. While a split occurred between teaching and research, scholarship has become the favoured route to success for legal academics, while teaching has declined in status, being increasingly assigned to a casualised precariat that is struggling to survive with little opportunity to realise its potential. The pressure to commercialise legal research through knowledge transfer may well be the next site of contest as universities struggle to re-establish their pre-Covid rankings, which are dependent on research that government is no longer willing to fund.

While we may be no closer to answering Birks' question *What is the law school for?* today than we were at the time that it was posed, we can see that the rapid pace of change incorporating responses to both neoliberalisation and Covid-19 has induced radically new ways of acting that preclude an unequivocal response to Birks' question. What can be discerned within the kaleidoscope of change over the past few decades is the remarkable resilience and agility of legal academics. While I have been critical of the excessive focus on financialisation and functionalism, committed academics are constantly creating new iterations of legal scholarship, as well as inspiring students who come to law school because they still believe in justice and want to change the world for the better. It may be, therefore, that we are able to reassure Birks that all vestiges of the idea of the law school as a public good have not been entirely eviscerated.

Bibliography

Allman K, 'The Burnout Profession' (2019) *Law Society Journal Online* <https://lsj.com.au/articles/the-burnout-profession/> accessed 21 July 2021.

Australia Department of Education, Employment and Workplace Relations, *Review of Australian Higher Education: Final Report* (2008).

Australia Department of Employment, Education and Training, *Higher Education: A Policy Statement* (Cmd 202, 1988).

Australian Government and Australian Research Council, 'Excellence in Research for Australia' <https://www.arc.gov.au/excellence-research-australia> accessed 26 July 2021.

Beck U, *Risk Society: Towards a New Modernity* (Mark Ritter tr, Sage 1992).

Birks P, 'Editor's Preface' in Peter Birks (ed) *Pressing Problems in the Law: What Are Law Schools For?* (Oxford University Press 1996).

Birks P (ed), *Pressing Problems in the Law: What Are Law Schools For?* (Oxford University Press 1996).

Bolton P, 'Tuition Fee Statistics' (Briefing paper no.917, UK House of Commons Library, 19 February 2018) <https://researchbriefings.files.parliament.uk/documents/SN00917/SN00917.pdf> accessed 21 July 2021.

Bolton P and Hubble S, 'Coronavirus: Financial Impact on Higher Education' (Briefing Paper, House of Commons Library, UK Parliament, London, 2020) <https://commonslibrary.parliament.uk/research-briefings/cbp-8954/> accessed 26 July 2021.

Bond University, 'Bond Canadian Law Program' (*Bond University*, 2021) <https://bond.edu.au/intl/future-students/study-bond/search-program/law/information-students-canada> accessed 26 August 2021.

Bourne R, 'The Coming Crash in Legal Education: How We Got Here, and Where We Go Now' (2011/2012) 45 *Creighton Law Review* 690–691.

Bradney A and Cownie F, 'The Changing Position of Legal Academics in the United Kingdom: Professionalization or Proletarianization?' (2020) 47(52) *Journal of Law and Society* S227–S243.

Brett J, 'The Bin Fire of the Humanities' (*The Monthly*, March 2021) 20–27.

Brown W, *Undoing the Demos* (Zone Books 2015).

Brown W, *Undoing the Demos: Neoliberalism's Stealth Revolution* (MIT Press 2015).

Burrows R, 'Living with the H-Index? Metric Assemblages in the Contemporary Academy' (2012) 60(2) *The Sociological Review* <https://onlinelibrary.wiley.com/doi/abs/10.1111/j.1467-954X.2012.02077.x> accessed 26 July 2021.

Cahill D, 'Wage Theft and Casual Work Are Built into University Business Models' (*The Conversation*, Sydney, 27 October 2020) <https://theconversation.com/wage-theft-and-casual-work-are-built-into-university-business-models-147555> accessed 26 July 2021.

Cahill D, 'Wage Theft Is Core University Business' (November 2020) 27(3) *Advocate* 28–29.

Chapman B, Timothy Higgins, and Joseph E Stiglitz (eds), *Income Contingent Loans: Theory, Practice and Prospects* (International Economics Association, Palgrave Macmillan 2014).

Clark E and Tsamenyi M, 'Legal Education in the Twenty-First Century: A Time of Challenge' in Peter Birks (ed), *Pressing Problems in the Law: What Are Law Schools For?* (Oxford University Press 1996).

Collier R, 'Anxiety and Wellbeing Amongst Junior Lawyers: A Research Study' (Presentation at 'Mind your Head', *Anxiety UK*, London 2019) <https://www.lawcare.org.uk/files/Junior-Lawyer-Collier-Anxiety-UK-Briefing-Report.pdf> accessed 27 August 2021.

Collier R, '"Left Pessimists" in "Rose Coloured Glasses"? Reflections on the Political Economy of Socio-Legal Studies and (Legal) Academic Well-Being' (2020) 47(52) *Journal of Law and Society* S244–S261.

Collier R, 'Reflections on the UK Experience of Legal Academic Wellbeing and the Legal Profession: Moving Across Silos' in Michael Legg, Prue Vines, and Janet Chan (eds) *The Impact of Technology and Innovation on the Wellbeing of the Legal Profession* (Intersentia 2020).

Comaroff J, 'The End of Neoliberalism? What Is Left of the Left' (2011) 637 *Annals, AAPS* 141–147.

Cooper D, Jackson S, Mason R, and Toohey M, 'The Emergence of the JD in the Australian Legal Education Marketplace and Its Impact on Academic Standards' (2011) 21 *Legal Education Review* 23–48.

Davis K, 'A Federal Lawsuit against the University of San Diego Is the Latest Asking for Prorated Tuition and Fees to Reflect the Switch to Online Learning' (*The San Diego Union-Tribune*, 18 October 2020) <https://www.sandiegouniontribune.com/news/courts/story/2020-10-18/lawsuits-refunds-coronavirus-universities-san-diego> accessed 26 July 2021.

Demleitner N, 'Colliding or Coalescing: Leading a Faculty and an Administration in the Academic Enterprise' (2010/2011) 42 *University of Toledo Law Review* 605–617.

European Migration Network, European Commission, *Inform #2: Impact of COVID-19 on International Students in EU and OECD Member States* (2020) <https://www.oecd.org/migration/mig/00_eu_inform5_return_en.pdf> accessed 26 July 2021.

Ferguson H and Love S, 'The Impact of COVID-19 on Australian Higher Education and Overseas Students – What Do the Numbers Say?' (Parliamentary Library, Parliament of Australia, 12 August 2020) <https://www.aph.gov.au/About_Parliament/Parliamentary_Departments/Parliamentary_Library/FlagPost/2020/August/Universities_and_COVID> accessed 26 July 2021.

Firang D, 'The Impact of COVID-19 Pandemic on International Students in Canada' (2020) 63(6) *International Social Work* 820–824.

Flew T, 'Michel Foucault's *The Birth of Biopolitics* and Contemporary Neo-Liberalism Debates' (2012) 108(1) *Thesis Eleven* 44–65.

Foucault M, 'Governmentality' in Graham Burchell, Colin Gordon, and Peter Miller (eds) *The Foucault Effect: Studies in Governmentality, with Two Lectures by and an Interview with Michel Foucault* (University of Chicago Press 1991).

Foucault M, *The Birth of Biopolitics* (Macmillan USA 2010).

Foucault M, *The Birth of Biopolitics: Lectures at the Collège de France, 1978–1979* (Michel Senellart ed, Graham Burchell tr, Palgrave Macmillan 2008).

Freire P, *Pedagogy of the Oppressed: 30th Anniversary Edition* (Continuum Press 2005).

Friedman M and Friedman R, *Capitalism and Freedom* (University of Chicago Press 1962).

Friedman M and Friedman R, *Free to Choose: A Personal Statement* (Harcourt Brace Jovanovich 1980).

256 *Margaret Thornton*

Froomkin M, 'The Virtual Law School 2.0' University of Miami Legal Studies Research Paper No. 3728114.

Garrett P, 'Revisiting "The Birth of Biopolitics": Foucault's Account of Neoliberalism and the Remaking of Social Policy' (2018) 48(3) *International Journal Politics, Culture & Society* 1–19.

Gil N, 'One in Seven Students Work Full-Time While They Study' (*The Guardian*, London, 12 August 2014) <https://www.theguardian.com/education/2014/aug/11/students-work-part-time-employability> accessed 26 July 2021.

Golshan T, 'Bernie Sanders's Free College Proposal Just Got a Whole Lot Bigger' (*Vox*, Washington DC, 23 June 2019) <https://www.vox.com/policy-and-politics/2019/6/23/18714615/bernie-sanders-free-college-for-all-2020-student-loan-debt> accessed 22 July 2021.

Goodman J et al., *Scholarly Teaching Fellows as a New Category of Employment in Australian Universities: Impacts and Prospects for Teaching and Learning: Goodman Report* (Department of Education, Skills and Employment, Australian Government, Canberra, 2020).

Gudmand-Høyer M and Lopdrup Hjorth T, 'Liberal Biopolitics Reborn' (2009) 7 *Foucault Studies* 99–130.

Hepple B, 'Some Concluding Reflections' in Peter Birks (ed) *Reviewing Legal Education* (Oxford University Press 1994).

Higher Education Statistics Agency, 'Higher Education Student Statistics: UK, 2018/19' <https://www.hesa.ac.uk/news/16-01-2020/sb255-higher-education-student-statistics> accessed 21 July 2021.

Jackson K, 'The Higher Education Contribution Scheme' (*e-Brief, Parliament of Australia*, December 2000, updated March 2001, July 2003, August 2003) <http://www.aph.gov.au/About_Parliament/Parliamentary_Departments/Parliamentary_Library/Publications_Archive/archive/hecs> accessed 21 July 2021.

James C, Stevens C, and Field R, 'Law Teachers Speak Out: What Do Law Schools Need to Change?' in Michael Legg, Prue Vines, and Janet Chan (eds) *The Impact of Technology and Innovation on the Wellbeing of the Legal Profession* (Intersentia 2020).

James N, 'More than Merely Word-Ready: Vocationalism versus Professionalism in Legal Education' (2017) 4(1) *UNSW Law Journal* 186–209.

Jayasuriya K, 'COVID-19, Markets and the Crisis of the Higher Education Regulatory State: The Case of Australia' (2020) 18(4) *Globalizations* <https://www.tandfonline.com/doi/pdf/10.1080/14747731.2020.1815461> accessed 01 September 2021.

Joseph R, 'The Cost of Managerialism in the University: An Autoethnographical Account of an Academic Redundancy Process' (2015) 33(2) *Prometheus* 1–25.

Keyes M and Johnstone R, 'Changing Legal Education: Rhetoric, Reality and Prospects for the Future' (2004) 26(4) *Sydney Law Review* 537–564.

Kniest P, 'Students Pay More; Staff Do More; Universities Get Less' (November 2020) 27(3) *Advocate* 25–27.

Krugman P, 'All the President's Zombies' (*The New York Times*, NYC, 24 August 2009) <https://www.nytimes.com/2009/08/24/opinion/24krugman.html> accessed 22 July 2021.

Lantry L, 'Harvard Law Student Sues University over Tuition Prices as Classes Remain Online' (*ABC News Exclusive*, 23 June 2020) <https://abcnews.go.com/US/abc-news-exclusive-harvard-law-student-sues-university/story?id=71345292> accessed 26 July 2021.

Law Council of Australia, Law Admissions Consultative Committee, *Prescribed Areas of Knowledge* (Australia\SDCL\657475579.01, 2019).

Le Barbanchon T, Ubfae D, and Araya F, 'The Effects of Working While in School' (*VOX. CEPR Policy Portal*, 16 December 2019) <https://voxeu.org/article/effects-working-while-school> accessed 26 July 2021.

Le Brun M and Johnstone R, *The Quiet (R)evolution: Improving Student Learning in Law* (Law Book Company 1994).

Legal Line, 'Bond University, Australia' (*Legal Line*, 2021) <https://www.legalline.ca/legal-answers/bond-university/> accessed 26 August 2021.

Lyotard J, *The Post Modern Condition: A Report on Knowledge* (Manchester University Press 1984).

Marginson S, 'Covid-19 and the Market Model of Higher Education: Something Has to Give, and It Won't Be the Pandemic' (*Centre for Global Higher Education Blog*, 17 July 2020) <https://www.researchcghe.org/blog/2020-07-20-covid-19-and-the-market-model-of-higher-education-something-has-to-give-and-it-wont-be-the-pandemic/> accessed 26 July 2021.

Marginson S and Considine M, *The Enterprise University: Power, Governance and Reinvention in Australia* (Cambridge University Press 2000) 30–33.

Marklein M, 'New International Student Enrolments Drop by 43% in US' (*University World News*, 23 November 2020) <https://www.universityworldnews.com/post.php?story=20201116050900954> accessed 26 July 2021.

Martin L, 'From Apprenticeship to Law School: A Social History of Legal Education in Nineteenth Century New South Wales' (1986) 9 *UNSW Law Journal* 111–143.

Mason R, 'Labour Pledges to Abolish Tuition Fees as Early as Autumn 2017' (*The Guardian*, London, 30 July 2017) https://www.theguardian.com/education/2017/may/21/labour-abolish-university-tuition-fees-jeremy-corbyn-eu-uk-europe> accessed 22 July 2021; US Presidential candidate, Bernie Sanders, made a similar proposal in 2019.

Mavelli L, 'Governing the Resilience of Neoliberalism through Biopolitics' (2017) 23(3) *European Journal of International Relations* 489–512.

McNay L, 'Self as Enterprise: Dilemmas of Control and Resistance in Foucault's *The Birth of Biopolitics*' (2009) 26(6) *Theory, Culture & Society* 55–77.

Morrish L, 'Academic Identities in the Managed University: Neoliberalism and Resistance at Newcastle University, UK' (2017) 59(2) *Australian Universities Review* 23–25.

Newman J, *The Idea of a University* (1st published 1852, Ian T Ker (ed), Oxford University Press 1976).

Oliver D, 'Teaching and Learning Law: The Pressures on the Liberal Law Degree' in Peter Birks (ed) *Reviewing Legal Education* (Oxford University Press 1994).

Organisation for Economic Cooperation and Development, 'The Knowledge-Based Economy' (1996) <https://www.basicknowledge101.com/pdf/KNOWLEDGE-BASED%20ECONOMY.pdf#:~:text=The%20term%20%E2%80%9Cknowledge-based%20economy%E2%80%9D%20stems%20from%20this%20fuller,traditional%20economics%2C%20as%20reflected%20in%20%E2%80%9Cnew%20growth%20theory%E2%80%9D> accessed 26 August 2021.

Owens D, 'Yale Student Sues University Claiming Online Courses Were Inferior, Seeks Tuition Refund, Class Action Status' (*Hartford Courant*, 4 August 2020) https://www.courant.com/coronavirus/hc-news-coronavirus-student-sues-yale-20200804-eyr4lbjs2nhz7lapjgvrtnyyea-story.htmlhttps://www.courant.com/coronavirus/hc-news-coronavirus-student-sues-yale-20200804-eyr4lbjs2nhz7lapjgvrtnyyea-story.html> accessed 26 July 2021.

Parker J and Cahill D, 'The Retreat from Neoliberalism That Was Not: Australia's Building the Education Revolution' (2017) 52(2) *Australian Journal of Political Science* 257–271.

Parliament of Australia, 'Schedule 2 of the Higher Education Support Amendment (Job-Ready Graduates and Supporting Regional and Remote Students) Act 2020 and the Explanatory Memorandum to the Act' <https://www.legislation.gov.au/Details/C2020A00093> accessed 26 July 2021.

Purcell M, *Recapturing Democracy: Neoliberalization and the Struggle for Alternative Urban Futures* (Routledge 2008).

Research Excellence Framework, 'Research Excellence Framework' <https://www.ref.ac.uk/> accessed 26 July 2021.

Riddell S, 'Widening Access to Scottish Higher Education: Unresolved Issues and Future Challenges' (2016) 48(1) *Scottish Educational Review* 3–12.

Ross J, 'Foreign Students "Disproportionately Impoverished" by Pandemic' (*Times Higher Education*, 10 August 2020).

Rowbotham J, 'HELP for Nations Looking at Income-Contingent Loans' (*The Australian*, New South Wales, 2 July 2019).

Rudd K, 'The Global Financial Crisis' (*The Monthly*, Melbourne, February 2009).

Sanchez-Gelaberi A, Figueroa M, and Elias M, 'Working While Studying in Higher Education: The Impact of the Economic Crisis on Academic and Labour Market Success' (2017) 52 *European Journal of Education* 231–244.

Savage N and Watt G, 'A "House of Intellect" for the Profession' in Peter Birks (ed), *Pressing Problems in the Law: What Are Law Schools For?* (Oxford University Press 1996).

Self P, *Government by the Market: The Politics of Public Choice* (Macmillan 1993).

Shattock M and Horvath A, 'The Decentralisation of the Governance of UK Higher Education: The Effects of Devolution to Scotland, Wales and Northern Ireland, and on England' (2020) 2(2) *Policy Reviews in Higher Education* 164–178.

Shore C and McLauchlan L, '"Third Mission" Activities, Commercialisation and Academic Entrepreneurs' (2012) 20 *Social Anthropology* 267–286.

Skead N, Elphick L, McGaughey F, Wesson M, Offer K, and Montalto M, 'If You Record, They Will Not Come – But Does It Really Matter? Student Attendance and Lecture Recording at an Australian Law School' (2020) 54(3) *The Law Teacher* 349–367.

Smalley A, 'Higher Education Responses to Coronavirus (COVID-19)' (*National Conference of State Legislatures*, 28 December 2020) <https://www.ncsl.org/research/education/higher-education-responses-to-coronavirus-covid-19.aspx> accessed 26 July 2021.

Smith E, 'Casual Wage Theft Par for the Course' (*Saturday Paper*, Melbourne 30 January 2021).

Smith J (ed), 'Law Apprenticeships' (*Prospects*, May 2021) <https://www.prospects.ac.uk/jobs-and-work-experience/job-sectors/law-sector/law-apprenticeships> accessed 26 July 2021.

SMYTHSYS, 'Online Classes Should NOT Be Cheaper than Face to Face Classes' (*Teachers Madrid*, 20 October 2020) <https://teachersmadrid.es/10238/

online-classes-should-not-be-cheaper-than-face-to-face-classes/> accessed 26 July 2021.

Solicitors Regulation Authority, 'Solicitor Apprenticeships' (*SRA*, April 2021) <SRA | Solicitor apprenticeships | Solicitors Regulation Authority> accessed 26 July 2021.

Tadros E, 'Law Degree the New Arts Degree, Students Warned' (*Financial Review*, 14 February 2014).

Tadros E and Walsh K, 'Too Many Law Graduates and Not Enough Jobs' (*Financial Review*, 22 October 2015) <www.afr.com/business/legal/too-many-law-graduates-and-not-enough-jobs-20151020-gkdbyx> accessed 21 July 2021.

Tamanaha B, *Failing Law Schools* (Chicago University Press 2012).

The Higher Education Student Experience, *2019 Student Experience Survey* (Department of Education and Training, Canberra, 2020).

Thomasset C and Laperrière R, 'Faculties under Influence: The Infeudation of Law Schools to the Legal Professions' in Fiona Cownie (ed) *The Law School: Global Issues, Local Questions* (Ashgate 1999).

Thornton M, 'Deregulation, Debt and the Disciplines of Law' (2014) 39 *Alternative Law Journal* 213–216.

Thornton M, *Privatising the Public University: The Case of Law* (Routledge 2012).

Thornton M, 'The Challenge for Law Schools of Satisfying Multiple Masters' (2020) 62(2) *Australian Universities Review* 5–13.

Thornton M, 'Towards the Uberisation of Legal Practice' (2019) 1(1) *Law, Technology and Humans* 46–63 <https://doi.org/10.5204/lthj.v1i1.1277> accessed 26 July 2021.

Thornton M and Shannon L, '"Selling the Dream": Law School Branding and the Illusion of Choice' (2013) 23(2) *Legal Education Review* 249–271.

Universities Australia, '2020 Higher Education Facts and Figures' (2020).

Universities Australia, 'Data Snapshot 2019' (2019).

Universities UK, 'Efficiency and Effectiveness in Higher Education: A Report by the Universities UK Efficiency and Modernisation Task Group' (Universities UK, 2011) <https://www.universitiesuk.ac.uk/policy-and-analysis/reports/Pages/report-by-efficiency-and-modernisation-task-group.aspx> accessed 26 July 2021.

Veblen T, *The Higher Learning in America: The Annotated Edition: A Memorandum on the Conduct of Universities by Business Men* (first published 1918, Richard F Teichgraeber III ed, annotated edn, Johns Hopkins University Press 2015).

Visentin L, 'Universities Facing $2 Billion Loss as Job Cuts Total More Than 17,000' *Sydney Morning Herald* (Sydney, 3 February 2021) <https://www.smh.com.au/politics/federal/universities-facing-2-billion-loss-as-job-cuts-total-more-than-17-000-20210202-p56yqc.html> accessed 26 July 2021.

von Hayek F, *The Road to Serfdom* (Routledge and Kegan Paul 1976).

Watts R, *Public Universities, Managerialism and the Value of Higher Education* (Palgrave Macmillan 2017).

Webley L, Flood J, Webb J, Bartlett F, Galloway K, and Tranter K, 'The Profession(s)' Engagements with LawTech: Narratives and Archetypes of Future Law' (2019) 1(1) *Law, Technology and Humans* 6–26 <https://lthj.qut.edu.au/article/view/1314/841> accessed 26 July 2021.

Whitham B, 'Post-Crash Neoliberalism in Theory and Practice' (2018) 16(4) *Political Studies Association* 252–264.

260 *Margaret Thornton*

Wikipedia, 'Legal Education in the United Kingdom' <https://en.wikipedia.org/wiki/Legal_education_in_the_United_Kingdom> accessed 21 July 2021.

Wilson J, 'A Survey of Legal Education in the United Kingdom' (1966) 9(1) *Journal of the Society of Public Teachers of Law* 29.

Zaglas W, 'Student Accommodation Providers Prepared to Charter Flights and Quarantine Students' (*Campus Review*, 18 January 2021) <https://www.campus-review.com.au/2021/01/student-accommodation-providers-prepared-to-charter-flights-and-quarantine-students/> accessed 26 July 2021.

Index

Note: **Bold** page numbers refer to tables, *italic* page numbers refer to figures and page numbers followed by "n" refer to footnotes.

academic/educational identity 204–205, 207, 210
Adebisi, F. xxxii, xxxiii, xxxv, 85–107, 130
Advisory Committee on Legal Education and Conduct (ACLEC) xx, xxn6, xxi, xxin9, xxii, xxix, 144
albeit xxvii, 19, 119, 121, 232, 247
anti-foundationalism 171–179, 188–190
antiracism 85, 87, 89
antiracist/decolonial approach xxxiii, 85, 87, 90, 96–107
Ashford, C. 148
Auerbach, E. xxviin35
Augustine xxvi
Austin, J. L. 182
Australia 86, 232, 234, 234n27, 235, 238–240, 243, 246, 248–249, 251, 253
Australian National Tertiary Education Union, The 250
authenticity xxxiii, 129, 138–139, 141, 149–155, 157–158, 161

Bachelor of Laws (LLB) 61, 63, 66, 124, 178, 240, 240n64
Bach, K. 182
Bakhtin, M. xxxiv, 196, 198
Bales, K. xxxiii, 85–107
Barnett, R. 189
Barrett, B. 177n41
Bar Standards Board (BSB) 6n15, 11n32, 12
Baxter, J. A. 209
Beech, D. 43–44
Beinart, S. 144
Bennett, M. J. 74–79

Bereiter, C. 181–182, 184–187
Berytus (Beirut) xxxii, 7–9, 9n25, 17–19, 20n65
Bhattacharyya, G. 102
Biggs, J. 185–186
Birks, P. xix, xixn1, xixn2, xx, xxn4, xxn6, xxi, xxii, xxiin9, xxiii, xxiiin18, xxiv, xxv, xxvii–xxx, xxxii–xxxvi, 3, 25–27, 27n20, 30, 32, 46, 51, 60, 62, 67, 80, 86, 106, 111–124, 132, 133, 138, 139, 142, 150, 155, 160, 167, 169–170, 179n49, 188, 190–191, 195, 196, 221–224, 231–232, 234, 244, 252, 253
Birth of Biopolitics, The (Foucault) 234
Black Lives Matter xxxiii, 85, 100, 113, 124, 128
Blackness 90, 100
Blankenberg, E. 78
Bleak Legal Realism 19n59, 125–126, 132
Bleasdale, L. xxxiv, 167n2, 195–224
Bloom, H. xxvii
Boas, F. 88
Bond University 240
Boon, A. 2, 13
Bradney, A. 151, 247
Brett, J. 249
Britishness 72
Brown, A. 181–182
Browne Review 69
Brown, R. 200
Brown, W. 239, 241n69
Burridge, R. 148
Burrows, R. 245

262 Index

Campione, J. 182
Canto-Lopez, M. xxxii, 25–52
capital accumulation 232, 234–242, 253
Cartwright, N. 104
Cartwright, T. O. 104
Christie, H. 210
civil procedure 212, *213,* 216, 218, 221
Clark, E. xxv, xxvii, xxxii, xxxiv, 25,
 28–29, 31, 45–46, 60–61, 86, 106,
 167n2, 232
Collins, A. xxvii, 167n2, 184
Collins, H. xxvii
colonial histories xxxiii, 85, 87, 89, 91,
 94, 96, 98–99, 101–103, 106
colonialism 76–77, 90, 93–94, 96,
 103, 106
coloniality 90–93, 96–98, 104–106, 130
colonisation 86, 90, 92, 98, 104
competence 19, 73–75, 77, 80, 89–90,
 140, 177n41, 182, 237, 241
consumerisation 98, 100, 106, 143
Consumer Right Act (CRA) 26
Corbyn, J. 233
Couture, B. 180
COVID-19 pandemic xxiin12, xxiv,
 xxxvi, xxxix, 10, 28, 34, 45, 47, 67, 95,
 113, 124, 130–131, 140, 156, 159–160,
 200, 202, 210, 234–235, 243, 248–253
Cownie, F. xxvi, 247
credentialism 243
Crenshaw, K. 98
Critical Legal Studies (CLS) approach
 xxiv, 172–173
Critical Race Theory 89
critical thinking 97, 114, 126, 208
critical university studies (CUS) 245, 247
Cui, V. 43–44
cultural awareness 77–78, 80
cultural difference 73–74, 77
curriculum: decolonising the 86–87,
 97, 104, 129–130; design xxxi, 2, 4,
 14; hidden 71; interdisciplinary 65;
 internationalized xxxii, 60, 61, 63–68,
 64n20, 69, 72, 80; legal xxxii, 12, 19,
 63–68, 76, 79, 126, 139, 142, 146–147,
 178; Scottish 67, 68; undergraduate
 law 63–68, 70n47, 76–77, 78, 142

Da Lomba, S. 67–68
Dawkins, H. J. S. 235, 235n31
De Beaugrande, R. 182
decoloniality/decolonisation xxxiii, 85,
 87, 90, 97–107, 130

'Decolonise UoK' 104–105
dehumanisation 91, 94–95, 96
Dekker, S. xxv
democratisation 253
Department for Education (DfE) 35
Destination of Leavers Survey from HE
 (DLHEA) 36–37, 36n91
Dewey, J. 171, 176, 188–189
digital lecture 201, 212, *213,* 216–217,
 223–224
digital skills 140, 154–157
disciplinary learning 15–16, *16*
Donaldson, J. F. 48
Donovan, T. R. 179
downsliding 184, 187
Du Bois, W. E. B. 88
Duncan, N. 152
Dutton, K. 127

educational technology 214, 222–223
Ehrmann, H. 78
El-Enany, N. 94
emotional skills xxxiii–xxxiv, 140, 155,
 157–160, 161
engagement: academics and LTs 30, 32,
 41, 45; layers of 216, *216*
English Legal System 80–81
equality 91, 99, 127
Eraut, M. 16, 19, 177
Excellence in Research for Australia
 (ERA) 245, 247

face-to-face (f2f) 131, 202, 203, 209,
 211–212, 216–218, 217n71, 220–221,
 223, 251
Fields, B. J. 93
Fields, K. E. 93
Fish, S. 171–179, 172n19, 185,
 185n72, 188
Fletcher, M. 67–68
Flood, J. 13, 13n39
Flower & Hayes model 181, 183,
 186–188
Flower, L. 181, 183, 186–188
Floyd, G. 85, 128
Foucault, M. xxxiv, 234, 241–242
Frankham, J. 42
Franks, J. 188
Friedman, M. 233, 238

General Certificate of Secondary
 Education (GCSE) 117, 117n30
Gentner, D. 184

Index

Gilbert, A. 66–67
Gilmore, R. W. 89
Gilroy, P. 88, 94
Glasgow 167, *213*, 216
Gledhill, K. 18
global citizenship xxxiii, 60, 63, 68–73, 69n40, 75, 79, 81
global financial crisis (GFC) xxiv, 233, 239
Global North 92–93, 101, 169
Global South 86–87, 92–94, 101–102, 105
Goelman, H. 186
good citizen xxxii, 69, 148–150, 154–161
Goodman, J. 246
Goodrich, P. xxix, xxxv, 123–124, 168, 172–175, 177n41, 190
governmentality xxiii, xxxii, xxxiv, 25–27, 32, 41, 46–47, 49, 68, 143, 234
Graduate Outcome (GO) survey 36n91
Graham, S. W. 48
Grey, T. 171
Grosfoguel, R. 88–89
Group of Eight (Go8) 240, 248
Guardian University Guide 5
Guth, J. xxxiii, 45, 67, 76, 111–133, 129n82, 140, 146, 148

Hall, E. 1–21
Harnish, R. M. 182
Harrison, N. 61, 69, 72
Harris, P. 144
Harvey, D. 94
Hayek, F. 233
Hayes, J. R. 181, 183, 188
Heidegger, M. 168n7, 214n69, 224
Hervey, T. 67, 76, 128
Hickel, J. 93
higher education (HE): consumerisation of 25, 26, 98, 106, 143; ecology of 14; employability xxxii, 143, 146, 151; English 32, 42, 43n140, 69, 70; internationalisation of xxiii, 61–63; marketisation of xxxii, xxxiii, 25, 32, 51, 98, 143; massification of xxiii, 10, 98; neoliberalisation of 231–235, 242, 253; policies xxxii, 28–32, 39, 46–52; *see also* Australia; COVID-19 pandemic
Higher Education and Research Act (HERA) 26, 36
Higher Education Contribution Scheme (HECS) 237, 250, 253

Higher Education Funding Council for England (HEFCE) 35
Higher Education Institutions (HEIs) 25–52, 85, 209
Higher Education Loan Programme (HELP) 237, 250, 253
Higher Education Statistical Education, The 64n17
Higher Education Statistics Agency (HESA) 36n91, 37, 60n2, 122–123
Hirsch, E. D. 179
Hoj Jensen, D. 207
'home' jurisdiction 73
homo oeconomicus 241, 241n69
Hughes Report xxin9
human capital 233–235, 241–248, 253
Hunt, A. 178–179
Husa, J. 71
Hussey, T. 127
Hutchinson, T. 152
hybrid learning 203, 211

Ibarra, H. 203, 205
identity formation 203–212, 221, 224
identity frame 214, *214*
imperialist thinking 96
indigenous populations 90–93
inequality xxxii, 10, 15, 20–21, 86–87, 91, 95–96, 105, 107, 149, 161, 199
informal learning 200, 211, 224
intercultural education 61, 73–79
internationalisation xxxii, 60–70, 72, 80
International Monetary Fund (IMF) 94

James, C. 12
Jetten, J. 207
Jivraj, S. 104–105
Joint Statement xxii, 65–66, 65n25
Jones, E. xxxiii, 138–161
Jones, M. 144
Juris Doctorate (JD) 240

Kintsch, W. 181
Klemp, G. 177
Knight, J. 61
knowledge acquisition 148, 218, **219**, 244
knowledge frame 215, *215*
Koo, J. 12
Krugman, P. 233
Kuznetsova, O. 31

264 *Index*

Langbein, J. H. 113–114, 128
Law Admissions Consultative Committee (LACC) 237, 237n41
law and race 85, 101
Lawrence, S. 86
law school xx, xxn4, xxii, xxiin11, xxiin12, xxiii–xxiv, xxvi–xxxii, xxxiv–xxxvi, 1–21, 25–30, 45, 47, 60–62, 60n2, 66, 67, 74, 80, 85–87, 97, 98, 100, 102, 104–106, 111–133, 138–161, 167, 169, 188, 190, 191, 199–203, 221n78, 222–224, 224n82, 231–253; Birks and xxii, xxiii, xxiv, xxviii, xxix, xxx, xxxiii, xxxiv, xxxv, xxxvi, 67, 86, 111, 112, 113–124, 132, 133, 169, 170, 190, 191, 221–224, 231, 232, 234, 244, 252; crisis 124–131; curriculum xxxi, xxxiv, 7, 20, 60, 61, 66, 86, 97, 126, 129, 139, 144, 147, 160; English xxii, 18, 74, 113, 123, 145, 161; problems 7–15; *see also* COVID-19 pandemic
Law Society of Scotland 68
law teachers (LTs) xxxi, xxxii, 11, 16, 17, 25–52, 98, 105, 106, 247; needs for 46–51; role of 17; and teaching 32–46; and TEF 41–51
Law Teachers' Voices (LTVs) xxxii, 25–52; in HE policies 46–51
legal academics 9, 21, 28n28, 100, 112n8, 116–117, 124, 124n56, 132, 170, 177n41, 189, 232, 235, 245–248
legal education xixn1, xx, xxn4, xxi, xxin7, xxi–xxiin9, xxiii, xxv, xxvi, xxvii, xxviii, xxx–xxxv, 1–21, 26, 27n22, 28, 46, 65, 67–72, 80, 86, 87, 89, 111–114, 116n26, 124, 132, 138–141, 148, 150–161, 167; 167n1, 168n7, 196, 214n69; 217, 222, 223, 234, 242, 244, 252, 253; antiracist/ decolonial approach xxxiii, 85, 87, 90, 97–107, 130,; Birks 26–27, 67, 222–224; chronotopes of 196–203; contemporary 139, 149, 154–155, 161, 175, 252; English 2, 70, 140, 168; integration of skills 141–147; intercultural 73–79; internationalisation in 65, 68; as jurisprudential activity 167–191; liberal 65, 132, 139, 148–149, 151, 154, 158, 161, 242, 244; rhetoric 179–188
legal enterprise 138–139, 141, 147–149, 150–155, 161
legal pedagogy 17, 171, 177n41, 189, 196, 203

Legal Practice Course (LPC) 11, 14, 117
legal profession 6, 10, 12, 14, 19, 27n20, 63, 65, 67, 73, 87, 96, 100, 111, 113, 115–117, 126, 139, 139n39, 141, 143–147, 147n59, 150, 153, 160, 236–237, 252
legal skills xxxiii, 114, 126n65, 138–161, 188, 189; authentic 138–139, 141, 149–150, 152–155, 157–158, 161; emotions xxxiii, 140, 157–160; within legal education 141–147
LETR Report xxin7, xxii
liberal education 115, 148, 151, 155, 158–159
Lifelong Learning UK 122
Livings, B. 18
Llewellyn, K. 188
Locke, J. 91
Longitudinal Education Outcome (LEO) 37, 37n93

McClelland, B. W. 179
MacCormick, N. 178–179
McGlynn, C. 120n40
McGregor, J. 198
Mackie, K. 177n41
McNamee, K. 17
Maharg, P. xxx, xxxi, xxxiv, 3, 167n2, 167-191, 168n5–7, 169n8, 195–224, 219n73
Malec, A. 210
Marginson, S. 252
Marton, F. 180, 186
Mason, L. 19n59, 125, 126n62
Master of Arts (MA) 118
Matsuhashi, A. 183
Memon, A. R. 105
Menis, S. 65
Mertz, Beth xxvi
Mignolo, W. D. 103
minimisation 77
modernity 92
Modiri, J. 96, 99
Morrison, D. xxxiii, 10n27, 45, 111–133

national citizenship 69
National Student Survey (NSS) 28, 32, 37, 37n92
navigation frame 215, *215*
neoliberalism xxiv, 143, 232–235, 241, 253
Newbery-Jones, C. xxxiv, 167n2, 195–224

Ninety-Three Percent Club 127n74
Nussbaum, M. 68–72, 71n49, 159, 160

Office for Students (OfS) 36, 39–41,
41n122, 50, 52
Oliver, D. 244
Organisation for Economic
Co-operation and Development
(OECD) 237, 248n111
OSCOLA referencing 156

Pask, G. 185–187
Paterson, A. xxin9
Pearce Review 38–40, 40n117, 49
Phirangee, K. 210
Post Graduate Research (PGR) 119
Post Graduate Taught (PGT) 119
Pressing Problems in the Law School 1–2
Priestley 11 237, 237n41, 252
professional identity 12, 205–207,
210–211
Pue, W. W. 148–149

Qualifying Law Degree (QLD) xxin9, 6,
6n15, 10–13, 11n32, 13n39, 65–66, 80,
124–125, 147
Quality Assurance Agency (QAA)
11n34, 36, 64–65, 68, 80, 146, 146n52,
153

race/racism/racialisation 85–97, 99–102,
105–106
Rasiah, S. xxxi, 1–21
rationality 92, 96, 115, 149, 158, 169n8
Renshaw, P. 200
Research Assessment Exercise (RAE)
27n15, 32
Research Excellence Framework (REF)
xxxii, 26–27, 32, 44, 60, 60n3,
62, 245
return on investment (ROI) 219n73
rhetorical turn xxiin11, xxix, 99, 127,
132, 171–176, 179–190, 232
Rich Law, Poor Law 101, 102
Rigney, S. 104
Romgens, I. 151
Rorty, R. 171
rule of law 71–72, 91
Russell Group 15n45, 118, 123
Rutazibwa, O. 101

Sadock, J. 182
Savage, N. 113, 114, 115
Scardamalia, M. 181–182, 184–187

Scholarly Teaching Fellow 246
Schön, D. 177
School of Oriental and African Studies
(SOAS) 85
Science, Technology, Engineering, and
Math (STEM) 236, 246, 248n113,
249, 250
Searle, J. R. 182
self-awareness 77, 176, 185n72
Shannon, L. 65
Shaughnessy, M. 180
Shields, R. 47
Shilliam, R. 89
Shulman, L. 169, 223n81
skill 11, 140, 160
Smith, F. 183
Smith, K. 30
Smith, P. 127
social construction 88, 101
social identity 203–212
Society of Public Teachers of Law
(SPTL), xix–xx
soft skills 126, 126n65, 154–155,
157, 160
Solicitors Qualifying Examination
(SQE) xxiv, xxivn23, xxxi, 27–28,
27n22, 66–68, 113, 124–126, 125n57,
126n65, 132, 145–147, 151
Solicitors Regulation Authority (SRA)
xxiv, xxivn23, 6n15, 11n32, 13n39,
15n48, 27, 27n21, 61, 67–68,
80, 125
Stevens, R. xxv, 188
Stevens, W. 172
Stier, J. 62
student: activities 18, 36, 61, 202, 220,
221; as human capital 235, 241–245;
identity 95, 203–211, 221; population
99–100, 102; and tutors 17, 18, 211,
250; and university 104–105, 210, 249;
voice on legal education 3–7; *see also*
COVID-19 pandemic
Student Law Office 7n16
Stychin, C. F. 75–76
Subject Benchmark Statement for Law
64–65, 68, 146, 153
Svensson, L. 186, 187

Teaching Excellence Framework (TEF)
xxxi, xxxii, xxxv, 28–29, 32–41, 51–52,
238n53; HE policies 46–51; LTs and
41–46
Thornton, M. xxiii, xxxi, xxxiii, xxxiv,
25, 65, 112n6, 231–253

266 *Index*

Toddington, S. xxix, xxxiii, 114, 138–139, 139n9, 140–142, 143, 146, 147–156, 158, 160–161, 168, 188
Tsamenyi, M. xxv, xxvii, xxxii, xxxiv, 25, 28–29, 31, 45–46, 60–61, 86, 106, 167n2, 232
Tuck, E. 90
Twining, W. xxiin12, xxvi, xxxv, 30, 71, 73, 80, 119, 140, 142, 177n41
Twitter xxixn39

UN Commission on Human Rights 103
undergraduate law 3, 61, 63–66, 63n13, 64n17, 70n47, 68, 76, 78, 80, 142, 147, 207
undergraduate legal curriculum 63–68, 146
Universal Declaration of Human Rights 103
University and College Union (UCU) 31, 31n55, 35, 38, 42, 44–47
University College London (UCL) 85
University of Bristol 87, 101, 127n74
University of California, Los Angeles (UCLA) 239

Valverde, M. 198–199, 224
Van Dijk, T. 181
Vaughan, S. xxxi, 13
Veblen, T. 231
Vicker, B. 172
Voltaire & Rousseau 167, 170, 170n9, 191

Wallace, C. xxxii, 60–81
Watermeyer, R. 47
Watt, G. 113, 114, 115
Watts, R. 234
Webb, J. 2, 13, 142, 148
Weinberger, D. xxviii
West, C. 171, 172
Whiteness 87, 89–90, 100
white supremacy 77, 93
Wiltsche, H. 190
writing process 175, 179–189
Wynter, S. 91

Yang, K. W. 90
Young, R. E. 180

Zahn, R. 67–68
Zander, M. xxivn18

Printed in the USA
CPSIA information can be obtained
at www.ICGtesting.com
LVHW021125170924
791293LV00002B/401